CW00632004

The Excavation of Khok Phanom Di,

A Prehistoric Site in Central Thailand

Volume III : The Material Culture (Part I)

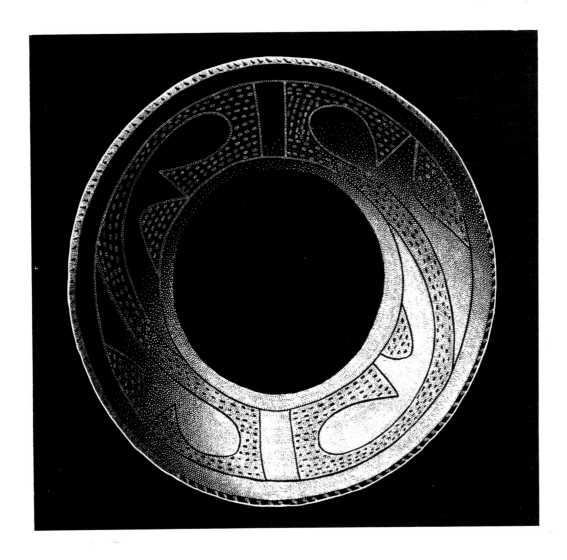

Frontispiece: Pottery vessel from burial 11

Reports of the Research Committee

of the

Society of Antiquaries of London

No. L

The Excavation of Khok Phanom Di

a Prehistoric Site in Central Thailand

Volume III : The Material Culture (Part I)

Edited by

C.F.W. Higham, Sc.D., F.S.A. & R. Thosarat, M.Sc., Ph.D.

with contributions by M.D. Hall, M.A., C.F.W. Higham, Sc.D., F.S.A.,
D.M. Higham, B.A., T.F.G. Higham, M.A., M.N. Moore, B.A., J.S. Pilditch, M.A.
and P. Pisnupong, M.A.

Published by The Society of Antiquaries of London
Distributed by Oxbow Books Ltd.
1993

British Library Cataloguing in Publication Data
A catalogue record for this book is available from the British Library

The excavation of Khok Phanom Di: a prehistoric site in central
   Thailand.
   Vol. II, The material culture (part I)
   (Reports of the Research Committee of the Society of
   Antiquaries of London) No. 50
   1. Thailand, Antiquities. Excavation of remains
   I. Higham, Charles, 1939 - II. Thosarat, R. (Rachanie), 1955 - III.
   Series 959. 3021

   ISBN 0-85431-262-5 ISSN 0953-7163

PRINTED IN NEW ZEALAND BY

THE UNIVERSITY OF OTAGO

CONTENTS

LIST OF FIGURES

LIST OF TABLES

AUTHORS

W E owe a deep debt of gratitude to the authors of this volume, who have contributed their skill and time towards an understanding of the environment and activities of the occupants of Khok Phanom Di.

During the preparation of this volume, Jacqui Pilditch died following a long illness. All those who worked with her at Khok Phanom Di will remember her enthusiasm, dedication and the many hours she devoted to studying the jewellery. We would like this volume to serve as a memorial to her membership of our team.

D.M. Hall, Department of Anthropology, University of Otago, P.O. Box 56, Dunedin, New Zealand.

C.F.W. Higham, Department of Anthropology, University of Otago, P.O. Box 56, Dunedin, New Zealand.

T.F.G. Higham, Radiocarbon Laboratory, University of Waikato, Hamilton, New Zealand

D.M. Higham, Department of Anthropology, University of Otago, P.O. Box 56, Dunedin, New Zealand.

M.N. Moore, Department of Anthropology, University of Otago, P.O. Box 56, Dunedin, New Zealand.

J.M. Pilditch

P. Pisnupong, Research Division, Fine Arts Department, Sri Ayutthaya Road, Theves, Bangkok 10300, Thailand.

PREFACE

K HOK Phanom Di is a large prehistoric site located in Chonburi Province, Central Thailand. This is the third of a series of volumes which will report on the excavations we undertook there in 1985 as part of our project on the prehistory and early history of the lower Bang Pakong Valley. This volume is concerned with the non-ceramic artefacts recovered, with the exception of the decorative motifs on the pottery vessels and the clay netweights. Dr B. A. Vincent will report separately on the other ceramic material. We have adopted the policy of describing the material, reserving for the final volume in this series of reports, the overall interpretation and place of Khok Phanom Di within its wider setting. Details of the site's stratigraphy, chronology, environmental setting and subsistence economy may be found in preceding volumes in the series.

We are deeply indebted to many individuals and their institutions for the support which has made this project possible. First, we owe a debt to our respective institutions, the University of Otago and the Fine Arts Department, for allowing us the time and resources to devote to research in the Bang Pakong valley. To Sir Robin Irvine, Vice-Chancellor of the University of Otago, and Thaweesak Senanarong, then Director General of the Fine Arts Department, we can only reciprocate with our thanks, coupled with this volume and its companions.

Financial support for the programme and subsequent analyses was provided by a number of institutions. The Ford Foundation through Dr Thomas Kessinger, then representative in the South-East Asian Regional Office in Jakarta, provided funds to underwrite excavation costs and for Pirapon Pisnupong, Rachanie Thosarat and Phrapid Choosiri to undertake research on the data in New Zealand. The University of Otago also provided a research fellowship which supported Amphan Kijngam in New Zealand.

The Shell Company of Thailand Limited assisted by the provision of a vehicle, a computer and a generous subsidy to defray the costs of producing this series of volumes. To M.R. Sarisdiguna Kitiyakara, Chairman, and Precha Phonpraserth, Public Affairs Manager, we offer our thanks for such support, and for the enthusiasm of their visits to the site.

Major assistance was also provided by Earthwatch and its Research Corps, the Wenner-Gren Foundation, the University of Cambridge through its Evans Fund, New Zealand University Grants Committee and the British Academy.

We acknowledge the invaluable contribution made by Elizabeth Nichols, of the Society of Antiquaries of London, Margaret Sharman and Ruth Daniel in improving this volume. Leslie O'Neill and Martin Fisher prepared the illustrations. Last, but by no means least, we owe a considerable debt of gratitude to Graeme McKinstry of the University of Otago Computing Centre Advisory Service for his guidance and advice in using the Latex typesetting programme.

I. THE BONE, ANTLER AND TURTLE CARAPACE TECHNOLOGY

C. F. W. Higham

THE FISHING TECHNOLOGY

The fish-hooks

APART from the rare occurrence of fish-hooks in association with Bs 30 and 102, all fish-hooks were found in non-mortuary contexts in layers 11 and 10 (Fig. 1). This does not imply that fishing declined in significance, rather that the build-up of layers 2–9 resulted from different activity patterns than those in the lower horizons at the site.

All the twenty-four fish-hooks found in layers 11 and 10 were made of bone. Only one was found complete, the most common point of weakness leading to breakage being across the bend between the shank and point. It is, however, clear that all the hooks belong to the same form. They are one-piece bait hooks. Wherever sufficient has survived, it is evident that there were two barbs. One was situated on the inner part of the point and the other at the outer part of the point where it began to curve into the bend (Fig. 1).

The shank and point legs of the better-preserved specimens are virtually parallel with each other, though the point leg was given a gentle curving shape. The shank terminates with a pronounced shank knob for securing the line. Examination of the bone surfaces reveals that the final procedure in shaping the hook was to run the bone across an abrasive surface in one direction, thereby leaving fine parallel striations along individual surfaces. Many fine-grained grinding stones were recovered from Khok Phanom Di. In some cases, the shank leg was left faceted and irregular in cross section, but some hooks were given a circular shank cross-section. No unfinished hooks were found which might reveal the initial stages in roughing out the hook from the original tab of bone.

Fig. 2 shows a plot of the size of the fish-hooks based on two measurements, the depth and the width at the bend. All these measurements are shown in Table 1. It is suggested that there might be two different groups based purely on size. Most of the hooks belong to the larger putative group.

Net sinkers

A number of pierced clay artefacts have been found, the most likely use for which is held to be as net sinkers (Fig. 3). Because of their association with fishing, they will briefly be referred to here although this section refers specifically to implements made of bone or antler. They appear to fall into two groups on the basis of size. Most, irrespective of size, were roughly moulded into a circular shape, but a few of the larger specimens are more oval. Three have been damaged, allowing inspection of the interior of the central holes. We find that in two cases there are linear striations combined with fine lateral striations, as if a probe was inserted through the clay prior to

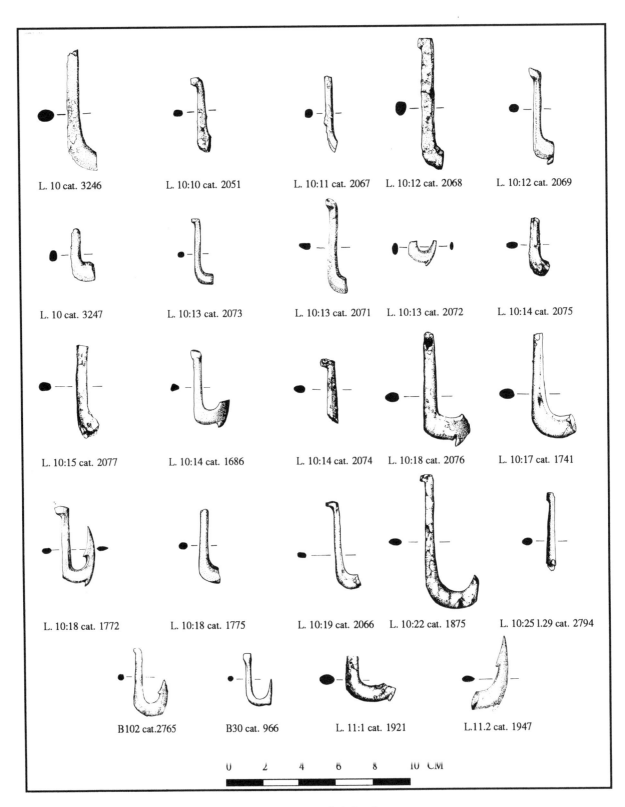

L. 10 cat. 3246

L. 10:10 cat. 2051

L. 10:11 cat. 2067

L. 10:12 cat. 2068

L. 10:12 cat. 2069

L. 10 cat. 3247

L. 10:13 cat. 2073

L. 10:13 cat. 2071

L. 10:13 cat. 2072

L. 10:14 cat. 2075

L. 10:15 cat. 2077

L. 10:14 cat. 1686

L. 10:14 cat. 2074

L. 10:18 cat. 2076

L. 10:17 cat. 1741

L. 10:18 cat. 1772

L. 10:18 cat. 1775

L. 10:19 cat. 2066

L. 10:22 cat. 1875

L. 10:25 1.29 cat. 2794

B102 cat.2765

B30 cat. 966

L. 11:1 cat. 1921

L.11.2 cat. 1947

0　2　4　6　8　10 CM

FIG. 1.　The fish-hooks

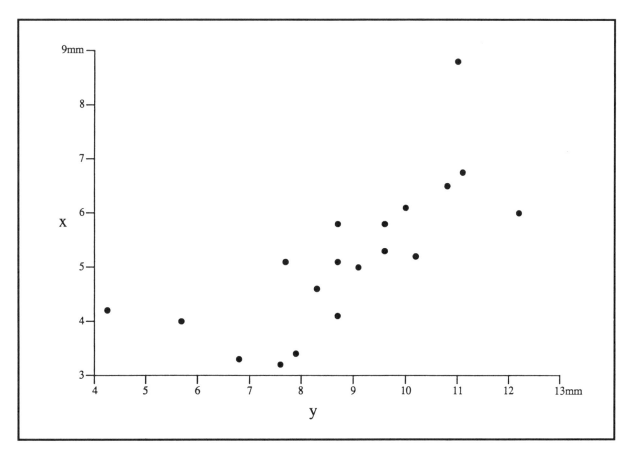

FIG. 2.   The distribution of the fish-hooks on the basis of maximum width (X axis) and maximum depth at the bend (in mm)

firing, and twisted from time to time. There is a slight projection of clay round each hole where the stick forced out clay during this operation. These two sinkers come from 8:7 (cat. 1257) and 7:4 lens 5 respectively. A third such broken sinker from 10:3 (cat. 1224) has only the lateral striations within the perforation.

Bone harpoons

There are four harpoons from Khok Phanom Di, of which two are complete (Fig. 4). All come from layer 10:12. The first complete specimen, cat. 1563, has two barbs and a swelling at the base to secure the line. The grinding marks which result from fashioning the implement are clearly visible even to the naked eye. This complete harpoon is 124.5 mm in length. The second specimen (cat. 1633) had been subjected to intense burning. Its basal end is identical with cat. 1563, and it is *c* 120 mm long. The third harpoon, represented by the base only (cat. 1539), has a swelling all round the surface of the bone. The basal section only of the fourth harpoon (cat. 2381) has

TABLE 1:   *The fish-hooks*

Context	Cat. no.	Dimension A	Dimension B	Dimension C
11:2 feature 2	1947	5.2	10.2	-
11:1	1921	5.8	9.6	-
10:25 lens 29	2792	-	-	-
10:22	1875	6.5	10.8	73.7
10:19	2066	3.4	7.9	47.1
10:18	1772	3.2	7.6	41.5
10:18	1775	5.1	8.7	-
10:17	1741	6.8	11.7	-
10:15	2076	6.0	12.2	-
10:15	2077	-	-	-
10:14	2074	-	-	-
10:14	2075	4.6	8.3	-
10:14	1686	4.1	8.7	39.9
10:13	2071	5.8	8.7	51.1
10:13	2073	4.0	5.7	35.9
10:13	2072	3.3	6.8	-
10:12	2069	5.0	9.1	48.2
10:12	2068	6.1	10.0	69.9
10:11	2067	-	-	-
10:10	2051	5.3	-	39.9
10	3246	8.8	11.0	-
10	3247	5.3	9.6	-
10:11 B102	2765	5.1	7.7	37.0
8:5 B30	966	4.2	4.2	28.7

A: maximum width at bend; B: maximum depth at bend; C: maximum length
from the shank knob to the bend

survived. These implements could have been used in hunting marine or terrestrial species as well
as for fishing. The faunal spectrum discloses the remains of crocodile, large fish and turtle as well
as large and small deer.

TECHNOLOGY OF WEAVING AND FABRIC PROCESSING

Bone bobbins (Fig. 5)

There is a group of bone artefacts having several features in common. They have a clear curvature, the convex side being described as the lower, and the concave surface being called the upper,

TABLE 2: *The net sinkers*

Context	Cat. no.	Max. L	Max. W	Context	Cat. no.	Max. L	Max. W
10:20	1857	30.0	30.9	10:19	1833	-	29.8
10:18	1799	41.9	27.7	10:18	1771	46.2	30.1
10:17	1769	43.0	37.7	10:17	1765	24.2	20.9
10:16	1746	26.2	25.5	10:15	1752	36.5	36.4
10:15	1710	25.6	24.7	10:15	1711	25.2	24.7
10:15	1693	38.2	35.4	10:15 f.8	1644	26.0	23.6
10:14	1669	25.3	22.5	10:14	1661	30.4	28.0
10:14	1646	23.2	22.4	10:13	1612	24.8	19.7
10:12	1586	27.6	21.6	10:12	1576	31.4	25.3
10:12	1541	45.1	30.7	10:12 f.15	1590	21.8	20.8
10:11	1552	36.8	34.9	10:11	1490	25.7	21.1
10:11 f.27	1589	-	33.3	10:10	1588	24.0	19.8
10:9	1496	44.3	29.9	10:9	1494	23.8	18.4
10:4	1278	36.8	38.4	10:3	1229	20.3	18.9
10:3	1224	26.9	23.3	10:3 1.2	1209	27.7	19.8
9:7	1143	40.2	32.8	9:4	1321	26.1	19.6
9:3 1.7	1316	32.4	22.2	8:7	1257	-	-
8:3	1137	26.6	18.6	8:3	939	51.4	30.0
8:2	906	21.3	19.7	8:2	1180	-	-
7:4 1.5	1015	41.2	25.8				

L: length; W: maximum width

surface. The contour of the lower surface is continuous to the working edge, whereas the upper surface has a slight facet. Each of the two surfaces at the sharpened or working end bears a high gloss reflecting repeated rubbing across a resilient medium. A recurrent characteristic of this class of artefact is the presence of a carefully cut 'U' shaped groove down one side. In some cases, the edges of the grooves bear polishing which suggests that some substance was repeatedly run across them. In the better preserved examples, such as cat. 1184, there are also clear polishing lines within the groove itself, which run as straight parallel lines along the length of the artefact. There is also some polishing present on the body of the artefact. This indicates that it is unlikely that the implements were hafted because this would have ruled out the polishing marks on the edges of the groove, which extend over the complete length of the groove, and on the body of the artefact. Clearly, however, the sharpened facets received the most intensive contact with the medium which imparted the bright gloss to the surface of the bone. In one case (cat. 1611), a hole had been bored through the base, though there was no clear indication of wear within it. Some of these implements are very slightly waisted at the base as if, with time, a depression has been worn due to the narrow filamentous substance being tied there.

While interpreting the use of such artefacts as these is beset with problems, there are some variables which, when taken in conjunction, indicate a plausible function for them. In the first instance, the presence of grinding marks partially smoothed over with subsequent use indicates careful shaping to provide the smooth curvature on the convex side of the finished implement. The leading edge is sharp and burnished, but shows no signs of heavy wear which would indicate its use as a chisel or cutting implement used on an abrasive substance. This tends to rule out the possibility that these tools were used in, for example, the caulking of boats. Semenov (1964) has stressed the widespread use of bone implements in the processing of leather, but this application would not account for the grooves, nor the polishing along the edges and within the grooves. The presence of slight waisting in some of the tools suggests that a filament or yarn was attached to them, while the high gloss at the leading edge was imparted by continual movement across a resilient surface. These factors lend support to the possibility that these tools served as bobbins in weaving. Modern Thai bobbins are made of wood, and have the same curvature at the working ends to facilitate the penetration of the bobbin between the warp and the weft of the fabric. It remains necessary, however, to account for the polish along the edges and within the groove. The modern Thai, and indeed any weaver, must compress the weft. The groove would have encompassed the weft with the act of compression, while the polish along the leading surfaces of the groove could have resulted from passage across the warp threads in the act of compression. Unless a more plausible interpretation is identified, therefore, these implements will be described as bone bobbins used in weaving.

There are three specimens from layer 11. The provenance and size are set out in Table 3. Cat. 1953 has lost its leading edge and the bone surface has deteriorated, but the side groove is still clearly apparent and there is some slight evidence for notching at the base to secure the filament. The specimen numbered cat. 1967 has lost its basal end, but the leading edge retains a high gloss on both surfaces which has partially obscured lateral and rather coarse scratches which reflect the shaping of this part of the implement. The edges of the groove have a gloss which stands out above the less pronounced polish in the body of the groove itself. In the case of cat. 1924, the leading edge suffered damage in antiquity, but it otherwise presents all the characteristics of these artefacts, with gloss running along the edges of the groove and a high polish on the surviving surfaces of the leading edge. Layer 10 has furnished 4 examples. The earliest, cat. 2359, is complete although the bone surface has been rather badly pitted with time. Parts, however, still reveal traces of polish on the leading edge over transverse groove marks which, it is held, result from the initial procedure of shaping the tool with a stone abrader. Cat. 1464, while having the slight curvature and groove, has a narrower leading edge produced by filing back an angled facet on which the file marks clearly survive. The edges of the side groove retain a clear polish. The next example, cat. 1611, is complete and has all the hallmarks of this type of implement. In addition, there is some indication that a hole had been bored transversely through the base to assist in securing thread. Unfortunately, this part of the tool has broken and only a part of this possible hole survives. Cat. 1184 is the most complete and best preserved bobbin from the site. The polish along the edges of the grooves is particularly clear, and there are linear streaks of polish still within the groove. The upper and lower body of the bobbin are also burnished with use, but the most intensive area of polishing is on the surfaces of the leading edge. About 10 cm from the basal end, there are some barely discernible grooves which probably result from attaching the thread.

No bobbins were found in layers 6, 8 or 9, and only one specimen, cat. 2379, was found in layer 7:2. As has been explained, these were built up at a time when the area excavated was used exclusively for burials and attendant mortuary ritual, and implements associated with weaving were never incorporated as grave offerings. When we encounter further bobbins in layers 3 to 5, we find that the essential elements were the same as for those encountered in layers 10 and 11, but there is a tendency for them to be shorter. That from layer 5 (cat. 591), for example, has the same smooth contour from the body of the artefact to the leading edge on the basal side, and a facet on the top. It has a pronounced groove with polished edges, but the tool is hardly more than half as long as the earlier examples, and has a slight shoulder or cut notch on each side which may have served to attach the thread. Cat. 494 from layer 4 is one of the few in this late group which has the same length as the earlier examples. Polish on the leading edge is particularly pronounced, and vestiges of polishing remain on the body of the tool and along the edges of the groove. The other two examples from layer 4 are quite badly preserved although both have heavy polishing at the leading edge. The first of the six specimens from layer 3 (cat. 241) is particularly short, attaining a length of only 36 mm. The striations on the leading edge are very marked, but those on the upper edge run in the contrary direction to those on the lower, showing that they could not result from use in the same direction. Their disposition is, however, consistent with abrading in one direction before turning the artefact over onto its other side and proceeding to abrade it in the same direction as before. Cat. 322 also has a very highly polished leading edge but the groove and its margins have been badly corroded. A further specimen from layer 3 (cat. 2475) has perhaps the clearest indication of lateral grooving to attach a yarn, while cat. 341 has a well-preserved edge to the groove which still bears polish. This latter specimen also has a depression for attaching yarn. A further bobbin from layer 3 (cat. 213) has a marked polish on the leading edge and along the groove, together with a central depression for yarn attachment. The last example from this layer, cat. 216, is complete although the surface of the body of the artefact is rather corroded. These bobbins were found virtually to the surface of the mound, as one specimen, albeit broken (cat. 2376), was found within a few centimetres of the top of the site in layer 2. Despite its broken condition, it still displays all the characteristics of those found almost 7 m lower down in layer 11.

Bone awls (Fig. 6)

The next class of artefact has many factors in common with the group described as bobbins, but also a number of important differences. Both were equipped with a groove running down the side, and both have a convex or curved outline. Whereas bobbins had an asymmetric leading edge with a chisel-like end, the tools described here as awls terminate at the leading edge with a sharp point, behind which there was no sign of faceting. It is, however, the case that the sharp point with its high gloss extended back only to a distance of about one third of the total length before usually expanding into the broader body of the tool. At this point the high gloss terminated, though the edges of the groove bore polish along their entire length. When viewed from the side, the contour of these tools reveals a beaked outline, the basal grooved edge being much straighter than the upper or beaked surface. In most cases the shiny pointed end was covered with striations which suggest that it was periodically sharpened. This, combined with the reduction in the working surface through use, probably accounts for the greater bulk of the body of the tool compared with the smaller polished tip. It is conceivable that we are confronted with no more than a small and pointed bone bobbin used in fine weaving. This seems unlikely on two counts. First, it is hard to visualise a smaller and finer bobbin than those already so classified as being necessary or even workable. Secondly, the sharpness of the points, curvature of the artefact as a whole and high gloss on the reduced pointed surface are compatible with repeated puncturing of a somewhat resilient medium such as fabric or leather. In this context, the groove would facilitate the threading of a yarn

TABLE 3:   *The provenance and dimensions of the bone bobbins*

Prov.	Cat. no.	Max. L	Max. W	Max. D
11:2 f.2	1953	-	16.6	9.1
11:2 f.1	1967	-	12.1	6.0
11:1	1924	54.5	12.4	5.7
10:16	2359	68.0	18.5	9.9
10:13	1611	63.1	15.1	8.2
10:10	1464	60.0	13.0	6.6
10:1	1184	66.3	10.2	10.0
7:2	2379	-	16.1	9.4
5:4	591	43.9	17.0	10.7
4:2	2341	56.0	-	9.8
4:1 f.1	494	68.3	16.2	8.3
4:1	1525	41.5	14.2	8.3
3:3	322	50.0	16.6	9.9
3:3	2475	-	-	8.9
3:3	341	47.8	13.5	7.8
3:1	213	59.6	19.2	12.1
3:1	216	51.2	13.9	9.1
3:1	241	36.0	16.6	10.2
3:1	2420	-	10.0	6.7
3:1	2661	-	-	11.5
2:2	2376	-	-	10.2
2:2	2318	-	-	5.6

through the hole just created with a thrust of the hand on the awl itself, though it remains hard to explain the polish which runs the length of the groove edges. In some of these artefacts, however, the polish is rather greater at the leading end of the groove than towards the end. At present, the balance of the evidence favours a use rather distinct from that suggested for the bobbins, but still related to the working of some sort of fabric.

The distribution of bone awls is very similar to that for bobbins. They are present in layer 11, and are particularly common in layer 10 contexts. There was then a hiatus with only one being present in layer 9 and none in layers 6–8. We again encounter the awls in layer 5, with several coming from layers 2–4. The provenance, sizes and catalogue numbers are set out in Table 4.

The example from basal layer 10 (cat. 1936) has a burnt tip and a clear lateral groove on both sides of the awl, which may have been to attach a yarn of some sort. In the case of cat. 1868 from a slightly higher context in layer 10, there is a cut notch in the side of the tool, just less than half way up from the point, along which there are vestigial traces of fine grooves which may have been caused by a yarn running laterally along the length of the notch. One specimen, from upper layer 10, only has a groove on the first third of its length and the groove at the leading point has almost worn right away (cat. 1474). In the case of one of the specimens from layer 3 (cat. 2592), there is a notch on the top of the awl within which there are signs of wear.

TABLE 4:   *The provenance and size of the bone awls*

Prov.	Cat. no.	L	W	D	Prov.	Cat. no.	L	W	D
10:25	1936	-	14.1	5.8	10:24	1993	54.2	11.5	5.4
10:21	1868	45.0	7.6	3.9	10:16	2457	-	7.0	3.1
10:15	1729	35.9	6.0	3.2	10:14	1660	51.2	7.3	3.8
10:14	2389	-	7.0	3.1	10:14	2388	-	4.4	2.7
10:11	2470	32.5	7.3	3.9	10:11 f.23	1546	52.3	10.0	4.9
10:10	1471	50.0	9.9	4.7	10:9	2202	40.0	9.3	5.0
10:7	1441	56.2	11.3	9.2	10:3 1.2	1474	35.4	6.2	3.2
10:3 1.2	1473	50.9	10.3	5.1	10:3 1.2	2353	-	9.8	5.2
10:3 1.2	2353	-	9.8	5.2	9:7	1475	47.3	8.6	4.0
5:4 f.2	1530	-	-	4.4	4:3	1529	51.6	9.8	5.1
4:1	1526	48.6	10.6	5.0	3:4	367	-	9.5	-
3:3	343	53.5	11.4	5.8	3:3	2366	-	-	-
3:2	2592	37.4	9.7	3.9	3:2	287	-	9.0	4.2
3:1	2339	-	-	-	3:1	281	-	-	-
2:2	123	53.1	10.2	5.1	2:2	2465	-	11.4	5.5
2:2	125	51.0	11.9	5.8	2:2	2317	-	10.2	5.0
2:1	2311	45.9	9.1	4.9					

L: length; W: maximum width, D: maximum depth

The micro-awls

Implements described as micro- or miniature bone awls are confined to layers 2–4 (Fig. 7). Implements ascribed to this class of awl have in common an asymmetric form, with one edge usually being relatively straight, and the other more beaked. There is often a bevel or ridge half way down the length of the tool. From this ridge to the point, there is a polished surface. The gloss on the surface has all but removed the striations formed when the tool was first ground to shape. The ridge or bevel may have assisted in hafting, but it is also possible that it represents the limit of penetration into a soft medium, such as leather. Viewed laterally, these micro-awls have a slightly curved shape. All save a small sample of broken fragments are set out in Table 5. The fragments are from 2:1(3), 2:2(2), 3:2(1), 3:3(2), 4:1(1) and 4:2(1).

Bone needle

The bone implement from 2:2 (cat. 2342) is strikingly long and narrow. Unfortunately, one end is missing but it still retains a length of 51.8 mm, while it is 1.5 by 2.0 mm in maximum diameter. It has all the characteristics of a needle. The sharpened tip is asymmetrical in cross-section (Fig. 8).

TABLE 5:   *The provenance and size of the micro bone awls*

Prov.	L	W	D	Prov.	L	W	D
4:4	22.1	3.8	2.1	4:3	23.6	4.1	2.6
4:3	22.0	4.3	2.3	4:3	-	4.1	2.3
4:3	22.3	4.5	2.2	4:3	17.0	3.2	2.0
4:3	20.0	4.3	2.1	4:3	21.0	4.3	2.4
4:3	22.0	4.1	2.4	4:3	18.6	5.0	2.6
4:3	-	5.1	2.2	4:2	19.2	3.5	1.9
4:2	24.0	4.1	2.8	4:2	24.0	4.8	2.2
4:2	21.9	3.7	2.0	4:2	23.5	5.2	2.7
4:2	16.0	3.5	1.9	4:2	-	3.8	2.0
4:1	23.6	3.7	1.7	4:1	-	4.1	2.2
4:1	22.2	4.5	2.4	4:1	16.0	3.1	2.0
4:1	-	-	1.9	4:1	-	3.8	2.0
4:1	15.5	3.0	1.8	4:1	20.5	4.0	1.9
4:1	14.1	3.5	2.0	4:1	18.5	3.2	2.0
4:1	-	5.0	2.7	4:1	-	5.0	2.6
4:1	15.5	3.6	2.0	3:5	25.9	4.8	2.3
3:4	16.0	3.0	1.2	3:4	27.5	5.6	3.2
3:4	-	5.0	2.6	3:4	17.5	4.9	2.6
3:4	-	5.2	3.0	3:4	21.2	4.5	2.0
3:3	22.1	4.0	2.1	3:3	28.9	5.0	2.7
3:3	19.5	3.4	2.0	3:3	18.5	3.0	1.8
3:3	22.0	5.0	2.5	3:3	20.0	3.1	1.9
3:3	15.0	2.8	1.2	3:3	-	2.9	1.8
3:3	-	4.1	2.5	3:3	-	4.6	2.6
3:3	-	3.0	1.7	3:3	17.0	3.2	1.9
3:3	19.0	3.2	2.0	3:3	26.5	5.5	2.7
3:3	24.0	-	2.0	3:3	-	4.0-	2.0
3:3	24.5	4.5	2.3	3:2	23.3	4.6	2.3
3:2	23.7	4.1	2.0	3:2	20.0	3.8	2.0
3:2	17.6	3.2	1.8	3:2	24.0	4.3	2.2
3:2	12.5	2.1	1.0	3:2	-	2.3	1.2
3:1	25.2	4.0	2.0	3:1	23.6	4.0	2.0
3:1	23.1	4.8	2.0	3:1	23.5	4.6	3.5
3:1	-	3.4	1.8	3:1	16.3	3.6	2.0
3:1	-	3.0	1.8	3:1	-	3.5	1.8
3:1	15.0	2.2	1.3	3:1	19.8	3.2	1.6
3:1	18.8	3.1	1.8	3:1	18.3	3.1	1.8
3:1	-	2.8	1.8	3:1	15.5	3.2	1.8
3:1	-	-	2.3	3:1	18.3	3.2	2.0
3:1	18.0	3.2	2.0	3:1	18.2	2.8	2.0
3:1	-	5.0	2.0	3:1	26.0	4.2	2.5
3:1	25.0	4.8	3.0	2:2	22.2	4.0	2.0
2:2	-	4.0	2.2	2:2	-	3.2	2.0
2:2	17.0	4.0	1.8	2:2	26.0	4.4	2.2
2:1	26.0	-	3.1	-	-	-	-

THE WORKED STINGRAY SPINES

The faunal remains from the site include a large sample of the remains of stingrays. These have been identified as either *Dasyatis sephen* or *Dasyatis bleekeri*. They are found in all layers of the site. Some of the caudal spines of these rays have been modified at the base (Fig. 9). This appears to have been undertaken by grinding in order to produce a flattened surface at the base of the proximal end. Most have been broken at about the midpoint. Details of the illustrated specimens are as follows:

- 10:20 cat. 3257. The proximal end of this specimen has been fashioned to a flattened and rounded form. The point is missing, but there is no sign of further working on the middle or distal surfaces.

- 10:20 cat. 3254. This is a small and nearly complete specimen, having lost only its final tip at the distal end. The proximal end has been modified to produce a smoothed and flattened surface.

- 10:20 cat. 3255. Modification to the proximal or butt end of this artefact has produced a flattened, spatulate form with a rounded tip.

- 10:20 cat. 3256. This is the only complete specimen to survive. The butt or proximal end has been fashioned to a flattened form with a blunt edge. The point end bears a series of striations running both laterally across and on the long axis of the implement, but there is no clear pattern to them. The first four or five barbs on both sides at this pointed end, incorporating the first 10 mm of the artefact's length, have been planed down, and the surfaces reveal faint traces of striations running on the long axis of the implement, as if the point had been inserted into a soft medium. This finding is supported by the fact that a slight wear facet has been formed on one of the sides abutting the point. This, too, has a depth of 10 mm.

- 10:15 cat. 1719. This item is also fractured below the tip. The proximal end has been fashioned to a blunt point. There are no signs of grinding on the surface, which is slightly polished.

- 10:11 cat. 1489. The proximal end of this specimen has been worn or modified to a rather more pointed form than the previous two examples. It is also smoothed or slightly polished.

- 10:10 cat. 1462. Just as with cat. 1489, the proximal end has a rather pointed form. No signs of use are visible on the middle part of the artefact.

- 9:2 cat. 3258. Again, the proximal end has a rather pointed form which is markedly flattened in cross-section.

Further examples of broken modified stingray spines come from 10:10 (5), 10:14 (1), 8:6 (1) and 6:6 (3). On the basis of the one complete example, it is not possible to be other than speculative on the possible uses to which these spines were put. It may be the case that they were used as awls. This, however, is not considered to be likely in view of the number of bone awls which have been found. The implements appear to have been inserted into soft tissue. An alternative use, therefore, could have been for scarification during mortuary rites. As is well known, stingray spines were prized for this purpose in prehistoric Mesoamerica (Flannery, 1976).

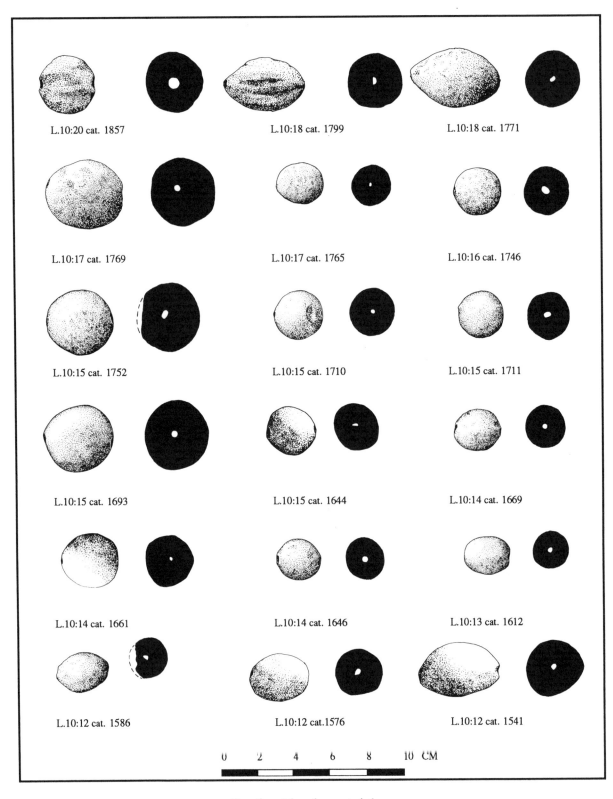

FIG. 3.   The clay net sinkers

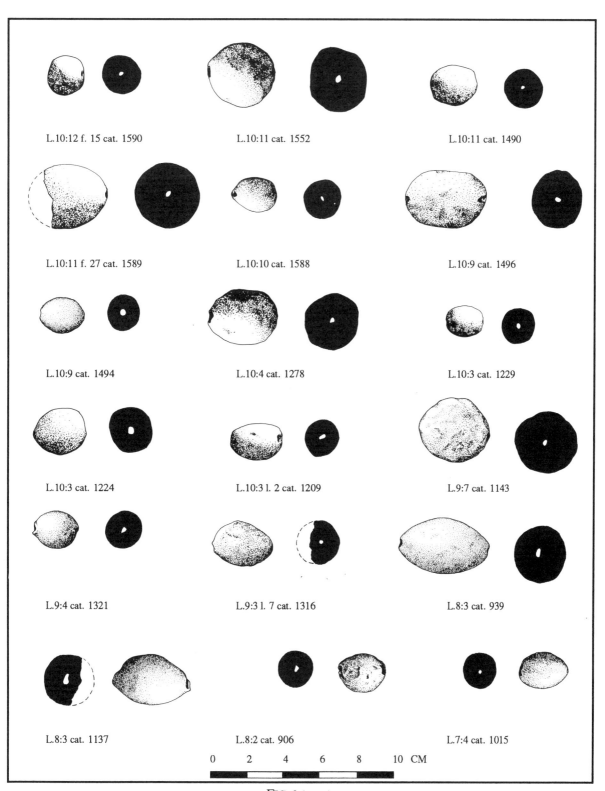

L.10:12 f. 15 cat. 1590   L.10:11 cat. 1552   L.10:11 cat. 1490

L.10:11 f. 27 cat. 1589   L.10:10 cat. 1588   L.10:9 cat. 1496

L.10:9 cat. 1494   L.10:4 cat. 1278   L.10:3 cat. 1229

L.10:3 cat. 1224   L.10:3 l. 2 cat. 1209   L.9:7 cat. 1143

L.9:4 cat. 1321   L.9:3 l. 7 cat. 1316   L.8:3 cat. 939

L.8:3 cat. 1137   L.8:2 cat. 906   L.7:4 cat. 1015

0   2   4   6   8   10   CM

FIG. 3 (cont.)

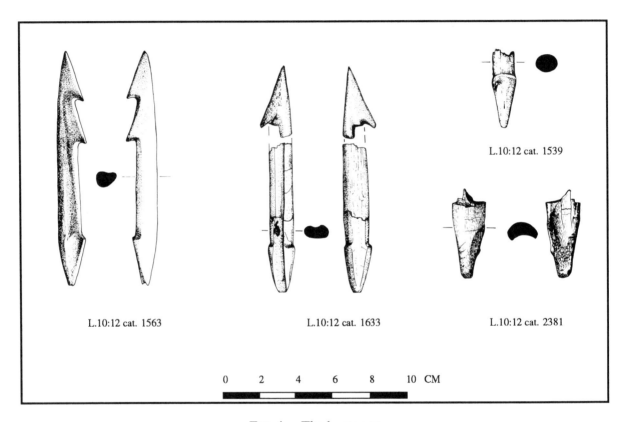

L.10:12 cat. 1539

L.10:12 cat. 1563   L.10:12 cat. 1633   L.10:12 cat. 2381

0   2   4   6   8   10 CM

FIG. 4.   The harpoons

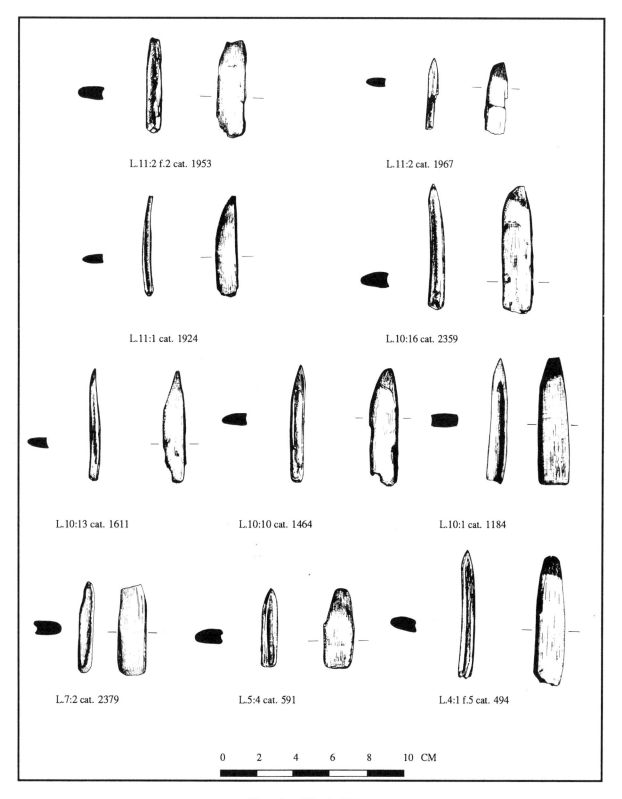

L.11:2 f.2 cat. 1953

L.11:2 cat. 1967

L.11:1 cat. 1924

L.10:16 cat. 2359

L.10:13 cat. 1611

L.10:10 cat. 1464

L.10:1 cat. 1184

L.7:2 cat. 2379

L.5:4 cat. 591

L.4:1 f.5 cat. 494

0   2   4   6   8   10 CM

FIG. 5.   The bobbins

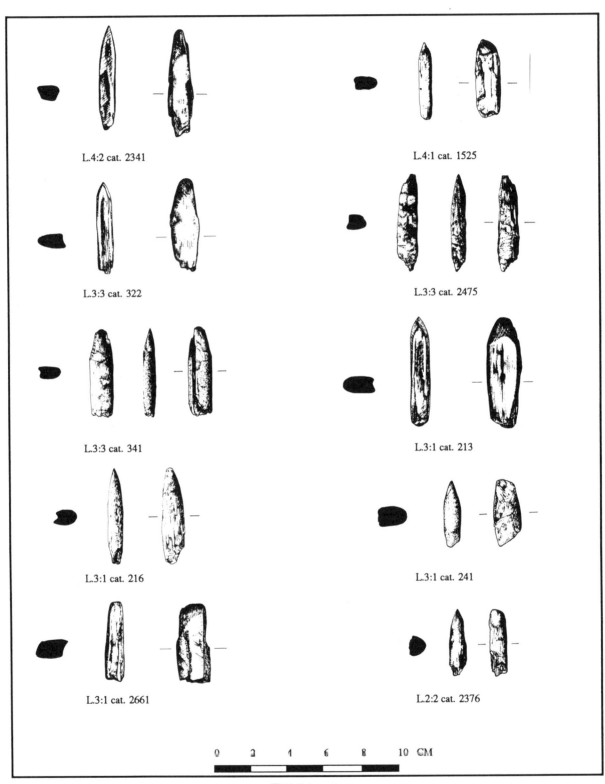

L.4:2 cat. 2341

L.4:1 cat. 1525

L.3:3 cat. 322

L.3:3 cat. 2475

L.3:3 cat. 341

L.3:1 cat. 213

L.3:1 cat. 216

L.3:1 cat. 241

L.3:1 cat. 2661

L.2:2 cat. 2376

0   2   4   6   8   10 CM

FIG. 5 (cont.)

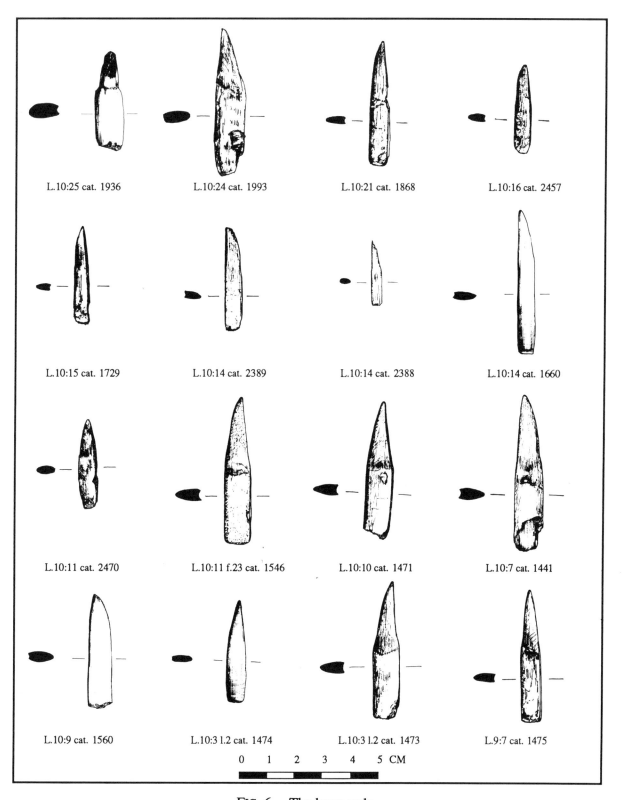

L.10:25 cat. 1936   L.10:24 cat. 1993   L.10:21 cat. 1868   L.10:16 cat. 2457

L.10:15 cat. 1729   L.10:14 cat. 2389   L.10:14 cat. 2388   L.10:14 cat. 1660

L.10:11 cat. 2470   L.10:11 f.23 cat. 1546   L.10:10 cat. 1471   L.10:7 cat. 1441

L.10:9 cat. 1560   L.10:3 1.2 cat. 1474   L.10:3 1.2 cat. 1473   L.9:7 cat. 1475

0   1   2   3   4   5 CM

FIG. 6.   The bone awls

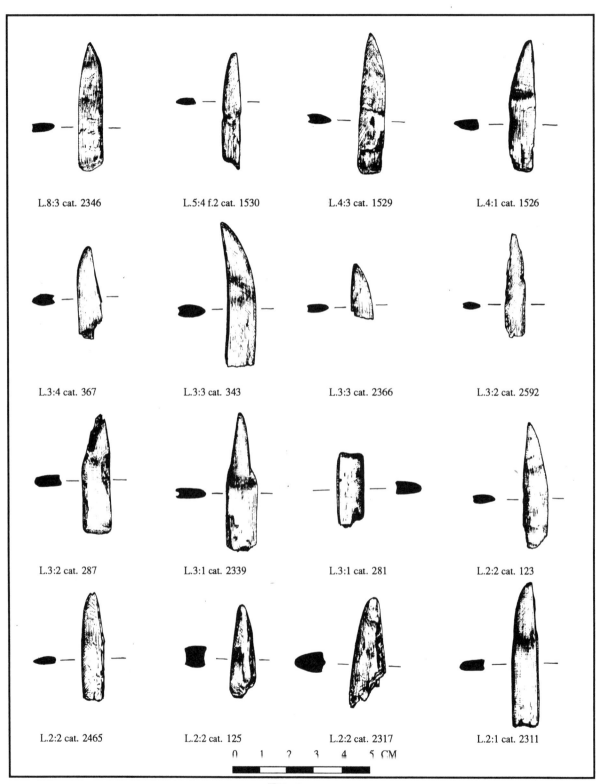

L.8:3 cat. 2346   L.5:4 f.2 cat. 1530   L.4:3 cat. 1529   L.4:1 cat. 1526

L.3:4 cat. 367   L.3:3 cat. 343   L.3:3 cat. 2366   L.3:2 cat. 2592

L.3:2 cat. 287   L.3:1 cat. 2339   L.3:1 cat. 281   L.2:2 cat. 123

L.2:2 cat. 2465   L.2:2 cat. 125   L.2:2 cat. 2317   L.2:1 cat. 2311

0   1   2   3   4   5 CM

FIG. 6 (cont.)

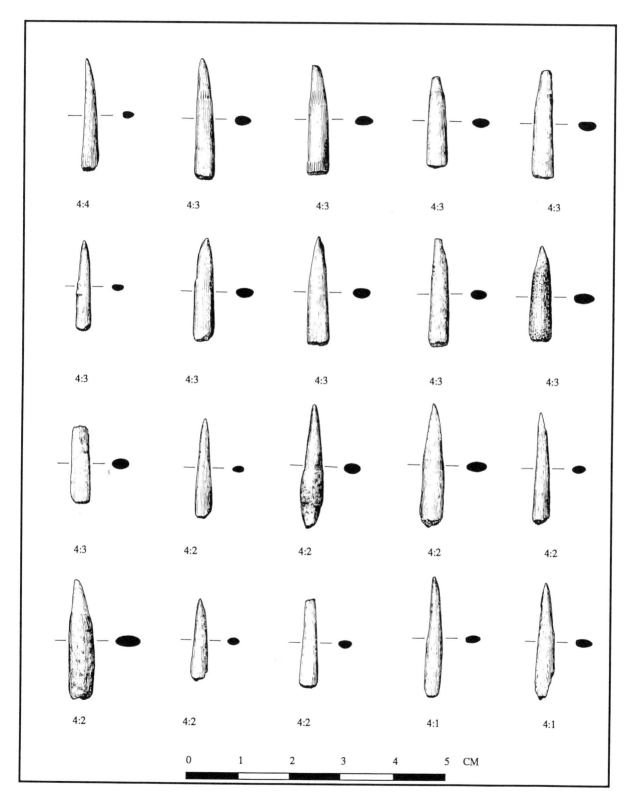

FIG. 7.   The bone micro-awls

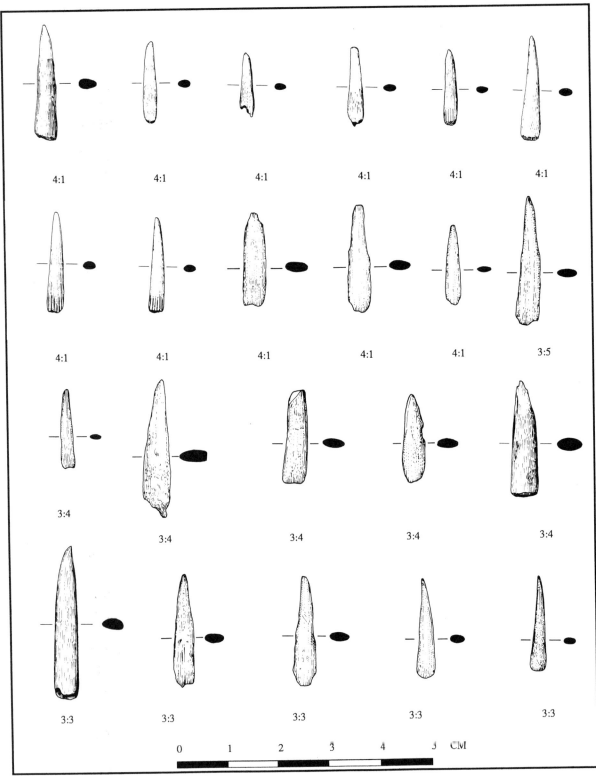

FIG. 7 (cont.)

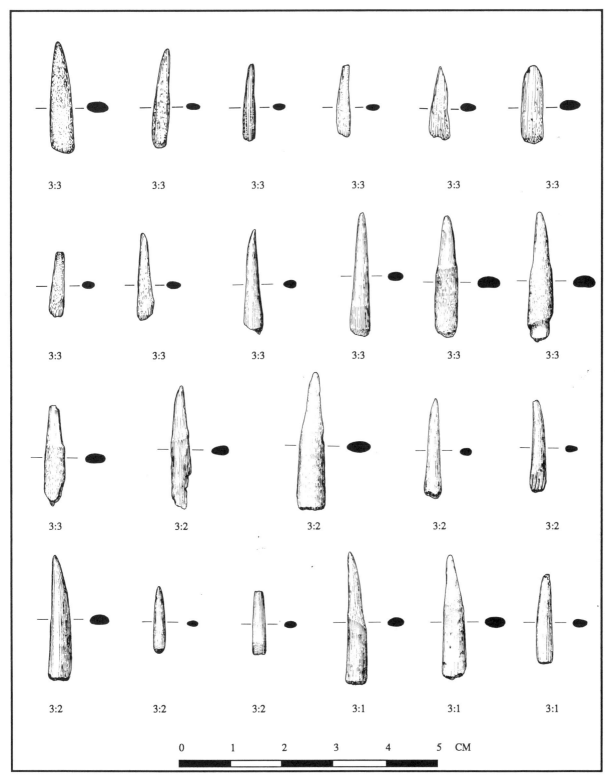

FIG. 7 (cont.)

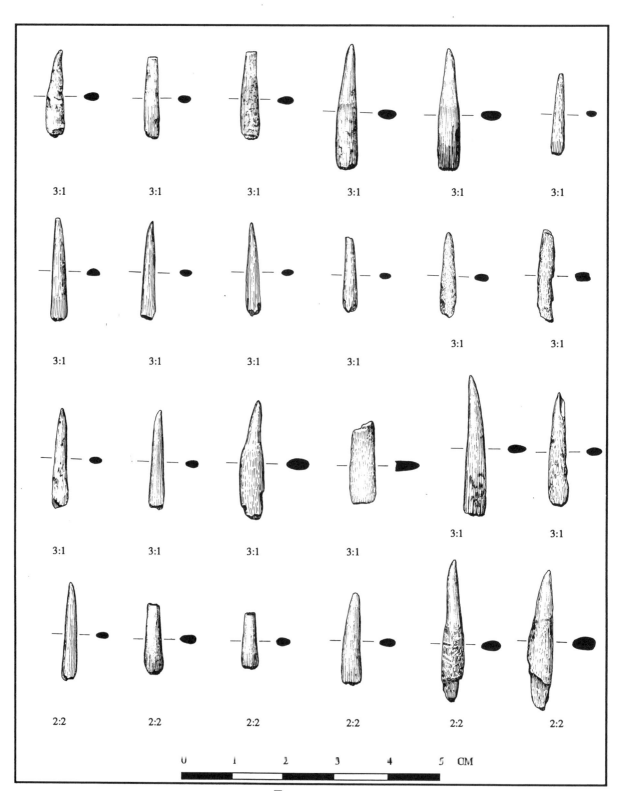

FIG. 7 (cont.)

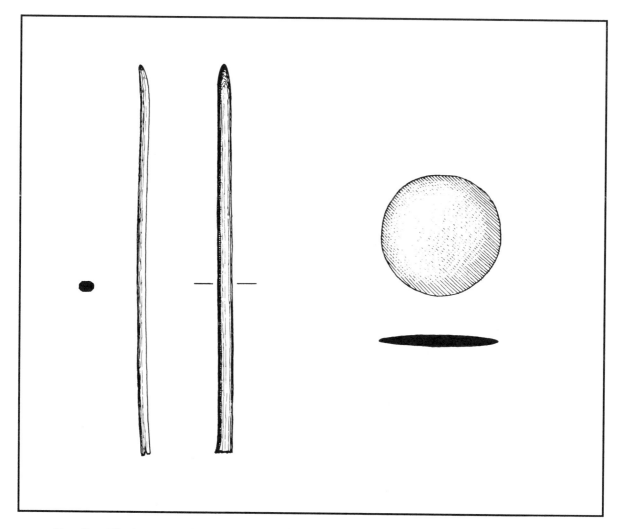

FIG. 8.   The bone needle (L. 2:2 cat. 2342, x2) and bone disc (L. 4:1 cat. 523, actual size)

THE WORKED FISH VERTEBRAE

A small sample of worked fish vertebrae has been identified (Fig. 10). They have in common the drilling of a central hole and grinding and smoothing of the edge of the rim. These edges reveal both the grinding which shaped them, and subsequent smoothing over and polishing of the worked surfaces. There is no consistent pattern of wear in the vicinity of the perforation to suggest that they were strung and worn as beads. Some specimens have been modified beyond the stages mentioned. Cat. 1704 (10:15) has been slit longitudinally down the middle. Both exposed surfaces were then ground and polished. The interior surface is polished all over, the exterior is polished only in a narrow band about 2 mm deep which runs as an exposed facet round the rim. The polished interior surface is slightly convex. The example from 10:3 lens 2, of which only a segment survives, has had the central area removed to leave what is, in effect, a band or ring. This treatment has also been applied to the example from 10:13 cat. 1329. Four were found in association with burials, three with B102 and a single specimen with B58. While the first three reveal little modification, the last was cut axially and the remaining half has a greatly enlarged central hole. Details are given in Table 6.

Mansuy (1902, 1923) identified similarly modified fish vertebrae at Samrong Sen, and suggested that they had been used as discs set into distended ear lobes. This is a possible use, but no such discs have been found in appropriate areas of the head in any of the burials from Khok Phanom Di.

TABLE 6:   *The provenance and size of the modified fish vertebrae*

Provenance	Cat. no.	Max. L	Max. D	Provenance	Cat. no.	Max. L	Max. D
11:1	3296a	34.1	15.0	11:1	3296b	23.2	10.2
11:1	3296c	22.2	10.2	11:1	3296d	23.0	10.1
11:1	3296e	22.7	10.1	11:1	3296f	23.0	10.1
11:1	3296g	23.1	10.1	11:1	3296h	23.6	10.6
11:1	3296i	23.1	10.2	11:1	3296j	22.0	9.8
11:1	3296k	36.1	15.1	10:19	1864	34.2	14.2
10:16	2571	54.0	20.2	10:16	2568	34.1	14.1
10:15	1704	34.5	-	10:15	1718	57.0	21.0
10:14	3297a	26.5	12.0	10:13	1329	-	-
10:3 1.2	1265	-	-	6:4	2555	24.0	-
5:3 f.5	617	18.5	6.3	4:2	2568a	16.6	-
4:2	2568b	10.0	3.8	4:2	2568c	9.2	4.6
B102	1584a	34.3	15.5	B102	1584b	34.5	14.9
B102	1584c	22.8	11.0	B58	1286	38.0	6.1

L: length; D: maximum depth

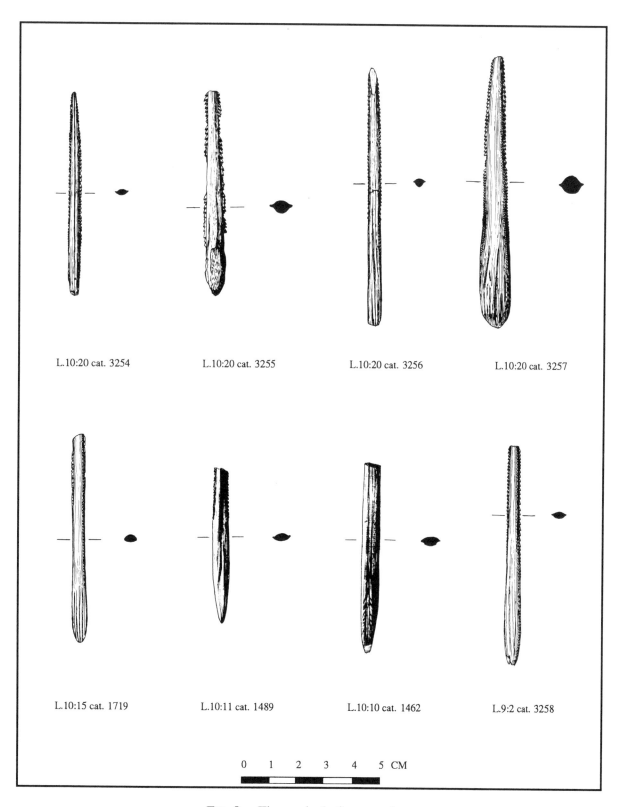

| L.10:20 cat. 3254 | L.10:20 cat. 3255 | L.10:20 cat. 3256 | L.10:20 cat. 3257 |

| L.10:15 cat. 1719 | L.10:11 cat. 1489 | L.10:10 cat. 1462 | L.9:2 cat. 3258 |

0   1   2   3   4   5 CM

FIG. 9.   The worked stingray spines

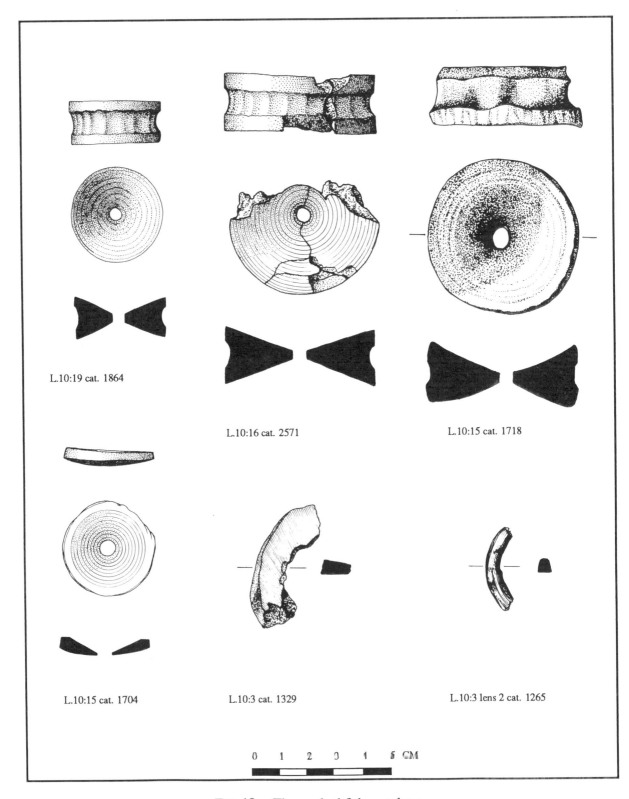

L.10:19 cat. 1864

L.10:16 cat. 2571

L.10:15 cat. 1718

L.10:15 cat. 1704

L.10:3 cat. 1329

L.10:3 lens 2 cat. 1265

0   1   2   3   4   5 CM

FIG. 10.   The worked fish vertebrae

Burial 102 cat. 1584b

Burial 102 cat. 1584a

Burial 102 cat. 1584c

Burial 58 cat. 1286

L.5:3 cat. 617

0 1 2 3 4 5 CM

FIG. 10 (cont.)

BONE BURNISHERS

The distinction between layers 5 and 4 is very clear. In the former, the deposits were soft, sandy and contained relatively few items of material culture. It has been argued that this reflects the use of this part of the site as a cemetery. The fauna from this layer indicates that coastal resources were still accessible. This situation changed with layer 4. The quantity of artefactual material rose sharply, marine resources diminished in favour of larger terrestrial mammals and no burials were encountered. Within this context, we also encounter a proliferation of bone tools, some of which can be ascribed with confidence to the deer, *Cervus unicolor*. The group of such artefacts to be described share a flat, convex working end worn to a polished surface (Fig. 11).

A particularly well-preserved and complete example, fashioned from the metapodial of a large deer, comes from layer 3:1 (cat. 223). It is 74.5 mm in length and 16.5 mm wide. The body of the implement bears the coarse abrasions left by the shaping of the artefact, probably with a grinding stone. The working surface, which is slightly convex, bears striations which run parallel with the long axis of the implement. The whole surface has a burnish which may result from regular handling, but this is accentuated on the two facets which make up the working end. A similar but unprovenanced tool revealed that attention was given, through grinding, to the provision of parallel sides behind the convex working surface. The marks of abrasion against a grinding surface are clearly visible on the body of the tool. The present length is 72.2 mm, and it is 19.0 mm wide. There is a polish, probably imparted by regular use, on both the upper and lower surfaces of the leading edge. The specimen from layer 3:2 (cat. 312) was again ground from a segment of deer's metapodial with attention being given to the provision of parallel sides. This tool is about 79.0 mm long and has a maximum width of 17.0 mm. Again, the working surface is markedly convex and bears a use-polish, whereas the body of the tool bears the striations resulting from initial manufacture. A broken specimen from layer 4:1 (cat. 501) has a width of 13.2 mm. The lower working surface has a clear facet with transverse striations which probably reflect shaping with an abrader. These lines are partially obliterated by the subsequent polishing on the working surfaces.

There are a further five such implements provided with parallel sides and a convex working end. Cat. 2512 from layer 4:1 was made from deer metapodial, but was broken axially in antiquity. This particular bone is straight in nature, and was preferred as a source of making these polishers. The small and broken tool from layer 2:3 (cat. 1504) has transverse striations on the body of the tool, but on the working surface, the striations run about 15–20° from the long axis. These may result from re-modelling the working edge rather than from actual use. A shallow flake of bone had been removed from one of the working facets, but the broken surface bore traces of polish which indicates continued use after the break occurred. Cat. 2479 from layer 2:2 was probably fashioned from a deer metapodial and has a maximum width of 14.2 mm, the surviving length being 70.6 mm. The two remaining examples of parallel-sided bone polishers, both of which are fragmentary, come from layer 3:3 (cat. 2365) and 3:2 (cat. 291).

There are, however, several examples of bone tools with convex working ends. These were made from bone or antler which does not provide parallel sides. A good example is a worked deer ulna (layer 4:1 cat. 2466). With the exception of the shape difference imposed by the different bone used, the grinding striations and polish match that described for the tools made from metapodials. Again, the convex, polished working edge is present on a section of antler from layer 3:5 (cat. 457). The piece of antler measures 55 by 28 mm. Of the eight remaining fragmentary examples, five come from layer 3 and two from layer 4. There is also a possible example from layer 8:5, which was probably made from a deer's metapodial. It has the characteristic polished convex working end, but lacks the careful forming of the parallel sides found with later examples. A shallow concavity along one edge, however, bears a polish indicating habitual movement across a soft medium.

Semenov (1964) devoted much attention to the configuration and use of convex-ended bone implements from Soviet sites, and has cited ethnographic parallels in Inuit contexts. He has concluded that these polished surfaces were used to concentrate pressure on the surface of hides to make them more attractive, stronger and more water-resistent. The class of tools from Khok Phanom Di, which are described as burnishers, have all the features which led Semenov to ascribe to some of the bone tools with which he was familiar, a function in preparing animal skins. It is held likely that attention to skins as a useful resource at Khok Phanom Di followed the environmental changes which accompanied a falling sea level.

BONE GROOVERS

There are six artefacts which have deep U-shaped straight grooves (Fig. 12). The earliest comes from layer 11:1 (cat. 2491). The sides of this implement have been ground down to form a thin (6 mm) tab of bone, along both surfaces of which there are U-shaped grooves. Within each of these, striations run parallel with the long axis. That from layer 10:14 (cat. 2387) has been worked in several ways. One lateral side has been ground to a cutting edge, which bears a mirror-like gloss. There are numerous fine striations running back almost at right angles from the cutting edge. These may have been the result of shaping and sharpening the blade, but some could also be due to use as a knife. The cutting blade is interrupted at one end by a narrow U-shaped groove within which there are many striations running across the long axis of the artefact. At the opposite end, and also running laterally across the bone, there are two much longer grooves located opposite each other. These also have numerous fine parallel striations. The edges of these grooves are also polished as if something was regularly run along them. In the absence of locally available fine-grained stone, the occupants of the site turned in this case to bone to supply a cutting edge and provided the tool with three grooves for reasons which are not easy to identify. It is conceivable that the cutting edge, with its marked gloss, resulted from use in cutting plant material as in harvesting or preparing fibres for cord or net making.

Another implement (layer 10:6 cat. 2397) matches that just described in virtually all respects. This item was ground to a very flat and thin configuration, being parallel-sided, 17 mm wide and just over 2 mm in thickness. At one end, there is a groove which runs diagonally across the tool, and against which it broke in antiquity. The groove is covered by parallel striations. Each of the long sides of the tool have been ground to a sharp cutting edge along which there is some gloss resulting from cutting. Like cat. 2387, this tool could have been used in cutting fibres, but a programme of experimentation would be necessary before more light is thrown on the possible use or uses to which such tools were put.

The fourth grooved bone tool comes from layer 10:16 (cat. 1731). Unlike the preceding examples, it has no surviving prepared edge for cutting, but it had been ground to a flat cross-section and it is possible that the battered edge on one side had formerly been honed to a cutting surface.

There are two grooves at one end. These are located opposite each other. One runs laterally across the tool and is 22 mm long. The other lies opposite and on the other side of the implement, which broke at the point of weakness between the two. There is a high gloss at the base of the groove and at the edges, as if a filament or yarn of some sort was moved along it.

A fifth specimen from layer 10:12 (cat. 3286) has two grooves on opposite sides of the flattened surfaces of the bone. Each has parallel striations running along the long axis of the groove. It is evident that something habitually ran along these grooves. Again, breakage came at the weak point where the two grooves almost met in the middle of the artefact.

The last grooved bone tool comes from a much later context in layer 2:2 (cat. 1492). It was made on a metacarpal of *Cervus unicolor*, the outer surfaces of which bear the marks of lateral abrasions on a grinding stone. In this instance, the groove has worn right through the bone to the medullary cavity. There are many fine, parallel striations within the groove.

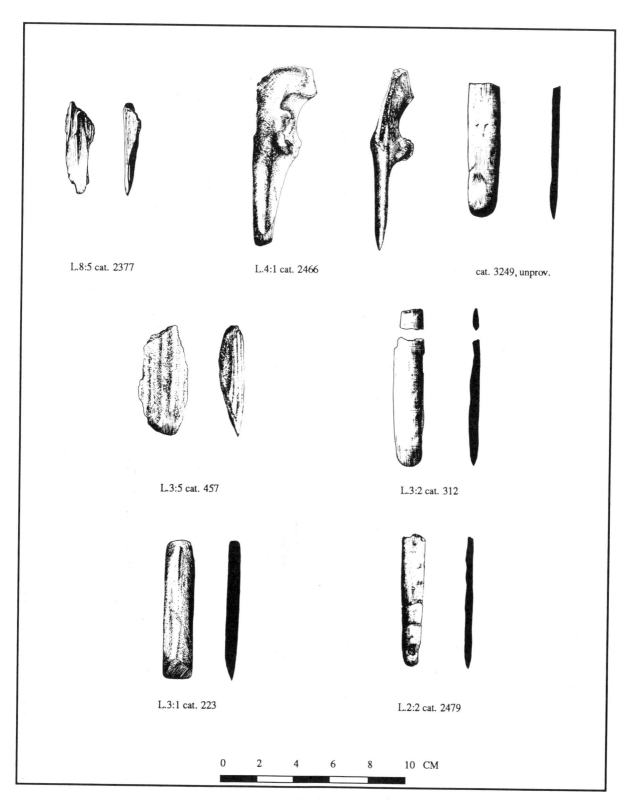

L.8:5 cat. 2377   L.4:1 cat. 2466   cat. 3249, unprov.

L.3:5 cat. 457   L.3:2 cat. 312

L.3:1 cat. 223   L.2:2 cat. 2479

0   2   4   6   8   10 CM

FIG. 11.   Examples of bone burnishers

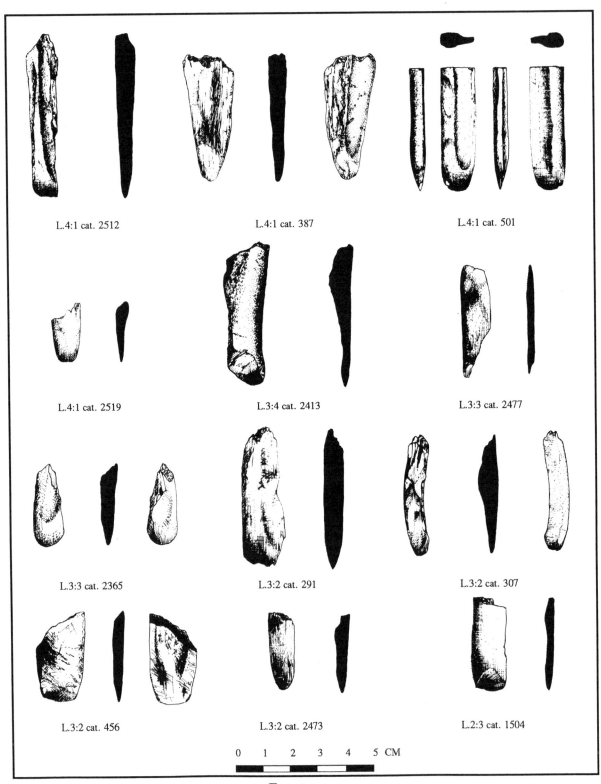

L.4:1 cat. 2512   L.4:1 cat. 387   L.4:1 cat. 501

L.4:1 cat. 2519   L.3:4 cat. 2413   L.3:3 cat. 2477

L.3:3 cat. 2365   L.3:2 cat. 291   L.3:2 cat. 307

L.3:2 cat. 456   L.3:2 cat. 2473   L.2:3 cat. 1504

0   1   2   3   4   5 CM

FIG. 11 (cont.)

BONE DISC

There is one circular bone disc. It was found in layer 4:1, cat. 523 (Fig. 8). The maximum diameter is 32.5 mm and the minimum diameter, 31.5 mm. It has a greatest thickness of 3 mm. The underside bears the grinding striations involved in shaping it. Those on a slight bevel round the outer surface were later partially obliterated by hatched striations which cover the rest of the artefact. On the upper surface, these striations have almost been obliterated by subsequent polishing, perhaps as a result of use or friction against another medium. Its use is unknown.

MISCELLANEOUS BONE AND ANTLER ARTEFACTS

There are a number of bone or antler artefacts which do not display sufficient similarity with others to be grouped together. These are described below in the sequential order in which they occurred in the site, beginning with the earliest (Fig. 13).

- 10:17 lens 15 cat. 2355. This is a segment of the long bone probably derived from a bird. It has transverse striations over most of its surface, perhaps to shape it.

- 10:16 cat. 2357 (Fig. 13a) shares many of the features of the tools described above as bone polishers. It has a convex working end, which reveals traces of polish. It was excluded from the above group only because it occurred in a much earlier context in the site's sequence.

- 10:11 cat. 1632 (Fig. 13b) was probably shaped from a deer's metapodial bone. At one end, there is a convex working surface bearing marked polishing. The other end has a semicircular groove within which there are many parallel striations which run across the long axis of the implement. The inside of the groove has a polished surface. Unfortunately, the tool has fractured along its long axis.

- 9:5 cat. 2048 (Fig. 13c). The functional end of this implement has been ground to a chisel-like working surface not dissimilar from the bone bobbins described above. The artefact lacks the parallel sides of the bobbins, however, as well as the groove down one side. It is quite possible that it fulfilled a similar function to the polishers which became so prevalent from layer 4.

- 7:1 cat. 1631(Fig. 13e). This long and narrow artefact was probably never completed. Its surface bears longitudinal scars indicating that a heavy implement had been used for rough shaping. There is a stepped tang at one end, indicating the possibility of intended hafting, and the shape overall hints at an end use as a projectile point.

- 6:4 cat. 2471. This specimen, which probably comes from a fish bone, has been ground to the form of a point. There are several deep notches cut across the pointed end.

- 6:1 cat. 603 (Fig. 13f) was ground to a point at one end, and a spatula shape at the other. It is 75 mm long, and has a maximum width of 12.3 mm. The obvious care which has been applied to the shaping of each end indicates more than one application for the one tool. No other implement from Khok Phanom Di is similar. Both the top and underneath surfaces are polished.

- 4:4 cat. 2438 is 37 mm long, though it has been broken at both ends. It has been ground to a convex outer surface, while one end was pointed. The outer surface is smooth and, where not eroded, the surface bears striations running along the main axis.

- 4:4 cat. 2440 (Fig. 13i). comprises a section of bone ground to a curved form, the outer surface being shiny. Manufacturing striations have been smoothed.

- 4:3 cat. 2508 (Fig. 13g). After having been detached from the parent tine by grooving and splitting, this section of antler was subjected to a process which left shallow striations laterally across the central area which produced a waisted effect as the antler was gradually worn away. This waisted area reveals traces of polish on the surface.

- 4:3 cat. 667 (Fig. 13j). This broken piece has a rectangular cross section, ending with a blunt point. It has slight polishing on the surviving surface.

- 4:2 cat. 2516 (Fig. 13r). This highly polished fragment of bone has been ground to a hooked end.

- 4:2 cat. 2517 (Fig. 13s). comprises a half section of a small bird bone. Its tip is missing, but the rest has been ground, resulting in fine striations, some of which are hatched.

- 4:1 cat. 2522 (Fig. 13u). has been first ground to a sharp point, which was subsequently used is such a manner as to produce a high sheen over all the surviving surface.

- 4:1 cat. 2484 (Fig. 13k). has been ground to the form of a blunt point, leaving striations all over its surviving surface. The tip is polished, partially obliterating the striations.

- 3:4 cat. 360 (Fig. 13h). This piece, which probably derives from fish bone, has been ground to the form of a point, below which is a long, straight edge. This edge is smoothed and polished, which argues against its having been used as a knife or cutting surface. The artefact gives the impression of having been used both as an awl and some sort of polisher on a soft medium.

- 3:3 cat. 2333. This section of bone has been ground to a flat, disc-like shape. Fine striations and polish cover the flat surface.

- 3:3 cat. 325 (Fig. 13m) has been ground to the form of a point. It bears many deep striations, many of which run across the long axis of the tool, making it likely that they result from shaping it rather than from use.

- 3:3 cat. 3266. Only a sliver of this artefact survives, but it contains a sharp edge from which striations run at 90° to the cutting surface as if it was used as a knife.

- 3:2 cat. 310 (Fig. 13n) was fashioned from a fish bone. It has the form of a hollow-ground chisel with a working surface 13.3 mm wide. The cutting edge has a small facet, and bears fine striations running back at 90° to its surface.

- 3:2 cat. 313 (Fig. 13l) has a slight curvature and rounded rectangular cross-section. One edge bears manufacturing striations, but the other is smooth and polished.

- 3:2 cat. 298 (Fig. 13v). This short (21.5 mm) length of bone has been ground to a sharp point at one end, the point itself having a polished surface.

- 3:1 cat. 2463 (Fig. 13w) has been half-sectioned longitudinally, and has a polished, hollow-ground working edge.

- 3:1 cat. 251. This comprises a section of long bone which has been ground all over into a sub-rectangular form.

- 2:3 cat. 174 (Fig. 13x) was ground all over to produce a convex working end, where the grinding striations have been smoothed over, partially obliterating them.

- 2:3 cat. 172 (Fig. 13y). There are grinding marks along the surface of this implement, which were later smoothed over as the artefact was used. This has resulted in a polished surface. The point end is missing, but the surviving section probably came from a pointed implement like an awl.

- 2:3 cat. 1503 (Fig. 13o). This tool, which has been broken such that the cutting end only survives, has a sharp and polished end. In addition to a sharpened end worn to a mirror-like gloss, the working end also has a set of three parallel grooves running at an angle of about 45° to the long axis on each surface. The tops of these grooves are polished, but the valleys are not. They may result from repetitive sharpening of the blade, although it is hard to see how this could have produced such pronounced grooves. One edge of the tool has been broken, but there is a hint that there was once a broad groove down it in the manner of the bobbins and awls described above.

- 2:2 cat. 2312 (Fig. 13aa). Again, grinding striations cover this implement, many being cross-hatched. The blunted point has been ground and smoothed over with use.

- 2:2 cat. 3248 (Fig. 13z). This is a piece of bone with a semi-circular cross-section, the surface of which is smoothed and polished.

- 2:1 cat. 1629 comprises a broken mid section of rounded length of bone, the diameter being 12 by 10.5 mm. The surviving section bears a relief carving of two wing-like elements.

The presence of grinding striations on sections of long bone has also been noted, though in none of the following items was there a completed form. Nor was any possible use apparent. It is possible that these specimens reflect a stage in the preparation of artefacts which remained incomplete. They come from the following contexts: 10:25 l. 29, cat. 2356; 10:25 l. 29, cat. 1888; 10:23, cat. 2549; 10:23, cat. 3267; 120:23, cat. 3268; 10:18, cat. 2354; 10:14, cat . 2392; 10:12, cat. 2069; 9:6, cat. 2462; 9:6 lens 9, cat. 3270; 8:2, cat. 2446; 8:1, 2375; 7:7, cat. 3271; 7:7, cat. 3272; 7:4, cat. 3274; 6:4, cat. 3292; 4:2, cat. 3277, 3:2, cat. 2460.

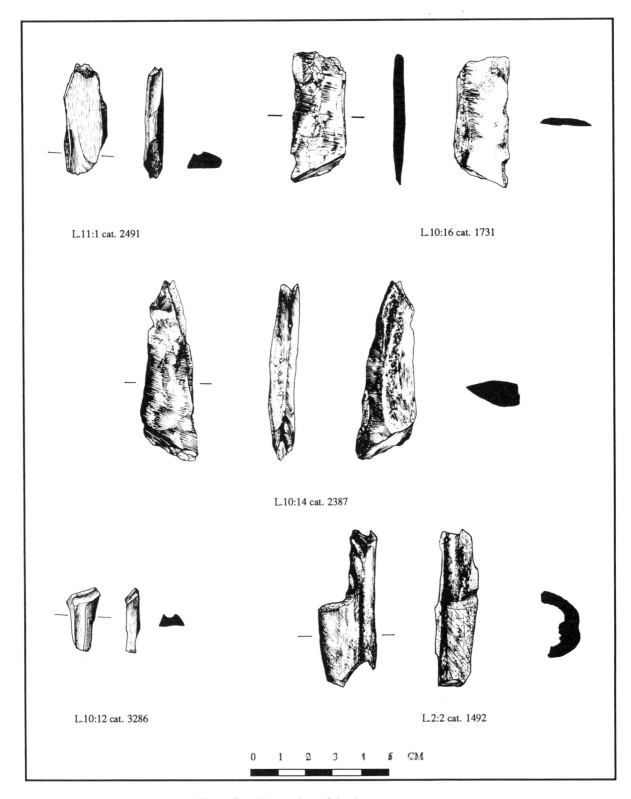

L.11:1 cat. 2491   L.10:16 cat. 1731

L.10:14 cat. 2387

L.10:12 cat. 3286   L.2:2 cat. 1492

0   1   2   3   4   5   CM

FIG. 12.   Examples of the bone groovers

THE WORKED ANTLER

The development of an antler industry commenced in layer 4 contexts. There are fifteen pieces of worked antler from layers 2–4 of which some are too fragmentary to describe. This is very probably related to the change in the environment which occurred at the end of layer 5. At that part of the sequence, the dominance of marine species fell away, to be replaced by an increase in land mammals among which *Cervus unicolor* was prominent. The remains of worked antler tell us more of the method of obtaining tabs or blanks than complete artefacts, if any. Perhaps the most informative specimen in this respect comes from layer 2:2 (cat. 182, Fig. 14). This is a large piece of antler incorporating the junction of the two main tines. At the base of this junction, at least seven firm but carefully placed cuts with a sharp and heavy implement, such as an axe, had severed the outer surface of the antler before it was detached from the cranium. About 25 mm above this break, an abrasive implement had been used to file a V-shaped groove round the circumference of the antler. In another example from layer 2:3, cat. 2430, an identical conjunction of heavy cut marks associated with a groove about 25 mm up the tine is present. It is, of course, possible that the grooves were worn not with the intention of cutting off a tab from the antler, but rather as a result of use-wear of some sort. Indeed, there are two small grooves with parallel striations at the junction of the two tines in cat. 182. In another example, cat. 459, there is a groove still bearing many parallel striations above that one which in due course severed the tine. A similar double grooving is present on cat. 2444 from layer 2:3. On the other hand, in some cases, similar grooving has been noted right round the tine, followed by a break. This is seen in another example from layer 2:2 (cat. 118) where the groove penetrates to a depth of 5 mm and the fracture of the tine occurred at the base of the 'V'. There is a second example from 3:4 (cat. 2443), where a series of cuts had succeeded in detaching a 86 mm length of tine. Subsequent use had converted the outer surface to a smooth and polished condition. A specimen from 3:1, cat. 1629, also has the cut grooves to break a length of tine associated with a notably smoothed surface. Further examples of this grooving technique come from 4:1 f. 5, cat. 3283; 3:2, cats. 431 and 2467; 2:2, cat. 2449 and 1:3 cat. 2474. While it is acknowledged that the grooves may result from use-wear, the interpretation that they represent attempts to cut the antler into workable segments is preferred at present.

THE WORKED TURTLE CARAPACE

During mortuary phases 3 and 4, males were often interred in association with turtle carapace ornaments. A number of fragments of cut and shaped turtle carapace, which might have come from these ornamental plaques, have been found. The only one which reveals features other than cut edges was found in layer 8:4 lens 7. This has a circular shape, and had a small hole cut in the middle. The cutting of such holes in the middle was a recurrent feature of these plaques, and this artefact has the appearance of a miniature version (Fig. 15). The diameter of the surviving piece is 88 mm. Other fragments of cut carapace come from the following contexts: 11:1, cat. 3262; 11:1, cat. 3263; 10:25 cat. 2563; 10:25 lens 29, cat. 2390; 10:24, cat. 2562; 10:22, cat. 2393; 10:21, cat. 2352; 8:5, cat. 993; 6:2 cat. 894; 3:1, cat. 2410; 2:2, cat. 3291; 2:2, cat. 2368.

A further section of carapace from 2:2 cat. 202 has two parallel lines cut across the surface (Fig. 15).

PELLET-BOW PELLETS

TABLE 7: *The provenance and size of the clay pellets*

Prov.	Diam.	Prov.	Diam.	Prov.	Diam.	Prov.	Diam.	Prov.	Diam.
11:1	20.0	11:1	17.5	10:23	18.0	10:23 1.26	19.0	10:23 1.26	19.4
10:22	20.4	10:20	12.6	10:20	16.0	10:20	15.2	10:19	20.2
10:18	21.2	10:18	17.0	10:16	21.5	10:16	19.0	10:15	16.2
10:14	17.0	10:14	17.8	10:13 f. 13	22.0	10:13	-	10:13	19.8
10:12	21.0	10:12	21.5	10:11	17.6	10:11	20.8	10:11	18.6
10:11	16.0	10:11 f.2	19.0	10:10	21.3	10:10	16.5	10:10	20.2
10:9	17.2	10:8	-	10:6	23.0	10:6	19.1	10:6	22.5
10:4	20.1	10:3 1.2	19.1	10:3 1. 2	19.6	10:3 1.2	20:0	10:3 1. 2	19.4
9:6	19.2	9:4	21.2	8:3	24.5	8:1	19.0	6:7 f. 11	17.5
6:6	18.6	6:5	15.8	6:5	18.2	6:5	14.6	6:4	20.1
6:3	19.4	6:3 f. 49	20.2	6:2	19.9	6:2	20.0	6:2	21.0
6:2 f.5	17.0	6:1	17.6	6:1	20.0	6:1 1.2.	17.3	5:5	16.5
5:5 f.2	16.2	5:4	20.5	5:4	19.8	5:2	19.4	5:1	12.0
5:1	17.8	5:rs.24	21.0	4:5 f.1	21.0	4:4	20.0	4:4	17.2
4:4 f.1	14.2	4:4 f.4	17.3	4:3	15.2	4:3	17.9	4:3	12.3
4:3	17.0	4:3	20.1	4:3 f.8	20.1	4:3 f.8	20.1	4:3 f.6	20.2
4:2	21.6	4:2	20.3	4:2	21.0	4:2	11.2	4:1	21.1
4:1 f.1	20.5	4:1 f.5	20.0	4:1 f.5	20.2	4:1 f.5.	21.2	3:5	18.0
3:5	15.2	3:5	13.2	3:4	19.0	3:4	19.8	3:4	16.0
3:4	17.9	3:4	15.0	3:4	21.0	3:4	18.0	3:4	18.3
3:4	14.5	3:3	13.0	3:3	19.5	3:3	17.9	3:3	17.0
3:3	11.2	3:2	14.0	3:2	14.5	3:2	15.1	3:2	17.1
3:2	17.3	3:2	20.1	3:2	14.0	3:2	18.6	3:1	20.0
3:1	20.0	3:1	18.9	3:1	14.2	3:1	16.9	3:1	17.0
3:1	18.5	3:1	11.4	3:1	20.3	3:1	17.1	3:1	14.2
3:1	14.6	3:1	14.8	2:3	10.6	2:3	19.2	2:2	15.0
2:2	18.9	2:2	19.4	2:2	23.0	2:2	14.1	2:2	17.0
2:2	17.4	2:2	21.0	2:2	20.2	2:2	17.0	2:2	12.0
2:2	15.8	2:1	14.5	2:1	17.2	2:1	19.1	2:1	15.2
2:1	17.6	2:1	17.2	2:1	14.2	2:1	17.0	2:1	18.2
1:4	15.8	1:2	21.6	1:2	24.2	1:2	19.5	1:1	17.8

These small balls of clay are thought to have been used as ammunition for the pellet bow. They are common at Ban Na Di and Ban Chiang, where one burial included a heap of them near the skull. The numbers of pellets declined sharply between layers 5 and 9, but rose during layers 2 to 4.

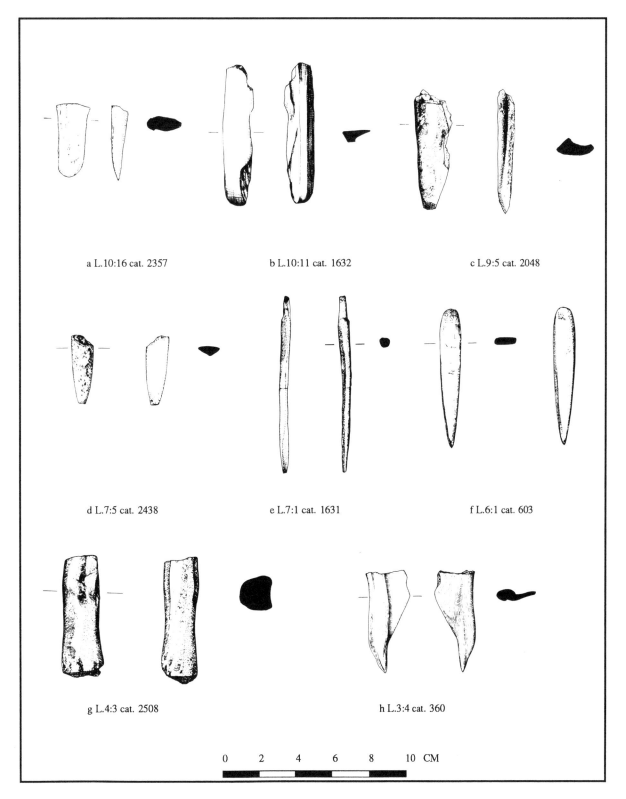

a L.10:16 cat. 2357   b L.10:11 cat. 1632   c L.9:5 cat. 2048

d L.7:5 cat. 2438   e L.7:1 cat. 1631   f L.6:1 cat. 603

g L.4:3 cat. 2508   h L.3:4 cat. 360

0   2   4   6   8   10 CM

FIG. 13.   Examples of miscellaneous bone artefacts

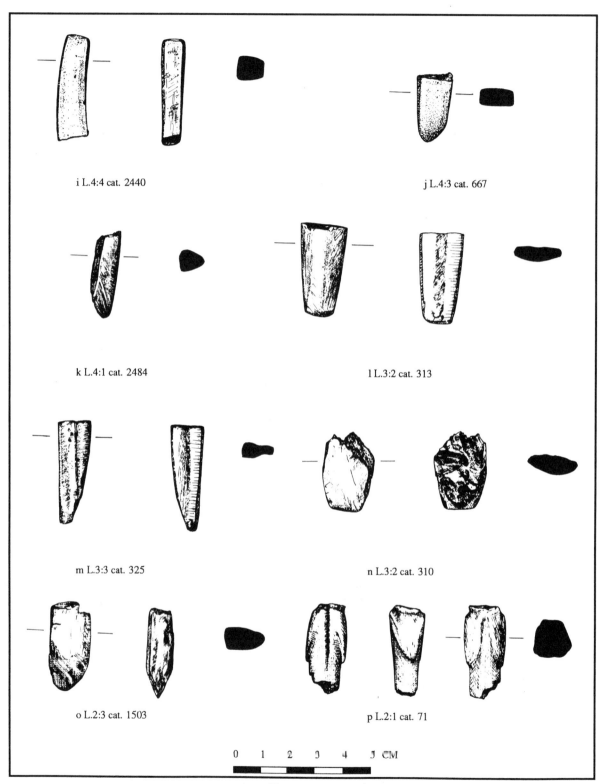

i L.4:4 cat. 2440

j L.4:3 cat. 667

k L.4:1 cat. 2484

l L.3:2 cat. 313

m L.3:3 cat. 325

n L.3:2 cat. 310

o L.2:3 cat. 1503

p L.2:1 cat. 71

0   1   2   3   4   5 CM

FIG. 13 (cont.)

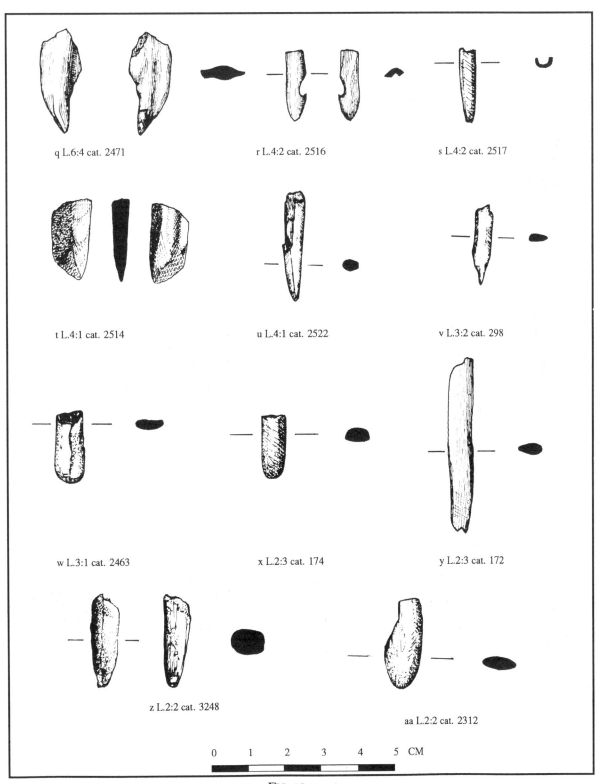

q L.6:4 cat. 2471   r L.4:2 cat. 2516   s L.4:2 cat. 2517

t L.4:1 cat. 2514   u L.4:1 cat. 2522   v L.3:2 cat. 298

w L.3:1 cat. 2463   x L.2:3 cat. 174   y L.2:3 cat. 172

z L.2:2 cat. 3248

aa L.2:2 cat. 2312

0   1   2   3   4   5   CM

FIG. 13 (cont.)

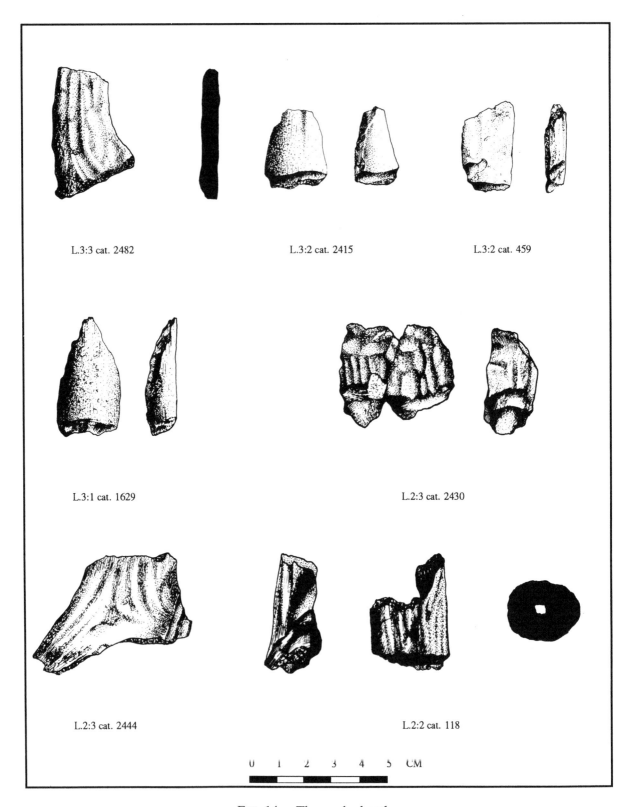

L.3:3 cat. 2482   L.3:2 cat. 2415   L.3:2 cat. 459

L.3:1 cat. 1629   L.2:3 cat. 2430

L.2:3 cat. 2444   L.2:2 cat. 118

0   1   2   3   4   5   CM

FIG. 14.   The worked antler

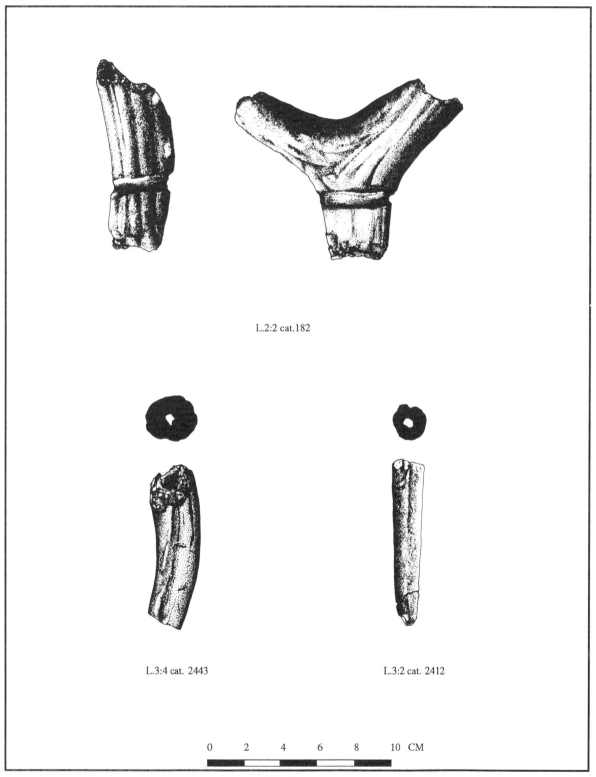

L.2:2 cat.182

L.3:4 cat. 2443

L.3:2 cat. 2412

0   2   4   6   8   10 CM

FIG. 14 (cont.)

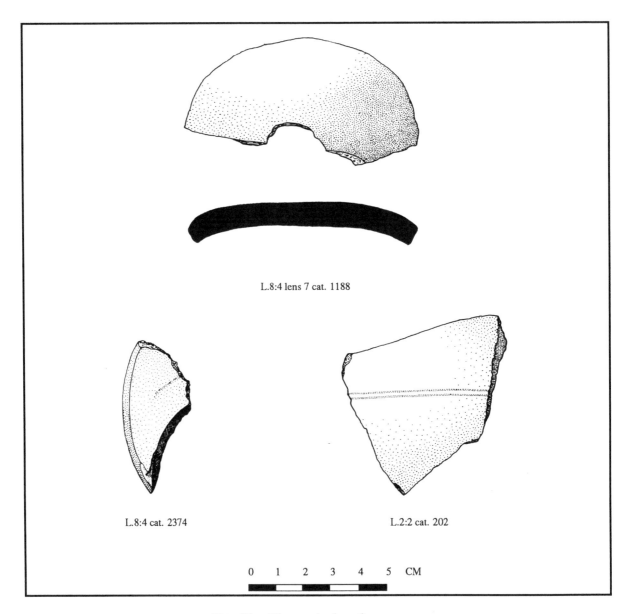

L.8:4 lens 7 cat. 1188

L.8:4 cat. 2374

L.2:2 cat. 202

0   1   2   3   4   5   CM

FIG. 15.   The worked turtle carapace

II. THE INDUSTRIAL STONE TECHNOLOGY

Pirapon Pisnupong

INTRODUCTION

THE general area in the vicinity of the site is flat, comprising former marine and brackish-water deposits. These give way to the slightly elevated low-terrace alluvial soils. Khao Kirirom, a prominent hill about 7 km southeast of Khok Phanom Di, is made of phyllite and it dominates this part of the lowland plain (Figs. 16 and 17). About 70-100 km from the mound, the coastal plain gives way to elevated uplands. On the north and the northeast, they are Khao Kheo, Khao Had Yao, and Khao Yai. The mountain ranges of Khao Cha Mao, Khao Cha Mun, Khao Ang Lue Nai and Khao Takrub lie to the south and the southeast. There are several smaller hills on the plain between the mountains and Khok Phanom Di. These are known as Khao Dong Yang, Khao Cham Ra Kham, and Khao Mun Ted (Fig. 17).

The earliest rock formation in the surrounding uplands is Pre-Cambrian amphibolite. It trends in a northwest to southeast direction from Chachoengsao Province to the coastal area of Rayong Province (Fig. 17). The Ordovician rocks are quartzite, slaty shale, slate, quartzitic sandstone and limestone located on the coastal area of Chonburi Province. The Silurian-Devonian rocks are quartzite, limestone, shale, slaty shale, and quartzitic sandstone located from Chachoengsao and Prachinburi Provinces to the Rayong and Chanthaburi coasts. The Carboniferous siltstone, slaty shale, rhyolitic tuff, limestone, quartzite, and tuffaceous sandstone are located in the south of Amphoe Kabinburi in Prachinburi Province, expanding southward to Amphoe Klaeng in Rayong Province. The Permo-Carboniferous rocks and the red-black rocks such as sandstone, mudstone and tuffaceous shale, are formed on the Rayong and Chanthaburi coasts and trend northwards. Permian grey and dark grey limestone is found in the central area of this region. On the coastal plain and the high valleys, the sedimentation of sand takes place while laterite, gravel, silt, and clay particles have been deposited on the river terraces (Nakinbodee *et al.*, 1976).

Soils in this area are regarded as a part of the deposition of the Bangkok Plain. They comprise brackish-water deposits on former tidal flat, which was recently 2–3 m above sea-level. These soils are fine-textured, very high in acidity, and have a high sulphate content. Radiocarbon dates indicate that deposition commenced from about 6,700 BP and ended about 3,000 BP (Fig. 17).

Most of the Khok Phanom Di polished stone adzes, chisels and polished flakes from the 1982 excavation were made from extrusive igneous rocks, especially andesite and andesitic tuff (Maranet and Boonsue, 1984). These outcrop in the uplands about 60-100 km east of the site. Petrographical analyses of the polished stone material from that excavation indicate that andesite was the most abundant raw material. It is a fine-grained, porphyritic greenish-grey to dark grey rock composed of plagioclase- oligoclase-andesine feldspar with actinolite-tremolite amphibole as the major minerals. The minor minerals include quartz, chlorite and magnetite. The nearest andesite outcrop is found on Khao Luk Chang, Khao Mai Kaew and Khao Chin about 65-70 km northeast of Khok Phanom Di (Fig. 16). The andesitic tuff has a similar composition, but andesitic tuff contains rock

45

fragments of shale, sandstone, andesite, and has coarse to medium grains. This rock is usually found in the same source areas as andesite. Rhyolitic tuff was also identified, this being a very fine-grained, greenish-grey rock containing quartz, feldspar, muscovite, chlorite, and iron oxide (magnetite). Quartz and feldspar are the principal components. This type of rock is found at Khao Yai Moa Noi and Khao Tham Rat along the boundaries of Chonburi and Rayong Provinces about 90-100 km east of Khok Phanom Di.

The geological structure of this area is complicated, due to the occurrence of contact metamorphism in restricted zones adjacent to the bodies of plutonic rocks and regional metamorphism which developed over large areas, and is related to igneous intrusion (Turner and Verhoogen 1960). These metamorphisms alter igneous to metamorphosed igneous rocks. On the coast, rock beds slope downward to the west, while rock formations on the central and east of the area slope to the east due to folding and unconformity (Nakinbodee *et al.*, 1976). The stone samples from the 1985 excavation were selected and sent to the Department of Geology, University of Otago, to be thin-sectioned and identified. Most are identified as metamorphosed igneous rocks comprising volcanic sandstone and tuffs. The volcanic sandstone is poorly sorted with angular and subangular grains of coarse silt and sand tightly packed in an argillite matrix coloured green by chloritic material. About half the grains are particles of volcanic rock, chiefly andesite, and volcanic siltstone is similar, but has smaller grains. Fragments of various kinds of andesitic tuff predominate. These metamorphosed igneous rocks were formed by the mingling of pyroclastic and non-volcanic sedimentary materials (clay, silt, sand and gravel) before being lithified (Williams *et al.*, 1958). However, the sources of these metamorphosed igneous rocks are found in the Kaeng Krachan formation of Carboniferous rocks (Fig. 16), the same area as the extrusive igneous rocks described in the identification of materials from the 1982 excavation. The resources of fine-grained volcanic rocks along the boundary of Bangkok Plain are found in the east and northeast, hills containing outcrops of andesite, a dark greenish-grey to purple, fine-grained rock. These extrusive igneous rocks were found as volcanic flows over the sedimentary rocks of the Kaeng Krachan formation (Carboniferous rocks) at Khao Babaroon and Khao Chin in Chachoengsao Province. These hills are about 60 km to the east, and extend southward to about 5 km from Khao Cha Mao, the area upstream of the Phang Raad River in Rayong Province about 170 km from Khok Phanom Di. This particular outcrop contains fine-grained, dark greenish-grey to purple andesite. The Kaeng Krachan formation can be divided into 2 units, Cb1 in the lower layer comprising micaceous siltstone, slate, shale, rhyolitic tuff, limestone, quartzite, sandstone, chert and conglomerate. Cb2 comprises tuffaceous sandstone, greywacke shale and slaty shale. They are found in the middle and eastern parts of Southeast Thailand. In the Kanchanaburi formation of Silurian-Devonian rocks, the extrusive igneous rocks are found among quartz mica schist, medium-grained and yellowish-brown sandstone interbedded with tuffaceous sandstone and chert beds at Khao Mai Kaew and Khao Luk Chang in Prachinburi Province 64 km to the north-east. Further east in Prachinburi Province, about 100 km from Khok Phanom Di, the Triassic rocks at Khao Sam Sip, Khao Tham Ma Kok and Khao Yai Laem contain andesite, welded tuff, tuff, agglomerate, andesitic basalt and minor rhyolite.

A few ground hoes were found during the 1982 and 1985 excavations. They were made of leucogranite, an intrusive igneous rock which is a yellowish-brownish grey, medium grained, altered rock composed of quartz, feldspar (partly to mostly altered to kaolinite), and, less frequently, tourmaline, mica and iron oxide. It is a light-coloured granite which contains less than 30% of mafic or dark minerals. This type of Carboniferous rock is found at Khao Kheo and Khao Chomphu about 50 km south of Khok Phanom Di (Fig. 16, Nakinbodee *et al.*, 1976).

Apart from the polished stone artefacts, the prehistoric people on Khok Phanom Di also used various types of rock suitable for different functions. Most of the grinding stones and whetstones were made of sedimentary rocks such as sandstone, siltstone and mudstone. The stone disc/bangles derive from metamorphic rocks like siltstone, shale, or slaty shale. Reddish brown shale was used for the stone polishers. The pounders are made of quartzite. The detailed description of these rocks and their most likely sources follow.

1. Sandstone. Most of the grinding stones and whetstones were made of varieties of sandstone which vary according to their grain, texture and composition. The principal composition comprises quartz, feldspar, mica and iron oxide.

2. Siltstone. A dark grey, more highly silicified, very fine-grained rock (finer than sandstone), mainly composed of fine-grained quartz, sericite, feldspar and in some cases iron oxide.

3. Mudstone and claystone. A reddish-brown, very fine-grained, rather compact rock composed of iron oxide, sericite, chlorite, and minor quartz and feldspar. It is the finest sedimentary rock among the sandstones and siltstones.

4. Shale. A reddish-brown, fine-grained rock composed of sericite, iron oxide, chlorite, quartz and feldspar.

5. Slate and slaty shale. A greenish to dark greenish-grey, fine-grained rock with a slaty cleavage composed chiefly of chlorite, sericite, feldspar, quartz, chlorite and quartz, and less commonly of iron oxide.

6. Quartzite. A compact rock varying in colour, and composed chiefly of quartz and feldspar.

The most probable sources of the sandstone from Khok Phanom Di may be located on two formations in the Korat group of Jurassic rocks. First, the Pra Wihan formation comprises white, brown and yellowish-brown, medium-grained, well-cemented sandstone, purplish-red siltstone and white grey claystone. Second, the Phu Kradung formation comprises calcareous, micaceous, reddish-brown, purplish-red siltstone and greenish-grey to yellowish-brown sandstone. These formations are located on the Khao Yai ranges about 80 km northeast of Khok Phanom Di. Reddish-brown shale, greenish-grey to brownish-grey slaty shale and dark grey slate were used to make stone disc/bangles which concentrated in zone C. Reddish-brown shale was also used for polishers and sources of red pigment. They are sedimentary and metamorphic rocks, for example the greenish to dark greenish-grey slaty shale and dark grey slate are found in the Thung Song formation of Ordovician rocks. This Thung Song formation is located along the coast from Chonburi Province to Rayong Province about 30 km southwest from Khok Phanom Di. Most quartz and quartzite burnishers are river pebbles.

Although the raw material resources have not been definitely located and the stone quarries have not yet been found, there is no doubt that the sources are in the areas where the volcanic materials were deposited. These are located on the east of the Bangkok Plain, especially among the Carboniferous rocks. Although there are igneous outcrops in the north of this plain, for example near Saraburi and Lopburi Provinces, the polished stone artefacts found in those areas are made of different materials from the sample from Khok Phanom Di. Apart from these, the next available source of igneous rocks is to be found at the Kra Isthmus, 300 km to the southwest in a direct line across the Gulf of Siam. It is, therefore, predicted that the sources for the Khok Phanom Di stone artefacts will be identified in the highlands in and near the headwaters of the Bang Pakong River. This situation poses a number of questions. These include the probable location of the stone quarries, the forms of raw materials, the means of transportation and the consumption of materials. Petrological factors make it likely that prehistoric people in this area obtained raw material for making stone adzes from the valley of the Klong Si Yat, a tributary of the Bang Pakong River. The rarity of stone flakes suggests that stone adzes were imported as rough-outs, in the case of cats. 2723 and 2057 (Fig. 30d), or as finished adzes. This would save transporting surplus material (Ericson, 1984). They may have been transported to the site along the Bang Pakong River, which was then probably wider than at present due to the higher sea-level. Sandstone, siltstone and claystone are abundant in the Khao Yai Ranges (Korat Group). Two varieties have been identified as deriving from either the Pra Wihan or the Phu Kradung formations. The closest area yielding these two varieties is upstream of the Prachinburi River which is, in effect, the upper reach of the Bang Pakong River itself. This stone, however, may not have been quarried because the raw materials could have been picked up from the river bed where boulders or cobbles of stone were naturally transported.

THE ADZES

In describing the polished stone adzes, the following system of nomenclature is employed (Fig. 18):

1. Front face: the ventral side of a tool which faces the user when handling the tool.

2. Back face: the dorsal side of tool, opposite the front face.

3. Cutting edge or edge: the blade of a tool formed by the intersection of the front and back sides.

4. Bevel: a platform above the cutting edge.

5. Bevel chin: a ridge where the bevel platform meets the face of a tool.

6. Blade corner: the angles on both ends of the cutting edge where the cutting edge intersects the side.

7. Side: the area of intersection between the front and back faces. It usually forms the edges on each side, but in some cases the edges were ground into narrow platforms.

8. Butt or tang: a handle or hafted part of a tool.

9. Poll: the opposite end to the cutting edge. It is either an edge or a platform.

The main characteristics which Duff used in his classification of such tools are the cross-section and modification to the butt. The cutting edge, size and shape are less important in undertaking a classification, but they provide some information for an understanding of lithic technology. The cross section has an important role in the classification of polished stone adzes. In Duff's system, cross-sections vary from simple rectangular to triangular (Duff, 1970). The sample from Khok

Phanom Di includes specimens with elliptical, oval to rounded rectangular and sub-triangular cross-sections. These fall into Duff's type 2. The predominant form (65%) has an elliptical section tending towards the semi-lenticular as the implement was truncated through constant sharpening of the blade. A third of the adzes have an oval to rounded rectangular cross-section wherein the side platforms are clearly defined and are either rounded or straight. Only one adze (cat. 1682) has a sub-triangular or virtually plano-convex section.

The cutting edge is the working part or the blade of an adze formed by the intersection of the front and the back faces. About 60% of the Khok Phanom Di adzes have asymmetrical bevels in which the back is wider than the front. Only 12 adzes have symmetrical bevels. The polished adzes from zone A, however, either have a vestigial bevel or none at all. In terms of shape, there are three different forms of cutting edge. One has a unilateral bevel with the cutting edge being formed by the intersection of the front face with the back bevel. The second has one bevel considerably broader than the other, and the third has no bevel at all. The bevels might have been formed unintentionally as a result of constant resharpening. The occurrence of bevels, therefore, has a minor role in the classification and is used to define sub-varieties after the consideration of the cross-section. From Khok Phanom Di, most of the adzes have asymmetrical bi-bevels which are assigned to type 2D, based on their rectangular section, and type 2G based on an elliptical section. There are also a few examples of types 2A, 2E and 2F, and only one sample of type 2B.

The butt is the handling or hafting part of the tool. Most of the adzes from Khok Phanom Di have butts which taper from the blade up to the poll, but in some cases it was modified in the form of a waist or shoulder to suit the intended function. The tool possibly had a quadrangular shape and was then ground on both sides of its butt to form a waist or shoulders. The modification of the butt is also an important variable in the classification of adzes. There are 16 complete and 7 incomplete shouldered adzes comprising 1 double shouldered, 12 open-curved shouldered, and 10 right-angled shouldered specimens. These, according to Duff's classification, are varieties of type 8. Most have an elliptical section and asymmetrical bi-bevels as in type 2G described above. Indeed, but for the shoulders, these two types are very similar. These are described below as type 8D, of which nine were recovered during the 1985 excavation. There is also one example of a type 8B, which has two hafting grooves on the sides of the tang (cat. 90, Fig. 24).

There are also some shouldered adzes with symmetrical features, which have been classified by Duff as axes, belonging to type 8F (cat. 1034) and type 8E (cats. 1945, 1836). One of these (cat. 1836), was reworked into a typical 2D adze. Most of the incomplete shouldered adzes have either right-angled or open-curved shoulders with an elliptical section, and these are classified as type 8D, but a round adze with a short and massive tang (cat. 1946) has been assigned to type 8H.

Apart from the shoulders, the characteristics of the poll are important in the lithic technology. They reflect the weight and possible uses of the tools, and how they were hafted or handled. Some display evidence for regrinding the poll after the adze suffered transverse fracture. This involved a radical change in the shape of the tool, and would have required a modification to the method of hafting.

According to these characteristics, the Khok Phanom Di polished stone adzes have been classified within the Duff system as set out in Table 8.

The detailed characteristics of the Khok Phanom Di adzes are as follows:

TABLE 8: *The distribution of adzes*

Layer	2A	2B	2D	2E	2F	2G	8B	8D	8E	8F	8H	No.
1	-	-	-	-	-	1	-	-	-	-	-	1
2	-	-	-	-	-	12	1	2	-	-	-	15
3	-	-	3	-	-	13	-	2	-	-	-	18
4	-	-	2	-	-	6	-	1	-	-	-	9
5	-	-	1	-	-	2	-	-	-	-	-	3
6	-	-	1	-	-	2	-	-	-	-	-	3
7	-	-	-	-	-	1	-	1	-	-	-	2
8	-	-	-	-	-	1	-	-	-	-	-	1
9	1	-	-	-	-	2	-	-	-	1	-	4
10	-	-	1	1	-	17	-	5	2	-	-	26
11	-	1	-	2	1	8	-	7	1	-	1	21
Total	1	1	8	3	1	65	1	18	3	1	1	103

- Type 2A. Rectangular to rounded rectangular section; unilateral bevel; the cutting edge formed by the intersection of front face and back bevel.

- Type 2B. Rounded rectangular section; back and front mutually concave longitudinally which reduces the quality of bevels; butt unmodified; poll of deep rectangular section.

- Type 2D. This type has a rectangular section; bi-bevels; the axis of the cutting edge created by the intersection of the back bevel and front bevel; front bevel wider than back; unmodified butt.

- Type 2E. The cross-section is either sub-rectangular or sub-elliptical with flattened sides; unilateral bevel; strongly curved cutting edge with everted corners.

- Type 2F. Shallow elliptical section with unilateral bevel.

- Type 2G. Elliptical to oval section, or round sub-triangular section, sides tapering to a rounded or flattened poll, unilateral bevel somewhat weakened by the downward descent of the front.

- Type 8B. A double-shouldered adze.

- Type 8D. A right-angled or open curved shouldered adze which may have types 2D and 2G as its prototype.

- Type 8E. A right-angled shouldered tool with symmetrical bilateral bevels which may be regarded as a shouldered axe.

- Type 8F. An open-curved shouldered tool with symmetrical bilateral bevels which may be regarded as a shouldered axe.

- Type 8H. Round-shaped, right-angled, shouldered adze, with a short tang and robust poll.

The following descriptions of polished stone adzes is presented according to the stratigraphical sequence. The complete or almost complete samples which form the basis of the detailed descriptions are grouped in the section on their tool types. Specimens which have lost an important part, but still provide information relating to the identification and classification of tool-types, are included.

Layer 11

Type 2B

- 11:2 f.1 cat. 1965. This specimen has an oval section; oval shape; straight cutting edge; symmetrical figure; no bevel chins; rounded sides; deep and straight poll. Its cutting edge was formed at the intersection of front and back faces which have equal convexity and give a symmetrical appearance. It was broken into 4 pieces when found, possibly after subjection to heat. This adze was made of fine volcanic sandstone and has a sharp edge. Damage is present only on the blade corners. There are flake scars on the butt near the side-edges and on the poll platform. Deep use-striations are not evident behind the cutting edge but there are faint fine striations at right-angles to the edge on both faces (Fig. 22b).

Type 2E

- 11:2 f.2 cat. 1942. This volcanic sandstone adze has a rectangular section; rectangular shape; symmetrical bi-bevels with unclear or no chins; flattened and straight poll with a poll platform and everted blade corners. Striations reflecting use at right-angles to the edge extend back to above the bevel chin. The cutting surface is blunt and the grinding striations lie against the axis in several directions (Fig. 22c).

- 11:1 cat. 1911. A volcanic sandstone adze with a rectangular cross-section; a rectangular shape with the front face wider than the back; no bevel chin; a slightly concave cutting edge; flattened and straight poll. The cutting edge has everted corners formed by grinding both sides of the butt. This sample has a symmetrical cutting edge according to the equal convexity of both faces (Fig. 22d). It has been resharpened so often that the shoulders have all but disappeared. The cutting edge is blunt and there are large flake scars along it. There are clear use striations behind the blunt cutting edge. Polishing striations are present on the sides and the butt.

Type 2F

- 11:1 cat. 1910. An elliptical-sectioned adze with an oval shape; unilateral bevel; round cutting edge and a flattened and rounded poll. The cutting edge was formed by the intersection of both convex front and back faces. The convexity of the front face is greater than the back one. It is made of fine volcanic sandstone and reveals very little damage to the cutting edge. In contrast to the polished surface of the butt, the poll bears peck marks which might result from percussion with the wooden haft. There are clear use striations on both sides of the cutting edge and these overlie previous resharpening striations which lie at 40° to the cutting edge and fade near the edge due to use. There is a slight facet between the resharpening and use striae (Fig. 22f).

Type 2G

- 11:2 f.2 cat. 1943. A truncated, triangular-shaped adze with an elliptical section; asymmetrical bi-bevels with suppressed bevel chins and a flattened and blunted point poll. Its cutting edge is slightly convex and it was ground, forming a narrow facet on the edge. It is made of fine volcanic sandstone. The cutting edge has been blunted by grinding in order to form a long, narrow facet about 1.3 mm wide. This was probably to obtain an appropriately convex shape of the edge prior to resharpening. A large flake scar at one end of the blade, resulting from damage in use, has been partially obliterated by grinding. Surface damage on the poll, caused it is felt by the impact there of the haft in use, has also been partially ground over. Fine striations (40°) on both sides of the bevel overlie 90° striations. It is felt that this pattern reflects sharpening applied over use-marks (Fig. 23a).

- 11:2 f.2 cat. 2042. This specimen comprises the cutting edge of a symmetrical, elliptical adze with no bevel (Fig. 26a).

- 11:2 f.2 cat. 1966. The differences between this volcanic siltstone adze and cat. 1920 lie only in its straight cutting edge, which runs obliquely from one blade corner to the other, and a deeper poll. It is made of volcanic siltstone, is blunt, and has the characteristic use marks running back at 90° from the cutting edge. The butt bears fainter striations at a series of angles. A large flake scar at the side of the butt has been partially obliterated by polishing (Fig. 23b).

- 11:1 cat. 1908. This trapezoid adze with elliptical or oval section has a convex cutting edge, no bevel chins and a flattened and straight poll. Both sides are round. It is made of altered andesitic tuff. More than half the cutting edge and most of the poll were broken in antiquity. There are large flake scars on both sides of the adze. The surviving part of the adze blade is only 12 mm wide, but bears short and deep use-wear striations. There are traces of grinding all over the butt, the striations being parallel or almost parallel to the edge. The poll surfaces are not highly polished.

- 11:1 cat. 1920. This oval-shaped adze has an elliptical section with asymmetrical bi-bevels, the bevel chins being reduced. Its has a round cutting edge. On both sides, the convex front and back faces intersect and form the edges which were subsequently blunted. It is made of fine volcanic sandstone and is blunt through use. Deep use striations run back from the edge. The tool was due for resharpening. A particularly large flake scar on the edge has been partially obliterated by subsequent grinding. There are 40° striations on the butt, but the surface is not highly polished (Fig. 23d).

- 11:1 cat. 1925. An oval adze with an elliptical to oval section; asymmetrical bi-bevels; no bevel chin; convex cutting edge; edged sides; and flattened and round poll. This adze was made of volcanic sandstone and has been subjected to heavy use and it has a blunt edge on which there are no scars. Large flake scars are present on both sides and deep 90° striations run back from the cutting edge. These are particularly long on the back, reaching about 20 mm back from the edge (Fig. 23c).

- 11:1 cat. 1927. An oval to round adze with elliptical cross-section; suppressed bi-bevels; blunt-edged sides and flattened and rounded poll (Fig. 23f). This specimen is made of andesitic tuff and is quite blunt. Deep gouged 90° striations run back from the length of the edge. There is a bevel chin on each side. Working striations extend back only as far as the ridge which demarcates the bevel chin from the secondary bevel. Both butts are well polished and the edges bear flake scars.

- 11:1 cat. 1928. An oval to round shape; elliptical section; asymmetrical bi-bevels; suppressed bevel chins; blunt-edged sides and round flattened poll (Fig. 23h). It is made of fine volcanic sandstone. The edge is blunt and 90° striations are clear on both of its faces. A facet has been formed along the front bevel chin as a result of continual working followed by resharpening.

Type 8D

- 11:2 f.2 cat. 1941. This shouldered adze has a rectangular section at its butt and elliptical section at its blade; asymmetrical bi-bevels; a faint bevel chin can be recognised on the blade corners; convex cutting edge and a flattened round poll. It possibly had a prototype similar to cat. 1920 (Fig. 23d) and was then ground to a form with right-angled shoulders on both sides. The tang of this sample was cracked, probably due to the heat from burning after it was buried, and it was found in 2 pieces. It is made of volcanic siltstone, has a blunt edge and 90° striations on both faces of the cutting edge. The ends of the cutting edge bear large flake scars suggesting that the adze had been subjected to heavy-duty use (Fig. 25a).

- 11:2 f.2 cat. 1944. A rectangular-shouldered adze with a rounded rectangular section; asymmetrical bi-bevels with suppressed bevel chins; convex cutting edge and a flattened straight poll. This adze is made of volcanic sandstone. It is a further example of a shouldered adze resharpened so often that the shoulders are vestigial. Deep striations representing use are apparent at 90° to the edge. Relatively faint 40° striations can be recognized on both butts (Fig. 25b).

- 11:2 f.2 cat. 2043. Similar to cats. 1920 and 1964, this sample probably has an oval to round-shaped adze as its prototype. It has an elliptical section at the blade, a rectangular section at its tang, and no bevel chins. The shoulders are at a right angle to the axis. Made of volcanic siltstone, this shouldered adze has a sharp edge with damage only on a corner of the blade. There are 90° striations on the back face and faint transverse striations on the butt which probably reflect manufacture (Fig. 25c).

- 11:2 f.1 cat. 1964. This is another shouldered example with an oval to round section similar to and possibly having cat. 1920 (Fig. 23d) as its prototype. Its shoulders form a right angle with the sides (Fig. 25d).

- 11:1 cat. 1929. This sample is almost complete. It is a trapezoid adze with an elliptical to oval cross-section; asymmetry; no bevel chins; and flattened convex poll. It was made of a low quality rock which explains its present weathered surface.

- 11:1 cat. 1926. This severely weathered shouldered adze made of a low quality rock has open-curved shoulders, oval section, and deep round poll.

Type 8E

- 11:2 f.2 cat. 1945. An unusual shouldered adze with no bevel chins and a symmetrical figure. It has a rectangular section; rectangular shape; convex cutting edge; deep and straight poll and right-angled shoulders. This large shouldered adze was made of volcanic siltstone and has a blunt cutting edge from which use striations originate. There has been damage to the edge and back face of the poll represented by large flake scars (Fig. 24b).

Type 8H

- 11:2 f.2 cat. 1946. This incomplete shouldered adze has a round shape; elliptical section; asymmetric figure; no bevel chins; possibly a short tang and a robust poll. The deepest part of this sample is its poll, which tapers down to the cutting edge. It is the only example of type 8H (Fig. 24d).

Layer 10

Type 2E

- 10:25 cat. 1900 is shouldered and has a rectangular section; symmetrical figure with no bevel chins; rectangular shape; everted blade corners and flattened straight poll with a poll platform. It is similar to cats. 1911 and 1942 in layer 11, but is wider and shorter. It is made of volcanic siltstone and has been resharpened to the point that only vestigial shoulders have survived. It is blunt and use marks are present at 90° to the edge. There is a large scar on the poll and clear grinding striations are present on the butt (Fig. 22e).

Type 2G

- 10:25 cat. 1904. This trapezoid adze has an elliptical section; symmetric figure with no bevel chins; convex cutting edge; rounded sides and massive and straight poll. It has lost one corner of the blade. It is made from andesitic tuff. There are several large flake scars on both sides and the blade corners. Smaller scars are present on the edge and the surface of the poll has been ground and polished. Striations occur on the butt, varying from parallel to about 40° to the cutting edge. The edge itself, at least away from the flake scars, is still sharp and there are no signs of use-wear (Fig. 23j).
- 10:25 l. 31 cat. 1931. This triangular-shaped adze has a rounded rectangular section; symmetric figure; no bevel chins; round cutting edge and a massive and straight poll. It is made of volcanic siltstone. Three small flake scars on the edge have been partially obliterated by subsequent sharpening, although the edge itself has been blunted by use, and clear use striations are present on both bevels. The adze was broken laterally in antiquity and the present poll still bears the flake scar modified by grinding to permit rehafting (Fig. 23i).

- 10:24 cat. 1885. A triangular adze with an elliptical section; unilateral bevel; slightly convex cutting edge and flattened pointed poll. This sample was made of calcareous sandstone which is heavily weathered and no damage or striations can be observed due to the nature of raw material and the weathered surface (Fig. 23k).

- 10:21 l. 23 cat. 1856. This trapezoidal adze has an elliptical section; symmetric figure; no bevel chins; flattened and straight butt end. It is made of what looks like a decayed calcareous sandstone marked by extensive pitting. On the front face, there are fragments of wood adhering to the surface of the adze which are interpreted as a surviving part of the haft. There are also a few strands of bark fibre within the interstices of the implement. No damage or striations can be observed due to the condition of the surface (Fig. 23l).

- 10:18 cat. 1422. This sub-triangular adze has an elliptical section; asymmetrical bi-bevels; slightly convex cutting edge; flattened round poll and no platform on either its sides or poll. The tool has lost a corner of the blade. It was made of fine volcanic sandstone. This small adze was seriously damaged in antiquity when it lost half the cutting edge. The remaining part of the edge has a few scars, the striations lying at 25° to the edge on both bevels. They probably result from resharpening before the fracture rendered the adze useless (Fig. 23m).

- 10:18 cat. 1808 is a triangular-shaped adze made of a coarse grained rock, which has an oval to rounded rectangular section; unilateral bevel on the back; a front face curved to the cutting edge intersection and a pointed poll. This adze is made of what looks like a decayed sandstone. The surface is highly pitted, and this has removed any signs of use. The interstices of the decayed surface have, however, retained fragments of bark cloth. These are found from the poll to the cutting edge, which makes their use as part of the hafting procedure unlikely. It is suggested that the adze was wrapped in cloth prior to its being lost or set aside (Fig. 23n).

- 10:17 cat. 1748. This triangular-shaped, open-curved shouldered adze has a rectangular cross section; straight cutting edge; bilateral bevels with vestigial bevel chins and a deep and blunted point poll. Large flake scars are present on the edge but no striations can be seen due to the nature of the raw material, which is altered calcareous sandstone (Fig. 23o).

- 10:17 cat. 1758. This trapezoid adze has a bi-truncated elliptical section; bilateral bevel with the front bevel chin reduced; straight cutting edge; flattened and straight poll; one side has a groove at the middle which may be an attempt to make a shouldered adze or alternatively its shoulders were worn out. It is made of fine volcanic sandstone. There is severe damage on the edge, especially on both blade corners. Large to small scars mostly lie on the back bevel, while scars around the poll were polished probably by its haft. Striations at 30–35° are present on both bevels, but on the back bevel there were two sets of striations of 30–35° and 120–125° which cut across each other. This tool was very well polished, especially at its poll (Fig. 23p).

- 10:16 cat. 1723. This trapezoid adze has an elliptical section; asymmetrical bi-bevels; straight cutting edge and a round poll. This small adze of volcanic siltstone has a blunt edge bearing a few small scars on the back bevel and larger scars on the butt and poll. Striations at 90° occur on both faces, though these are blurred by resharpening wear, especially on the back bevel. The surface of the tool is very well polished (Fig. 23q).

- 10:16 cat. 1734 has an oval section; round cutting edge; symmetrical figure; no bevel chins and a thick and straight butt end. It is widest at the middle of the body, and deepest at its poll. Like cat. 1702, this is a large adze of volcanic siltstone much damaged on the edge and both sides. There has also been damage on the poll, treated by grinding to a uniform surface. One large flake scar is also located on the butt itself. Both butt surfaces bear striations at 80–90° to the edge (Fig. 23r).

- 10:16 B140 cat. 1702. This adze is sub-triangular with elliptical to oval section; asymmetrical and convex cutting edge; prepared round sides; no bevel chins and a flattened and blunted point on the poll. The cutting edge of this volcanic siltstone adze is blunted by a series of small scars along the edge. Striations at 80–90° are found on both faces from the edge to a distance of about 9 mm (Fig. 23s).

- 10:15 cat. 1707. A large polished stone adze which has a rounded rectangular section at its butt and an oval section at the cutting edge; asymmetric figure; no bevel chins; trapezoidal shape and a massive, straight poll. The cutting edge was formed where the curve of its front face intersects its flat back. The deepest part of this sample is its poll. It may be regarded as a heavy chopper. When compared with other specimens from Khok Phanom Di, this adze of volcanic siltstone is massive, weighing 197 gm. Severe damage is present on the edge, sides and poll, represented by large flake scars. Faint 90° striations are visible on the small surviving section of the edge (Fig. 23t).

- 10:9 f.7 cat. 1439. This shouldered adze has a bi-truncated elliptical section; suppressed bilateral bevels; trapezoidal shape; prepared side and poll platforms; round cutting edge and deep and straight poll. It has tiny shoulders which are open-curved and possibly formed by grinding or polishing on both side platforms of the tang (Fig. 23u).

- 10:1 cat. 1165. This polished stone adze has a flattened straight poll and elliptical section (Fig. 26e).

- 10:7 cat. 1378. The poll of this triangular-shaped adze has a flattened and blunted point. It has an elliptical cross-section (Fig. 26c).

- 10:3 cat. 1380. The poll of this triangular-shaped and elliptical adze has a flattened and blunted point (Fig. 26d).

- 10:12 cat. 1564. The body of this shouldered adze lost its cutting edge and poll in antiquity. It has an oval shape, elliptical section, and open-curved shoulders.

Type 8D

- 10:25 cat. 1992. This shouldered adze has a rectangular cross-section at the flattened and rounded poll. It has lost a corner of the blade (Fig. 25j).

- 10:20 cat. 1860. This shouldered adze of volcanic siltstone has a rectangular section at its tang and elliptical section at its cutting edge; bilateral bevels with prominent bevel chins and a convex cutting edge with a flattened round butt. Its shoulders are right-angled and one has lost its blade corner. This adze possibly had an oval or rounded form as in cat. 1920 (layer 11) before the shoulders were added (Fig. 25h). The edge has been blunted and it has small flake scars all over it. One shoulder has been broken and a large area is missing. Fine resharpening striations lie at 40–50° to the edge and 90° use striations are present on both bevels. A secondary bevel has been formed on the front. The adze is well polished especially on the hafted area. There are some small areas bearing what may prove to be the resin used in hafting.

- 10:19 cat. 1831 is a shouldered adze of volcanic tuff, similar to cat. 1941 in layer 11. It has an elliptical section at its cutting edge and rectangular section at the butt; front bevel reduced; no bevel chins on its back face; convex cutting edge; right-angled shoulders and a flattened and convex poll (Fig. 25g). It has been shortened through constant resharpening. The cutting edge bears a number of flake scars which have been partially ground away. A large scar is present on the tang, which was also polished after flaking. The poll has been subjected to jarring in use, resulting in a series of flake scars. Grinding wear is present across the axis of the tool on its butt and use wear is seen in the striations running back from the edge. It is highly polished.

- 10:17 l.15 cat. 1739. This shouldered adze has a bi-truncated elliptical section; suppressed bilateral bevels; oval shape and flattened round poll. The bevel chins were ground to reduce their ridges, which made the front and back faces convex. It has small open-curved shoulders and has lost one blade corner (Fig. 25f). This specimen, made from volcanic siltstone, was formerly shouldered, but only one vestigial shoulder survives. The other broke in antiquity and its location is now covered with a large flake scar. There is a row of flake scars along the cutting edge. Deep striations at 80–90° are present behind the cutting edge.

- 10:14 cat. 1682. A shouldered adze with a sub-triangular section with apex downward. It is asymmetrical with a unilateral bevel; no bevel chin; trapezoidal shape and straight flattened poll. It has open-curved shoulders (Fig. 25e). No traces of use are evident.

Type 8E

- 10:19 cat. 1836. This small surviving stump of an adze made of fine volcanic sandstone underwent much modification. It probably began as a shouldered specimen, as a shoulder edge is still just discernible. What would have been the edge has been deliberately blunted into a poll the surface of which bears transverse grinding striations. What had formerly been the poll was then converted into the cutting edge. The transverse striae involved in this conversion are clearly visible and the newly fashioned edge is still sharp (Fig. 21a).

- 10:22 cat. 1869. The tang of this shouldered adze has lost its cutting edge. It has a long rectangular shape, rectangular section and a flattened straight poll with a narrow poll platform (Fig. 26b).

Layer 9

Type 2A

- 9:4 cat. 1043. This oval adze of volcanic siltstone has a bi-truncated elliptical section; unilateral bevel; convex cutting edge and blunt pointed poll. It has a polished facet on the cutting-edge intersection. Its edge was blunted by grinding and polishing. However, damage and striations can be observed on the remains of its bevels. Damage is seen on the blade corners and the poll with small scars on the edge. There are clear striations at a sharp angle to the edge on both bevels (Fig. 22a).

Type 2G

- 9:4 cat. 1318. A rectangular-shaped adze with an elliptical section and bilateral bevels with the front bevel wider than the back; slightly convex cutting edge; prepared side platforms and flattened straight poll with a narrow poll platform. It is broader than it is long (Fig. 23v). This is a very small implement, probably due to regular sharpening. Large and small scars over the blade and the blade corners are missing. Half the poll is damaged. Striations at 30 to 40° are obvious on both bevels which partially obliterate the larger 90° striations behind the edge, as if the implement was being resharpened when it was finally set aside. The tool was very well polished and made of fine volcanic sandstone.

- 9:4 cat. 1349. This is the finest polished stone adze found at Khok Phanom Di. Of volcanic siltstone, it has a high triangular shape; elliptical section; bilateral bevel front wider than back; flattened, pointed poll and slightly convex cutting edge (Fig 23w). Of all the adzes from Khok Phanom Di, this is the most complete. Indeed, its condition is nearly pristine. Given the clear evidence for major, and often drastic modification to adzes during use, this implement tells us much about the artefact during the initial stages of this process. It is 88.0 mm in length and has a maximum width of 40.6 mm. On the front surface, a mirror-like sheen covers the upper half of the butt, reaching 48 mm from the poll to the end in a straight transverse line across the butt. This sheen then gives way to very fine transverse striations which cover the surface down to the bevel edge. This bevel reaches back to a maximum of 13 mm from the edge. The back lacks the mirror sheen on the upper half, but the surface from poll to bevel edge is polished such that striations are barely visible under x20 magnification. The bevel is also deeper, reaching 24.5 mm from the edge. There is a slight facet down each edge, attaining a maximum width at the cutting end of 2.2 mm and disappearing at the poll end. Striations at 30° are present on the back bevel while some very small flake scars and faint 90° striations are present on the front, suggesting that the tool had been hafted and used. Given this finding, it is proposed that the junction between the mirror-like surface and the area covered by fine striations on the front indicates the hafting line, the haft itself having protected the covered surface from abrasion during episodes of resharpening.

Type 8F

- 9:3 cat. 1034. A shouldered adze of fine volcanic sandstone. The shoulders are open-curved and it has a trapezoid shape; elliptical section at its cutting edge and rounded rectangular at its poll with a poll platform and a convex cutting edge (Fig. 24c). Small scars are present along the edge and larger scars are found on the sides and poll. Striations at 75 to 90° are present on both bevels.

Layer 8

Type 2G

- 8:6 cat. 1222. A flattened pointed poll of an adze with a possible triangular shape and elliptical section.

Layer 7

Type 2G

- 7:7 cat. 846 comprises the poll of a triangular-shaped, elliptical cross-sectioned adze which has a flattened and pointed butt.

Type 8D

- 7:2 cat. 845. The tang of this shouldered adze has an oval to rounded rectangular section and open curved shoulders. The poll is rectangular in shape and has the same thickness as the body. There is a poll platform.

Layer 6

Type 2D

- 6:4 B11 cat. 766. This polished volcanic siltstone adze was found as a mortuary offering. It has a trapezoidal shape; rectangular section; asymmetrical bilateral bevels; convex cutting edge and deep and straight poll. Its sides are slightly concave and curving towards the blade corners, thus expanding the width of its cutting edge (Fig. 21b). Two large scars are present on the back bevel near the blade corners and smaller scars are found on the edge. Two scars on the poll have been partially obliterated by grinding and the poll surface is polished. Striations at 70° are present on the front bevel and 90° striations are present on the back bevel. The edge is still sharp.

Type 2G

- 6:2 cat. 615. A triangular-shaped adze of volcanic siltstone with an elliptical section; asymmetrical bilateral bevels with the front bevel wider than the back one; a straight cutting edge and a flattened point poll. The edged sides were blunted (Fig. 23x). Damage is present on the edge and the poll. Striations at 90° are clearly apparent on the back bevel, though these are faint. Resharpening has formed a secondary bevel at the middle of the back edge.

- 6:3 cat. 627 comprises the flattened poll of a triangular adze with an elliptical section (Fig. 26f).

Layer 5

Type 2D

- 5:4 cat. 584. A sub-triangular shaped adze with an oval or rounded rectangular section; bilateral bevels; a straight cutting edge and flattened, blunt poll. Its back face is convex while its front is flat (Fig. 21c). This small volcanic siltstone adze had been resharpened, as is apparent from the transverse fine and parallel striations visible on both bevels. Serious damage along the length of the edge thereafter is seen in the two large and deep flake scars. This damage seems to have ended the working life of the adze. Earlier scars on both the poll and butt surfaces had been partially obliterated with grinding and polishing.

Type 2G

- 5:4 cat. 585. This round to oval-shaped adze, similar to cat. 1920 from layer 11, has an elliptical section; bilateral bevels with front wider than back; round cutting edge with asymmetrical bevels; blunt-edged sides; and flattened round poll. Its back bevel is very steep, possibly caused by resharpening. It has lost its blade and poll corners (Fig. 23y). This andesitic tuff adze has been severely damaged and there are flake scars on the body with larger scars on the poll. The edge is blunt, bears many flake scars, and use striations originating at the edge cover the surviving bevel surfaces.

- 5:1 cat. 570. A trapezoid adze with elliptical section and bilateral bevels of which the front is wider than the back; a cutting edge oblique from one blade corner to another; and flattened straight butt end (Fig. 23z). It is made of andesitic tuff and the edge is still sharp, a series of vestigial scars having been virtually ground away with resharpening. Part of the poll is polished, but the balance has been bruised and damaged with use. There are faint 80 to 90° striations on both bevels and these reduce the bevel chins.

Layer 4

Type 2D

- 4:1 cat. 357. A trapezoid adze with unilateral bevel; rounded rectangular section; straight cutting edge and deep and straight poll. It has a narrow back bevel and prepared side platforms (Fig. 21d). Small scars are present on the edge and larger ones are found on the sides and the poll. No striations have been observed.

- 4:1 f.1 cat. 524. This small polished stone adze has an oval section; asymmetrical bilateral bevels; slightly convex cutting edge and convex poll (Fig. 21e). There is a large flake scar on the poll which has been partially obliterated by reworking. Both bevels bear 90° striations, but these have been partially obliterated by resharpening striations. It is made of fine volcanic sandstone.

Type 2G

- 4:3 f.7 cat. 535. This adze, which is made of andesitic tuff, has a triangular shape; asymmetrical bilateral bevels; elliptical section; straight cutting edge; and blunted point poll. Its front face is convex and its back face is flat (Fig. 23aa). Large scars are present on one blade corner and on the poll, 25° and 80 to 90° striations criss-cross each other on the back bevel and on the very edge of the front bevel. These are fine and parallel, and the others are considered likely to represent resharpening rather than use. The edge is still sharp. The front bevel chin was reduced by wear at the middle of the edge. This adze resembles cat. 1349 save that it has been sharpened until it is only 38 mm long.

- 4:3 f.7 cat. 552. A trapezoid-shaped adze of fine volcanic sandstone with an elliptical section; bilateral bevels; the front bevelled chin was ground but its previous chin still occurs near the blade corner. It has a convex cutting edge. This sample is possibly similar to cat. 551 in that its previous shape was high triangular before the poll was broken. Subsequently, the broken area was reground, markedly changing the shape of the tool (Fig. 23bb). Just the same comments on the modification of a broken form originally resembling cat. 1349 apply to this adze. Similarly, the signs of working have been partially obliterated by resharpening striations. One blade corner bears a large flake scar. Both bevel chins have been reduced by wear.

- 4:2 cat. 551 is a trapezoidal adze which has an elliptical section; bilateral bevels; slightly convex cutting edge; and flattened straight poll. A large flake scar on the poll surface was probably polished after the poll was broken (Fig 23cc). This fine volcanic sandstone adze has an identical shape with the lower end of cat. 1349. It is evident that it formerly matched cat. 1349, but that it broke across the middle and was therefore modified to a trapezoid-shaped implement. The edges of the flake scar which resulted from the fracture have been ground to shape. Small flake scars are present. Some deep striations at 90° to the edge have been partially obliterated by the marks of resharpening. The edge is still sharp.

- 4:2 cat. 683 is a triangular-shaped adze of fine volcanic sandstone with an elliptical section; asymmetrical bilateral bevels; straight cutting edge and flattened and blunted point poll. It has a large flake scar at the middle of the cutting edge. Both blade corners were broken (Fig. 23dd). This adze is similar in shape to the poll end of cat. 1349, and has a length of only 35.5 mm. Both blade corners and the centre of the edge itself have been severely damaged. Striations at 80° are present. The surviving areas of both bevels reveal use striations.

- 4:1 cat. 393. A poll of a poorly polished adze with an elliptical section. It was relatively long (Fig. 26g).

- 4:1 cat. 496 is the poll of a long adze with a trapezoid, sub-triangular section. It was poorly polished.

- 4:3 cat. 556. The poll of this triangular-shaped adze has an elliptical section which is flattened and pointed.

Type 8D

- 4:3 cat. 500. This shouldered adze has right-angled shoulders, a rectangular shape; rounded rectangular section; round cutting edge and deep round poll. It has lost a shoulder and the blade corners (Fig. 25i). It was made of shell, probably giant clam shell. It has lost a shoulder and both blade corners. No striations have been observed.

Layer 3

Type 2D

- 3:2 cat. 258. This sample has a trapezoid shape; round rectangular to oval section; symmetrical figure; bilateral bevel; slightly convex cutting edge; prepared side platforms; and deep and straight poll. It may be considered as an example of an axe (Fig. 21f). It is made of fine volcanic sandstone. Small scars are present on the back bevel and there are peck marks on both sides and the poll. There is a flake scar across the poll, suggesting that it was remodelled after a break at the midpoint. This was subsequently ground. Clear striations varying between 70 and 90° to the edge are apparent.

- 3:1 cat. 208. An oval adze of volcanic siltstone with an oval to rounded rectangular section; bilateral bevel; straight cutting edge and deep and straight poll. A corner of the blade and the poll have been damaged. It possibly had a trapezoidal shape before being broken (Fig. 21g). Only one side of this large adze has survived without major damage. Little is left of the original edge of the reverse side, although an attempt had been made to regrind its broken surface. No striations can be observed.

- 3:1 cat. 226. A rectangular-shaped adze of andesitic tuff with an elliptical section; bilateral bevel with front wider than back; rounded side; and deep and straight poll. Its butt was broken, leaving a large flake on the poll surface which possibly shows that this sample was a triangular adze before breakage occurred (Fig. 21h). Like so many other specimens, this adze was modified after fracture at the approximate midpoint. Several small scars are present on the edge and large scars are found on both sides. The poll, especially on the front margin, bears the marks of reworking following fracture. Striations lie at 90° to the cutting edge.

Type 2G

- 3:4 cat. 405. A trapezoidal adze of fine volcanic sandstone with a bi-truncated elliptical section; asymmetrical bi-bevels; prepared side platform and flattened convex poll platform most of which is broken (Fig. 23ee). It was remodelled after fracturing near the former poll. The flake which resulted has been partially obscured by reworking. The bevels bear the signs of resharpening, but the edge reveals small flake scars which may result from subsequent use.

- 3:3 cat. 439. This is a trapezoid adze made of amphibolite with a slightly irregular section due to the weathered surface. The cutting edge is oblique to one side and it has asymmetrical bi-bevels (Fig.23ff). Severe damage is present on the cutting edge, especially on the blade corners. This adze has lost most of its poll. Resharpening striations at 80 to 85° are present on what remains of both bevels.

- 3:2 cat. 260. An oval-shaped adze of fine volcanic sandstone with an elliptical to oval section; asymmetrical bi-bevels and flattened point or round poll. The poll was broken off. The possible shape is either oval or rounded triangular (Fig. 23gg). Although fractured at the midpoint, there are no signs that it was later remodelled. It was sharpened not long before it was set aside, for the bevels have resharpening striations, but no clear sign of use.

- 3:2 cat. 267. This specimen of fine volcanic sandstone has a trapezoidal shape; elliptical section; asymmetrical bi-bevels and a deep poll. Its poll was broken and repolished which made an oblique poll platform. This sample was possibly triangular-shaped before the poll fractured (Fig. 23hh). It was remodelled after a fracture across the butt. The edges of the flake scar across the poll have been ground and polished after the fracture occurred, resulting in a short implement, measuring only 30.5 mm in length. There are some small flake scars on the edge which concentrate near its blade corners and 80 to 90° striations are present on the front bevel. They are rare on its back and expand to above the bevel chins.

- 3:2 cat. 276. A trapezoid adze with an elliptical to oval section and asymmetrical bi-bevel (Fig. 23ii). The poll of this fine volcanic sandstone adze has been ground, suggesting that it had been remodelled in prehistory following fracture. Damage has occurred only as a few small scars on the edge and larger scars on the blade corners. Fine striations lie across its axis on the front bevel and 80 to 90° use striations are obvious on the back bevel.

- 3:2 cat. 279. A trapezoid volcanic sandstone adze with an elliptical to oval section; asymmetrical bi-bevel and a deep straight butt end. Its cutting edge is oblique to one side. The butt has almost the same thickness as the body, and due to the damage on the body the cross-section of this sample is slightly irregular (Fig. 23jj). This adze has a series of striations which track across each other at right-angles and are seen as the result of resharpening. There are, however, still a series of small flake scars on the edge. This implement was probably remodelled after a fracture at the midpoint, since the poll has been ground across to remove the resultant flake scar.

- 3:1 cat. 229. This oval fine volcanic sandstone adze has a round butt with flake scars around its edges. It has a straight cutting edge blunted by a number of small scars, an elliptical section; bilateral bevel with front wider than back and a deep and round poll (Fig. 23kk). This adze was abandoned during an early stage of remodelling. There is a series of steep flake scars along all the edges. These obliterate the polished surfaces along the edges of the implement. The surviving areas of both bevels bear use striations.

- 3:1 cat. 253. This is a triangular adze of volcanic siltstone which has an elliptical section; asymmetrical figure; asymmetrical bi-bevels and a flattened pointed butt end (Fig. 23ll). It is only 43.5 mm in length, and has probably been continually sharpened from an adze originally resembling cat. 1349. There are several small flake scars along the edge, as well as use striations on both bevels.

- 3:1 cat. 221 and layer 2:2 cat. 170. The butt of an elliptical-sectioned adze which has lost its cutting edge and poll.

- 3:1 cat. 210. A flattened, pointed butt of a triangular-shaped adze with elliptical section.

- 3:1 cat. 238. A flattened, round butt of a probable triangular or oval-shaped adze with an elliptical section.

- 3:2 cat. 294. A flattened and pointed butt of a triangular-sectioned, ground stone adze.

- 3:3 cat. 330. A robust poll of a trapezoid-shaped and elliptical-sectioned adze with an unpolished surface.

Type 8D

- 3:1 cat. 230. This shouldered adze made of volcanic siltstone has an elliptical section; bilateral bevels, front wider than back; trapezoid shape; open-curved shoulders and deep and straight poll. A corner of the tang was broken as well as a blade corner. Flake scars occur on the edges around its body (Fig. 25l). The cutting edge of this adze bears a series of small flake scars, behind which the bevels reveal use striations. One blade corner is broken and there are larger scars near the sides.

- 3:1 cat. 247. A tang of a shouldered adze which has right-angled shoulders. It has lost its cutting edge and has a rectangular section at the butt and elliptical section above the shoulders (Fig. 26h).

Layer 2

Type 2G

- 2:3 cat. 178. A sub-triangular adze of fine volcanic sandstone with a broken poll, an elliptical section and unilateral bevel. Similar to cat. 152, the poll of this sample was possibly flattened and pointed, then the poll was broken and left the hollow flake scar which was subsequently ground (Fig. 23mm). The poll is represented only by a flake scar as if it broke in antiquity. Its edges were then polished to form a smooth groove. Large and small scars on the edge mostly lie on the back bevel. Use striations at 90° to the edge are obvious on both bevels. They extend to about the middle of the tool. Grinding striations are also clear across the axis of the tool.

- 2:3 cat. 195. This volcanic sandstone adze has an elliptical section; asymmetrical bi-bevels; trapezoid shape. It was possibly a triangular-shaped adze with a pointed poll before the poll was broken (Fig. 23nn). This tool has lost its blade corner and the poll fractured in antiquity to leave a flake scar in its place. Small scars are visible on the edge. No striations can be observed leading from the edge.

- 2:2 cat. 147. A ground adze of volcanic sandstone with similar characteristics to cat. 276 in layer 3. Its shape is almost oval due to its convex cutting edge and convex poll. Flake scars occur on its cutting edge while there are larger flake scars on the poll and a blade corner (Fig. 23oo). A large scar and several small scars are present on the edge. Grinding striations lie in various directions across the axis of the tool and use-wear is found at 90° to the edge.

- 2:2 cat. 152. Similar to cat. 551 in layer 4, this volcanic sandstone adze was triangular-shaped. It has lost its point poll and was modified to a trapezoid shape. The flattened butt was possibly pointed and formed a triangular shape but was then broken to a hollow scar on the butt end (Fig. 23pp). This adze was fractured near the original poll, since the present poll is a hardly modified flake scar. There is also a large flake scar on the edge, the surviving portions of which are still sharp.

- 2:2 cat. 155. A small ground adze of volcanic sandstone with an oval shape; oval to elliptical section; asymmetrical bi-bevels; straight cutting edge and flattened, rounded poll. Flake scars are present on its blade corner and its poll (Fig. 23qq). Faint scars on the edge mostly lie near the blade corners of the front bevel. Striations are obvious on the front bevel and less common on the back.

- 2:2 cat. 162. A trapezoid adze of volcanic siltstone with a flat back face and a clear elliptical cross-section. It has asymmetrical bi-bevels and a hollow on the back bevel which was probably formed by polishing against objects while in use. The butt end was broken, leaving a hollow poll (Fig. 23rr). A few small scars are found on the edge, mostly on the back bevel. Clear 90° striations occur on both bevels, the bevel chin and above the chin on the front.

- 2:1 cat. 50. A flattened and pointed poll of a triangular-shaped, elliptical-sectioned adze.

- 2:2 cat. 61. A flattened and rounded poll of a possible oval-shaped adze which has an elliptical section.

- 2:1 cat. 73. The cutting edge of an adze which had an elliptical section, asymmetrical bi-bevels and edged sides (Fig. 26i).

- 2:1 cat. 75. Half of the cutting edge of an elliptical asymmetrical-sectioned adze (Fig. 26j).

- 2:1 cat. 83. A flattened and rounded poll of an oval-shaped, elliptical-sectioned adze.

Type 8B

- 2:1 cat. 90. This is the only sample of a double-shouldered adze found at Khok Phanom Di. It is made of volcanic sandstone and has a truncated triangular shape; asymmetrical bi-bevels; elliptical section at the cutting edge and oval section at the butt. This tool has lost one blade corner, has large flake scars on the body and butt end, and a few small scars on its cutting edge (Fig. 24a). The edge has been blunted by a series of small flake scars. The poll is pecked and bears large scars. There is a secondary bevel on the back. Striations are faint and unclear.

Type 8D

- 2:1 cat. 94. An open-curved, shouldered adze of volcanic sandstone with an elliptical section at its cutting edge and oval section at its poll; asymmetrical bi-bevels; convex cutting edge and deep and straight poll. Its tang possibly shows an attempt to make double shoulders. This sample has lost a shoulder and a side platform (Fig. 25k). It retains a sharp edge associated with wear marks at 90° on both bevels. The ventral side retains most of the original flake scars, though these have been worn with use.

- 2:1 cat. 99. This open-curved, shouldered adze has a triangular shape; elliptical or plano-convex section; asymmetrical bi-bevels; and sharply straight back-bevelled chin; slightly convex cutting edge; and flattened and rounded poll. It was formed by simply grinding both sides of the tang into shoulders (Fig. 25m). It is possible that this volcanic sandstone adze originally had the form of cat. 1394, but that after being considerably reduced in length through sharpening, small shoulders were added in order to assist in hafting. Both bevels display clear use striations.

Layer 1

Type 2G

- 1:3 cat. 29. The only polished stone adze found in this layer has a trapezoidal shape, and elliptical section, asymmetrical bi-bevels; round sides, and a deep convex poll and well-polished poll platform (Fig. 23ss). It is made of volcanic sandstone. There is one flake scar on the margin of an otherwise sharp edge. Striations at 90° to the edge are present on both bevels, but on the body they lie across the axis of the tool. Clear grinding striae are visible on the butt, which may well represent modification following breakage during use.

TABLE 9: *The measurements of polished stone adzes (cm)*

Prov.	Cat. no.	ML	MW	WP	MD	DP	Angle	Prov.	Cat. no.	ML	MW	WP	MD	DP	Angle
11:2	1941	5.21	4.75	2.53	1.60	0.42	59°	11:2	1942	4.55	›2.20	1.96	1.32	0.71	52°
11:2	1943	3.84	3.23	-	1.10	0.52	45°	11:2	1944	4.53	3.00	2.24	1.50	0.57	56°
11:2	1945	6.55	5.17	4.07	1.43	0.88	51°	11:2	1964	4.79	4.76	1.96	1.45	0.52	54°
11:2	1965	6.28	4.04	2.07	2.16	1.07	61°	11:2	1966	4.70	4.04	-	1.37	1.00	46°
11:2	2043	3.93	4.61	1.91	1.09	0.43	56°	11:2	1946	›5.47	4.96	2.74	-	2.22	61°
11:2	2042	-	5.03	-	1.45	-	50°	11:1	1929	5.94	4.15	2.10	1.59	-	
11:1	1908	4.57	3.04	1.70	1.24	0.71	50°	11:1	1910	7.22	4.06	2.08	1.76	0.68	50°
11:1	1911	4.53	›2.50	2.10	1.42	0.51	48°	11:1	1920	5.10	4.24	-	1.43	0.34	50°
11:1	1925	6.31	4.08	-	1.57	0.71	50°	11:1	1927	5.03	4.37	-	1.95	0.30	59°
11:1	1928	5.33	4.68	-	1.52	0.59	61°	10:25	1904	4.86	4.12	2.77	1.41	0.76	51°
10:25	1931	3.16	3.68	2.01	1.27	1.10	45°	10:25	1900	4.00	›2.82	2.61	1.06	0.45	53°
10:24	1885	5.58	3.26	-	1.24	-	51°	10:21	1856	3.63	3.16	1.35	0.82	0.31	61°
10:20	1860	4.36	4.16	2.58	1.22	0.31	61°	10:19	1831	4.66	4.86	2.80	1.43	0.55	54°
10:19	1836	3.11	2.18	2.07	0.97	-	57°	10:18	1422	4.35	2.61	-	1.01	0.28	42°
10:18	1808	3.37	2.78	-	1.14	-	62°	10:17	1739	4.49	›3.13	2.88	0.96	0.33	55°
10:17	1748	4.61	2.95	0.61	1.60	1.23	53°	10:17	1758	4.24	3.09	1.92	1.16	0.39	49°
B140	1702	4.76	3.76	1.76	1.39	0.51	48°	10:16	1723	3.80	3.04	1.59	0.93	0.58	49°
10:16	1734	8.09	4.94	3.72	-	1.95	39°	10:15	1707	8.54	6.43	4.30	2.48	-	50°
10:14	1682	4.49	3.22	1.97	0.52	-	41°	10:9	1439	5.62	3.88	3.36	1.65	1.24	60°
B72	2049	3.91	1.60	1.03	0.41	-	18°	9:4	1043	3.33	2.02	0.94	0.80	0.28	45°
9:4	1318	2.44	2.93	2.30	0.88	0.28	57°	9:4	1349	8.82	4.06	-	1.29	-	49°
9:3	1034	4.88	4.43	2.44	1.72	0.85	61°	B11	766	4.25	3.30	2.21	1.24	0.91	51°
6:2	615	4.01	2.89	-	0.99	-	55°	5:4	584	3.70	2.82	1.27	1.32	0.68	67°
5:4	585	4.57	4.06	2.20	1.49	0.59	81°	5:1	570	3.37	2.55	1.79	1.20	0.78	62°
4:3	500	4.44	2.99	1.81	1.30	1.30	60°	4:3	535	3.79	3.57	-	1.12	0.21	59°
4:3	552	3.34	3.71	2.86	1.01	0.88	56°	4:2	551	3.88	4.26	2.63	1.36	0.85	67°
4:2	683	4.05	›2.94	-	0.99	0.28	59°	4:1	357	4.66	4.37	2.67	1.17	1.05	68°
4:1	524	2.94	2.23	1.40	1.21	0.65	65°	3:4	405	3.30	2.27	1.17	1.20	0.50	58°
3:3	439	4.53	3.01	1.15	1.10	0.54	69°	3:2	258	4.74	4.23	2.89	1.41	1.10	70°
3:2	260	›2.82	2.48	-	1.10	-	59°	3:2	267	3.04	3.77	2.23	1.12	0.79	51°
3:2	276	4.43	4.28	3.00	1.51	0.85	66°	3:2	279	3.91	2.86	2.20	0.92	0.69	51°
3:1	208	5.60	4.35	-	1.90	-	66°	3:1	226	3.77	3.51	2.64	1.16	0.90	59°
3:1	229	5.42	4.22	-	1.52	1.03	61°	3:1	230	3.83	4.31	›2.50	1.47	0.80	59°
3:1	253	4.35	3.54	-	1.33	-	58°	2:3	178	4.10	3.15	1.62	1.28	0.65	65°
2:3	195	4.36	›2.35	2.42	1.39	1.04	65°	2:2	147	5.50	4.37	3.00	1.44	0.88	58°
2:2	152	3.17	3.60	1.92	1.21	0.76	56°	2:2	155	2.94	2.29	-	0.87	0.29	75°
2:2	162	5.74	4.70	3.43	1.07	1.11	71°	2:2	204	1.90	1.24	0.77	0.54	0.17	46°
2:1	87	3.11	1.88	1.56	1.02	0.84	64°	2:1	90	4.63	5.19	2.32	1.51	1.06	64°
2:1	94	6.21	4.53	3.40	1.51	1.71	60°	2:1	99	4.50	4.03	-	1.05	0.45	61°
1:3	29	3.23	2.97	1.94	1.15	0.67	59°	-	-	-	-	-	-	-	-

ML: maximum length; MW: maximum width; WP: width of poll; MD: maximum depth; DP: depth of poll

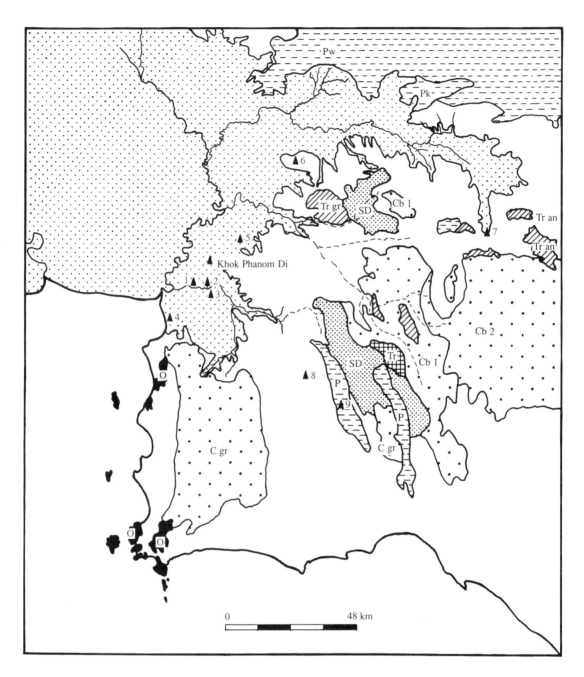

FIG. 16.   Geological map of the Bang Pakong Valley. 1: Khok Ra Kaa, 2: Khok Putsaa, 3: Muang Phra
Rot, 4: Muang Si Pharo, 5: Ban Samet Tai, 6: Muang Si Mahosot, 7: Khao Cha Kan, 8: Muang Phraya
Rae, 9: Khao Cha-Ang, P: Permian rocks, CP: Permo-Carboniferous rocks, Cb: Carboniferous rocks, SD:
Silurian-Devonian rocks, O: Ordovician rocks, C gr: Carboniferous granite, Tr gr: Triassic granite, Tr an:
Triassic andesite, Pw: Pra Wihan formation of Jurassic rocks, Pk: Phu Kradung formation of Jurassic rocks

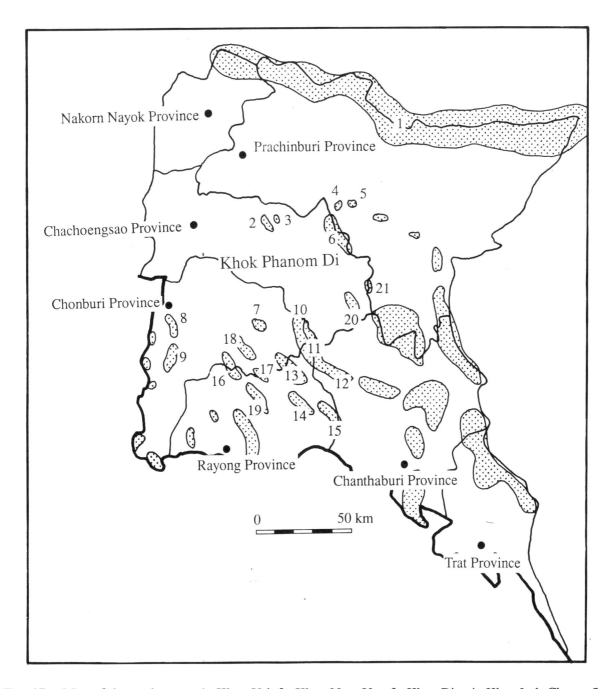

FIG. 17. Map of the study area. 1: Khao Yai, 2: Khao Nam Yot, 3: Khao Din, 4: Khao Luk Chang, 5: Khao Mai Kaew, 6: Khao Cham Ra Kham, 7: Khao Chong Khaeb, 8: Khao Kheo, 9: Khao Chomphu, 10: Khao Ang Lue Nai, 11: Khao Ra Chao, 12: Khao Plai Prakaet, 13: Khao Cha Mun, 14: Khao Cha Om, 15: Khao Cha Mao, 16: Khao Phai, 17: Khao Mod Ngam, 18: Khao Chao, 19: Khao Kong Keng, 20: Khao Rabom Pran, 21: Khao Takrub

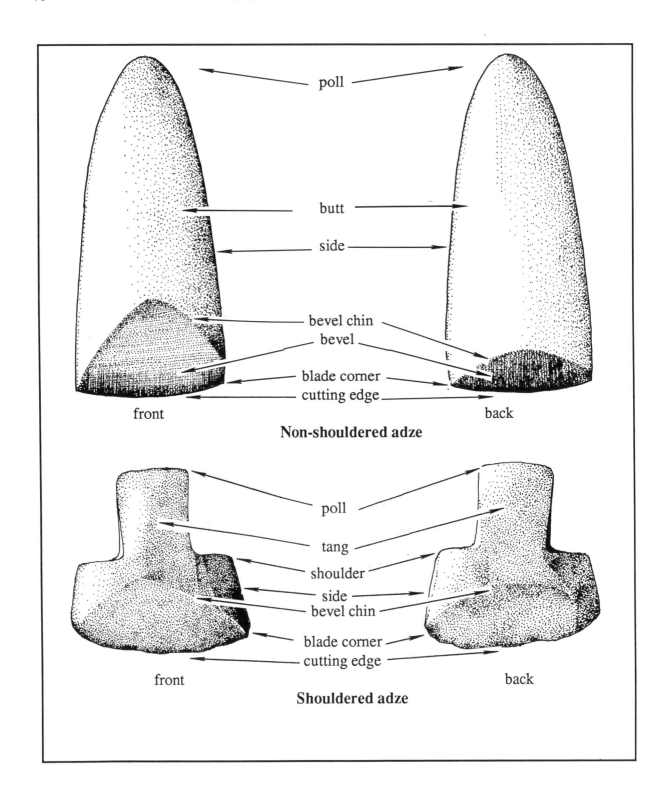

FIG. 18.   The polished stone adze terminology

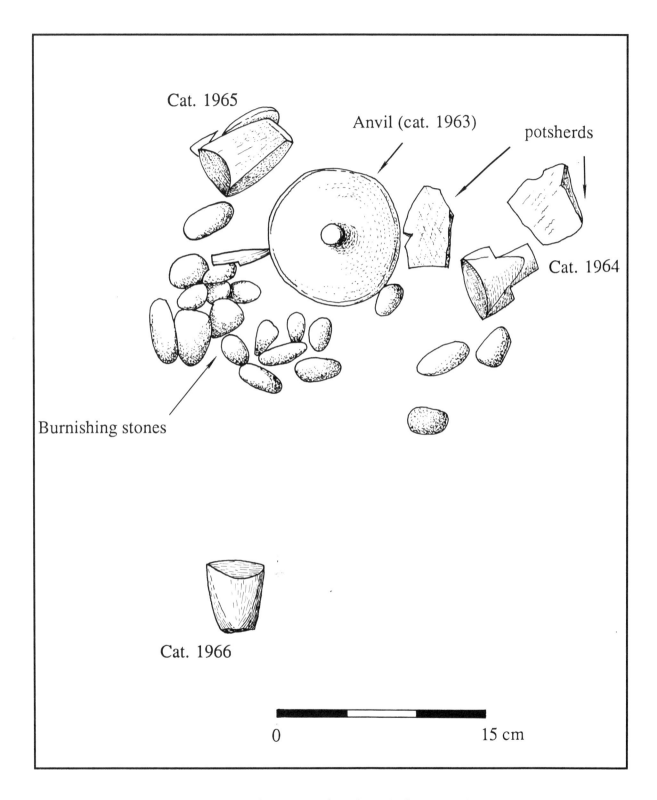

FIG. 19.   Cache 1 cut from layer 11 into natural

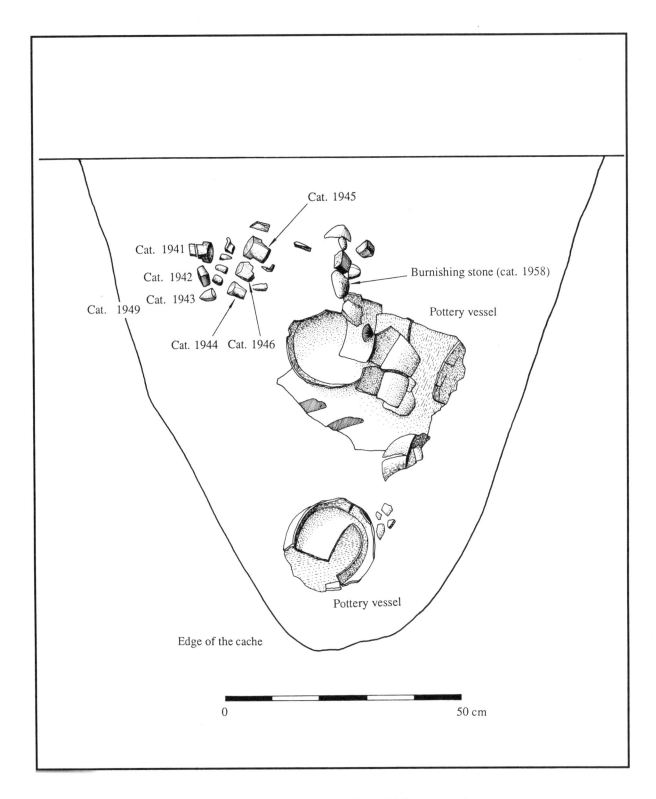

FIG. 20.   Cache 2 cut from layer 11 into natural

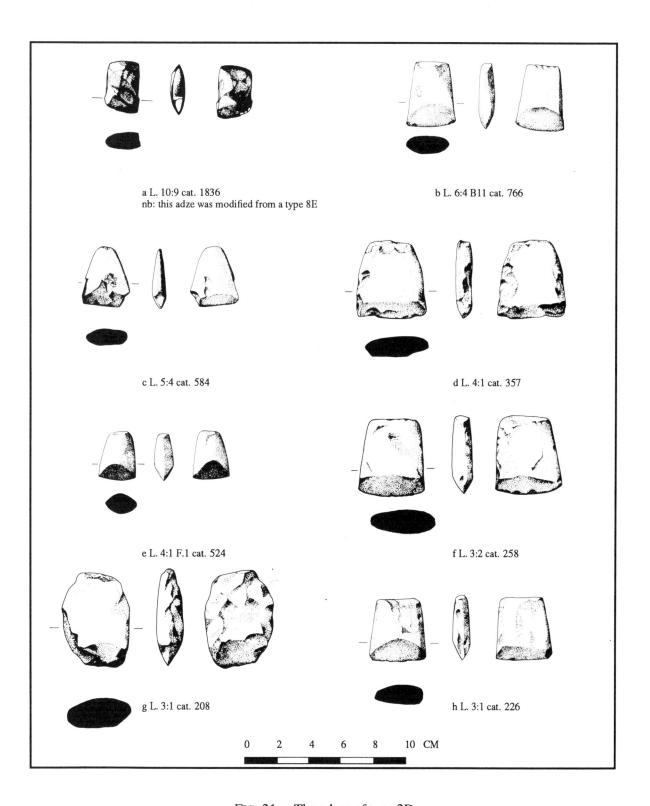

a L. 10:9 cat. 1836
nb: this adze was modified from a type 8E

b L. 6:4 B11 cat. 766

c L. 5:4 cat. 584

d L. 4:1 cat. 357

e L. 4:1 F.1 cat. 524

f L. 3:2 cat. 258

g L. 3:1 cat. 208

h L. 3:1 cat. 226

0   2   4   6   8   10 CM

FIG. 21.   The adzes of type 2D

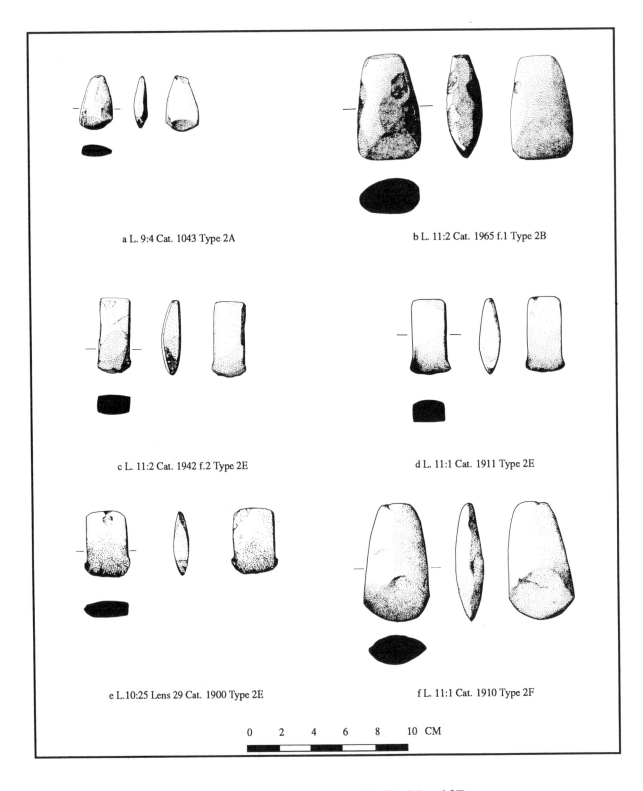

a L. 9:4 Cat. 1043 Type 2A

b L. 11:2 Cat. 1965 f.1 Type 2B

c L. 11:2 Cat. 1942 f.2 Type 2E

d L. 11:1 Cat. 1911 Type 2E

e L.10:25 Lens 29 Cat. 1900 Type 2E

f L. 11:1 Cat. 1910 Type 2F

0   2   4   6   8   10 CM

FIG. 22.   The adzes of types 2A, 2B, 2E and 2F

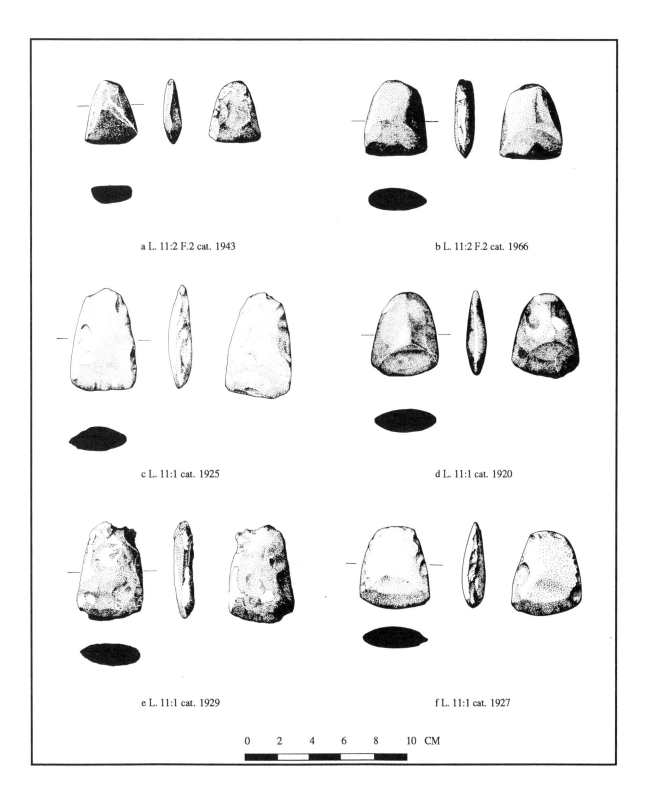

a L. 11:2 F.2 cat. 1943

b L. 11:2 F.2 cat. 1966

c L. 11:1 cat. 1925

d L. 11:1 cat. 1920

e L. 11:1 cat. 1929

f L. 11:1 cat. 1927

0 2 4 6 8 10 CM

FIG. 23.   The adzes of type 2G

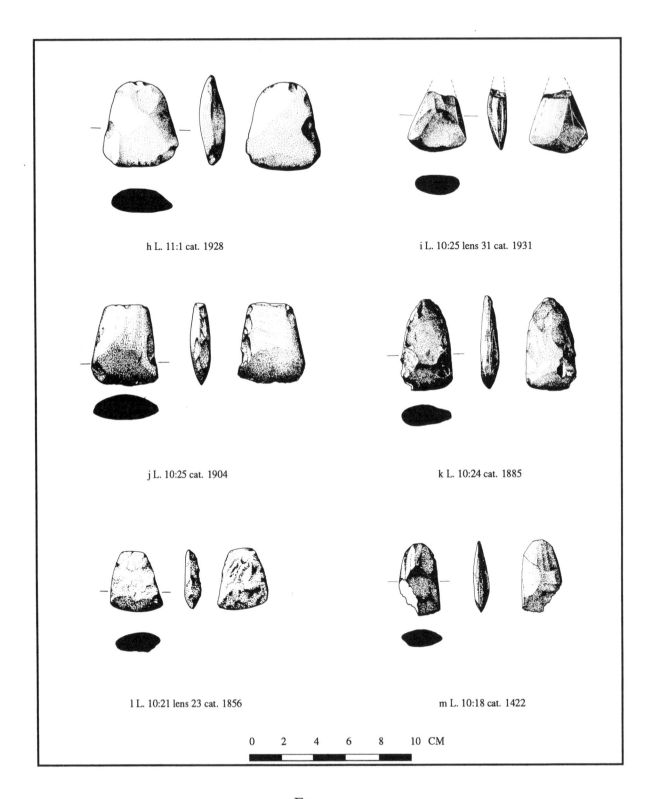

h L. 11:1 cat. 1928

i L. 10:25 lens 31 cat. 1931

j L. 10:25 cat. 1904

k L. 10:24 cat. 1885

l L. 10:21 lens 23 cat. 1856

m L. 10:18 cat. 1422

0   2   4   6   8   10 CM

FIG. 23 (cont.)

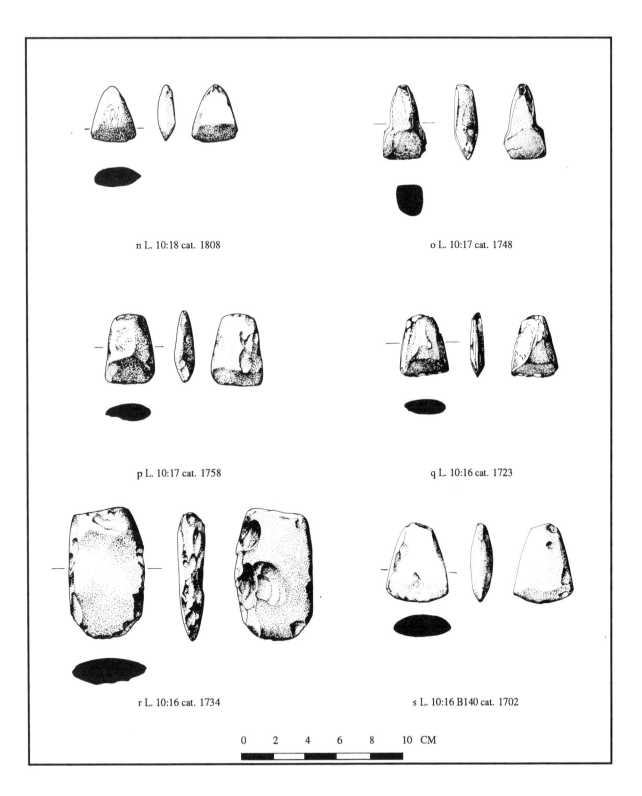

n L. 10:18 cat. 1808

o L. 10:17 cat. 1748

p L. 10:17 cat. 1758

q L. 10:16 cat. 1723

r L. 10:16 cat. 1734

s L. 10:16 B140 cat. 1702

0 2 4 6 8 10 CM

FIG. 23 (cont.)

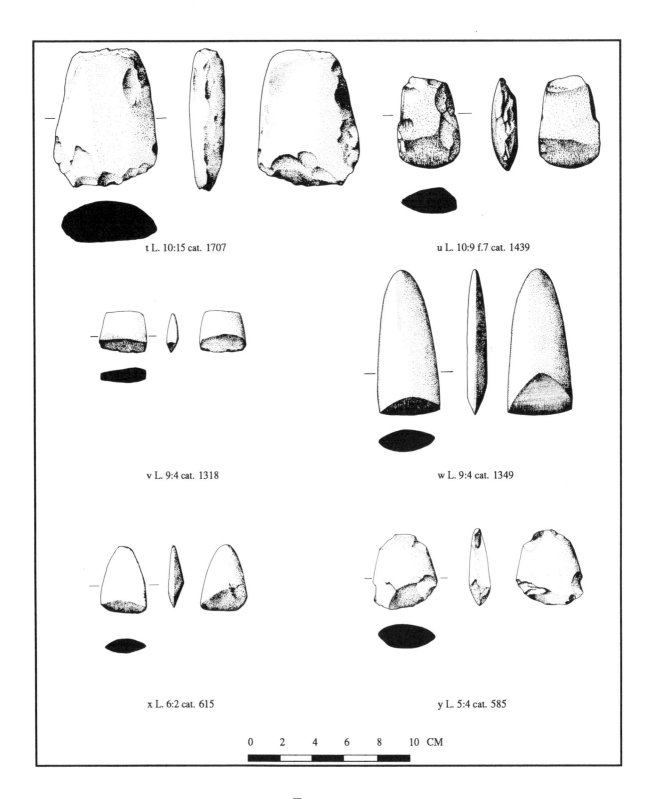

t L. 10:15 cat. 1707

u L. 10:9 f.7 cat. 1439

v L. 9:4 cat. 1318

w L. 9:4 cat. 1349

x L. 6:2 cat. 615

y L. 5:4 cat. 585

0   2   4   6   8   10 CM

FIG. 23 (cont.)

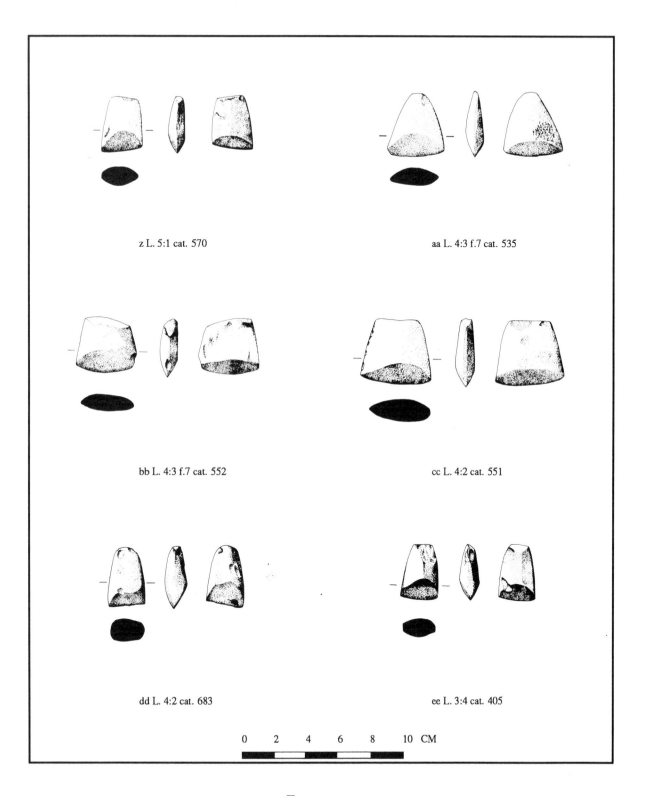

z L. 5:1 cat. 570

aa L. 4:3 f.7 cat. 535

bb L. 4:3 f.7 cat. 552

cc L. 4:2 cat. 551

dd L. 4:2 cat. 683

ee L. 3:4 cat. 405

0   2   4   6   8   10 CM

FIG. 23 (cont.)

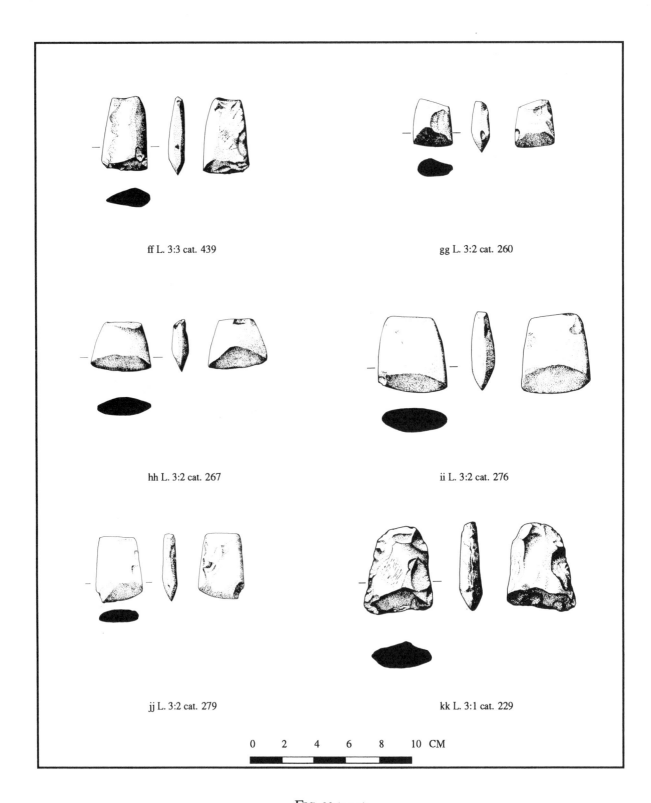

ff L. 3:3 cat. 439

gg L. 3:2 cat. 260

hh L. 3:2 cat. 267

ii L. 3:2 cat. 276

jj L. 3:2 cat. 279

kk L. 3:1 cat. 229

0   2   4   6   8   10   CM

FIG. 23 (cont.)

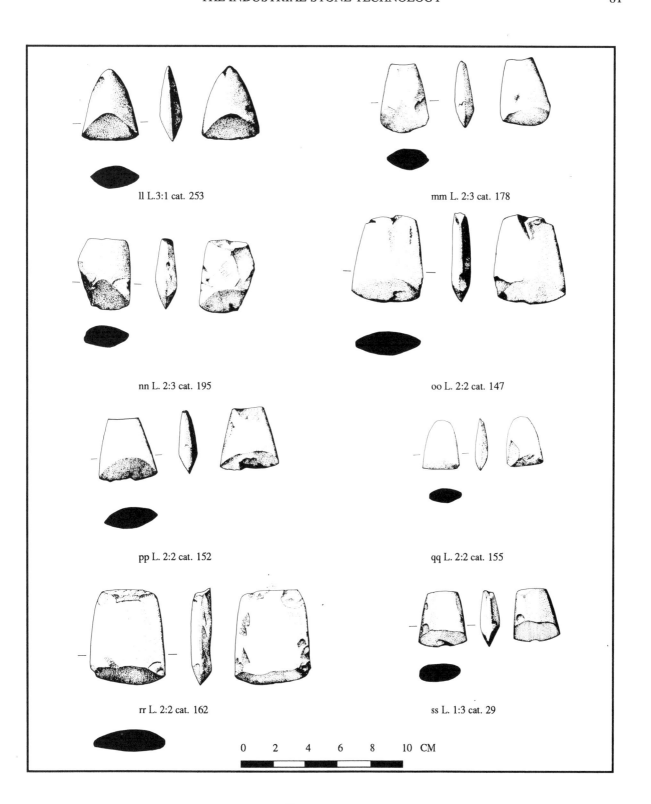

ll L.3:1 cat. 253

mm L. 2:3 cat. 178

nn L. 2:3 cat. 195

oo L. 2:2 cat. 147

pp L. 2:2 cat. 152

qq L. 2:2 cat. 155

rr L. 2:2 cat. 162

ss L. 1:3 cat. 29

0   2   4   6   8   10 CM

FIG. 23 (cont.)

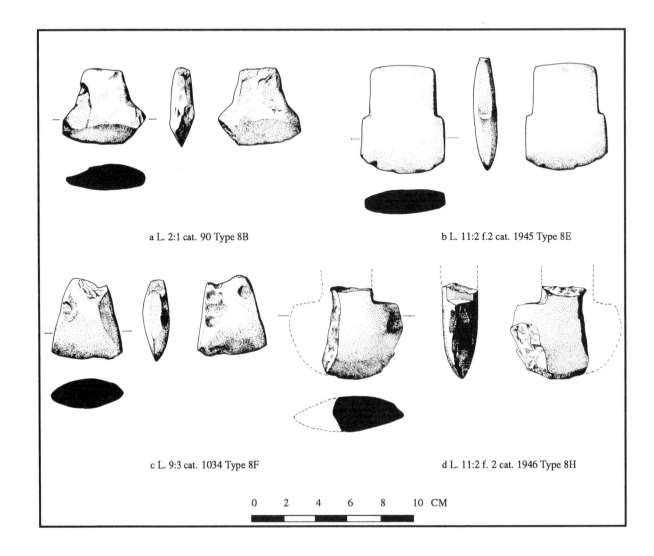

a L. 2:1 cat. 90 Type 8B

b L. 11:2 f.2 cat. 1945 Type 8E

c L. 9:3 cat. 1034 Type 8F

d L. 11:2 f. 2 cat. 1946 Type 8H

0   2   4   6   8   10 CM

FIG. 24.   The shouldered adzes of types 8B, 8E, 8F and 8H

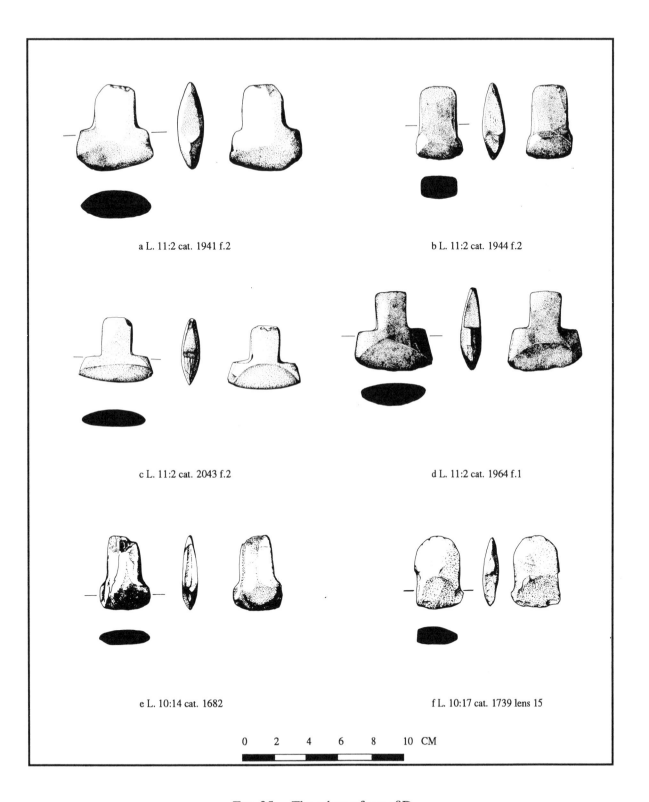

a L. 11:2 cat. 1941 f.2

b L. 11:2 cat. 1944 f.2

c L. 11:2 cat. 2043 f.2

d L. 11:2 cat. 1964 f.1

e L. 10:14 cat. 1682

f L. 10:17 cat. 1739 lens 15

0   2   4   6   8   10 CM

FIG. 25.   The adzes of type 8D

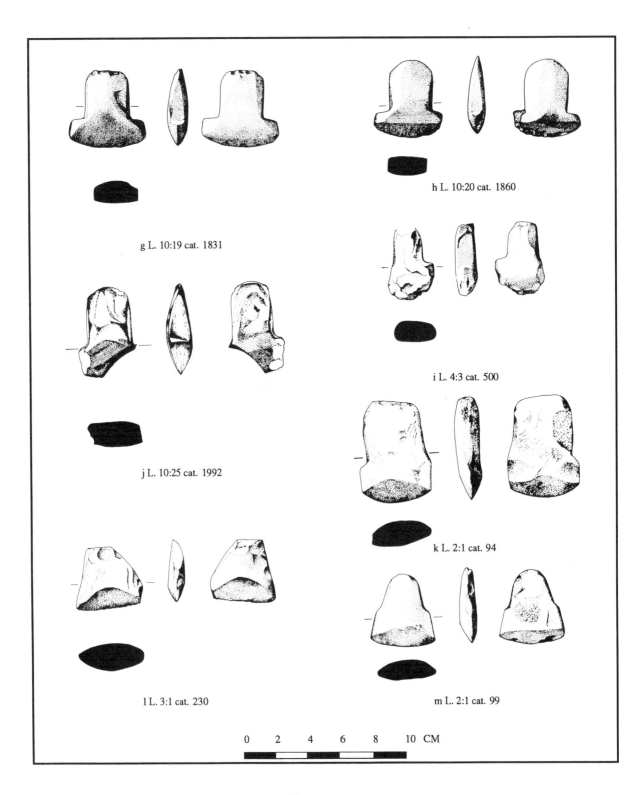

g L. 10:19 cat. 1831

h L. 10:20 cat. 1860

i L. 4:3 cat. 500

j L. 10:25 cat. 1992

k L. 2:1 cat. 94

l L. 3:1 cat. 230

m L. 2:1 cat. 99

0   2   4   6   8   10 CM

FIG. 25 (cont.)

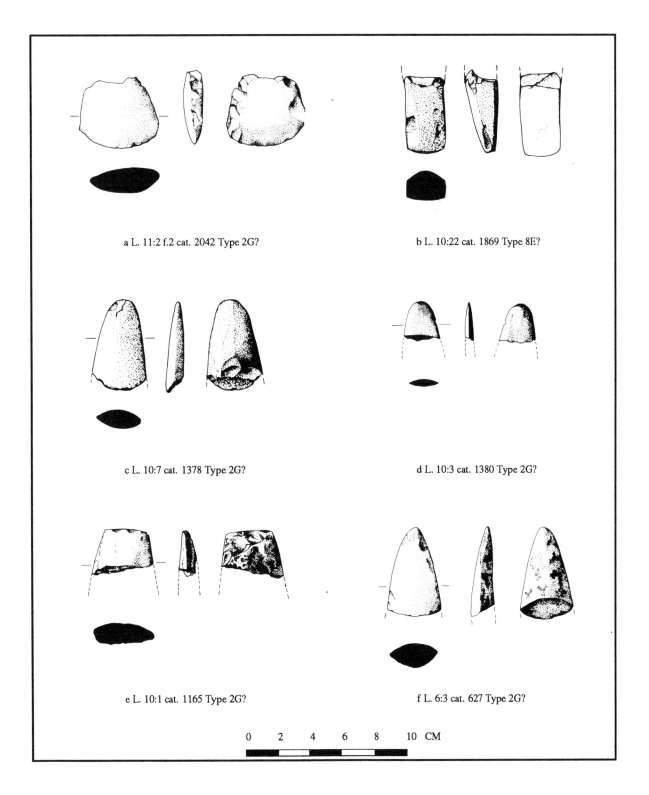

a L. 11:2 f.2 cat. 2042 Type 2G?

b L. 10:22 cat. 1869 Type 8E?

c L. 10:7 cat. 1378 Type 2G?

d L. 10:3 cat. 1380 Type 2G?

e L. 10:1 cat. 1165 Type 2G?

f L. 6:3 cat. 627 Type 2G?

0   2   4   6   8   10 CM

FIG. 26.   Adze fragments

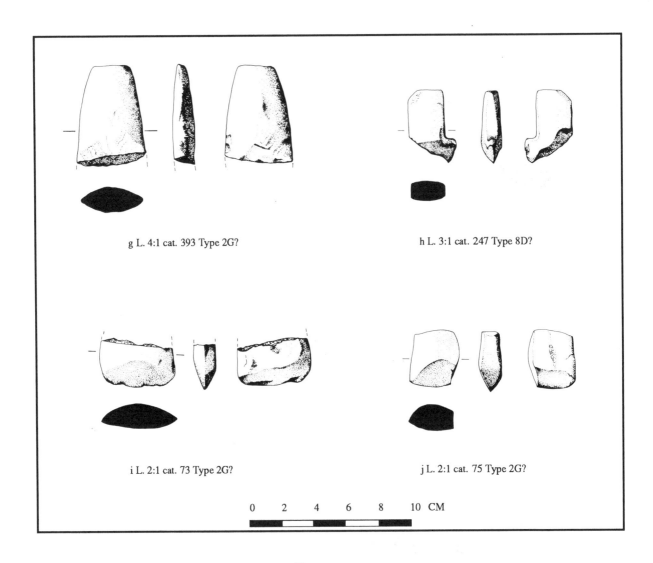

g L. 4:1 cat. 393 Type 2G?

h L. 3:1 cat. 247 Type 8D?

i L. 2:1 cat. 73 Type 2G?

j L. 2:1 cat. 75 Type 2G?

0　2　4　6　8　10　CM

FIG. 26 (cont.)

CHISELS

Some polished stone tools recovered at Khok Phanom Di are described as chisels due to their small size, nature of the cutting edge and clear evidence in their shape that they were neither handled nor used as adzes. They were, however, made of fine-grained stone similar to that employed for the adzes. These chisels were possibly used for the fine working of wooden or bone artefacts and hence there is less evidence for edge-damage.

TABLE 10: *The measurements of polished stone chisels (in cm)*

Context	Cat. no.	ML	MW	WP	MD	DP	Angle
10:1	1358	3.60	1.98	1.26	0.27	0.27	-
10:7 B72	2049	3.91	1.60	1.03	0.41	-	18°
10:12	1444	5.81	1.40	0.48	1.71	1.38	58°
2:1	87	3.11	1.88	1.56	1.02	0.84	64°
2:2	204	1.90	1.24	0.77	0.54	0.17	46°

- 10:8 cat. 1444. A unilateral bevelled gouge with a rectangular section; high triangular shape; obliquely straight cutting edge; front face wider than back and deep and pointed poll. The cutting edge was formed at the intersection of the curved front face and the back bevel. Neither side platform was well prepared and both have uneven surfaces (Fig. 27a). This specimen is made of calcareous sandstone. No traces of use are visible.

- 10:7 B72 cat. 2049. This polished slate chisel was found in association with B72. It has a round and sharp cutting edge; a sharp unilateral bevel; flat front face; round rectangular shape and a round poll. It is possibly similar to cat. 1358 (Fig. 27c) which was found in the same layer. No flake scars are present on the edge but one is present on the poll. Striations at about 50° to the edge are found on its back bevel and 90° striations are found on the front face (Fig. 27b).

- 10:1 cat. 1358. This small, roughly made chisel has an oval shape. The cross-section of its thin body is flat and rectangular; it has a round butt and working edge. It was made of fine volcanic sandstone. Half the cutting edge is missing, and the surviving section is very blunt. No striations can be observed (Fig. 27c).

- 8: cat. 895. The poll of a triangular-shaped adze or gouge which has a deep and pointed poll. This sample has the same thickness all over the body, which was broken at the middle, and a big flake has been chipped from the butt end.

- 3:3 cat. 328. The rounded poll of an oval gouge with an oval section.

- 2:2 cat. 204. This volcanic sandstone chisel is the smallest polished stone tool recovered. It has a trapezoid shape, oval to rounded rectangular section; symmetrical figure; no bevel chins; prepared side platforms and flattened poll. A few small scars are present on its edge. No striations can be observed (Fig. 27d).

- 2:2 cat. 942. The cutting edge of a barrel-shaped gouge with a narrow cutting edge and no bevel chins. Its side was possibly polished after damage (Fig. 27e).

- 2:1 cat. 87. A rectangular volcanic sandstone ground chisel with an oval section; asymmetrical bi-bevels; slightly convex cutting edge and deep and convex poll with a hollow flake scar on its poll platform. According to its size, it might have been used as a chisel (Fig. 27f). Its poll fractured during antiquity. One edge of the resultant flake scar has been reground and polished. No striations are visible.

GROUND STONE HOES

There are 14 incomplete ground stone tools which are bigger and longer than the adzes, and made of a coarse grained, leucogranite, probably obtained from Khao Kheo and Khao Chomphu about 40-50 km south of Khok Phanom Di. Most were found in zone A. Eight can be identified and grouped together. They comprise seven butts and one cutting edge and were probably used for relatively hard work and were commonly broken at the middle. They are regarded at the moment as hoes which were used in digging, the small number being, perhaps, explained because this type of tool was used outside the occupational area. These hoes are massive. They have a rounded to oval cross-section; the widest part at the middle, tapering toward the cutting edge and poll; a convex cutting edge and rounded deep poll with a poll platform. Since there is no clear damage on the poll platform, this type of tool was possibly hafted at the middle, the area most susceptible to breakage. The size of complete hoes has been estimated from the surviving fragments of polls and cutting edges as being approximately 30 cm long, with a round to oval section about 6 cm in diameter (Table 11).

- 10:3 1.2 cat. 1350. The body of this oval-sectioned hoe was found in a shell midden. It has a cylindrical shape, and was broken at both ends. It is the only sample which has provided the basis for an estimate of the tool's shape and length.

- 10:3 1.2 cat. 1351. The butt of this hoe has an oval cross-section; deep and rounded poll with an oval shape. It was broken at the middle. There is a relatively large poll platform at the butt end.

- 10:1 cat. 1162. The butt of an oval hoe with a rounded square section and a deep, round poll.

- 8:4 cat. 949. The butt of this oval-shaped hoe has a round section and large poll platform (Fig. 28a).

- 8:3 cat. 937. This is the only sample with the surviving working edge of a hoe. It has a round cross-section; round cutting edge and a possibly oval shape. The widest part is at the middle of the sample which then tapers to the cutting edge and the poll. The edge shows that its front face is narrower than the back, but more convex in shape (Fig. 28b).

- 8:2 f.38 cat. 1048. The butt of a trapezoid hoe broken at the middle. It has a round to oval section at the broken area and rounded rectangular section at its poll (Fig. 28c).

- 5:1 cat. 567. The butt of a trapezoid hoe with round section; round poll with the butt tapering from the middle to a convex poll platform.

- 4:2 cat. 419. The butt, which was broken at the middle, has an oval section, and a badly pitted surface due to the low-quality material of which it was made.

- 2:2 cat. 2594. The poll of this hoe has a round section.

TABLE 11: *The measurements of stone hoes (in cm)*

Context	Cat.no.	Width	Depth
10:3	1350	6.59	4.46
10:3 l. 2	1351	4.56	4.56
10:1	1162	3.35	3.35
8:4	949	3.20	3.20
8:3	937	5.20	5.20
8:2 f.38	1048	4.26	3.49
5:1	567	4.01	4.01
4:2	419	6.15	4.02
2:2	2594	4.35	3.94

FLAKES AND WORKED STONE

Thirty-five polished and 73 unpolished flakes were recovered. The type of stone suggests that they came from adzes. In some instances, it is possible to deduce from which part of the adze a particular flake came. Among 73 unpolished flakes, 51 appear to be natural. The 22 others are small waste flakes. Four samples are worked, but their characteristics indicate that they were rejected after an unsuccessful attempt to make a tool. They are described as follows:

- 3:5 cat. 2723. A fine-grained rock which joined with cat. 2053 from 1:1. It was probably a blank or the rough-out of a long, triangular adze. It has similar characteristics to cat. 1349 from layer 9, but it was unpolished. This sample possibly resulted from an attempt to make a polished adze. Failure to polish it may be due to the poor quality of the raw material (Fig. 30d).

- 3:2 cat. 2057. A quartzite cobble flaked around its circumference which makes a flat and round core (Fig. 30e).

- 3:1 cat. 2685. A piece of sandstone of triangular form.

GRINDING STONES AND WHETSTONES

During the 1985 excavation, 245 stone artefacts with grooves and smooth polished working surfaces were identified. They have been recorded as 145 grinding stones, 26 whetstones, 11 pounders,
62 fragments and 12 samples which cannot be grouped, on the basis of the working faces. Some
stone artefacts in this group, although fragmentary, were probably used for functions other than
grinding and whetting. Some examples reveal more than one function. The following classification defines each sample according to its presumed use.

TABLE 12: *The percentage of grinding stones, pounders, and whetstones by layer*

Layer	Grinder	Pounder	Stepped whetstone	V-shaped whetstone	Frag.
11	2.86	-	-	-	4.84
10	30.20	63.64	9.09	20.00	24.19
9	13.88	-	9.09	-	17.74
8	10.20	-	9.09	6.67	12.90
7	7.35	-	9.09	-	6.45
6	6.35	-	9.09	13.33	3.23
5	2.04	9.09	-	-	
4	4.47	-	18.18	33.33	3.23
3	13.47	27.27	9.09	20.00	17.74
2	9.39	-	18.18	6.67	9.67
1	0.82	-	9.09	-	
Total no.	145	11	11	15	62

Grinding stones

Most of the grinding stones from Khok Phanom Di were made of sandstone which varies
markedly in colour. Their most obvious characteristic is the U-shaped hollow or smooth-ground
working faces which in some implements have more than one hollow on one side or are worked on
both sides. Although most are fragmentary, complete or almost complete samples show that round,
square or rectangular blocks of sandstone of approximately 10 to 20 cm in length, 10 cm in width
and 5 cm in depth were formed before they were used (Fig. 29). The function of these grinding
stones is not clear. They were possibly used in resharpening stone or bone tools, or grinding or
powdering grain. Stone pounders with U-shaped grooves may have been used as anvils or querns
in grinding or powdering, while those with V-shaped grooves or stepped grooves were probably
used as resharpeners. However, they may be multi-functional due to the occurrence of different
types of groove on a sample. In addition to the grinding stones, some rounded pebbles have a worn
surface indicating use as stone pestles or pounders (Fig. 32).

Whetstones

Whetstones are important in the Khok Phanom Di lithic technology. They were used in edging and resharpening polished stone adzes. They were mostly made of a fine-grained sandstone formed as a rectangular block approximately 10 cm wide, 10-20 cm long and 2-4 cm deep. Two types of whetstone were recognized. The most characteristic has steep grooves which differentiates it from the concave hollow of grinding stones. These whetstones may be classified into 2 types according to the characteristics of their grooves. Type A is characterised by shallow stepped, U-shaped grooves formed around the end of a tool. The grooves are rectangular and usually curved at the end. This type was occasionally worked on both sides (Fig. 30). The curved and stepped edge on both margins of the grooves show that it was used in polishing the cutting edge of bone points and shell knives. Type B has a long and narrow V-shaped groove at the middle of either one or both faces, which was possibly formed by rubbing the cutting edge of an adze to and fro on the whetstone face (Fig. 30).

Apart from the grinding stones and whetstones, there are 12 samples which cannot be ascribed either to type A or B. Three have a cylindrical or conical shape and usually have one pointed end, for example cats. 1004 (Fig. 31b), 2627 and 2671. They were ground all around their body. It is considered likely that they were used for polishing or grinding, particularly grinding the inner ring of stone disc/bangles, which made the working face rounded and pointed at one end. One specimen (cat. 635, Fig. 31c) had been used as a combined tool by making a smooth round point for polishing or grinding the inner ring of a disc/bangle on one end of the whetstone, which has grooves and smooth working surfaces on its body. Some samples were found worked along the entire length of one side of the tool. The wear pattern indicates that one side was used to sharpen another artefact. A cylindrical pebble, cat. 481 (Fig. 31e), has one end polished and the other broken. It was possibly used in burnishing or polishing. Cat. 46 has a triangular shape with all the sides ground. It bears one obvious V-shaped groove. It was possibly a stone polisher for fine polishing or grinding purposes (Fig. 31f).

POUNDERS

Eleven pounders have been identified with a rounded shape and clear evidence of use around their edges. They have pecked surfaces around the body, and were probably used in conjunction with the grinding stones. The shape varies from a round to an oval ball. A few have a cylindrical shape with pecked surfaces on both ends. Most are about 4 to 7 cm in diameter, for example cats. 1210, 1514 and 1569. One specimen, cat. 2804, reveals stains of red ochre on its surface which indicate that it was used in crushing ochre. There are a few made of large pebbles or shaped as a large, oval-shaped stone ball with hollows on both sides (Fig. 32). These average about 15 cm in length, 9 cm in width and 6 cm in depth. These pounders are regarded as multi-functional, applications including use as hammers, anvils, crushing and grinding tools. Similar implements have been reported from Lower Mandailing, Sumatra (Tugby and Tugby, 1964) and from midden mounds in Tonga and Fiji (Birks, 1972).

RED OCHRE

There are 45 fine-grained, reddish-brown pebbles which have an irregular shape bearing polished facets on the surface (Fig. 32). Some samples reveal the natural surface before they were polished or partly polished. These comprise shale, a fine-grained sedimentary rock which provides a red powder when crushed. This rock is found along the coast about 30 km from Khok Phanom Di. These samples are probably the residue left after preparing red ochre for funeral rituals. However, some may have been used as fine polishers due to their planar facets. That some such material was also powdered is shown by the staining of red ochre found on a pounder.

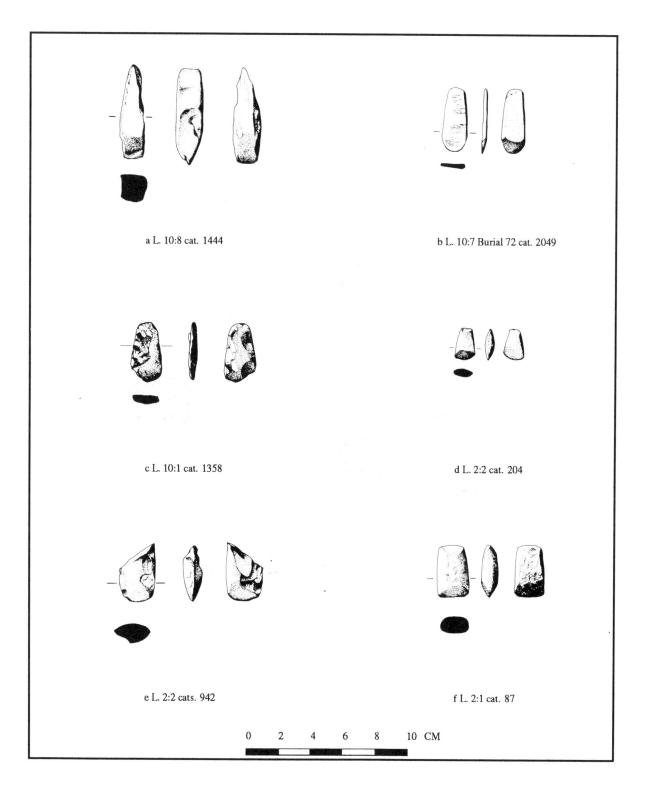

a L. 10:8 cat. 1444

b L. 10:7 Burial 72 cat. 2049

c L. 10:1 cat. 1358

d L. 2:2 cat. 204

e L. 2:2 cats. 942

f L. 2:1 cat. 87

0   2   4   6   8   10 CM

FIG. 27.   Polished stone chisels

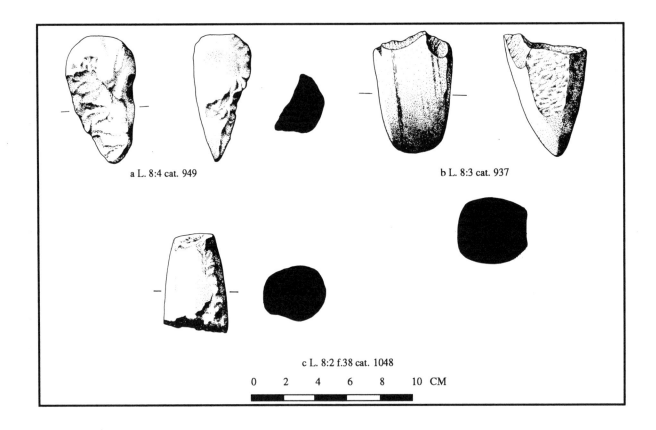

a L. 8:4 cat. 949

b L. 8:3 cat. 937

c L. 8:2 f.38 cat. 1048

0   2   4   6   8   10 CM

FIG. 28.   The ground hoes

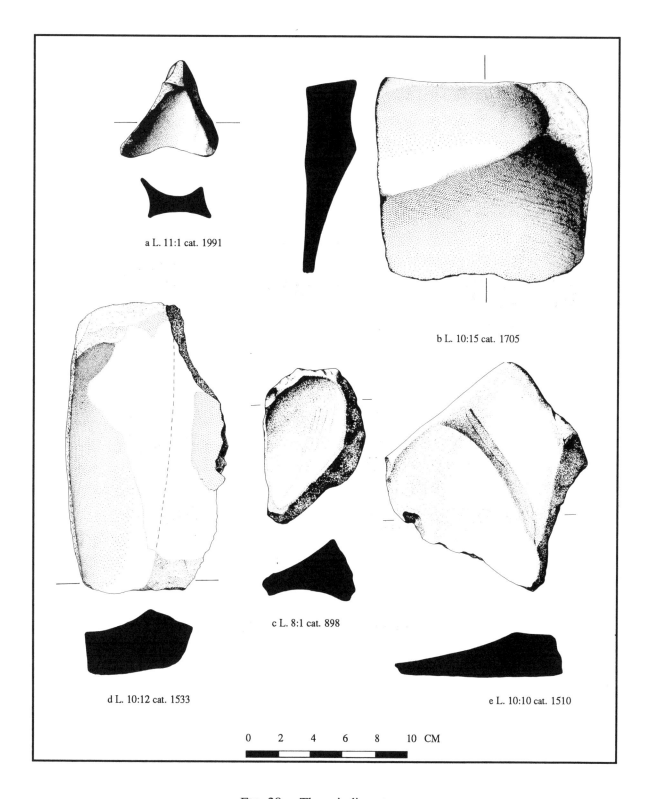

a L. 11:1 cat. 1991

b L. 10:15 cat. 1705

c L. 8:1 cat. 898

d L. 10:12 cat. 1533

e L. 10:10 cat. 1510

0   2   4   6   8   10 CM

FIG. 29.   The grinding stones

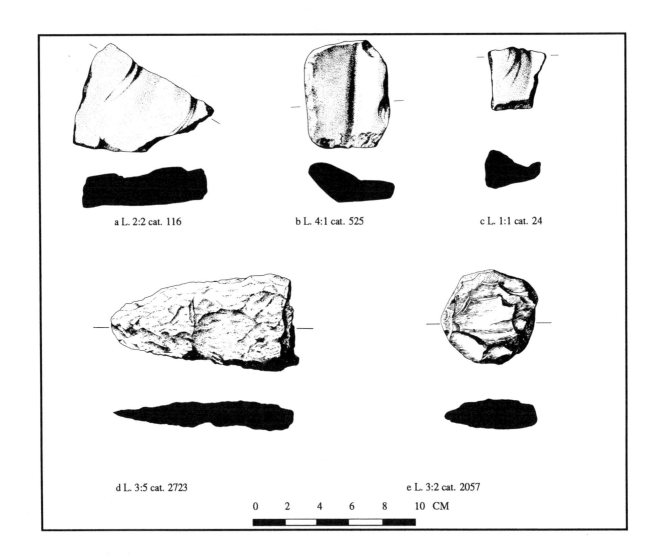

a L. 2:2 cat. 116   b L. 4:1 cat. 525   c L. 1:1 cat. 24

d L. 3:5 cat. 2723   e L. 3:2 cat. 2057

0   2   4   6   8   10 CM

FIG. 30.   Whetstones (top row), an adze rough-out (bottom left) and worked stone

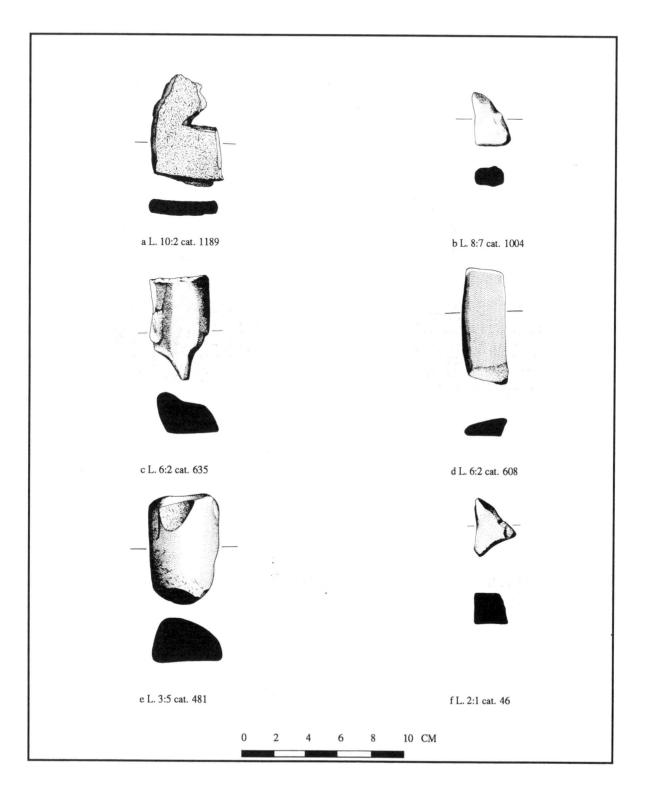

a L. 10:2 cat. 1189

b L. 8:7 cat. 1004

c L. 6:2 cat. 635

d L. 6:2 cat. 608

e L. 3:5 cat. 481

f L. 2:1 cat. 46

0 2 4 6 8 10 CM

FIG. 31.   The miscellaneous stone artefacts

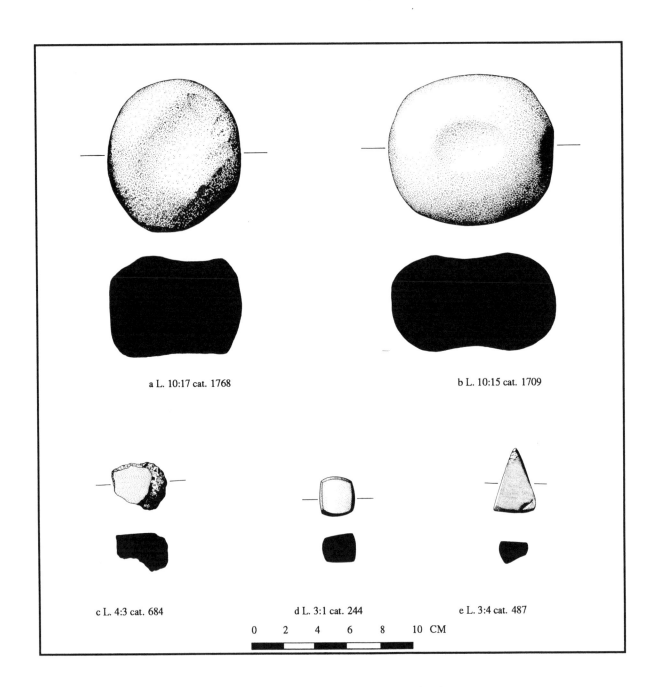

a L. 10:17 cat. 1768

b L. 10:15 cat. 1709

c L. 4:3 cat. 684

d L. 3:1 cat. 244

e L. 3:4 cat. 487

0   2   4   6   8   10 CM

FIG. 32.   The stone pounders and shale red ochre cores

SUMMARY AND CONCLUSIONS

Most of the polished stone artefacts are adzes, made from igneous or metamorphosed igneous rocks. Nearly all the adzes were broken, sharpened or modified during long-term use, but fortunately an adze found in layer 9 (cat. 1349) has survived in its original condition. It has a triangular shape, and is about 90 mm long, 40 mm wide and the maximum depth is 130 mm. This is a medium size for polished stone adzes (Semenov, 1964). Some trapezoidal adzes, for example cats. 152, 162, 267 and 552 (Fig. 23), apparently also had a triangular shape originally, but were modified into smaller implements after their polls fractured. Most such modifications of the poll were found in zone B and C contexts. There are also several short oval adzes at Khok Phanom Di (cats. 1927 and 1920). These are usually found in zone A. They have an elliptical cross-section, but in some cases both sides were ground, which formed truncated ellipsoid or rectangular sections. Bilateral bevels are common among them. They possibly had a unilateral bevel and then, due to constant use and sharpening, bi-bevels were formed. The bevel angle was mostly between 50° and 65°, a medium sharpness which possibly caused less edge-damage and yet was still effective.

Damage on the cutting edges, sides and polls is common. There are small flake scars on the cutting edges. Large flake scars are found on a few samples. These probably occurred as the adze was freed or moved when it was embedded in wood (Keeley, 1980). Large scars are also common on the blade corners and the middle of the cutting edges. A few samples, for example cat. 229, have large flake scars on their sides, possibly caused by a different method of hafting or by an attempt to fashion shoulders. Damage to the poll, apart from where it was broken or missing, is seen in the large flake scars and pecked scars probably caused by percussion against the wooden haft.

Certain types of wear on polished stone tools can be ascribed to wood-working. According to Semenov (1964), they are sharp, clear and visible to the naked eye. They are equally strong on both faces and the upper margin is usually very clearly defined. Adze wear usually took place on the back face, where the tool rubbed against wood. The results of working are seen as irregularly spaced grooves which are thicker at the bottom and narrow to fine lines along the axis of the tool. They occur at about 75° to 90° to the cutting edge (Keeley, 1980). Axe wear differs as the grooves occur on both cheeks of the axe and run diagonally. Another characteristic of wear which differentiates axes from adzes is the orientation of striae. They run in the same direction on both faces of adzes, while in the case of axes, they form angles or chevron-marks at the cutting edge. The implements from Khok Phanom Di have been investigated through both a hand lens and the binocular microscope. The striations can be ascribed to two types, thought to reflect traces of manufacturing and traces of wear. The former comprise fine parallel lines which run diagonally across the axis of the tool and mostly occur on the body. They are usually less than 70° to the cutting edge. There are two principal types of wear: use striations and polishing. The striae are clear on both bevels from the edge to the bevel chins. They are recognized as deep broken lines or grooves deeper at the edge and parallel or almost parallel to the axis of the tool. They are usually found above the chin on the back face and in some case they reduce the sharpness of the back bevel chin (Fig. 23). In some cases, both types of striation occur in the same area, for example, cat. 535 has very short striae about 65° to its edge along the very edge, and above them there is another set at 90° to the edge. The first set was possibly the result of resharpening over the use-striae. All the tools found in layer 11 have a blunt cutting edge and striations compatible with hard work before they were cached. The use-wear on most of these samples is deep, clear and crowded along the cutting edge. This evidence for heavy wear occurs among most of the implements from zone A. In zones B and C, although the edge damage and striations occur, the cutting edge was not completely blunted. There are some areas where a sharp edge survived. This may reflect the heavy nature of the initial clearance of the mound and its environs. According to Thompson (1992), much of the charcoal found in the early occupation layer comes from *Rhizophora*, a hard-wood mangrove species. The understanding of vegetation on and around the site contributes to an appreciation of why and how use-wear formed, and suggests how continual sharpening resulted in such small stone adzes. The polishing on the tool surface is another trace of wear. On the Khok Phanom Di materials it occurs on bevels as a glossy surface usually at the middle of the cutting edge. In some cases (cats. 615, 279 and 162), the polishing on the bevels formed grooves or facets at the middle of the cutting edge.

All polished stone tools from the 1985 excavation have been scrutinised using a binocular microscope at x 20 magnification. Observation commenced with the cutting edge to identify the wear which might have resulted from use rather than fashioning or resharpening the artefact. The butts and polls have also been examined under the microscope for evidence of grinding when it was manufactured and for hafting and use. Examples of this aspect of use could take the form of polishing and pecking against the haft and the residue of resin or other materials employed in hafting. Damage to the tool may involve large flake scars over 2 mm in width. In this case, it includes both Keeley's large deep scar and large shallow scar. Most of the scars in this category are found on the blade corners, sides and poll. Large scars are not common on the cutting edge. Small scars under 2 mm in width include Keeley's categories of small deep scar and small shallow scar (Keeley, 1980). They are very common on the cutting edges and are rare on the other parts of the tool.

Pecking marks were formed by the striking of the poll against its haft. In some cases, it may reflect direct percussion if the tool was used in the manner of a chisel. This reduces the edge damage but increases the damage on the poll. The pecking marks can be seen with the naked eye. It is suggested that, in contrast to these pecking marks, striations or scratch lines on the tool result from contact with an object when the adze was used, or as a result of grinding against a whetstone when it was made, resharpened or remodelled. In certain well-preserved examples, these striations can be observed with the naked eye. There are two groups of such striations. The first reflects use. Most of Khok Phanom Di tools are adzes and chisels which have a regular set of striations due to their method of use. They are located at about 90° to the edge, that is, parallel to the axis of the tool. They usually occur along the edge of both bevels in the form of deep V-shaped grooves. Apart from the cutting edges, such striations are also occasionally present on the bevel chin, indicating areas where the tool was rubbed. This type of striation is mostly in the form of a short and broken line. Striations due to manufacturing or resharpening were formed by rubbing the tool against another stone. They are fine, shallow and long, and run parallel to each other. They usually lie across the axis of the tool or parallel or nearly parallel to the edge. They are found on the butt, and sometimes the bevels. The latter probably reflect resharpening. The manufacturing striations are confined to the body of the tool.

Evidence for hafting methods is fugitive. In one case, fragments of wood survive in the haft area (cat.1856) and small spots of what may be resin are present on cats. 1349 and 1808. The use of a hardwood for hafting is likely. Blackwood (1950) has noted that in such cases the haft was probably cut from a tree with a branch attached at a convenient angle. The polished surface at the butt on the back face of cat. 1349 (Fig. 23) provides further evidence for the hafting method. It was probably polished through friction against the binding materials which, according to cat. 1808, may have included barkcloth. On the other face of this sample at the same part, the poll is coated by a greasy material, possibly resin used to fix the front face of the poll into a socket. Apart from those mentioned above, the recurrent damage to and pecking marks on the poll support this hafting method. Further evidence for hafting is the modification of the butt to form shoulders. Shouldered adzes have been found occasionally throughout the Khok Phanom Di sequence. The shoulders were formed by the reduction of the sides of the butt. They have been defined as a device to assist in hafting (Bulmer, 1977). The shouldered tool can be fixed more firmly in a wooden haft than the non-shouldered variety. Apart from that, both sides of its shoulders prevent damage to the socket of a haft as well as damage to the poll.

In considering the use of stone artefacts at Khok Phanom Di, it must be stressed that the site was located on the estuary of a major river with a hinterland comprising young marine and brackish-water clays. This low-lying area ultimately gives way to a series of uplands with highly variable stone resources. While the inhabitants had access to high-quality potting clay, wood and marine shell for jewellery manufacture, stone of any sort was not immediately available. The nearest potential sources of metamorphic stone suitable for adze manufacture are located between 60 and 100 km east of the site. The nearest source for the sandstone abraders is about 100 km to the north. Shale, quartz pebbles and leucogranite, all of which were used at Khok Phanom Di, are located at some distance from the site. Stone flakes are virtually absent from the excavated area, a situation which suggests that initial flaking was undertaken elsewhere, the adzes arriving at the site either as blanks or completed artefacts. Clearly, however, much grinding, modifying and sharpening of the stone implements was undertaken at the site.

The polished stone adzes and chisels from Khok Phanom Di concentrate in the basal three metres of the site and in the uppermost metre of deposit. Only one in ten of the adzes is found in zone B. During this cultural sequence, there is little evidence for typological change, nor indeed change in the way in which adzes were modified. The commonest form throughout is the lenticular cross-sectioned form, Duff type 2G, and its modified derivatives. The shouldered variety is also found from early and late contexts, especially the short, oval-shaped adzes similar to cat. 1920 (Fig. 23). The differences which have been noted between adzes from these two zones are the presence of type 2D and 8B in the upper part and types 2A, 2B, 2E, 2F, 8E, 8F and 8H in the lower part. It seems that the prehistoric people of Khok Phanom Di had more varieties of adze in the earlier period. A more restricted range is apparent for layers 1–4. Apart from polished stone adzes, other types of stone artefacts, for example the grinding stone, whetstones, pounders and hoes, also concentrate in zones A and C while they are rare in zone B.

The earliest polished stone artefacts were found as 2 caches placed in pits cut during the initial occupation. They contain polished stone adzes, burnishing stones, bone tools and pottery. The first contained 3 adzes and the second, 10 adzes or adze fragments including 5 shouldered examples. Although most of these adzes are of types 2G and 8D, types 2B, 2E, 2F, 8E, and 8H are also represented. This particularly wide variation occurs only in this layer although there was still considerable variation in adze form.

Adzes became rare in zone B, and there were fewer varieties. Most of them are type 2G. One example of type 2D and one of type 8D have also been uncovered. Polished stone adzes found in zone C continued the same tradition of raw material and form. Most of them are type 2G and 8D. However, a few changes did occur, in that adzes of type 2D became more common and there was an attempt to make a double-shouldered adze (cat. 90). One does not have to look far to account for the differences in the frequencies of adzes in these three successive zones. The build-up of cultural material in lower zone A resulted from the deposition of ash lenses and middens. There is much evidence of day-to-day domestic activity likely to have involved the loss of material items. With zone B, the nature of the archaeological deposits changed as the excavated area became a cemetery. Hence, the number of artefacts declined sharply. With zone C the situation changed again. No burials were found, but there was much evidence for industrial activity, particularly the manufacture of pottery vessels. The number of artefacts recovered increased.

The adzes found show much continuity. This may be due to the maintenance of stable exchange relationships with those specialising in the quarrying which provided the adzes at source.

Much attention has been devoted over the last few years to the presence and role of exchange in mainland Southeast Asia. Higham (1983) and Higham and Kijngam (1984) have noted the presence of exotic goods in mortuary contexts at Ban Na Di in Northeast Thailand, and suggested that such goods may have been correlated with the status of different social groups there. Exotic goods at Ban Na Di include marine shell and stone in the form of bracelets. That particular site also yielded bronzes and exotic ceramic vessels (Rajpitak and Seeley, 1984; Vincent, 1987). Ban Chiang is a further site revealing the presence of exotic objects in mortuary contexts (White, 1982). All three sites have yielded the remains of bronze dated to all or part of the prehistoric sequences. Khok Phanom Di has not yielded metal. It is, therefore, possible to examine the issue of regional exchange in a fresh context. This incorporates a site located in a rich marine/estuarine habitat for which there is no evidence for knowledge of metal.

The prehistoric occupants imported polished stone adzes as well as sandstone for manufacturing tools, leucogranite for hoes and shale for mortuary ritual purposes. There is a question, however, as to whether those materials were direct access (Renfrew, 1975) or exchanged materials. Prehistoric exchange has received much attention recently in order to describe behaviour reflecting similarities of artefacts in the form of raw materials distribution (Renfrew 1969, 1975; Webb, 1974; Ericson, 1981; Earle, 1982; Torrence, 1986). This has helped us to understand social, economic and political variables. There are four general stages in the exchange system including acquisition, production, distribution and use (Torrence, 1986). Acquisition applies to both raw materials and completed artefacts. Production is the process of material modification to form an artefact (Ericson, 1984). The distribution of either raw materials or completed artefacts can be defined in two different ways: exchange or direct access. Although these stages of an exchange system are based on the exchange of obsidian tools in Europe, West Asia and America, they can also be applied to the materials found at Khok Phanom Di.

The analysis of stone used in making implements demonstrates the exploitation of sources located between 40 and 140 km from Khok Phanom Di as the crow flies. It is felt that the rarity of adzes and hoes at the site may reflect acquisition of stone artefacts through a system of exchange rather than regular direct-access visits. Such exchange, if the suggested sources for the stone are shown to be correct, would have followed the advantages offered by riverine and coastal routes. The most likely sources for the stone converted into artefacts are located in the headwaters of the Bang Pakong River. Leucogranite came from 40 km and the nearest sandstone outcrops are between 100 and 140 km distant (Fig. 33).

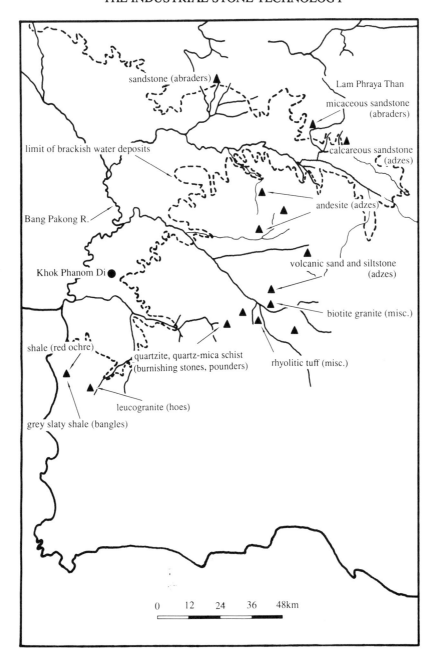

FIG. 33.   The location of the various proposed sources of stone used at Khok Phanom Di

Perhaps the most significant general finding to result from identifying the likely sources of stone found at Khok Phanom Di is that in the period when bronze-working was not locally in evidence, there existed an extensive exchange network. It linked coastal and inland communities. Future research may well reveal further such networks. If they linked with each other, a situation strongly hinted at by the presence of marine shell and some similar artefacts at Samrong Sen and Khok

Phanom Di, then the means whereby bronze and the associated casting skills disseminated can be more readily appreciated.

If it is the case that the stone adzes of Khok Phanom Di were obtained as part of a regional exchange network, then the possibility that further such networks might be identifiable on the basis of stone artefacts is posed. To isolate such regional patterns across Southeast Asia as a whole would then allow the reconstruction of interactive regions, and their geographic extent and characteristics could be considered. Thus, in the case of Khok Phanom Di, it is evident that the Bang Pakong River played a major unifying role in the exchange of stone. It could be anticipated that the waterways comprising the upper Chi catchment played a similar integrative role for such sites as Non Nok Tha, and the Songkhram River for Ban Chiang. In order to proceed with this possibility, it is necessary first to obtain and then source dated assemblages of stone artefacts. Clearly, *in situ* treatment and the careful use of typology also have an important bearing on this issue, as does the identification of quarry sources. As a very preliminary and incomplete exploration of this topic, the distribution of polished stone adzes around the Bangkok Plain has been considered.

It is found that the area can, on the basis of adzes, be classified broadly into two geographic regions. The first comprises the western region of this plain with an extension into peninsular Thailand. Its hinterland is rich in stone sources, and the most characteristic polished stone adzes of this region fall into types 2A and 8A. A large number of stone artefacts including chipped flakes have been found in both occupational and mortuary contexts there. The second region comprises the eastern area, incorporating Khok Phanom Di and the Bang Pakong Valley. In the latter, stone sources are further removed from the known lowland sites. Polished stone adzes in the lowland sites of this region are rare compared to those at sites like Ban Kao in the west. Very few adzes have been found in graves. Most are relatively small and belong to types 2G, and 8D. There is much evidence of resharpening, reusing, and modifying, a phenomenon suggesting scarcity.

III.   THE BURNISHING STONES

M. N. Moore

THIS section is concerned with a sample of 392 small, modified river pebbles found during the excavation of Khok Phanom Di (Figs. 38-44). The majority were quartz, and probably came from the stony bottomed streams which issue from Khao Kirirom, the highest hill on the margins of Bang Pakong flood plain, about 7 km southeast of Khok Phanom Di. These pebbles have diameters ranging from 1 to 5 cm. The modification on the pebbles involved facets worn by abrasive action, also unidirectional striations which are visible with the aid of a low-powered microscope.

The initial problem posed by the recovery of a hitherto unrecognised artefact type in a Southeast Asian prehistoric context is identifying its use. After considering other artefacts and materials found in the site, several options were considered. They may have been used to extrude rice from the husk, although their relatively small size casts doubt on this proposition, as a larger stone would have been more effective. They may have been used to hone the edges of other stone tools, or to grind red ochre. Other stones, however, have been identified which clearly fulfilled these functions. They may have been counters, or 'magic stones' used in a ceremonial context, but both these options are unlikely because of the extent of the wear. The most likely option appears to be that they were used to burnish pottery. This hypothesis will be tested in the first part of this chapter, and its implications will then be considered.

The proposition that the pebbles were burnishing stones was tested in six ways. The continuity of the wear pattern, any associations of the stones with items of a known use, both in mortuary and non-mortuary contexts, the prevalence and stratigraphic distribution of pottery in the site and ethnographic evidence from Thailand was considered. The reproduction of the wear patterns in a laboratory situation was also attempted. Various features and associations of the pebbles were studied: colour, size and type of stone, the provenance, the context in which the pebble was found (whether it was found in occupation material, in a lens or in a burial) and any association with other artefacts.

The wear pattern on the stones did not alter throughout the sequence, suggesting that they were used for the same purpose from the basal layer until the site was abandoned. This means that, whatever activity the stones were used for, it was independent of environmental fluctuations, as there was a change in the environment associated with a fall in sea-level with layer 4. An associated change in the economy and vegetation types evidenced in core samples taken in the vicinity of Khok Phanom Di is also present at this juncture. A raw material which would be unaffected by such a drop in the sea-level would be clay, and an industry that shows continuity throughout the sequence is pottery manufacture. The recurrent wear patterns, together with the continuity in clay availability and in the pottery industry supports the hypothesis that these pebbles were used as burnishing stones.

The stones were found in three different contexts: in the matrix of the deposition, in ash lenses and other features, such as caches, and placed in graves with a number of other artefacts. They were most common at the transition between zones A and B. The varied distribution of the stones

105

suggests that they were not only of industrial value, but as grave items they symbolised connection with pottery making, one of the most significant aspects of the technology of the site's inhabitants.

The stones were found in less than one-sixth of the burials at Khok Phanom Di. A repeated association between the stones and anvils is present. Of the eight clay anvils recovered in a burial context, six were found in graves close to these stones, which suggests associated functions. A good example of this is B15, the richest recovered. An anvil was found beside the body's right ankle together with a shell containing two burnishing stones (Fig. 34).

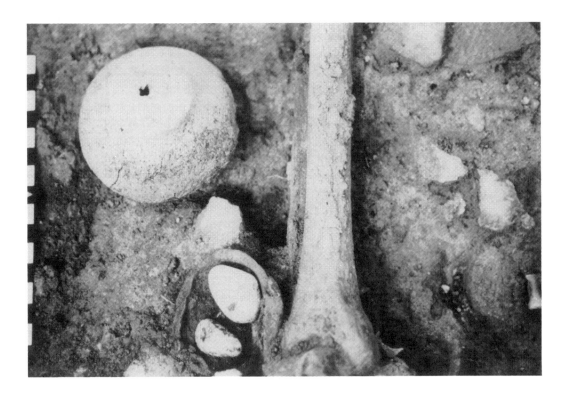

FIG. 34.   The right ankle of burial 15 showing the anvil and burnishing stones

Other mortuary offerings are also repeatedly found in graves containing the stones, but the frequency of these associations is no higher than for that of an item's total occurrence within all the graves at the site. Moreover, the relationships between the stones and the other items are not as clearly defined as with anvils. The close association in mortuary contexts between the stones with a tool used in pottery manufacture supports the hypothesis that the stones were used for burnishing.

When we turn to non-mortuary data, it is notable that the two caches in layer 11 contain burnishing stones, and one also includes a clay anvil. These are among the first signs of occupation at Khok Phanom Di. In addition to the 8 anvils found in a mortuary context, over 200 further anvils were recovered from Khok Phanom Di. Anvils were (and still are) used to support the wall of a pottery vessel on the interior as the exterior is beaten with a wooden paddle to shape the vessel.

Petrographic analysis indicates that most of the high-quality mortuary vessels were manufactured locally (Vincent, pers. comm.). At the same time, the occupation level sherds appear to have come from a wide range of sources. These, generally, do not have the same regularity of burnishing as those in a mortuary context. The occurrence of the stones is reduced from the end of zone B. This is paralleled by the cessation of the mortuary phase and an accompanying decline in high quality pottery.

Burnishing pottery was observed in Chiang Mai and Singburi Provinces in Northern Thailand in early 1986 by Bannanurag (pers. comm.) (Fig. 35). The potter uses the same implements as have been documented at Khok Phanom Di (Fig. 36).

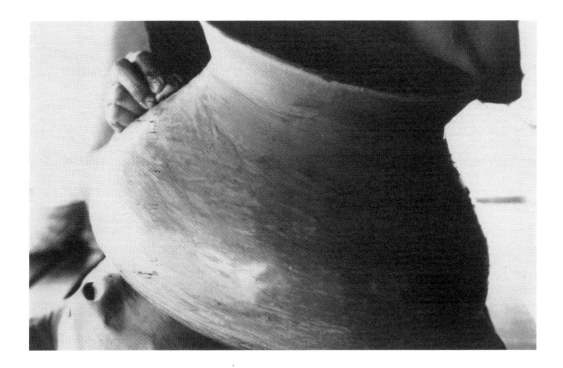

FIG. 35.   A woman from Bang Paeng, Singburi, Northern Thailand, burnishing a pot

Bannanurag also collected some of the burnishing stones from the women of the village. They were unwilling to part with the stones because it takes so long to wear a stone into a form which is needed to produce the smooth finish (Bannanurag, pers. comm.). When the stones were examined, they were found to exhibit almost identical wear-patterns to those from Khok Phanom Di. The modern examples are quite badly stained by the clay, which may have been the case for the stones from Khok Phanom Di when they were lost or buried at the site (Fig. 37).

The final indication that the pebbles are burnishing stones is the wear pattern exhibited on a previously unworn pebble from Khok Phanom Di. This was used to polish the surface of a clay tablet formed from clay similar to that used at the site in prehistory. After approximately 5 hours

FIG. 36.   Paddles and anvils used in forming pots, from Bang Paeng, Singburi, Northern Thailand

of burnishing over an extended period of time, striations were clearly visible and were identical to those on the prehistoric specimens. No sign of a facet was visible, indicating that a high output of pottery must have been achieved by the potters at Khok Phanom Di, and that the burnishing stones were used a great deal over a period of time.

All the information points to the use of the stones being to burnish pottery: the parallels between the wear patterns of those from Khok Phanom Di and the modern examples, the consistent form that the wear patterns exhibit, the association between anvils and stones in a mortuary context, the presence and distribution of pottery within the site, and the ethnographic analogy all support the hypothesis.

No other sites which evidence such a concentrated pottery industry as Khok Phanom Di are known in prehistoric Southeast Asia. By identifying the distribution of the burnishing stones among the burials, questions relating to the social and industrial organisation of the community who lived at Khok Phanom Di may be answered. Tracing the changing concentrations and associations of the stones may identify changes in the socio-political structures of the community.

The burnishing stones were found in all layers and contexts of the site. There appears to be no differentiation in the degree of wear present on stones found in different contexts. They were most commonly found in the occupation deposits, but the proportion of stones found in the various contexts changed. In layers 9-11, they were found mostly in the lenses or non-burial situations. In layers 5-8 the majority were found in burials, and in the uppermost layers, burnishing stones are

1x

FIG. 37. Burnishing stones from Khok Phanom Di and modern specimens from Northern Thailand. On the left are two stones from prehistoric Khok Phanom Di (cats. 2249 and 2160). In the centre are two modern burnishing stones from Northern Thailand, on the right is a previously unworn stone from Khok Phanom Di (cat. 2186) exhibiting wear marks created in the laboratory

found exclusively in occupation and pottery-making contexts. The numbers of stones recovered decreased with time throughout the deposition. Both points reflect the changing function of the area excavated, and the changing amounts of the highly burnished pottery which was produced.

Burnishing stones found in layers 9-11 were probably lost. About 240 were found this context. As has been shown in the ethnographic context, it takes a considerable time before a stone achieves the surface configuration necessary to create a well-burnished finish. In this context, it is possible that individual tools of significance were placed into the owner's grave. That they were also found in a number of infant burials may reflect on the skills or roles of the parents.

Twenty-three burials contained burnishing stones. They appear in all age and sex groups, but more commonly in female than in male or child burials. Some gender differentiation did appear between the clusters, for example in clusters A and C the burnishing stones were found mainly in female graves, and in clusters E and F they were found only in male graves (where sex has been identified). This appears to be of some significance as all these clusters have the same relative

proportions of adult males, adult females, juveniles and infants as in the whole of the sample recovered. This may represent a different approach to dividing labour within each cluster, a sampling
bias, or differentiation by the people who buried the bodies in these clusters in the selection of items
that were placed with the body.

TABLE 13: *A table of the burials in which burnishing stones were found. Note the distribution
of the genders among the clusters*

Burial no.	Age	Sex	Cluster	MP	No. stones	Burials in cluster	No. anvils
96	4	-	A	2	1	26	-
110	36	F	A	2	5	26	-
94	31	F	B	2	1	8	-
35	21	F	C	4	3	38	1
36	21	F	C	4	1	38	-
72	32	M	C	3	3	38	-
82	6 m	-	C	3	1	38	1
83	30	F	C	3	2	38	-
107	40	F	C	2	1	38	-
109	31	F	C	2	2	38	-
123	2	-	D	2	1	12	-
23	30	M	E	4	1	8	-
132	34	M	E	2	2	8	-
20	12	-	F	4	1	33	1
29	27	M	F	4	1	33	-
42	32	M	F	4	2	33	-
91	45	M	F	2	2	33	-
4	26	F	H	6	2	12	1
13	35	F	H	6	8	12	-
1	9	-	I	7	1	5	2
15	35	F	-	5	2	-	1
16	15 m	-	-	5	1	-	1
19	25	F	-	6	2	-	1
6	9	-	-	6	1	-	-

Within the burials, the burnishing stones are found in three recurring positions. Beyond the
head, beyond the feet, and in the mid-body region. The placement of the stones, while obviously
deliberate, does not appear to have been selected on age, sex or a cluster basis. The placement
may be more closely related to what other items were also placed in graves, many of which were
perishable and have decayed.

Other items were also found in burials. Especially relevant to this study is the distribution of
tools used in the manufacture of pottery, and of pottery vessels. Clay anvils have survived in an

archaeological context at Khok Phanom Di, the wooden paddles have decayed. Anvils were found in one infant burial (B82), three juvenile burials (Bs 16, 20, 33), and four adult female burials (Bs. 4, 15, 19, 35). No males were buried with anvils. Only three of the nine clusters had anvils present. Again, this could be due to the factors mentioned above. All but two of the burials containing anvils also contained burnishing stones in close association.

Funerary pottery was often of exceptionally high quality and stood out when compared with most of the pottery of the occupation layers. If we can assume that association with an artefact indicates ownership, then it appears that the formation of pottery vessels was performed by the females, but that decoration, and finishing of the vessels, was a universal occupation. If pottery vessels were a major exchange item, and if the finishing of the vessels was shared by all groups, then it may well have been a seasonal occupation as Vincent has suggested. This is because, during the different seasons, other gender-based activities would probably have occurred.

The evidence presented strongly suggests that the pebbles are burnishing stones. They were not obtained in the immediate vicinity of the site, but were collected or exchanged from some distance. They were of value to the inhabitants of the site, probably because of the time and effort involved in producing a surface on a stone that achieved a fine, burnished finish.

Unlike the shaping of the vessel, which appears to have been the exclusive domain of women, the finishing of the surface seems to have been an activity which was performed by all age and gender groups. There was no differentiation of labour between groups, as evidenced by the burial clusters, but some gender differentiation may have been present within specific clusters.

Although the positioning and distribution of the burnishing stones can independently give a small insight into part of the economy and social organisation of the site, as with many features and artefacts that are recovered from an archaeological site, the true value in studies such as this is revealed when all the conclusions gained are compared, and a complete picture is obtained.

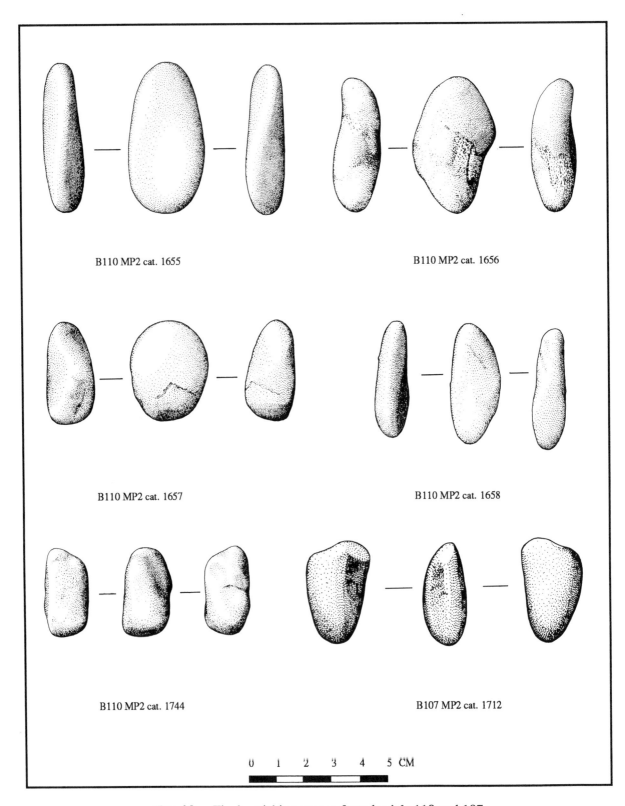

B110 MP2 cat. 1655

B110 MP2 cat. 1656

B110 MP2 cat. 1657

B110 MP2 cat. 1658

B110 MP2 cat. 1744

B107 MP2 cat. 1712

0 1 2 3 4 5 CM

FIG. 38.   The burnishing stones from burials 110 and 107

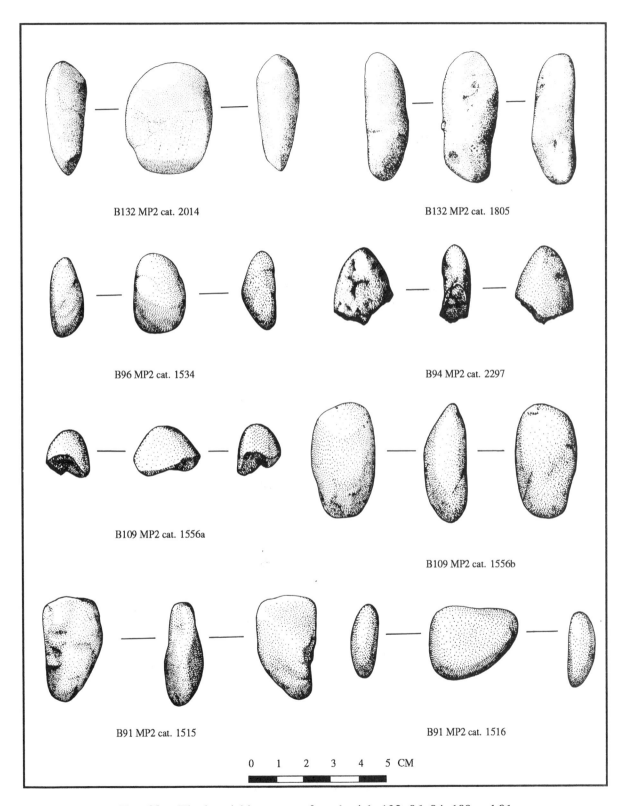

B132 MP2 cat. 2014

B132 MP2 cat. 1805

B96 MP2 cat. 1534

B94 MP2 cat. 2297

B109 MP2 cat. 1556a

B109 MP2 cat. 1556b

B91 MP2 cat. 1515

B91 MP2 cat. 1516

0 1 2 3 4 5 CM

FIG. 39.   The burnishing stones from burials 132, 96, 94, 109 and 91

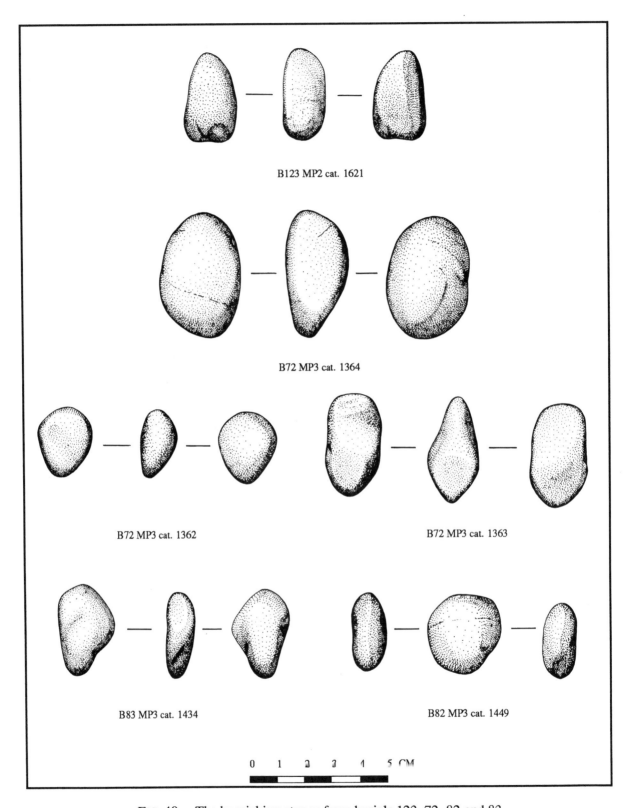

B123 MP2 cat. 1621

B72 MP3 cat. 1364

B72 MP3 cat. 1362   B72 MP3 cat. 1363

B83 MP3 cat. 1434   B82 MP3 cat. 1449

0   1   2   3   4   5 CM

FIG. 40.   The burnishing stones from burials 123, 72, 82 and 83

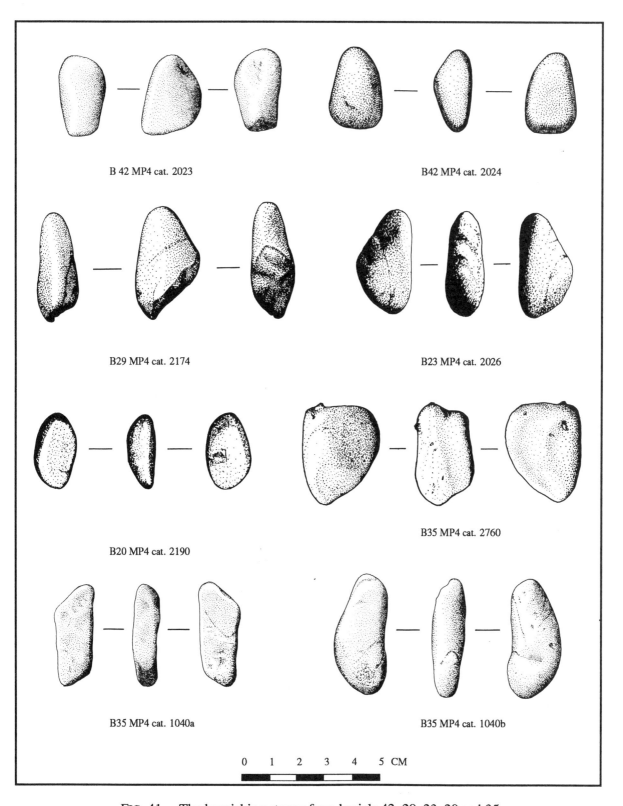

B 42 MP4 cat. 2023

B42 MP4 cat. 2024

B29 MP4 cat. 2174

B23 MP4 cat. 2026

B20 MP4 cat. 2190

B35 MP4 cat. 2760

B35 MP4 cat. 1040a

B35 MP4 cat. 1040b

0 1 2 3 4 5 CM

FIG. 41.   The burnishing stones from burials 42, 29, 23, 20 and 35

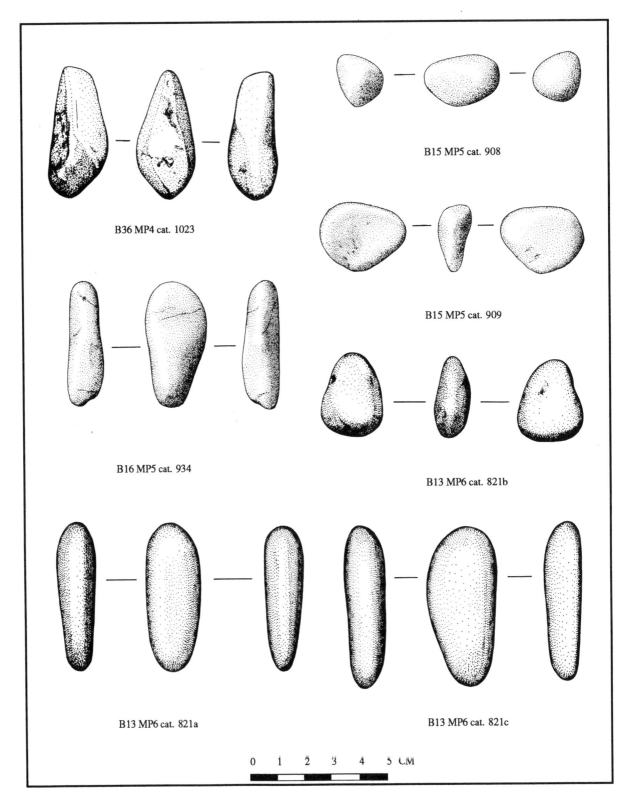

FIG. 42.   The burnishing stones from burials 36, 15, 16 and 13

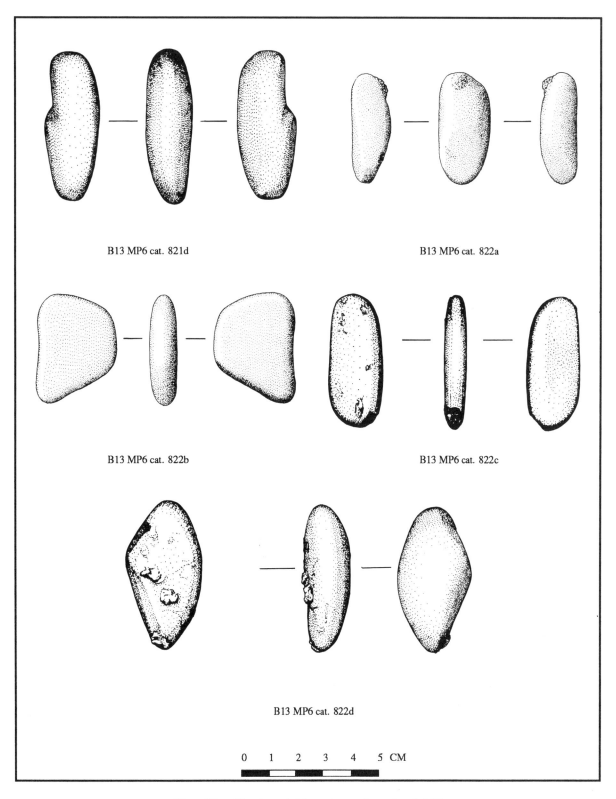

B13 MP6 cat. 821d   B13 MP6 cat. 822a

B13 MP6 cat. 822b   B13 MP6 cat. 822c

B13 MP6 cat. 822d

0   1   2   3   4   5 CM

FIG. 43.   The burnishing stones from burial 13

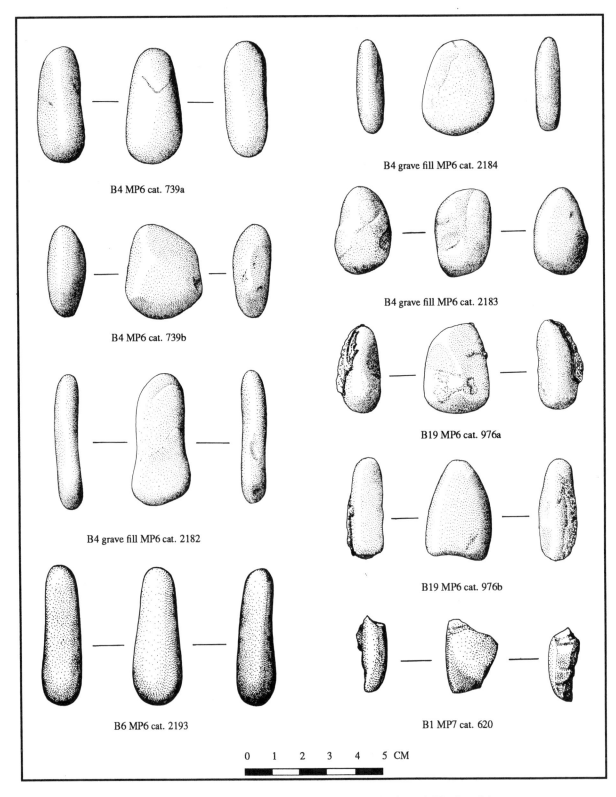

B4 MP6 cat. 739a

B4 grave fill MP6 cat. 2184

B4 MP6 cat. 739b

B4 grave fill MP6 cat. 2183

B4 grave fill MP6 cat. 2182

B19 MP6 cat. 976a

B19 MP6 cat. 976b

B6 MP6 cat. 2193

B1 MP7 cat. 620

0   1   2   3   4   5 CM

FIG. 44.   The burnishing stones from burials 4, and 19, 6 and 1

IV. THE PERSONAL ORNAMENTS

J. S. Pilditch

INTRODUCTION

THE personal ornaments recovered from Khok Phanom Di are made from a variety of materials and can be divided into three main types. The major ones are some form of bead or disc/bangle, but a third group, generally made from turtle carapace, has been tentatively identified as cod pieces or some sort of ornamental body plaque. The one or two objects in the site that may be called pendants are included in the bead classification, as are the perforated discoid objects which have external diameters of less than 1.5 cm, because they were found strung together for use in embroidery, necklaces or belts. All discoid objects with larger diameters are classed as disc/bangles regardless of their use. The ornaments are described according to the material they were made from. In many cases, there is a correlation between the material and the type of ornament, but this is not the case with the disc/bangles. In order to avoid repeatedly defining the classification of these ornaments they are only described in general terms in the text and a full classification of the styles is laid out in the final section of this chapter.

SHELL ORNAMENTS

Most ornaments at Khok Phanom Di are made from shell. There are various shapes of beads and bangles as well as discs. Although it has not yet been possible to identify all the species used, some families have been recognised. Most have been made from *Tridacna*, while others utilised *Conus* and many of the small disc beads have been produced from a nacreous bivalve. There is a chronological distribution in all styles of shell ornaments apart from disc beads, which are represented in all mortuary phases where jewellery is present.

Shell beads

There are six types of shell bead. The disc bead is the most numerous, and other styles include capstan or I-shaped, the smaller H-shaped and barrel- and cylinder-shaped beads.

Disc beads. These all have the same basic flat disc shape with straight outer surfaces and a central perforation. The size varies considerably. Some are almost 9 mm in diameter while others are as small as 1.2 mm. The majority have a diameter between 3 and 5 mm. There was a similar variation in thickness, ranging between 0.2 and 3 mm. Because of the large size of the sample, the beads

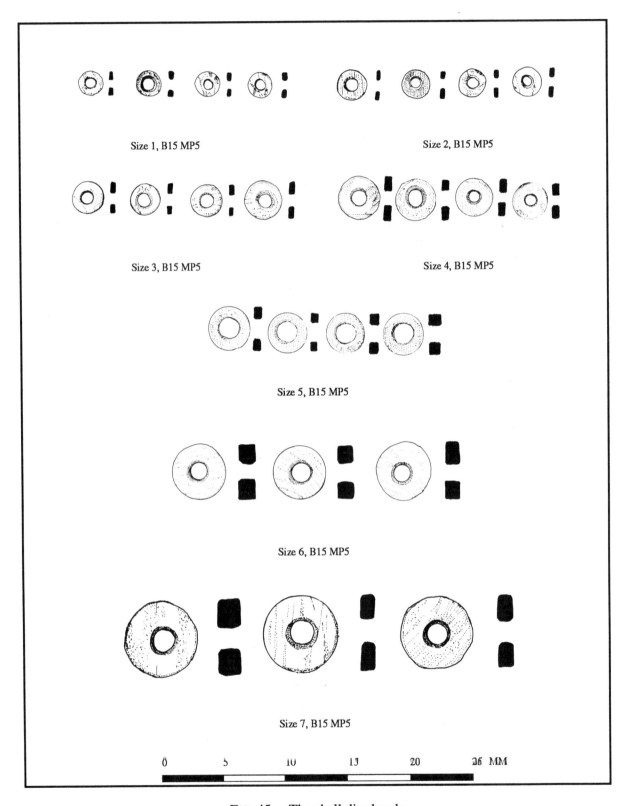

FIG. 45.   The shell disc beads

were sorted using graduated sieves into six size categories. Size 1 consists of beads in the range 1.2 to 2.29 mm, size 2 ranges from 2.3 to 2.79 mm, size 3 from 2.8 to 3.39 mm, size 4 from 3.4 to 3.89 mm, size 5 from 3.9 to 4.49 mm, size 6 from 4.5 to 6 mm and size 7 contains all disc-beads with diameters $\geq$ 6.0 mm (Fig. 45).

Although the total number of beads found was in excess of 250,000, the numbers recovered from individual burials varied from 2 (B 144) to over 120,000 (B 15).

The species of shell used in the production of these beads have not been positively identified, but at least four different types have been recognised, one of which has been tentatively identified as a giant clam. Most of the larger beads appear to be of this type, as they are generally much whiter than the other beads, and the shell is much denser in appearance. Many of the smallest beads still retained a nacreous sheen, while the remainder are either sandy or grey coloured or have been stained by the iron oxide powder that was such a prevalent part of the mortuary ritual.

Despite the variety of shell, the actual method of manufacture appears to be the same in all cases. The beads were bored from the shell using a small diameter cylinder, possibly of bamboo. It is not clear whether the central hole was drilled before or after the disc was removed, but it would have been simpler, especially in the case of the smaller beads, to have drilled it first. Beads taken from thick shells, such as clams, would either have been ground down or sliced to produce a fairly uniform thickness. These beads were used in a variety of ways, both as jewellery and for embroidering garments. In the majority of burials, they were strung into necklaces of one or more strands, often in conjunction with other beads (B 16 cat. 929, B 33 cat. 1098). In other cases the beads were recovered from around ankles (B 16) and wrists (B 90 cat. 1547). Small mother-of-pearl beads were found heavily encrusting the neck, vertebral and pelvic regions of two burials (B 15 and B 43). It appears that they decorated the edges of tunics. B 43 also had a belt made of several parallel strands of larger (size 5) clam shell disc beads. The beads were occasionally incorporated into head-dresses (B 113 cat. 1650).

Funnel beads. These beads are fairly long truncated cones with concave sides (Fig. 46). They are among the earliest beads found and come from B152 (MP1, n=1), B143 (MP2, n=2) and B132 (MP2 n=5). Their size range is between 1.85 and 3.95 cm. Neither the type of shell nor the exact method of manufacture has been identified, but it is clear that the perforation was made from both ends. They are found used as necklaces in conjunction with other types of beads including short barrel and disc beads.

Barrel beads. These beads range in shape from quite short fat barrels to cylinders (Fig. 46). Many have more or less pronounced lipped ends, which appear to be natural, and one or more flat planes on the sides which are apparently remnants of the original surface rather than a result of over grinding. Their length varies from < 6 mm to > 14 mm. They are all treated as the same type because they are made from the same species of shell and the differences are probably a result of the manufacturing technique rather than design elements. They were classified by size into 6 groups. Those under 6 mm in length are designated short barrel beads. The other groups range in lengths of 6.0–7.9 mm for size 2, 8.0–9.9 mm for size 3, 10.0–11.9 mm for size 4, 12.0–13.9 mm for size 5, and beads longer than 14 mm are classed as size 6. Chronologically, they occur throughout MPs 2 and 3.

The species of shell used is unidentified, but the presence of the lipped ends suggests that it is not one of the giant clams. Although these ends could have been manufactured, this seems unlikely,

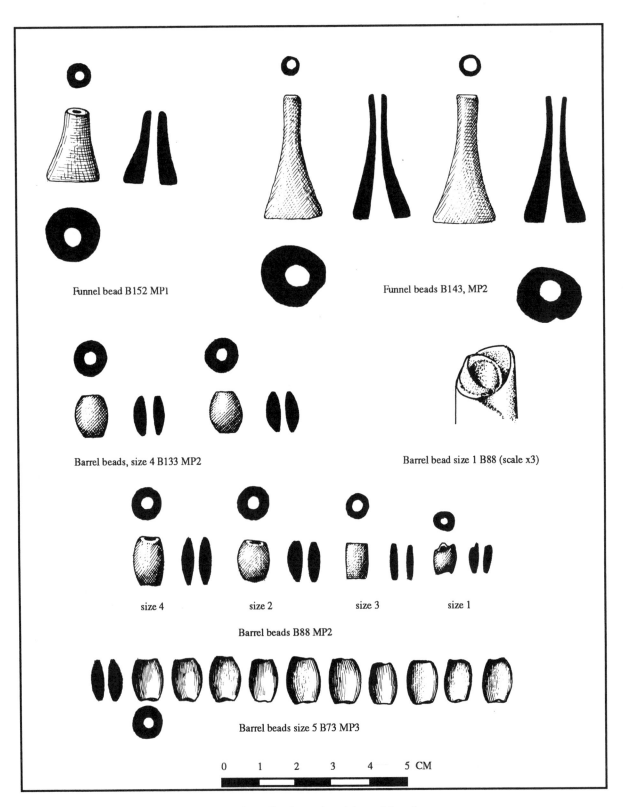

Funnel bead B152 MP1

Funnel beads B143, MP2

Barrel beads, size 4 B133 MP2

Barrel bead size 1 B88 (scale x3)

size 4   size 2   size 3   size 1

Barrel beads B88 MP2

Barrel beads size 5 B73 MP3

0   1   2   3   4   5 CM

FIG. 46.   The funnel and barrel beads

TABLE 14: *The distribution of disc beads*

Burial	MP	Cat. no.	Total no.	Sizes	Uses	Burial	MP	Cat. no.	Total no.	Sizes	Uses
152	1	1893	11	4	nk	144	2	1866	2	4	-
143	2	1745	50	3	nk	140	2	1703	610	3–4	nk
132	2	1804	39200	1–5	nk	126	2	1680	3	2–3	-
125	2	1652	2	5–6	-	123	2	1628	120	1–4	nk
122	2	2041	105	2–5	nk	120	2	1675	327	4	nk
114	2	1681	16	5	-	113	2	1650	224	4	hd & nk
112	2	1940	542	3	nk	109	2	1558	1588	3–4	gd
105	2	1535	1043	4	nk	103	3	1598	59	5	nk
101	2	1521	626	3	nk	100	2	1750	220	2	nk
99	2	1647	230	2–5	nk	93	3	1567	859	5	gd
91	2	1513	1294	4	nk	90	3	1547	1500	3–5	gd
89	2	1493	73	4	nk	88	2	1455	690	4	nk
87	2	1602	866	3,5	nk	73	3	1477	1260	4	nk
75	3	1376	189	3	bl or belt	72	3	1373	330	5	gd
57	3	2770	93	1–3	-	43	5	2035	56200	1–5	gd
41	4	1064	41	5	bl	35	4	2775	8	3–4	-
33	4	1098	7845	1–6	nk	19	6	1006	1600	1–4	bl
18	6	887	9969	1–6	nk	16	5	929	12247	1–4	nk
16	5	930	314	1–4	an	15	5	890	120787	1–5	gd
15	5	890	21	6	nk	14	5	788	269	3–6	belt
13	6	3075	3	2	-	12	7	1861	730	1–6	belt
11	6	772	12	4	nk	9	6	3076	3	3	-
7	6	2795	9	2	nk	6	6	808	17786	1–6	nk + belt
3	7	659	49	3–6	nk						

nk: necklace, hd: head-dress, gd: garment decoration, bl: bracelet, an: anklet

because when the beads are strung the lips cannot be seen and they do not alter the shape of the string. It seems more likely that the shape is natural and present because, by utilising that particular area of the shell, a minimum amount of grinding and polishing was required. These beads were worn as necklaces, belts and bracelets. They were not usually combined on the same strand with other types of beads, but in B133 they were found as a bracelet in conjunction with some bird bone beads.

Cylinder beads. Few of these beads were found at Khok Phanom Di (Fig. 48). Only six were made from shell. The diameters were similar to those of the disc beads and the impression is that they are either very thick versions of disc beads or are the tubular blanks from which they would have been made. They range in size from 3.4–6.8 mm in length and from 4.4–4.8 mm in diameter. All were found in MP5 (B 43 cat. 2035) but the other examples were made from bone and were from the MP2 B 133.

TABLE 15:   *The distribution of barrel beads*

Burial	MP	Cat. no.	Total no.	Sizes	Possible uses
133	2	1673	45	3–4	belt + bracelet
132	2	1804	11	1	necklace
130	2	2341	17	2–3	belt
129	2	1738	353	1–3	necklace
122	2	2041	13	2–4	necklace
121	2	1627	7	2–3	necklace
120	2	1675	13	2–3	necklace
117	2	2764	8	2–3	necklace
113	2	1650	143	3–4	necklace
105	2	1535	88	1–5	necklace
103	3	1598	56	1–5	necklace
101	2	1521	13	1–5	necklace
94	2	1687	55	1	necklace
91	2	1513	93	3–5	necklace
90	3	1547	37	1–5	bracelet
88	2	1455	16	1–4	necklace
73	3	1477	285	3–6	necklace

I–beads.   These are similar to capstan beads. They are round or ovoid in transverse section, and have concave sides. The longitudinal section is of a concave-sided cone with a thin flange on the narrow end that has roughly the same transverse shape as the other end, but lies on a slightly different transverse axis. The length of these beads varies from 5.9 to 45.4 mm and they are grouped here into eight size ranges (Figs. 47, 48, Table 16).

Size 1 are <7 mm long while size 2 ranges between 7 and 11.9 mm, size 3 between 12 and 16.9 mm, size 4 between 17 and 21.9 mm, size 5 between 22 and 26.9 mm, size 6 between 27 and 31.9 mm, and size 7 between 32 and 41.9 mm. All I-beads ≥ 42 mm are classed as size 8.

They occur in MPs 4–5 and predate the H-beads. They were recovered from five burials in numbers varying from 17 (B 29 cat. 995) to 950 (B 15 cat. 890). Some of the larger beads may have been made from the central spiral of a big gastropod, but most of the others seem to have been made from a shell with a similar density to clam. As with the other beads, these have been ground and polished into shape. Usually they were worn as necklaces, but in B 15 several hundred of them were used to decorate the bodices of the two garments the woman was wearing.

H–beads.   These beads have narrow, roughly-shaped oblong ends, and are longer than they are wide (Fig. 48). The two narrow, and one of the wide sides are deeply concave, but the other is usually flat. The ends are usually divergent in both directions and the perforations, which run along the bar of the H, are waisted. They range in length from 3.2 to 8.2 mm and have been grouped into three size ranges. The lengths of size 1 are ≤5 mm, of size 2 are ≤7 mm and of size 3 are >7 mm.

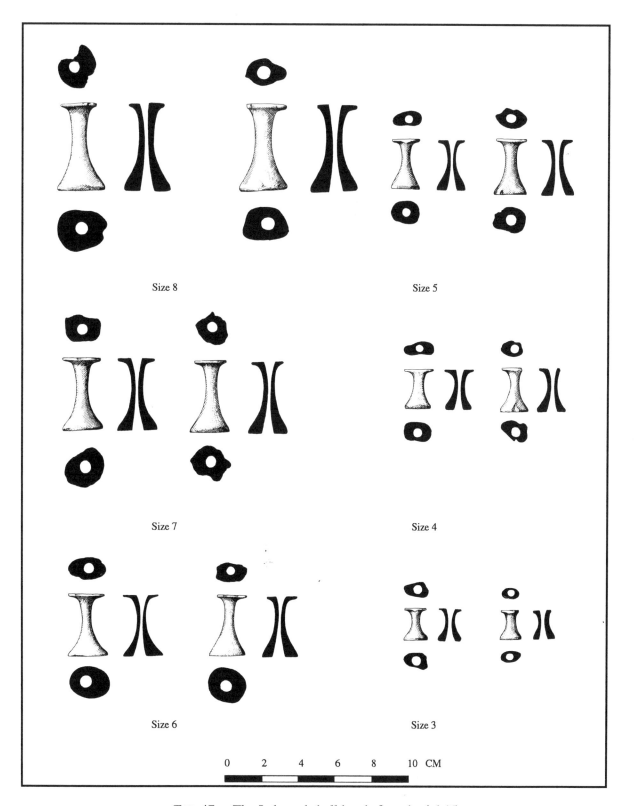

Size 8

Size 5

Size 7

Size 4

Size 6

Size 3

0　2　4　6　8　10　CM

FIG. 47.　The I-shaped shell beads from burial 15

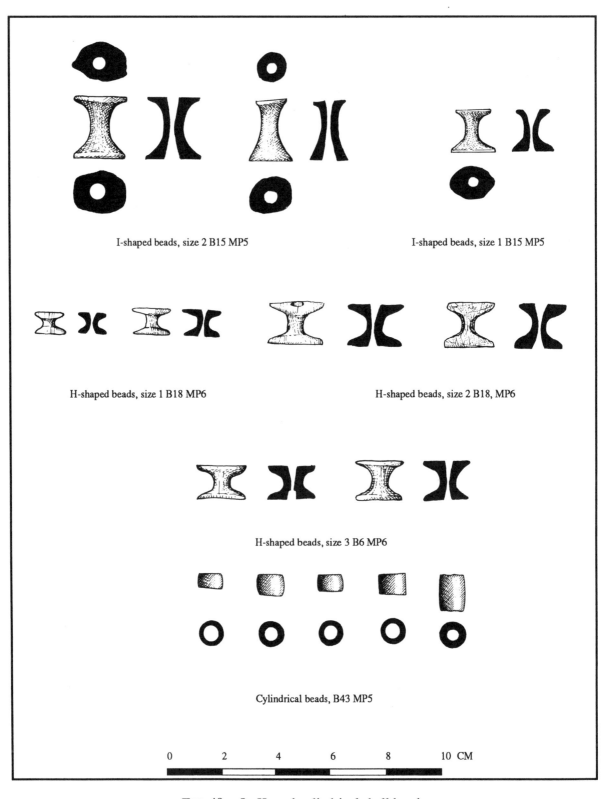

FIG. 48. I-, H- and cylindrical shell beads

TABLE 16:   *The distribution of I–beads*

Burial	MP.	Cat. no.	Total	Sizes	Possible use
43	5	2035	435	1–7	-
33	-	1098	107	3–4	necklace + anklets
29	-	995	17	2–4	necklace
16	-	929	200	1–4	necklace + anklet
15	5	890	950	1–8	garment decoration + anklets

H–beads were recovered in varying numbers from five MP6–7 burials. Numbers range from 12 (B 3 cat. 659) to 700 (B 18 cat. 887). They appear to have been fashioned from large *Anadara* shells or some other species of bivalve that has marked longitudinal ribs on the outer surface. Each tab of shell used had two ribs and a groove. This grooved area was ground away between the ribs until only a rounded bridge remained. The bead was finally perforated along the bridge's long axis. Although most of the beads were recovered from the neck region, in one of the burials they had been incorporated into a bracelet. They were usually worn in conjunction with other beads.

TABLE 17:   *The distribution of H–beads*

Burial	Layer	Cat. no.	Total	Sizes	Possible use
18	5	887	700	1–2	necklace
12	5	1861	30	1–2	necklace
11	6	772	57	1–2	necklace
6	5	808	656	1–3	necklace
3	6	659	12	1–3	necklace

Miscellaneous beads.   Beads recovered from B 33 were made from the portion of the *Nassarius* shell around the opening. Seventeen of them were worn as a necklace.

Disc/bangles

The shell disc/bangles show variety both in the style of ornament and in its use. Although some of them were apparently comparable to the stone bangles, others were used as portions of headgear and also as possible forms of garment decoration or even a type of ritualistic symbol.

Two unfinished ornaments recovered from B 43 show that circular tabs of shell were trepanned from the clam shell, probably by using a large piece of bamboo and grit. The rough original outer surface of the shell was then sliced off by concentric grinding of the outer edge and then breaking the resulting core once it was small enough. Producing the disc in this manner keeps the necessary amount of grinding to a minimum. It also is a limiting factor in the height of the central flange. The central core of the disc was removed by coring and the excess shell ground away until the required shape was produced.

Although these disc/bangles were the only shell specimens which were clearly unfinished, the method described above could easily have been adapted to produce them all.

Style 1   These artefacts were all probably bangles, because over half of them were found *in situ* on wrists in burials. They were all made from *Tridacna* and were found in layers 5, 6 and 7. The discoid bangles were all wedge-shaped, with a flange on one of the inner edges which gave the radial section the appearance of an L on its side. There does not appear to be a standard ratio between the depth and width or internal diameter and, in fact, the dimensions are more likely to be dictated by the thickness of the original disc blank and the size of the wearer. The largest bangle, cat. 2018, has an external diameter that is almost twice as wide as any of the others. It was found with B43 (Fig. 49). By comparison, the bangle associated with B16, a 15-month-old child (cat. 931) has an external diameter that, at 82 mm, is larger than most, yet the internal diameter is only 36 mm, the smallest in the group (Fig. 50).

Style 1a   All four of these objects were recovered from burials. The earliest was cat. 1688, a small disc made from the flat top of a *Conus* shell (Fig. 51). It was found beneath the ribs of B94, a female belonging to MP2. Two similar discs were recovered from each side of the head in the very rich female B 15. This was a much later burial from MP 5, and although one of the discs was made from *Conus* shell, the other was made from clam. The two later discs were part of some type of headgear, but the earlier one was more probably a pendant. Apart from its much larger dimensions and the fact that the central cylinder had a flat rather than curved top, the fourth artefact in this group, cat. 807, was the same as the others. It was found immediately above the skull of the child in B6, and may also have been part of a head-dress (Fig. 51).

Style 1b disc/bangles.   The two clam shell discs in this group, cat. 896a–b, differ from all the other finished disc/bangles in the site because they have no central perforation (Fig. 52). Apart from this lack, they are of the same general type as the disc/bangle from B 6 mentioned above. They are fairly large but thin discs having external diameters similar to that of the style 10 bangles. The central conical peg has slightly concave sides and a flat top. Their use is not clear as they were found, one on each shoulder, in B 15. While they could perhaps have been some type of garment fastener, it is considered more likely that they were a badge of rank.

Style 1c disc/bangles.   The three disc/bangles in this group are L–shaped in radial section and about as deep as they are wide, having only vestigial flanges. Two have the upper outer edge rounded off, while the third has a fairly deeply concave outer surface. Although fragmentary, this latter disc/bangle (cat. 723) was broken or cut in antiquity as it has an oblique transverse break with a broken hole that had been drilled laterally. The other end is flat and smooth, but because of deterioration, it is not clear whether the cut was deliberate. Cat. 974 was recovered from a layer 5 burial and the other two were from occupation areas in layers 5 and 6 (cats. 646 and 723, Fig. 52).

Style 4a disc/bangles.   These disc/bangles are wedge shaped with truncated outer surfaces. Only two of those tabled below are clearly from this category. Both are fragmentary and from layer 6. Cat. 616 was recovered from an occupation area. It has a small internal diameter which would only have been suitable for an infant to wear as a bangle, but its other dimensions are quite large, so it is possible that it served some other purpose (Fig. 53). The other came from a child's burial.

The two unfinished artefacts from B 43 were among the largest of the disc/bangles. Neither was perforated, but one had a central core partially removed. It is not clear whether they were to be further modified to become style 1 disc/bangles or remain wedge-shaped.

Style 5 disc/bangles.   The two fragments of disc/bangles of this type were found in non-mortuary contexts in layers 6 and 8. They were made from the top section of a *Conus* shell. Cat. 645 had been broken and a hole made to effect a repair. The wear polish on the end near the hole showed that this happened some time before the disc/bangle had been lost or discarded (Fig. 53).

Style 8b disc/bangles.   The single example of this style of shell disc/bangle was found in a burial in layer 6. All the edges were rounded and one of the radial breaks was through a diagonally-drilled hole.

Style 9b disc/bangles.   There were two examples of this flat rectangular style of disc/bangle. Both had small internal diameters. Cat. 636 was found in a non-mortuary context and it is therefore not possible to ascertain whether it was a very small child's bangle or served some other purpose. In comparison, cat. 658d was made from *Conus* shell and was found in close association with several other disc/bangles in B3 (MP7), that of an infant.

Style 10b disc/bangles.   Four of these square *Tridacna* bangles were recovered from non-mortuary contexts. Most were from layer 5, but cat. 533 was found near the bottom of layer 4 (Fig. 54). They were all fragmentary and chalky. Cat. 579 appears to have been the whole section, as a complete hole at one end was complemented by a partially drilled oblique one at the other. The corrosion is such that it is not possible to be sure whether the section was originally cut or broken.

The three disc/bangles from the burials were recovered from child burials in layer 6. They were all from groups of bangles. Cat. 658a and c, for example, were found with two others on the wrist of a very young infant. Cat. 658a had a comparatively small internal diameter making it more suitable for a child's bangle than cat. 658c. One portion of the outer surface is stepped as though the blank had been drilled out from both sides and the boring had not quite matched. Because of this the disc/bangle has both a square and L–shaped radial section. As the latter section is incidental it has been ignored for the purpose of stylistic classification.

Style 10c disc/bangles.   There was only one shell example of this fine square disc/bangle. It was recovered from layer 5 and was both fragmentary and chalky.

Style 11a disc/bangles.   Cat. 658b is a small and relatively wide disc/bangle which also came from the infant B 3 (Fig. 54). Like the others it is made from *Tridacna*. The inner surface is oblique which suggests that it was drilled out from one direction. The other two artefacts in this group came from non–mortuary contexts in layers 5 and 6. They have oblique surfaces and appear as severely truncated cones. Both are fragmentary.

Style 11b   The two artefacts in this group came from non-mortuary contexts in layers 6 and 4 (Fig. 54). They are fragmentary and have sloping surfaces that were similar to the 11a disc/bangles, but are narrower.

TABLE 18: *The distribution of shell disc/bangles*

Style	Context	Burial	MP.	Cat. no.	Diam.	Depth	Width	Material
1	7:7	43	5	2018	65.0	44.9	15.7	*Tridacna*
1	7:3	16	5	931	36.0	23.1	11.9	*Tridacna*
1	7:2	15	5	893	55.0	19.0	12.1	*Tridacna*
1	6:1	1	7	2039b	40.0	16.6	9.3	*Tridacna*
1	5:5	-	-	596	43.0	23.9	9.3	*Tridacna*
1	5:3	-	-	581	55.0	16.3	9.3	*Tridacna*
1	5:1	-	-	571	55.0	19.0	11.3	*Tridacna*
1a	10:11	94	2	1688	43.0	-	7.3	*Conus*
1a	7:2	15	5	892a	7.0	17.1	9.0	*Tridacna*
1a	7:2	15	5	892b	7.0	14.1	7.0	*Conus*
1a	5:3	6	6	807	5.0	51.5	27.0	*Tridacna*
1b	7:2	15	5	896a	98.0	-	29.0	*Tridacna*
1b	7:2	15	5	896b	78.0	-	19.7	*Tridacna*
1c	5:2	19	6	974	55.0	7.3	7.3	*Tridacna*
1c	6:4	-	-	646	53.0	9.2	9.0	*Tridacna*
1c	5:4	-	-	723	53.0	8.5	8.0	*Tridacna*
4a	6:2	-	-	616	35.0	19.7	7.0	*Tridacna*
4a	7:7	43	5	2036a	112.0	-	22.0	*Tridacna*
4a	7:7	43	5	2036b	125.0	-	16.0	*Tridacna*
4a	6:1	1	7	2039b	56.0	13.4	7.0	*Tridacna*
5	8:6	-	-	997	37.0	10.8	4.0	*Conus*
5	6:6	-	-	645	44.0	8.8	4.4	*Conus*
8b	6:3	3	7	1858	-	8.0	4.9	*Tridacna*
9b	6:3	-	-	636	32.0	7.0	5.5	*Tridacna*
9b	6:3	3	7	658d	38.0	8.4	3.4	*Conus*
10b	6:1	1	7	2039c	56.0	8.0	7.8	*Tridacna*
10b	6:3	3	7	658a	37.0	6.0	6.5	*Tridacna*
10b	6:3	3	7	658c	45.0	8.0	7.7	*Tridacna*
10b	5:2	-	-	681	55.0	6.9	5.9	*Tridacna*
10b	5:2	-	-	579	57.0	7.7	6.1	*Tridacna*
10b	5:1	-	-	572	55.0	6.9	6.0	*Tridacna*
10b	4:3	-	-	533	57.0	6.5	6.9	*Tridacna*
10c	5:2	-	-	577	56.0	5.6	5.0	*Tridacna*
11a	6:3	3	7	658b	37.0	6.1	10.2	*Tridacna*
11a	6:3	-	-	630	43.0	4.7	10.0	*Tridacna*
11a	5:4	-	-	589	43.0	6.9	11.0	*Tridacna*
11b	6:3	-	-	638	42.0	5.6	6.8	*Tridacna*
11b	4:2	-	-	420	44.0	4.4	8.0	*Tridacna*

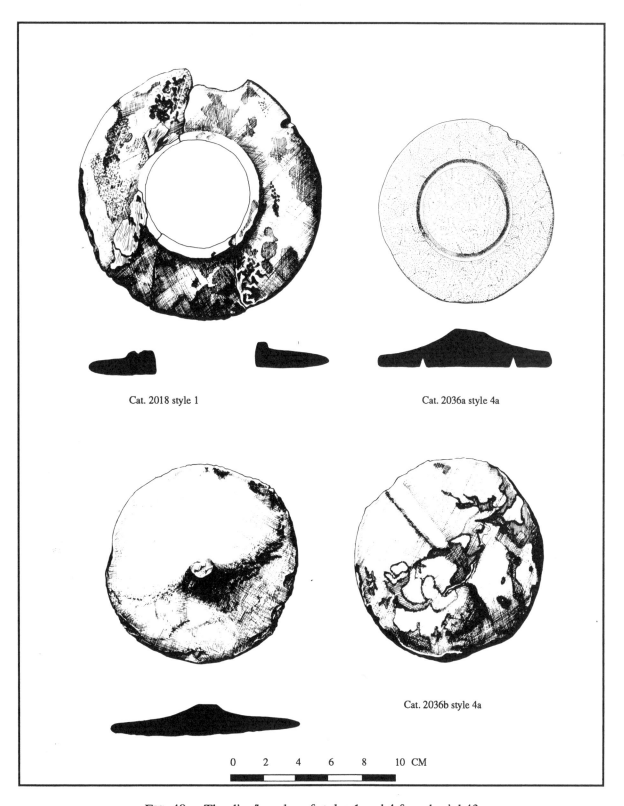

Cat. 2018 style 1

Cat. 2036a style 4a

Cat. 2036b style 4a

0   2   4   6   8   10 CM

FIG. 49.   The disc/bangles of styles 1 and 4 from burial 43

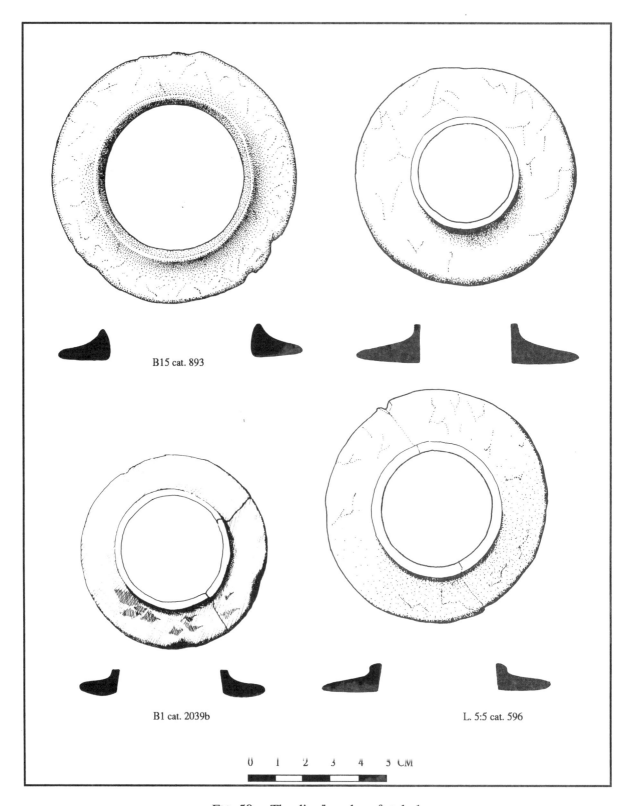

B15 cat. 893

B1 cat. 2039b   L. 5:5 cat. 596

0   1   2   3   4   5 CM

FIG. 50.   The disc/bangles of style 1

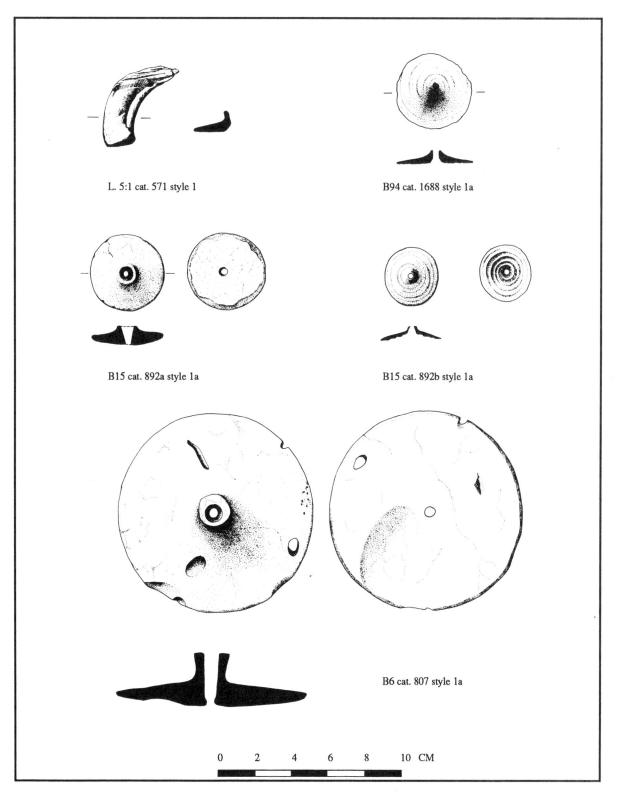

L. 5:1 cat. 571 style 1

B94 cat. 1688 style 1a

B15 cat. 892a style 1a

B15 cat. 892b style 1a

B6 cat. 807 style 1a

0   2   4   6   8   10 CM

FIG. 51.   The disc/bangles of style 1

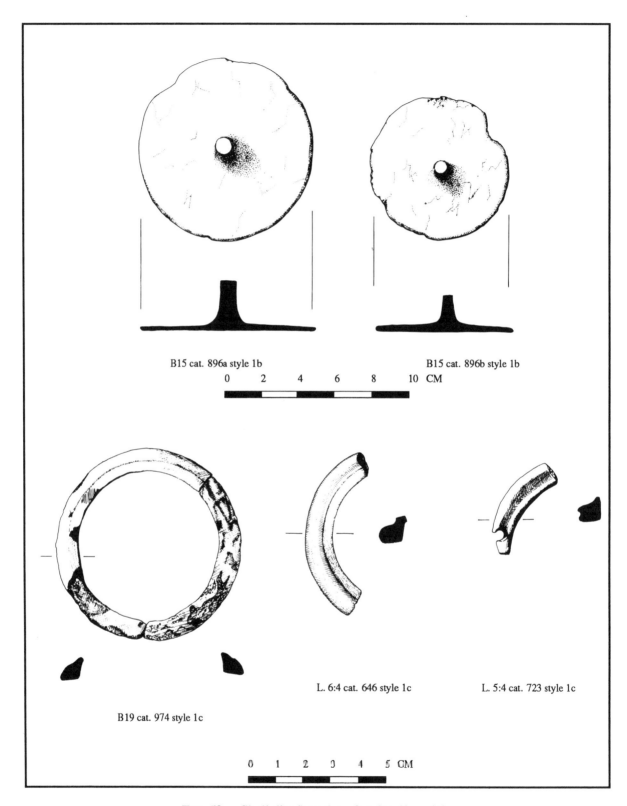

B15 cat. 896a style 1b   B15 cat. 896b style 1b

0   2   4   6   8   10 CM

L. 6:4 cat. 646 style 1c   L. 5:4 cat. 723 style 1c

B19 cat. 974 style 1c

0   1   2   3   4   5 CM

FIG. 52.   Shell disc/bangles of styles 1b and 1c

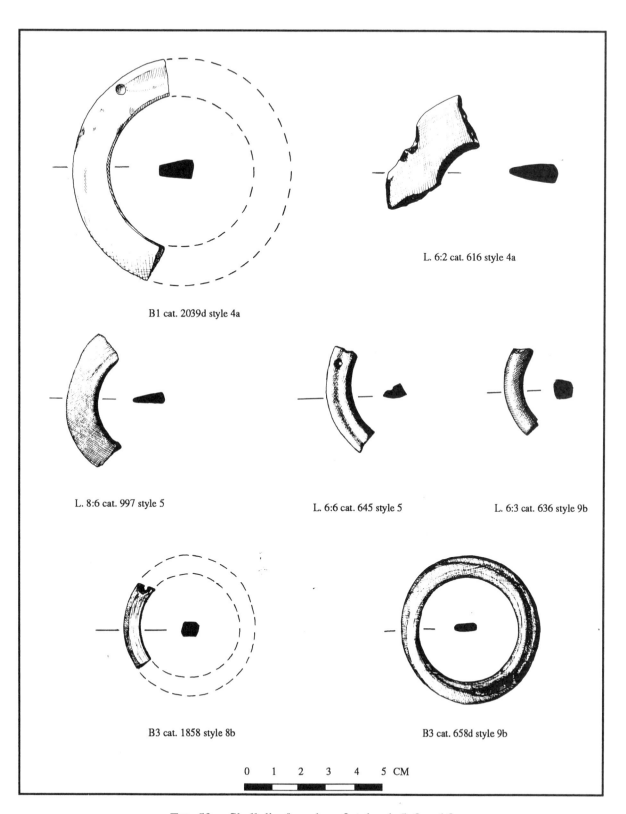

B1 cat. 2039d style 4a

L. 6:2 cat. 616 style 4a

L. 8:6 cat. 997 style 5

L. 6:6 cat. 645 style 5

L. 6:3 cat. 636 style 9b

B3 cat. 1858 style 8b

B3 cat. 658d style 9b

0 1 2 3 4 5 CM

FIG. 53.   Shell disc/bangles of styles 4, 5, 8 and 9

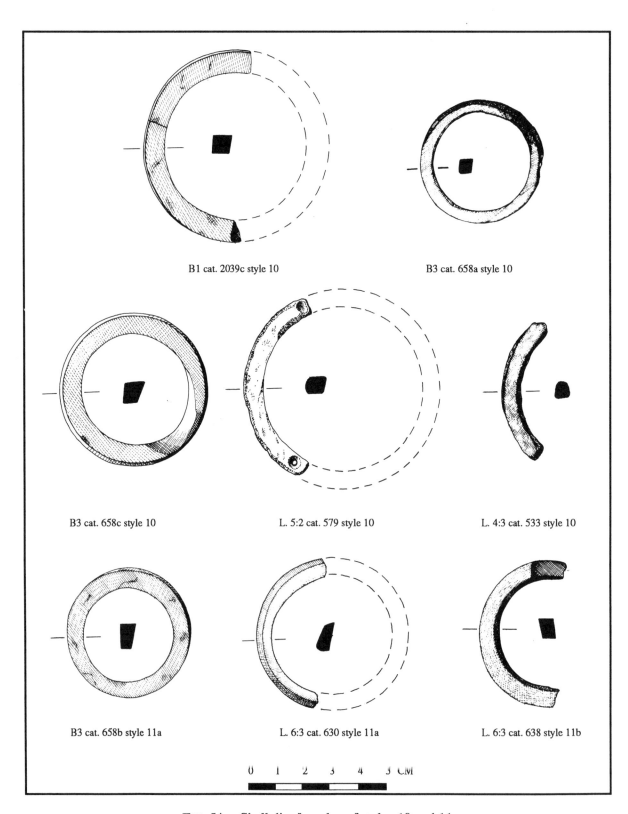

B1 cat. 2039c style 10

B3 cat. 658a style 10

B3 cat. 658c style 10

L. 5:2 cat. 579 style 10

L. 4:3 cat. 533 style 10

B3 cat. 658b style 11a

L. 6:3 cat. 630 style 11a

L. 6:3 cat. 638 style 11b

FIG. 54.   Shell disc/bangles of styles 10 and 11

STONE ORNAMENTS

The stone ornaments consisted of several different styles of disc/bangle and were made from three main types of stone (Fig. 55, Table 19). The majority were of slate, slaty shale, andesite and volcanic sandstone but three of the earliest pieces were fashioned from a mottled grey marble. All the disc/bangles were fragmentary and only in one case were all the pieces of a bangle recovered, although occasionally more than one piece of a disc/bangle was found. The range of shapes of disc/bangles are described below using the same style categories as for the shell artefacts.

The most common styles of bangle were nos. 8b, 9b and 10b, although all except styles 1 and 2 were represented. Examples of stone bangles were recovered from layers 1–9 and from layer 10:1, but a third of the entire sample was found in layer 3.

Only two fragments were found in association with burials. They were recovered from grave fill. All others were from the habitation or occupation areas. Two methods were used to manufacture these items. The majority were made by trepanning discs from the stone using large diameter bamboo canes and sand or grit. This was then ground and polished. As most of the stones used could be naturally split into flat plates and were not particularly hard, this was a fairly straightforward procedure. A few were made from marble or andesite and it would have required more labour to produce the flat blank. The central perforation would also have been removed by trepanning, using a smaller diameter cane, but, in a large percentage of cases, this inner area was not ground or polished and the rough edge left by the core breaking from the disc/bangle was still present. A few of the pieces were made by chipping or pecking at the stone to shape them before polishing. These were made from volcanic sandstone and, as they had not been carefully ground smooth, it was possible to recognise the manufacturing method.

Style 3   There are only three examples of this style from Khok Phanom Di. Two of them, cat. 1372 and cat. 1165, still retain the typical bulky concave triangular section, but cat. 967 is so small and damaged that only one of the original concave surfaces remains. The larger pieces are from layer 10 and are among the earliest stone ornaments recovered from the site, but the third artefact was recovered from layer 8. These three artefacts are the only examples of grey marble at Khok Phanom Di.

Style 4   Fragments of three wedge-shaped disc/bangles were identified. Although apparently of the same general shape, they differed quite markedly from each other. Two (cats. 647 and 2044) were made of volcanic sandstone and the third artefact was made of a grey slate that was beginning to disintegrate. Cat. 647 had chipped and uneven surfaces and the raised portions of the inner surface bore a fine polish. The outer surfaces were chipped in a way that could have been due either to deliberate flaking or to severe work-edge damage. This artefact was found in layer 6. All that remained of the original disc/bangle, cat. 2044, was a large chip that still retained part of the inner and one end surface. Because the outer surface was lost, the dimensions and the initial shape could not be gauged with any certainty. If the outer surface was bevelled, then this piece would have more accurately belonged in style 6. The third disc/bangle, cat. 199, differed from the other pieces in that it may have been a complete artefact. It comprised two fragments which formed a semi-circular object with deliberately cut radial ends. The internal diameter was the smallest recorded for a stone disc/bangle at this site.

Style 5   These disc/bangles were also wedge-shaped, but they were not as deep. Two of the three examples of this style found at Khok Phanom Di were roughly shaped by chipping and were made from the comparatively hard volcanic sandstone. Cat. 374 had its central core removed by boring which was unusual for disc/bangles made by this method. The third fragment, cat. 731, was made from slaty shale and was in a very friable state. The two volcanic sandstone pieces were from layer 4 and the shale piece was recovered from layer 6.

Style 5a   These disc/bangles are of the same general dimensions as the style 5 pieces but the apex of the triangles are truncated. Two of the fragments from this section are of special interest. Cat. 1092 is a small piece from a fairly bulky slate disc/bangle. One of the radial ends was deliberately cut tangentially. All the other surfaces, especially the inner, were well smoothed and polished. This was in marked contrast to cat. 643, which still has a chipped inner surface and roughly faceted and ground outer surfaces. The raised areas of the inner surface show some evidence of wear polish, but not as much as can be seen on cat. 647 (style 4). Cat. 1092 was recovered from layer 8 and the other two slate pieces were from layer 5.

Style 6   The surviving fragment of this disc/bangle (cat. 1109) has been broken from the outer rim of the disc and because of this it was not possible to assess the inner diameter. The external diameter would have been about 17 cm. This is larger than any other discoid ornament found at Khok Phanom Di. The artefact was made from black slate and was recovered from layer 9.

Style 7   There were five artefacts in this category. They consist of shallow disc/bangles with more or less pronounced bevels on the outer edge. Among them was the only complete bangle, cat. 623. It was made of slate and had been broken in antiquity as the pieces were found scattered through two quadrants and spits. It, and the slaty shale disc/bangle cat. 625, were recovered from layer 6. Two others were found in layer 7 and the fifth was found in layer 4. One disc/bangle, cat. 731, has been classified above as style 5, but, because of its friable state, it is possibly another style 7 piece.

Style 7a   These disc/bangles are generally slimmer than the style 7 pieces. They also have bevelled outer surfaces and are, with one exception, made from slate or slaty shale. The two fragments of cat. 184 were recovered from different spits. The other examples are all comparatively small. The slaty shale artefact, cat. 1414, has unpolished transverse surfaces. This is unusual and may indicate that both the original ends have flaked off and we are left with only the central portion of the disc/bangle. If this is the case, the piece could be classed as style 7. Cat. 687 is a fragment that just comes within the upper size limit of this category. It varies from others in the group in several other ways. The size, and the fact that it is made of volcanic sandstone allies it with cat. 647, as does the fact that it was apparently formed by chipping rather than grinding. The uneven inner surface is not polished, but the bevelled edge is chipped either in an attempt to manufacture the object or as a result of work damage. The artefacts were recovered from layers 6, 4 and 2.

Style 7b   The single example of this group is a well-polished fragment. The outer surface is convex rather than bevelled, and may be simply the result of over-exuberant rounding off of the corners. The shape has counterparts in Thai bronzes (Higham and Kijngam, 1984, vol.1, pp. 120, 144), so cannot be entirely excluded as a separate form.

Style 8a   These five fragments are among the bulkiest of the quadrangular stone disc/bangles recovered from Khok Phanom Di. All were made from black slate and two of them are of special interest. Cat. 179 has an apparently deliberate oblique tangential cut across one of the outer edges. Unfortunately, it is at one of the broken radial areas and so the extent and purpose of it is unknown.

The other, cat. 129, has an eccentric groove ground into one end where there was apparently a false start to the removal of the central perforation.

Style 8b   This type of rectangular disc/bangle was the most common at the site and only five of them were not made from black slate. Two made from slaty shale were the earliest examples (cat.768 from layer 7 and cat. 361 from layer 3). The other three, cats. 362, 266, and 89, were made from a dark grey slate and there was one from each of layers 2–4. The shape and state of manufacture was standard in all but cat. 77a, where there was an apparently deliberate oblique cut across one edge.

Style 8c   Five of these narrow rectangular disc/bangles were recovered from the site. They were all made from dark grey or black slate. One, cat. 840, came from layer 7 and layers 5 and 3 each yielded two.

Style 9a   Cat. 248 is one of two examples of this style recovered at Khok Phanom Di. It consists of two large and bulky fragments that are well polished and have one of the outer edges rounded. It is made of black slate and was recovered from layer 3.

Style 9b   Many disc/bangles were made in this style. They are fairly delicate, having flat rectangular radial sections that are less than 0.9 cm deep and 0.4 cm wide. Those from layer 6 and lower layer 5, for example cat. 637, were made of slaty shale, but the great majority of those recovered from layers 4–1 were made from black or dark grey slate. Cat. 280 was typical of this group with its sharp edges and its inner surface that had not been reworked after the core had been removed. By comparison, all the worked surfaces of cat. 327 had been ground smooth and cat. 369 had one of its outer edges rounded.

Style 9c   The two examples of this style, cats. 1421 and 180, were found in layers 5 and 2. They were both very narrow rectangles made of black slate.

Style 10b   These disc/bangles had a square radial section and a depth of about 0.6 cm. The earliest was recovered from layer 5 and the rest from layers 2–4. Four of them were made from grey andesite, though the majority were of black slate. Cat. 502 was one of the latter that had a slightly eccentric perforation, while cat. 404 varied in depth. The other artefacts in this group were apparently well made, although a few had not undergone smoothing of the internal surface.

Style 10c   With one exception, cat. 434, these square disc/bangles were made from black slate. They were recovered from layers 3–6 and cats. 382 and 583 are typical. They had larger than average or average internal diameters and radial dimensions smaller than those of other stone bangles, but reminiscent of the fish vertebra bangles.

TABLE 19: *The stone disc/bangles*

Style	Context	Cat. no.	Diam.	Depth	Width	Stone	Colour
3	10:1	1372	60.0	>36.0	18.2	marble	mottled grey
3	10:1	1165	68.0	>33.9	1.5	marble	mottled grey
3	8:4	967	-	-	-	marble	mottled grey
4	9:3	20.044	60.0	>40.0	>8.0	volc. sandstone	black
4	6:4	647	60.0	>22.0	9.5	volc. sandstone	black
4	2:3	199	37.0	14.5	6.5	slate	dark grey
5	6:5	731	60.0	11.2	6.0	slaty shale	brown
5	4:4	559	60.0	9.6	6.0	volc. sandstone	dark grey
5	4:1	374	59.0	11.3	4.4	volc. sandstone	black
5a	8:2	1092	60.0	18.0	7.0	slate	black
5a	5:rs.4	688		8.9	4.8	slate	dark grey
5a	5:6	643	58.0	8.1	5.3	slate	black
6	9:6 1.9	1109	170.0	>54.0	7.5	slate	black
7	7:6	1005	67.0	9.4	5.8	slaty shale	dark brown
7	7:5	812	40.0	8.0	2.7	slate	black
7	6:3	623	56.7	9.0	4.3	slate	dark grey
7	6:3	625	55.0	9.0	4.0	slaty shale	brown
7	4:2	436	60.0	8.0	4.0	slaty shale	brown
7a	6:3	687	65.0	>28.0	8.9	volc. sandstone	dark grey
7a	6:1	1414	-	7.5	>2.0	slaty shale	brown
7a	4:2	554	-	10.0	2.5	slate	dark grey
7a	2:3	184	58.0	9.7	2.7	slate	dark grey
7a	2:1	42b	60.0	7.3	1.7	slate	black
7b	3:1	255	55.0	9.7	5.1	slate	black
8a	3:3	337	62.0	11.0	6.0	slate	black
8a	3:2	304	59.0	9.4	5.2	slate	black
8a	2:3	179	63.0	9.4	7.2	slate	black
8a	2:2	129	59.0	10.0	7.7	slate	black
8a	1:1	18	56.0	11.7	6.4	slate	black
8b	7:2	768	58.0	6.0	4.2	slaty shale	brown
8b	6:4	626	55.0	7.1	4.3	slate	black
8b	5:1	1596	55.0	7.4	4.5	slate	black
8b	5:1	574	58.0	6.0	3.3	slate	black
8b	4:4	558	48.0	6.2	3.3	slate	black
8b	4:3	555	56.0	6.8	4.5	slate	black
8b	4:1	520	56.0	7.2	4.4	slate	black
8b	4:1	503	59.0	6.1	4.0	slate	black

rs: the fill layer comprising the raised mortuary structure for burials 6, 18 and 19

Table 19 (cont.)

Style	Context	Cat. no.	Diam.	Depth	Width	Stone	Colour
8b	4:1	362	67.0	6.0	3.1	slate	dark grey
8b	4:1	401	60.0	7.2	4.8	slate	black
8b	3:4	410	59.0	6.5	3.9	slate	black
8b	3:4	361	59.0	6.9	3.7	slaty shale	brown
8b	3:4	353	60.0	6.0	4.0	slate	black
8b	3:3	349	65.0	7.3	4.4	slate	black
8b	3:3	348	57.0	8.0	5.0	slate	black
8b	3:3	331	60.0	6.6	4.6	slate	black
8b	3:2	266	61.0	6.1	4.3	slate	dark grey
8b	3:1	254	64.0	6.0	4.3	slate	black
8b	3:1	222	59.0	7.3	4.3	slate	black
8b	2:2	203	59.0	7.0	4.5	slate	black
8b	2:2	161	58.0	6.4	3.5	slate	black
8b	2:2	109	56.0	7.5	4.5	slate	black
8b	2:1	89	57.0	7.6	4.0	slate	dark grey
8b	2:1	77a	57.0	7.0	4.3	slate	black
8b	2:1	77b	59.0	7.6	4.4	slate	black
8b	2:1	72a	53.0	7.0	3.6	slate	black
8b	2:1	72b	60.0	8.4	4.6	slate	black
8b	2:1	72c	56.0	7.0	4.7	slate	black
8c	7:5 f.5	840	56.0	5.5	3.3	slate	black
8c	5:5	597	55.0	4.5	3.0	slate	dark grey
8c	5:5	592	55.0	5.4	3.3	slate	dark grey
8c	3:3	321	55.0	5.3	3.0	slate	black
8c	3:2	306	60.0	5.8	3.2	slate	black
9a	6:3	612	65.0	9.3	4.0	andesite	dark grey
9a	3:1	248	54.0	13.8	6.3	slate	black
9b	6:3	637	55.0	7.0	2.8	slaty shale	dark brown
9b	6 f.44	613	55.0	6.8	2.6	slaty shale	dark brown
9b	6:2	610	55.0	7.3	3.3	slaty shale	dark brown
9b	5:3	644	56.0	8.9	4.0	slaty shale	dark grey
9b	4:3	548	-	8.9	2.5	slate	dark grey
9b	4 f.1	515	56.0	8.2	3.5	slate	black
9b	4:1	528	55.0	6.7	2.9	slate	black
9b	4:1	379	60.0	6.7	3.2	slate	black
9b	3:5	474	60.0	7.6	>2.8	slate	dark grey
9b	3:4	402	60.0	6.6	2.8	slaty shale	dark grey
9b	3:4	369	57.0	7.5	3.5	slate	dark grey
9b	3:3	344	60.0	8.2	3.9	slate	black

Table 19 (cont.)

Style	Context	Cat. no.	Diam.	Depth	Width	Stone	Colour
9b	3:3	327	60.0	8.0	2.0	slate	dark grey
9b	3:3	326	59.0	7.8	3.8	slate	black
9b	3:2	303	61.0	8.2	3.7	slate	black
9b	3:2	271	55.0	6.8	3.2	slate	black
9b	3:2	283	61.0	7.3	2.0	slate	black
9b	3:2	280	48.0	7.9	2.0	slate	dark grey
9b	3:2	264	56.0	7.5	2.0	slate	black
9b	3:1	250	62.0	8.7	3.0	slate	dark grey
9b	3:1	228	60.0	7.2	3.2	slate	black
9b	2:2	163	60.0	7.2	2.8	slate	dark grey
9b	2:2	140	58.0	6.0	>2.5	slate	dark grey
9b	2:2	139	60.0	6.6	3.0	slate	black
9b	2:2	120	59.0	6.4	2.8	slate	dark grey
9b	2:1	85	60.0	8.0	3.4	slate	black
9b	1:2	36	60.0	6.8	2.5	slate	dark grey
9c	5:3	1421	65.0	4.2	1.9	slate	black
9c	2:3	180	60.0	5.6	2.3	slate	black
10b	5:1	566	59.0	6.7	6.8	slate	dark grey
10b	4:3	502	61.0	8.0	6.9	slate	black
10b	4:1	368	61.0	6.0	4.9	slate	dark grey
10b	3:4	409	40.0	6.0	5.4	andesite	dark grey
10b	3:4	404	59.0	7.2	6.0	slate	black
10b	3:3	422	59.0	7.0	6.0	andesite	dark grey
10b	3:3	356		7.0	7.2	slate	dark grey
10b	3:2	284	56.0	7.4	6.8	andesite	dark grey
10b	3:1	220	60.0	6.2	5.5	andesite	dark grey
10b	2:3	198	55.0	7.0	6.3	slate	dark grey
10b	2:2	142	54.0	7.3	6.5	slate	black
10b	2:2	136	60.0	6.3	5.4	slate	black
10b	2:1	77c	54.0	7.0	7.0	slate	dark grey
10c	6:3	614	60.0	5.5	5.5	slate	black
10c	6:2	622	60.0	5.0	4.1	slate	black
10c	5:5	593	56.0	5.5	4.2	slate	black
10c	5:4	583	58.0	4.8	4.0	slate	black
10c	4:2	434	60.0	4.8	6.1	slaty shale	dark grey
10c	4:1	382	66.0	5.9	4.8	slate	black
10c	3:4	413	59.0	5.0	5.9	slate	dark brown
10c	3:2	270	65.0	4.4	3.8	slate	black
10c	3:2	259	60.0	4.2	3.5	slate	black

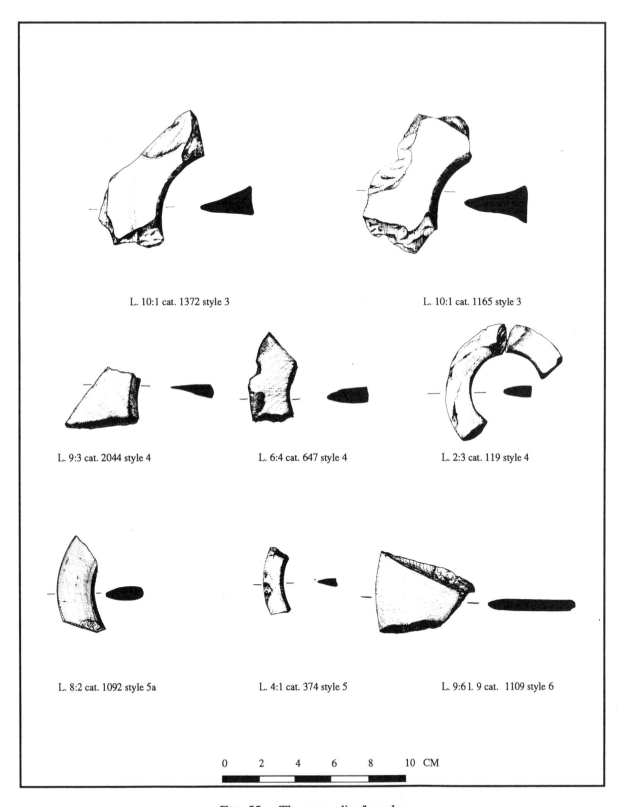

L. 10:1 cat. 1372 style 3   L. 10:1 cat. 1165 style 3

L. 9:3 cat. 2044 style 4   L. 6:4 cat. 647 style 4   L. 2:3 cat. 119 style 4

L. 8:2 cat. 1092 style 5a   L. 4:1 cat. 374 style 5   L. 9:6 l. 9 cat. 1109 style 6

0   2   4   6   8   10 CM

FIG. 55.   The stone disc/bangles

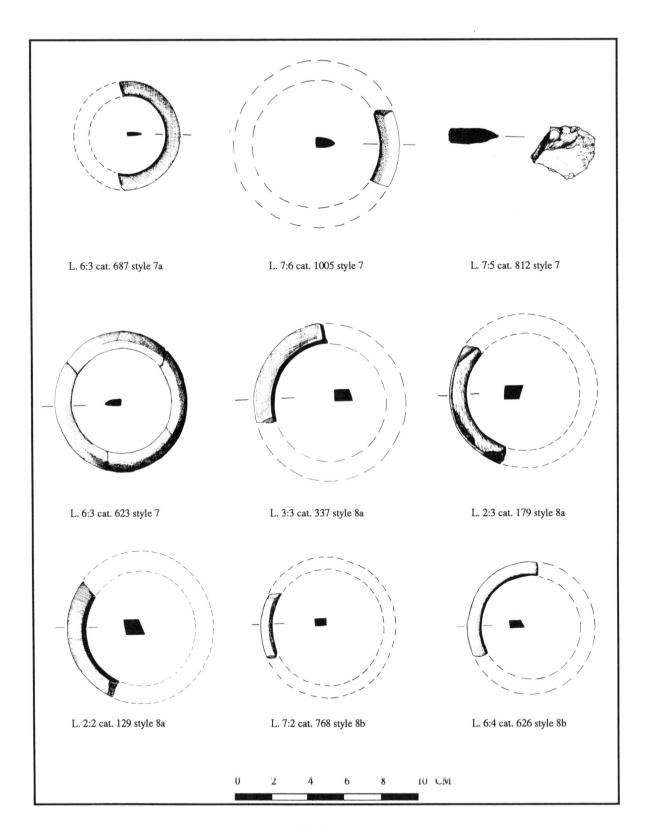

L. 6:3 cat. 687 style 7a   L. 7:6 cat. 1005 style 7   L. 7:5 cat. 812 style 7

L. 6:3 cat. 623 style 7   L. 3:3 cat. 337 style 8a   L. 2:3 cat. 179 style 8a

L. 2:2 cat. 129 style 8a   L. 7:2 cat. 768 style 8b   L. 6:4 cat. 626 style 8b

0   2   4   6   8   10 CM

FIG. 55 (cont.)

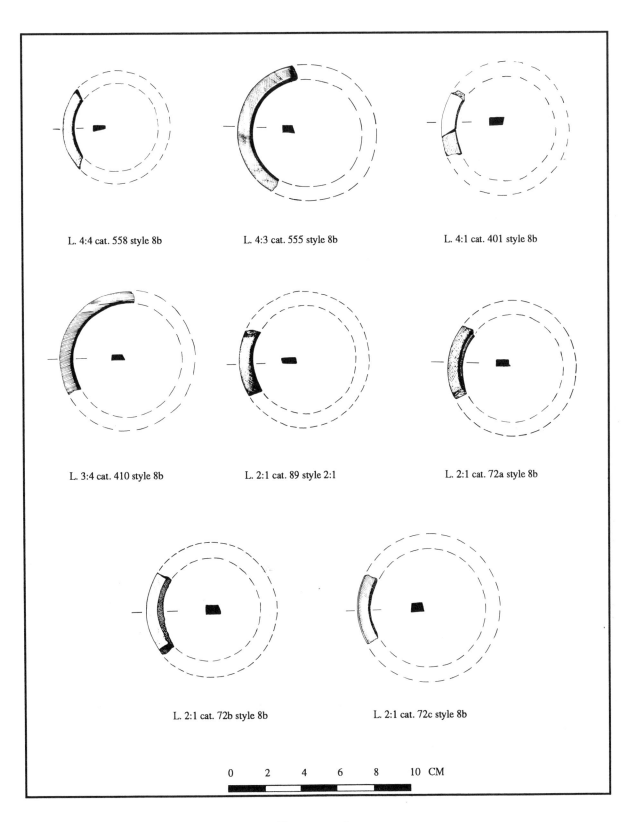

L. 4:4 cat. 558 style 8b   L. 4:3 cat. 555 style 8b   L. 4:1 cat. 401 style 8b

L. 3:4 cat. 410 style 8b   L. 2:1 cat. 89 style 2:1   L. 2:1 cat. 72a style 8b

L. 2:1 cat. 72b style 8b   L. 2:1 cat. 72c style 8b

0   2   4   6   8   10 CM

FIG. 55 (cont.)

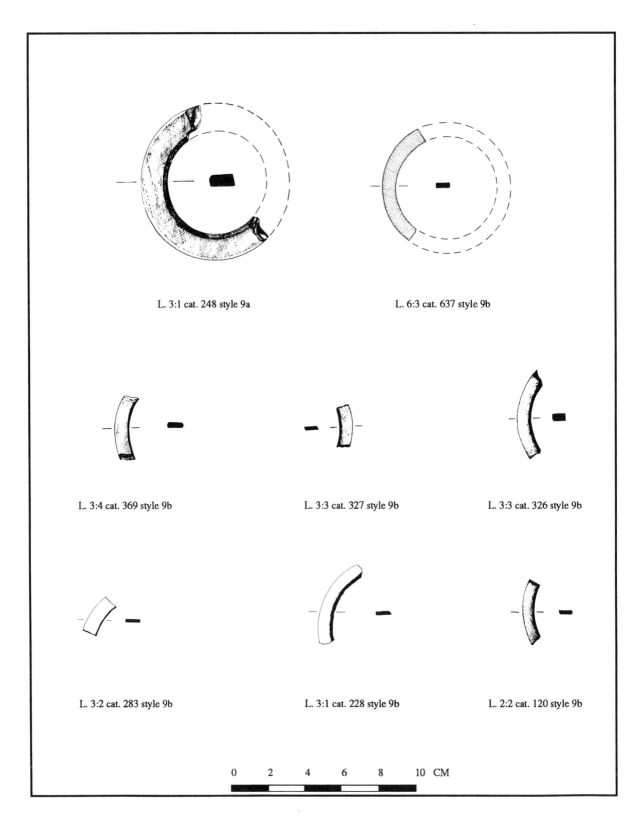

L. 3:1 cat. 248 style 9a

L. 6:3 cat. 637 style 9b

L. 3:4 cat. 369 style 9b

L. 3:3 cat. 327 style 9b

L. 3:3 cat. 326 style 9b

L. 3:2 cat. 283 style 9b

L. 3:1 cat. 228 style 9b

L. 2:2 cat. 120 style 9b

0   2   4   6   8   10   CM

FIG. 55 (cont.)

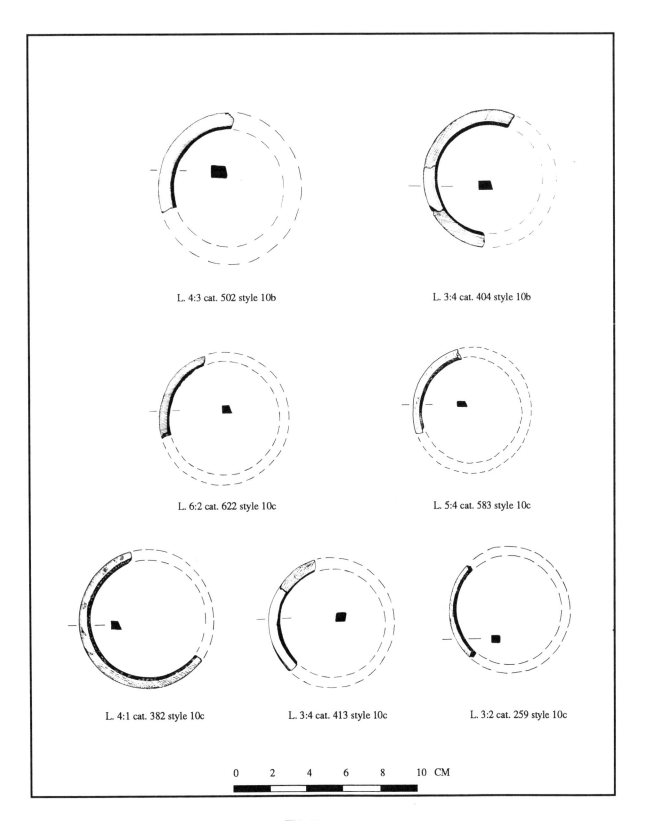

L. 4:3 cat. 502 style 10b

L. 3:4 cat. 404 style 10b

L. 6:2 cat. 622 style 10c

L. 5:4 cat. 583 style 10c

L. 4:1 cat. 382 style 10c

L. 3:4 cat. 413 style 10c

L. 3:2 cat. 259 style 10c

0   2   4   6   8   10 CM

FIG. 55 (cont.)

IVORY/TOOTH

The ivory ornaments in this group show some diversity, but the other tooth artefacts have minimal modification. Most simply have a hole drilled through a portion of the root, enabling them to be worn.

Ivory

Only very small fragments of the ivory artefacts remain, but they are large enough not only to indicate that they were all some type of disc/bangle, but also that several of them were decorated (Fig. 56). Two of the objects, cats. 451 and 295, had deep transverse grooves worked into the outer surface so that they would have had the appearance of several thin square-sectioned bangles rather than one deep one. Because they are broken transversely as well as laterally, we cannot be sure how many grooves were worked, but there must have been at least three on each. The other four decorated pieces, cats. 2426, 1578, 463 and 153 have designs using a combination of plain oblique bands and triangular areas with round indentations drilled at random into them. The plain fragments consist either of small, square-sectioned pieces or fairly wide thin rectangular sections. The dimensions of the disc/bangles suggests that they were taken from the region of the tusk nearest to the base. This would allow the delicate results to be obtained with the minimum of work. The smoothing process was still visible in the form of ground lines on all the surfaces.

Style 8c   There are the remnants of six of this style of disc/bangle. They are all plain and the grinding lines are usually clearly in evidence. Five of them were found between 3:3 and 4:1, but one was recovered from layer 6.

Style 9c   Only one ivory disc/bangle of this style was found. It was one of the earliest at the site and appears to have been damaged by fire.

Style 10c   Eight fragments of this square disc/bangle were recovered between layers 3:2 to 4:1. Their depth and width dimensions are all smaller than their stone counterparts. They show more similarity to the fish vertebrae disc/bangles found in several children's burials (Fig. 59).

Style 11   This group includes the four bangles with the indented triangle patterns. Only two of the group were plain. The decorated pieces were distributed in layers 2–4.

Style 11a   There are two examples of this style, one being decorated with deep concentric lines and the other plain. They both come from layer 3.

Style 11b   There was only one ivory artefact of this style found. It is the last of the decorated disc/bangles and has the deeply engraved parallel grooves running transversely around the outer surface.

Fish teeth

Six modified sharks' teeth were recovered (Fig. 57). Half were from layer 3, two from layer 2 and one from layer 6. They were modified by drilling a hole from both sides through the root

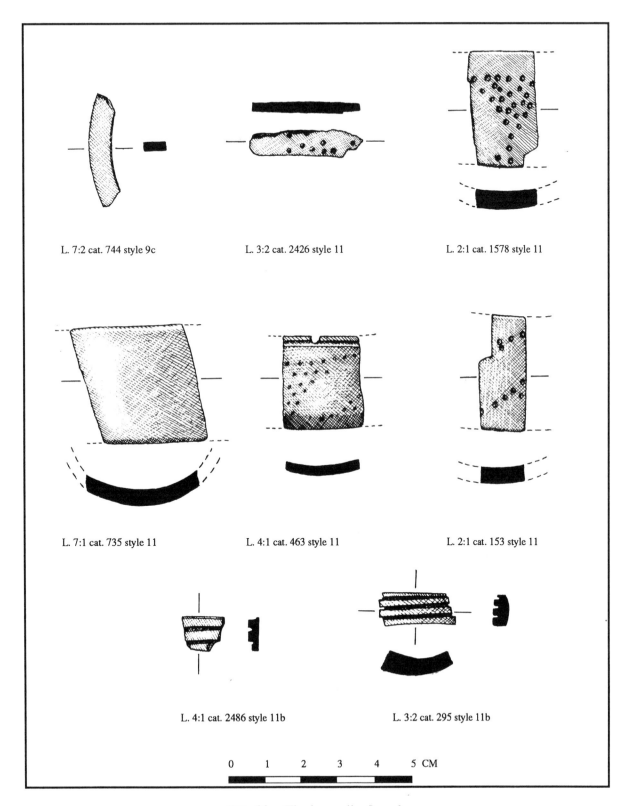

L. 7:2 cat. 744 style 9c

L. 3:2 cat. 2426 style 11

L. 2:1 cat. 1578 style 11

L. 7:1 cat. 735 style 11

L. 4:1 cat. 463 style 11

L. 2:1 cat. 153 style 11

L. 4:1 cat. 2486 style 11b

L. 3:2 cat. 295 style 11b

0   1   2   3   4   5 CM

FIG. 56.   The ivory disc/bangles

TABLE 20:   *The distribution of ivory disc/bangles*

Style	Context	Cat. no.	Diam.	Depth	Width	Dec./Plain
8c	3:3	2452c	-	3.0	4.1	plain
8c	3:4	2433a	-	3.9	3.5	plain
8c	6:4	1819	-	2.5	3.1	plain
8c	4:1	519	-	5.4	3.5	plain
8c	3:3	351	-	5.4	3.0	plain
8c	3:3	316	-	2.5	3.1	plain
9c	7:2	744	-	5.7	2.7	plain
10c	4:1	2513	-	3.2	3.3	plain
10c	3:3	2452a,b	-	3.6	3.7	plain
10c	3:3	2434	-	3.6	3.2	plain
10c	3:4	2433b	-	3.0	3.3	plain
10c	3:2	2428	-	3.5	3.5	plain
10c	4:1	518	-	3.5	3.4	plain
10c	3:4	363	-	3.8	3.4	plain
10c	3:2	301	-	3.7	4.2	plain
11	3:2	2426	-	4.4	>29.0	dec.
11	3:3	2425b	-	4.4	-	plain
11	2:1	1578	-	4.3	29.5	dec.
11	7:1	735	62.0	5.0	30.0	plain
11	4:1	463	-	-	-	dec.
11	2:1	153	60.0	4.5	29.4	dec.
11a	3:4	451	-	3.5	-	dec.
11a	3:3	332		2.9	13.4	plain
11b	3:2	295	37.0	4.3	8.2	dec.

base. One group of unmodified teeth was found in association with B 90, but the exact context is not known and they could be from grave fill.

Reptilian teeth

Two modified crocodile teeth were recovered from layer 10 (Fig. 57). They both had two holes drilled laterally opposite through the top of the root which had subsequently broken obliquely. Cat. 2472 came from layer 10:12, and cat. 2445 from layer 10:19. The surviving length of the former is 70.0 mm and of the latter, 47.0 mm.

Mammalian teeth

Modified canines from several mammalian species were found in both mortuary and occupation contexts. Unlike the ivory and shark teeth ornaments, these were all earlier than layer 5. Many of the teeth were incomplete and not identifiable to species (Table 22). The majority of the modified

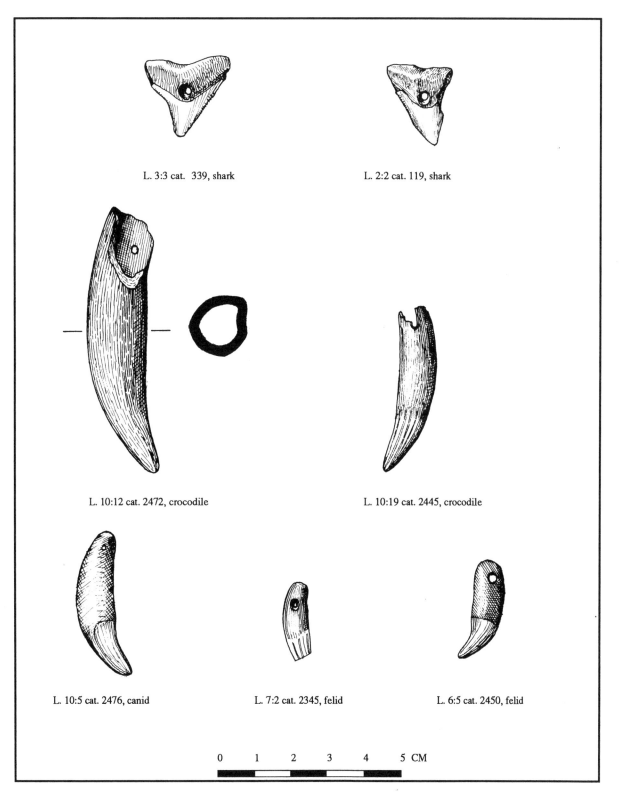

L. 3:3 cat. 339, shark   L. 2:2 cat. 119, shark

L. 10:12 cat. 2472, crocodile   L. 10:19 cat. 2445, crocodile

L. 10:5 cat. 2476, canid   L. 7:2 cat. 2345, felid   L. 6:5 cat. 2450, felid

0   1   2   3   4   5 CM

FIG. 57.   The modified teeth

TABLE 21: *The distribution of modified sharks' teeth*

Context	Cat. no.	Length	Whole/Frag.
2:3	2441	17.2	frag.
3:1	2418	>15.0	frag.
6:4	2343		frag.
3:3	339	19.0	whole
3:1	240	>15.0	frag.
2:2	119	20.2	frag.

mammalian teeth came from the burials. Some were single finds, but there were also several groups of teeth (Fig. 58). Three specimens come from non-mortuary contexts. One canid canine was found in layer 10:5 (cat. 2476) and the two felid canines were recovered from layers 6:5 (cat. 2450) and 7:2 (cat. 2345).

TABLE 22: *The modified mammalian teeth from mortuary contexts*

Burial	MP	Cat. No.	No.	Type	Whole/Frag.
132	2	2769	1	small mammal	frag.
120	2	1677	1	*Rhinoceros sondaicus*	frag.
102	2	1585	16	*Muntiacus muntjak*	frag.
72	3	2780	1	*Sus* canine	frag.
33	4	2778	2	small mammal	frag.
43	5	2768	1	small mammal	frag.
15	5	905	5	small mammal	frag.

BONE ORNAMENTS

Several different types of bone were used in the manufacture of personal ornaments. The pieces themselves also showed more variety than most of the other groups. As with the shell ornaments, the majority were recovered from mortuary contexts. It is not always clear how the pieces were utilised, but their position in the burials indicates that they had some specific significance and they are therefore included.

Fish bone

There are two types of fish-bone ornament. Large fish vertebrae were used to make children's disc/bangles and a large fish spine was also used as an ornament.

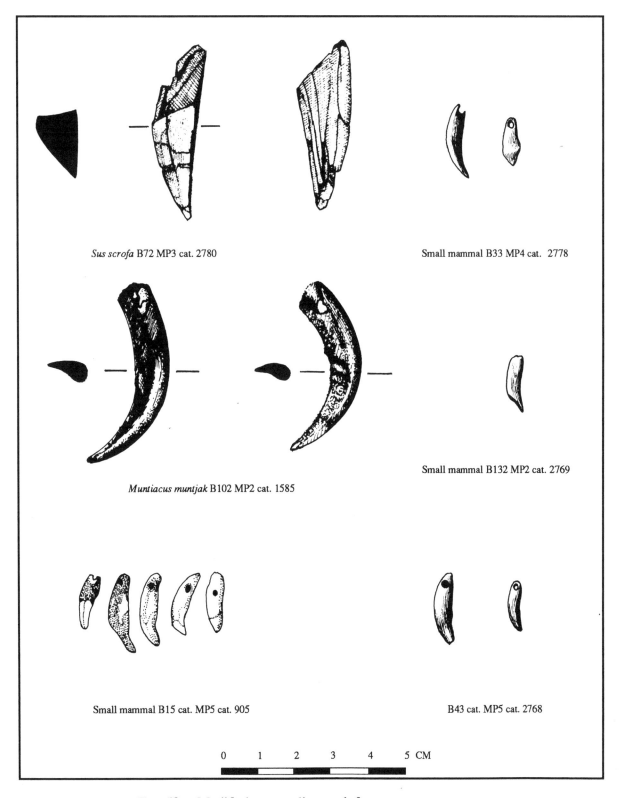

Sus scrofa B72 MP3 cat. 2780

Small mammal B33 MP4 cat. 2778

Muntiacus muntjak B102 MP2 cat. 1585

Small mammal B132 MP2 cat. 2769

Small mammal B15 cat. MP5 cat. 905

B43 cat. MP5 cat. 2768

0   1   2   3   4   5 CM

FIG. 58.   Modified mammalian teeth from mortuary contexts

The method of manufacturing the disc/bangles can be reconstructed from cat. 1671f, which appears to be a disc/bangle blank. Apparently the top or bottom of a large vertebra of a shark or ray was sliced off, the central area ground out and the other surfaces smoothed. This usually resulted in a square or triangular radial-sectioned disc/bangle with a rather small internal diameter. These bangles, like their shell and stone counterparts, were found in most layers in the site and also, like the shell, were found both in mortuary and other contexts. They are classified as children's ornaments because of their size and also because they were only found in infants' or young children's burials.

The fragments of three or four fish vertebra disc/bangles were found in the upper layers at the site. Two fragments were from layer 4 and the others were from layer 2. The very fragile state of these finds and of those recovered from the comparatively protected environment of the burials probably accounts for the lack of evidence of earlier pieces in a non-mortuary context. Unlike the burial pieces, which were usually very carefully worked, these fragments had roughly shaped cross-sections. This has meant that it is unclear whether the two fragments numbered cat. 2483 come from a single artefact. By contrast, it was possible to reconstruct all the seven fragmentary disc/bangles from B 133. At least 18 bone disc/bangles were recovered from burials. The styles varied from

TABLE 23:   *The non–mortuary fish bone disc/bangles*

Context	Cat. No.	Depth	Width	Style	No.	Whole/Frag.
4:1	2483	3.0	3.3	10c	2	frag.
2:3	1500	4.0	4.5	10c	1	frag.
2:2	165	6.1	3.0	9b	1	frag.

thin discs to square sections. Although most of them were broken, seven were complete. Most of them came from the early MP2 burials (Fig. 59). The amount of time spent on the production of individual disc/bangles varied greatly. Most were carefully made but at least one of them, from B 133, was no more than a rough slice taken from a vertebra. Although they were large enough to have been worn as bangles by the children, most were found across the pelvic region (cat. 698) or across the chest (cat. 1671a–g) and none is recorded as having been recovered from a wrist or arm. It is therefore possible that these were some form of amulet.   One fish-bone bead was found (Fig. 60). It is a large shark's dorsal fin spine from B 72 (cat. 2779), the length being 88 mm. It is curved and hollow, and has a triangular transverse section. One of the sides is very fragmented and has had to be reconstructed. The base of the spine has two holes drilled acentrically, but there appears to be no other modification.

Turtle carapace or plastron ornaments

A variety of objects made of turtle carapace or plastron was recovered (Figs. 61–63). As a general rule, the different types were not found in more than one context. None of the unusual body plaques was recovered from occupation areas and no disc/bangles were recovered from burials. Turtle carapace was apparently popular as ornamentation through most of the period of settlement. The earliest found is a body plaque from MP3 (B 57, Fig. 61) and the latest was a fragment of a star-shaped disc/bangle, cat. 2439, from the top of layer 3. The artefacts in this group had more complex

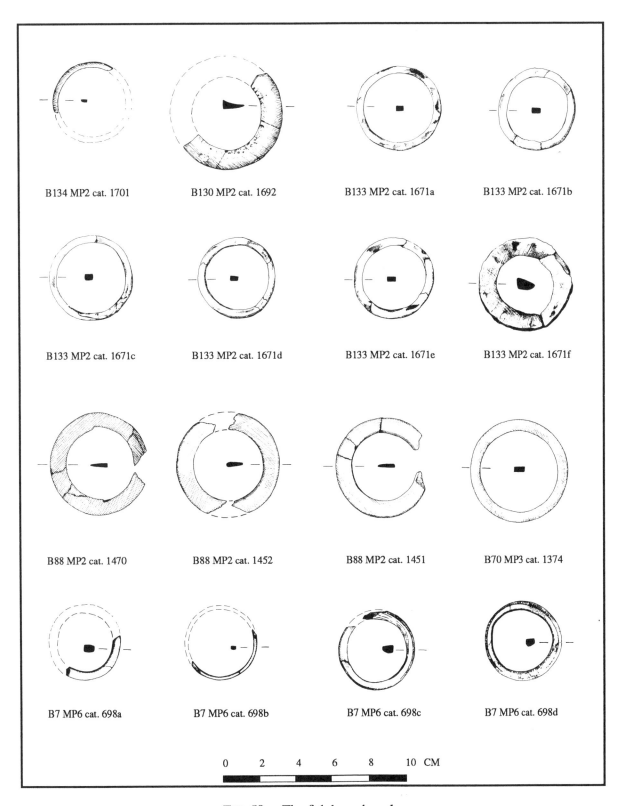

B134 MP2 cat. 1701   B130 MP2 cat. 1692   B133 MP2 cat. 1671a   B133 MP2 cat. 1671b

B133 MP2 cat. 1671c   B133 MP2 cat. 1671d   B133 MP2 cat. 1671e   B133 MP2 cat. 1671f

B88 MP2 cat. 1470   B88 MP2 cat. 1452   B88 MP2 cat. 1451   B70 MP3 cat. 1374

B7 MP6 cat. 698a   B7 MP6 cat. 698b   B7 MP6 cat. 698c   B7 MP6 cat. 698d

0 2 4 6 8 10 CM

FIG. 59.   The fish bone bangles

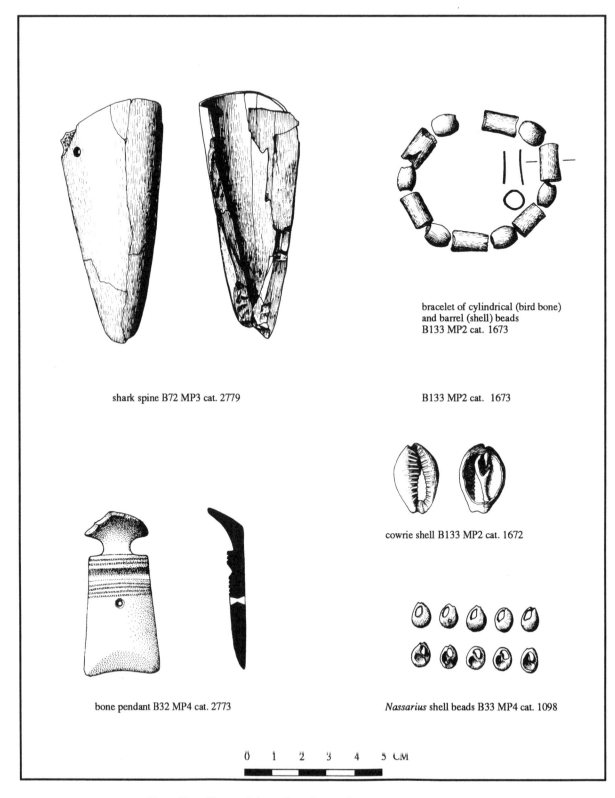

shark spine B72 MP3 cat. 2779

bracelet of cylindrical (bird bone)
and barrel (shell) beads
B133 MP2 cat. 1673

B133 MP2 cat. 1673

cowrie shell B133 MP2 cat. 1672

bone pendant B32 MP4 cat. 2773

Nassarius shell beads B33 MP4 cat. 1098

0   1   2   3   4   5 CM

FIG. 60.   Unusual jewellery items from mortuary contexts

TABLE 24: *The fish bone disc/bangles from mortuary contexts*

Burial	MP.	Cat. no.	Diam.	Depth	Width	Style	Whole/Frag.
134	2	1701	-	3.5	2.1	8c	frag.
130	2	1692	40.0	10.9	5.5	4	frag.
133	2	1671a	37.0	3.5	3.0	10c	whole
133	2	1671b	35.0	3.7	2.7	8c	whole
133	2	1671c	46.0	4.2	3.9	10c	whole
133	2	1671d	33.0	4.1	2.5	8c	whole
133	2	1671e	36.0	4.6	3.0	8c	whole
133	2	1671f	31.0	7.1	-	?	whole
133	2	1671g	-	4.1	2.6	8c	frag.
88	2	1470c	37.0	9.0	2.0	9a	frag.
88	2	1452b	38.0	8.6	2.1	9b	frag.
88	2	1451a	36.0	8.3	2.2	9b	frag.
70	3	1374	43.0	5.2	3.0	8c	whole
7	6	698a	35.0	4.5	4.5	10c	whole
7	6	698b	36.0	4.5	3.5	10c	frag.
7	6	698c	-	2.0	2.8	11c	frag.
7	6	698d	33.0	5.5	5.0	10c	frag.

forms than other ornaments. The plaques were cruciform (Fig. 62), and several of the bangles were star-shaped while a unique pendant was engraved. This may be due to the comparative ease with which this material can be worked. The majority of the stone and shell disc/bangles were produced using a trepan of bamboo. The star-shaped disc/bangles could also have been made by this method, but the deep concave between the two remaining points of the disc/bangle cat. 561 has sides that are too straight to have been obtained by trepanning. Another method must have been used. A possible alternative is indicated by the presence in the site of several small roughly circular discs of turtle bone (Fig. 64 cat. 2349) which appears to have been formed using a chisel. The two techniques of grinding and chiselling out perforations produce very different cores. The use of a chisel rather than a trepan to remove sections of unwanted material would certainly allow the artisan to produce much more complex shapes not only in the disc/bangles, but also in other ornaments.

Three small fragments of these star-shaped bangles were found in the site (Fig. 64). Two were just single points of a star, but the third had two points. This disc/bangle (cat. 561) was interesting in that it had apparently been broken in antiquity, and a hole drilled through one end just above the break showed that it had been repaired. It is, therefore, likely that it was valued. This style of disc/bangle may have been a late introduction, as none is found in the mortuary contexts. The earliest was found at the bottom of layer 4 and the latest was recovered from the top of layer 3.

There is one unfinished disc/bangle from layer 8:2 (cat. 2372). It comprises two fragments of a possible disc with the outer and inner surfaces cut and bevelled, but the ends unmodified. The diameter is 39.0 mm, depth 42.2 mm and width 10 mm. It is much earlier than the star-shaped

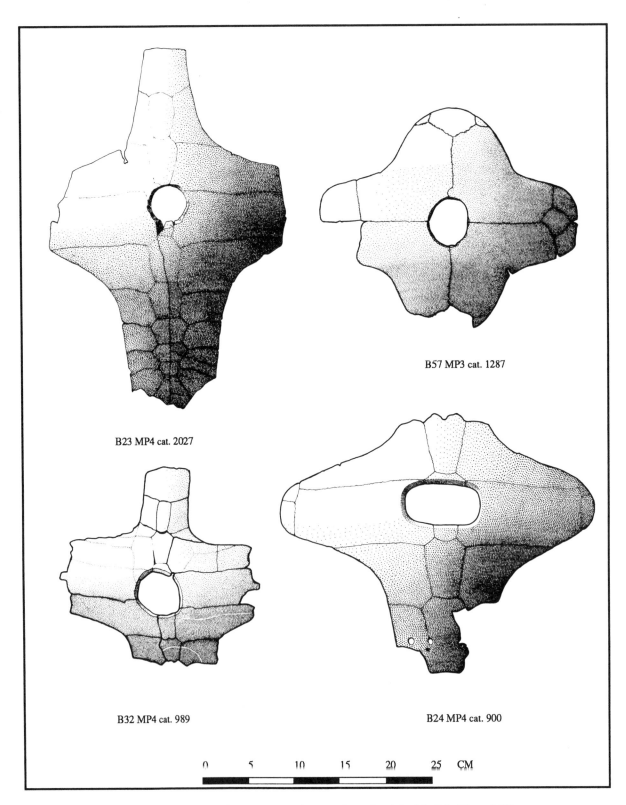

B57 MP3 cat. 1287

B23 MP4 cat. 2027

B32 MP4 cat. 989

B24 MP4 cat. 900

0   5   10   15   20   25   CM

FIG. 61.   The turtle carapace plaques from burials 23, 24, 32 and 57

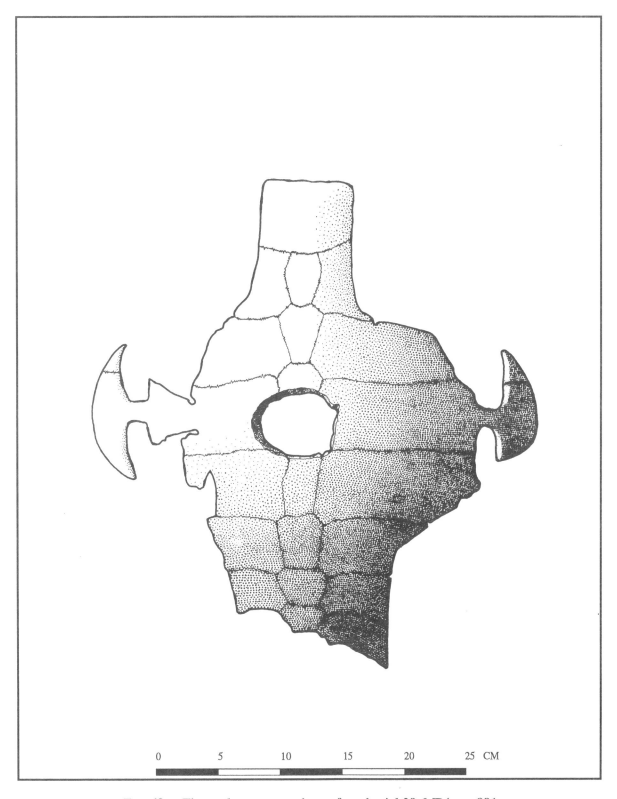

FIG. 62.   The turtle carapace plaque from burial 30, MP4 cat. 991

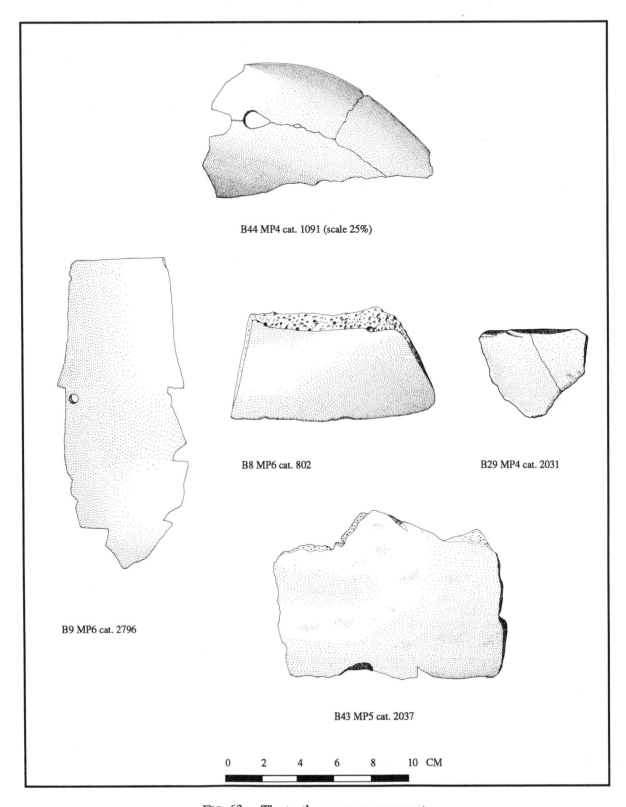

B44 MP4 cat. 1091 (scale 25%)

B8 MP6 cat. 802

B29 MP4 cat. 2031

B9 MP6 cat. 2796

B43 MP5 cat. 2037

0   2   4   6   8   10 CM

FIG. 63.   The turtle carapace ornaments

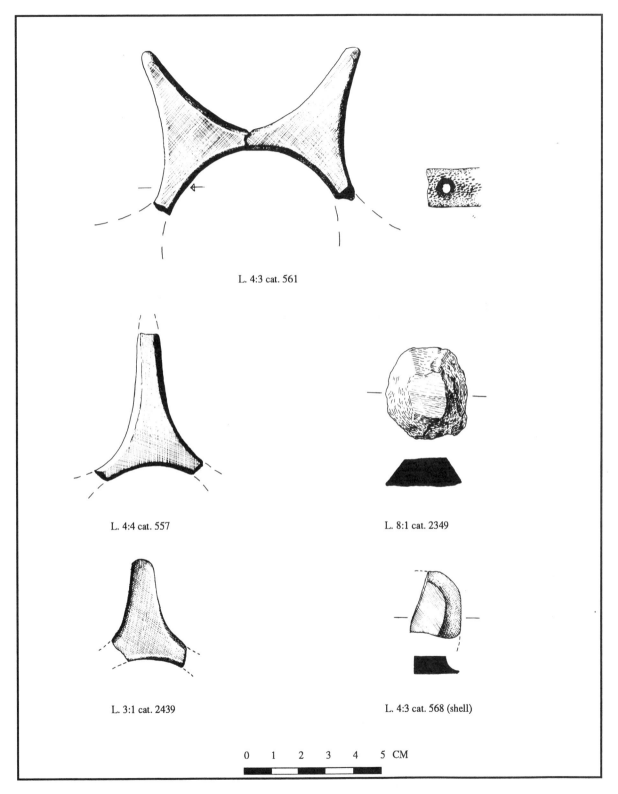

L. 4:3 cat. 561

L. 4:4 cat. 557

L. 8:1 cat. 2349

L. 3:1 cat. 2439

L. 4:3 cat. 568 (shell)

0   1   2   3   4   5 CM

FIG. 64.   The turtle carapace disc/bangles and cores. Note that cat. 568 is a bangle core made of shell

TABLE 25:   *The style 12 disc/bangles of turtle carapace*

Context	Cat. No.	Diam.	Depth	Width
3:1	2439	-	35.5	12.6
4:3	561	68.0	45.0	11.5
4:4	557	-	>5.0	13.3

bangles and therefore cannot be classed as an unfinished style 12 specimen. It is very similar to the fragmentary and incomplete cat. 2369 which was recovered from layer 8:7. This had a larger diameter, 65 mm and a depth of 54.6 mm but was otherwise the same. By comparison the bangle, cat. 2371, was worked on all surfaces and this had resulted in a style 5a disc/bangle with the diameter of 40 mm, a depth of 26.6 mm and a width of 46.3 mm (Fig. 65).

Cod pieces or body plaques

This group of objects was recovered from male or juvenile MP3-4 burials. Their precise use is not known though similar objects found in China suggest that they may be some type of ceremonial abdominal or pelvic shield. In the Khok Phanom Di burials, however, the broken pieces were usually placed over one side of the body in the general torso area and not over a specific region. For this reason, they are termed either cod pieces or body plaques.

They were all deliberately broken before interment and portions have disintegrated or are lost. By comparing all the examples, it is possible to reconstruct the basic shapes. Four segments were cut from the sides of the carapace leaving a domed cruciform. In four of the five cases, almost all of the carapace was used. The lateral arms were usually narrow and had rounded ends. The top projection was also narrow, but still had the original edge as did, in the case of cat. 2027 at least, the lower projection though it was broader than the others. All the plaques had large central holes gouged out of them. The tool used appears to have been awl-like rather than chisel-shaped as the scribing from them can still be seen. Two methods of attaching or securing the shields were used. Cat. 900 had three or, more likely, four holes bored parallel to and just below the top edge. An attempt to drill other holes slightly higher up did not meet with success. Three of the others had a deep oval cut on both sides of the arms just behind the curved end. This resulted in a toggle-like projection.

The example from B 57, cat. 1287, varied from the other shields in several ways. Like the others it was basically cruciform and had the central hole, but the top and bottom projections were squat and rounded. It was smaller than the others because of this. It also had no apparent method of attaching it though a portion of one end that could have had holes drilled in it is missing.

Miscellaneous: mortuary

Several amorphous pieces of turtle carapace were found in the burials. Not all were worked, but their deliberate placement indicates some significance. As one of the pieces could be an offcut from a body plaque they may relate to them in some way so are recorded here. One was recovered from an infant burial (cat. 802), but the others all came from male interments.

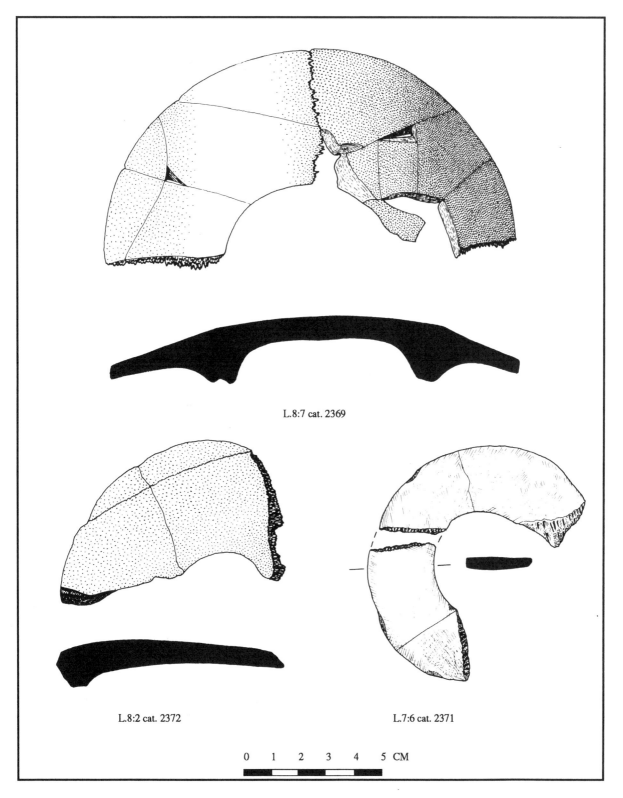

L.8:7 cat. 2369

L.8:2 cat. 2372

L.7:6 cat. 2371

0 1 2 3 4 5 CM

FIG. 65. The modified turtle carapace artefacts

TABLE 26: *The turtle carapace cod pieces or body plaques*

Burial	MP	Cat. no.	Length	Width
23	4	2027	500	>280
57	3	1287	300	>250
30	4	991	320	>220
32	4	989	>220	>220
24	4	900	>270	390

Two of the artefacts were clearly worked. Cat. 2796 was quite complex, consisting of a concave-sided rhomboid with a similarly-sized leaf-shaped portion on its base. Two holes were drilled into the outer edge of the leaf just above the junction with the rhomboid. The second worked piece (cat. 1091) consisted of a roughly triangular side section taken from the rear of a carapace. Apart from the inner side of the piece, which showed that it had been partially ground out and then broken, the only work seemed to be a series of differently shaped holes cut down a long suture line. The short side of the piece is damaged, but the original outer edge is still intact and unworked.

TABLE 27: *Miscellaneous turtle carapace artefacts*

Burial	MP	Cat. no.	Length	Width
9	6	2796	160	70
43	5	2037	120	90
29	4	2031	55	45
44	4	1091	290	145
8	6	802	110	60

Pendant or amulet

The size and shape of the unique object cat. 2773 suggests that it was probably either a pendant or an amulet. It was 55 mm long and 28 mm wide, and the base of the object was axe-shaped with a central hole in the upper portion. Above the perforation were two sets of engraved parallel lines separated by a deep groove and on a short neck above this was an angled piece shaped like a fan. It was found in the same juvenile's grave (B32) as one of the cod pieces (cat. 989). No other ornaments were associated with it.

Bird bone: beads

These six fragile beads were unique to the site though they have been found elsewhere. They were cylindrical beads made from the long bones of birds and they were found on an infant's wrist (B133).

SUMMARY AND CONCLUSIONS

Having discussed the various types of ornament individually, it is necessary to place them in the general context of the site. The jewellery was made from a variety of materials only fourteen of which were precisely identified and, as Table 28 shows, their distribution within the site varied with time. None of the layers had all fourteen materials. The number ranged from twelve in layer 6 to two in layers 1 and 9. The greatest changes in the types occurred in layers 7 and 6. Three new materials, including the earliest identifiable *Tridacna*, were recovered from layer 7 and two types of stone and the sharks' teeth were first found in layer 6. No new materials occurred after this time and almost all had disappeared by the top of layer 2.

Despite the range of materials identified, only five were represented in the burials. The shell beads formed the bulk of the mortuary jewellery but, although they were clearly made from several different species of shell, it was not possible to ascertain the species in many cases. They were not found outside the burial context. The presence of other shell ornaments in the non-mortuary areas suggests that this may be due more to their inability to survive in an unprotected environment than their original absence from it. The disc beads were found in all the mortuary phases (layers 10–5) and there seems to be little difference in size distribution. All the other bead types were restricted. The rare funnel beads were recovered from a MP1 and two of the earliest MP2 burials (lower layer 10), one of which, B132, also had some barrel beads. Barrel beads were recovered from 18 of the MP2 and MP3 burials (upper layer 10), but in MP4 and MP5, they were replaced by the I-beads. Although quite a large number of these I-beads were recovered, they were represented in only five burials. There were also only five burials in MP6 and MP7 which contained the H-beads (see Table 29).

TABLE 28: *The chronological distribution of identified jewellery materials*

Layer	1	2	3	4	5	6	7	8	9	10
Marble	-	-	-	-	-	-	-	*	-	*
Volcanic sandstone	-	-	-	*	-	*	-	-	*	-
Andesite	-	-	*	-	-	*	-	-	-	-
Black slate	*	*	*	*	*	*	*	-	*	-
Grey slate	*	*	*	*	*	*	-	-	-	-
Slaty shale	-	-	*	*	*	*	*	-	-	-
Tridacna	-	-	-	*	*	*	*	-	-	-
Conus	-	-	-	-	-	*	*	*	-	*
Turtle bone	-	-	*	*	-	*	*	*	-	*
Ivory	-	*	*	*	-	*	*	-	-	-
Fish vertebra	-	*	-	*	-	*	-	-	-	*
Mammalian tooth	-	-	-	-	-	*	*	*	-	*
Crocodile tooth	-	-	-	-	-	-	-	-	-	*
Shark tooth	-	*	*	-	-	*	-	-	-	-

TABLE 29: *The chronological distribution of the ornaments, based on presence and absence*

Non-Mortuary Ornaments	Layers									
	1	2	3	4	5	6	7	8	9	10
Beads										
Tooth–mammal	-	-	-	-	-	*	*	-	-	*
Tooth–reptile	-	-	-	-	-	-	-	-	-	*
Tooth–fish	-	*	*	-	-	*	-	-	-	-
Disc/bangles										
Stone	*	*	*	*	*	*	*	*	*	*
Shell	-	-	-	*	*	*	-	*	-	-
Fish	-	*	-	*	-	-	-	-	-	-
Ivory	-	*	*	*	-	*	*	-	-	-
Turtle bone	-	-	*	*	-	-	*	*	-	-
Mortuary										
Beads										
Tooth–mammal	-	-	-	-	-	-	*	*	-	*
Shell–disc	-	-	-	-	*	*	*	*	-	*
Shell–funnel	-	-	-	-	-	-	-	-	-	*
Shell–barrel	-	-	-	-	-	-	-	-	-	*
Shell–I	-	-	-	-	-	-	*	*	-	-
Shell–H	-	-	-	-	*	*	-	-	-	-
Pendants										
Tooth	-	-	-	-	-	-	-	-	-	*
Shell	-	-	-	-	-	-	-	-	-	*
Fish	-	-	-	-	-	*	-	-	-	*
Turtle bone	-	-	-	-	-	*	-	-	-	-
Disc/bangles										
Shell	-	-	-	-	*	*	*	*	-	*
Fish	-	-	-	-	-	*	-	-	-	*
Body plaques										
Turtle bone	-	-	-	-	-	*	*	*	-	*

The other beads and pendants found at the site were made from several types of tooth and turtle bone. Most were mammalian canines from different species. The majority were from burials in layers 10 and 7, but half-a-dozen came from non-mortuary contexts in layers 6–10 inclusive. Other teeth from non-mortuary contexts included some crocodile teeth and six drilled sharks' teeth, one of which came from layer 6 while the others were from layers 3 and 2. There were changes in the types of teeth used with time, and, although it is probable that the mammalian teeth were used as decoration, it is possible that the sharks' teeth were used as inlays where sharp edges were needed

Disc/bangles were the next most numerous group of ornaments, showing even greater variety of materials and styles. Some, like many of the beads, were used to decorate clothing. For example, most of the 1a style discs were from head-dresses and the 1b discs from B15 could have also been part of an outer garment. The great majority of disc/bangles, however, were probably used as bangles and they are discussed below. The bangles were made from six different types of stone, two species of shell, large fish vertebrae, ivory and turtle bone.

Most of the bangles were made from stone (Table 30). Approximately 30% of these were found during the period of mortuary activity, but despite this, none was directly associated with a burial. Black slate was the most common stone used and was recovered from the upper nine layers. Grey slate was also fairly common but was not found below layer 6. Nearly 80% of the stone bangles were made of these slates. Of the remainder, the three marble pieces are from layers 8 and 10 while the slaty shale, andesite and volcanic sandstone are distributed through the middle layers spanning both the mortuary and post-mortuary periods.

TABLE 30: *The chronological distribution of the different bangle materials*

Material	1	2	3	4	5	6	7	8	9	10	Non-mortuary	Mortuary
Stone												
Marble	-	-	-	-	-	-	-	1	-	2	3	-
Volcanic sandstone	-	-	-	2	-	2	-	-	1	-	5	-
Andesite	-	-	4	-	-	1	-	-	-	-	5	-
Slaty shale	-	-	2	2	1	6	2	-	-	-	13	-
Black slate	1	16	22	11	6	3	2	1	1	-	63	-
Grey slate	1	8	7	4	4	1	-	-	-	-	25	-
Shell												
Tridacna	-	-	-	2	10	12	5	-	-	-	16	13
Conus	-	-	-	-	-	2	-	1	-	-	2	1
Ivory	-	2	15	4	-	1	2	-	-	-	24	-
Turtle bone	-	-	1	2	-	-	-	3	-	-	6	-
Fish vertebra	-	2	-	1	-	1	-	-	-	16	3	17
Total materials	2	4	6	9	4	8	4	4	2	2	11	3
Total artefacts (+ two unknown styles)	2	28	51	28	21	28	11	6	2	18	165	31

The shell bangles are not as numerous despite apparently being popular as grave goods. Half came from the burials and only two were from non-mortuary layers (Table 30). Most were made from clam shell and varied in shape from L-shaped to narrow cylinders. The fish vertebra bangles were recovered from burials in layers 10 and 6 and were also found in the non-mortuary layers 4 and 2. They may have been more plentiful than the finds suggest as they are fairly fragile and might not have survived easily in the non-mortuary contexts. Six fragmentary disc/bangles made of turtle bone were recovered. The three conventional ones were found in non-mortuary contexts in the mortuary layers but the fragments of star-shaped disc/bangles were from the post-mortuary layers. So was the majority of ivory bangles. Two plain ones were found in layer 7, but the others were from layers 4-2. Four were decorated with incised lines and bored pits in triangular patterns. Apart from incising on a pendant (cat. 2773) these were the only decorated pieces. The same design motif was used to decorate pottery in layers 4 and 3.

Apart from occasional unique artefacts like the shark's spine pendant and the *Nassarius* shell necklace, the only other ornaments recovered from the burials were the body plaques and other shaped pieces of turtle bone. The pieces like the shark's spine are not included in the general style analysis as they are unique, but the turtle bone objects were found in several burials in layers 6–10.

Table 29 shows that not only are there chronological and numerical differences in the distribution of materials and types of ornaments but there is also a marked lack of similarity between the mortuary and non-mortuary artefacts even within the same layers. The absence of shell beads in the non-mortuary context may be due to their inability to survive in the harsher climate but the opposite cannot be true for stone or ivory, both found in the 'harsh' non-mortuary context but not in the burials. This suggests that availability of materials is not the only factor determining the distribution of ornaments within the site, so the relationships between material and style, and style and chronology were considered.

Chronological style distribution

The disc/bangles have the greatest variety of materials and styles. The stone disc/bangles were found in all layers though they proliferated in the post-mortuary ones. Despite the fact that they have been classified into 15 different styles, the basic shapes represented are triangular and quadrangular in radial section and do not show the variety of outline found in the shell pieces. The more varied stone shapes seem to be concentrated in the lower layers. The triangular and discoid styles were generally found no later than layer 4 and the square and rectangular ones increase after layer 5 (Table 31).

Other types of disc/bangle do not follow the same pattern. The *Tridacna* artefacts, for example, are all concentrated into layers 4–7 and there is no chronological difference in the styles. This was also probably the case for the five *Conus* disc/bangles, though the earliest piece, a 1a, was probably less difficult to produce than the last in the group, a 9b. With such a small sample it is not possible to say if it is significant but it is true that the amount of labour required to produce many of the ivory and turtle bone disc/bangles increased over time. All the ivory disc/bangles were made in the same way but six of the post-mortuary ones were engraved. Similarly, the turtle bone disc/bangles found in layer 8 were discoid and similar in shape to others in the same layer. The post-mortuary ornaments were all star-shaped. The only other type of disc/bangle was made from fish vertebra. Few are found outside burials but this is probably due to their fragility. Like the *Tridacna*, there appears to be no chronological distinction.

TABLE 31: *The chronological distribution of disc/bangle styles*

Style	1	2	3	4	5	6	7	8	9	10	Total	Percent
1	-	-	-	-	3	1	3	-	-	-	7	3.43
1a	-	-	-	-	1	-	2	-	-	1	4	1.96
1b	-	-	-	-	-	-	2	-	-	-	2	0.98
1c	-	-	-	-	2	1	-	-	-	-	3	1.47
3	-	-	-	-	-	-	-	1	-	2	3	1.47
4	-	1	-	-	-	1	-	-	1	1	4	1.96
4a	-	-	-	-	-	2	2	-	-	-	4	1.96
5	-	-	-	2	-	2	-	1	-	-	5	2.45
5a	-	-	-	1	2	-	-	1	-	-	4	1.96
6	-	-	-	-	-	-	-	-	1	-	1	0.49
7	-	-	-	1	-	2	2	-	-	-	5	2.45
7a	-	2	-	1	-	2	-	-	-	-	5	2.45
7b	-	-	1	-	-	-	-	-	-	-	1	0.49
8a	1	2	2	-	-	-	-	-	-	-	5	2.45
8b	-	9	9	6	2	2	1	-	-	-	29	14.21
8c	-	-	6	1	2	1	1	-	-	6	17	8.33
9a	-	1	-	-	-	1	-	-	-	1	3	1.47
9b	1	6	13	4	1	5	-	-	-	2	32	15.68
9c	-	1	-	-	1	-	1	-	-	-	3	1.47
10	-	-	-	1	3	3	-	-	-	-	7	3.43
10b	-	4	6	2	1	-	-	-	-	-	13	6.37
10c	-	1	9	5	3	5	-	-	-	2	25	12.25
11	-	2	2	1	-	-	1	-	-	-	6	2.94
11a	-	-	2	-	1	2	-	-	-	-	5	2.45
11b	-	-	1	1	-	1	-	-	-	-	3	1.47
11c	-	-	-	-	-	1	-	-	-	-	1	0.49
12	-	-	1	2	-	-	-	-	-	-	3	1.47
?	-	1	-	-	-	-	-	2	-	1	4	1.96
Total	2	30	52	28	22	32	15	5	2	16	204	

Although the shell disc beads are made from a variety of species, they vary very little over time, and, unless the shell can be assigned to its species, it will not be possible to demonstrate chronological changes. The distribution of other types of shell beads was limited and seems to have developed progressively but, again, until the types of shell are identified, it will not be clear if the similarity between the funnel, I- and H-beads is accidental or deliberate. It is not known whether they were completely new types or the result of adapting new materials because the source of the old ones was lost. The problem is compounded by the shell beads being restricted to burials, because their stylistic development cannot be traced beyond zone B.

The turtle-bone artefacts are all unusual and several are unique. They include the star-shaped disc/bangles discussed above, the cruciform body plaques and other often amorphous pieces. The earliest of these artefacts are the body plaques and the highly-worked pendant. These were recovered from male and juvenile burials in MPs 3 and 4, but the later pieces are simply roughly shaped offcuts from a carapace which in turn degenerate into unworked pieces. This is the opposite trend to that observed for the turtle-bone bangles.

The fact that the differing stylistic trends are due mainly to the changes in the types and amounts of materials available can be demonstrated if the changes in style are compared with the introduction and disappearance of the various materials. There is a clear correlation between them, despite the fact that several of the styles are made from more than one material (Table 32). There is little actual evidence for stylistic development, only change. Some of these changes appear to be due to the decline in availability, as in the case of the turtle bone and possibly *Tridacna*. Others, such as the changes in stone styles, may be due to this also, but the quantity of artefacts produced increased considerably with the comparative ease of workability of the new stones. With the cessation of burials in the area, most of the ornamental types became scarce or disappeared. In comparison, the number of slate bangles increased to what may almost be seen as a specialist production level.

To see if the move to simpler forms was as immediate as the cultural change in site use suggests, the non-burial disc/bangles were tabled comparing the complex and more rectilinear forms (Table 33). The fact that the square and rectangular forms were not represented in zone A, comprise over 71% of zone B disc/bangles and nearly 95% of the zone C group, suggests that the trend to the simpler forms was long term. The main interruption to this trend was found in the MP5 burials and later, where *Tridacna* was used.

SOCIAL IMPLICATIONS

There are various hypotheses about the methods of determining a prehistoric society's attitudes to non-utilitarian artefacts such as jewellery. The personal ornaments associated with the different cultures are always useful aids to the reconstruction of the social and economic organisation of the community and a recognition of the technical skills employed by them. The social organisation implicit in the distribution of the mortuary jewellery and other grave goods is discussed later in this report, but there are several other aspects which can be considered here.

Pottery making at Khok Phanom Di was a major industry, with clays locally available for the purpose. It is not so easy to make a case for the local manufacture of the personal ornaments because, in general, the raw materials used in their manufacture could not be obtained from the immediate environs. Much of the stone used, for example, originated in quarries over 100 km away and there are several other contemporary sites closer to the quarries that have clear evidence for the manufacture of disc/bangles from materials similar to those found at Khok Phanom Di.

In the case of shell, *Conus* and *Tridacna* inhabit sandy coralline waters rather than the muddy estuarine environment around Khok Phanom Di. Turtles were also not indigenous and would not have been easily obtainable.

This all seems to suggest that the ornaments were either obtained through trade or the exchange of prestige gifts (Dalton, 1977), but although this may have been true on occasion, it was not always the case. Central cores from turtle bone and shell were recovered (Fig. 64) indicating that some of these objects were made locally, and this was further supported by the presence in B43 of two partially made clam shell disc/bangles. One of these, cat. 2036a, had the central core only partially

TABLE 32: *The distribution of bangle styles*

Style	M	VS	An	BS	GS	SS	TR	CS	IV	TT	FV	Total mat.	Total bangles	%
1		-	-	-	-	-	7	-	-	-	-	1	7	3.54
1c	-	-	-	-	-	-	3	-	-	-	-	1	3	1.52
3	3	-	-	-	-	-	-	-	-	-	-	1	3	1.52
4	-	2	-	-	1	-	-	-	-	-	1	3	4	2.02
4a	-	-	-	-	-	-	4	-	-	-	-	1	4	2.02
5	-	2	-	-	-	1	-	2	-	-	-	3	5	2.53
5a	-	-	-	2	1	-	-	-	-	1	-	3	4	2.02
6	-	-	-	1	-	-	-	-	-	-	-	1	1	0.51
7	-	-	-	1	1	3	-	-	-	-	-	3	5	2.53
7a	-	1	-	1	2	1	-	-	-	-	-	4	5	2.53
7b	-	-	-	1	-	-	-	-	-	-	-	1	1	0.51
8a	-	-	-	5	-	-	-	-	-	-	-	1	5	2.53
8b	-	-	-	23	3	2	1	-	-	-	-	4	29	14.65
8c	-	-	-	3	2	-	-	-	6	-	6	4	17	8.59
9a	-	-	1	1	-	-	-	-	-	-	1	3	3	1.52
9b	-	-	-	11	11	5	1	1	-	-	3	6	32	16.16
9c	-	-	-	2	-	-	-	-	1	-	-	2	3	1.52
10	-	-	-	-	-	-	7	-	-	-	-	1	7	3.54
10b	-	-	4	4	5	-	-	-	-	-	-	3	13	6.57
10c	-	-	-	8	-	1	1	-	8	-	7	5	25	12.63
11	-	-	-	-	-	-	-	-	6	-	-	1	6	3.03
11a	-	-	-	-	-	-	3	-	2	-	-	2	5	2.53
11b	-	-	-	-	-	-	2	-	1	-	-	2	3	1.53
11c	-	-	-	-	-	-	-	-	-	-	1	1	1	0.51
12	-	-	-	-	-	-	-	-	-	3	-	1	3	1.52
?	-	1	-	-	-	-	-	-	-	2	1	3	4	2.02
Total	3	6	5	63	26	13	29	3	24	6	20	61	198	100.10
%	1.52	3.03	2.53	31.82	13.13	6.57	14.65	1.52	12.12	3.03	10.01			99.9

M = marble; VS = volcanic sandstone: An = andesite; BS = black or brown slate; GS = grey slate; SS = slaty shale; TR = *Tridacna*; CS = conus; IV = ivory; TT = turtle shell; FV = fish vertebrae

removed while the other was still in its rough discoid form. It is not easy to accept that these objects were traded or exchanged in their unfinished state. If, however, they were being made locally for a specific person who died before their completion, then their inclusion in the burial in that state would be understandable.

In general, the clam shell artefacts were carefully made and neatly finished, with the inner edges smoothed and polished. This was in marked contrast to the interior portions of many of the stone pieces. There, the rough edges remaining after the central core had broken away were either left

TABLE 33: *The chronological comparison between the rectilinear and more complex styles of bangles from non-mortuary contexts. Complex (C): types 1–5, 11. Simple (S): types 6–11*

Style	C Zone C	S Zone C	C Zone B	S Zone B	C Zone A	S Zone A	Ratio C:S
Tridacna	-	2	6	8	-	-	6:10
Conus	-	-	2	-	-	-	2:0
Marble	-	-	1	-	2	-	3:0
Andesite	-	4	-	1	-	-	0:5
Volc. sandst.	2	-	2	1	-	-	4:1
Slate	1	75	3	23	-	-	4:98
Ivory	-	21	-	3	-	-	0:24
Fish vert.	-	3	-	-	-	-	0:3
Turtle bone	3	-	1	2	-	-	4:2
Total	6	105	15	38	2	-	23:143
Zone %s	5.5	94.5	28.3	71.7	100		

unworked or had been only roughly ground down. This time the lack of finish could be accounted for if the artefacts had broken before completion.

Two other factors strengthen the argument for the local manufacture of some ornaments. These are: the recovery of a small unworked portion of the edge of a giant clam shell from the drain being dug along the side of the excavation, and the use of two different types of shell to make the discs for the head-dress in B15. One of the discs was made from the top portion of a *Conus* shell, utilising the basic natural shape, but the other was made from *Tridacna* and had been painstakingly formed as a copy of the *Conus* piece. The presence of clam as a raw material, and its use in producing copies in conjunction with the other signs of local manufacture, do little to help identify the goods used by the group as exchange of high-status gifts or even trade. It is possible that pots were traded for raw materials, but the fact that it was necessary to make a copy of the original disc from a species of shell from the same type of environment as itself indicates that the community did not have regular contact with a group that had easy access to the shells. The possibility remains that the people collected their own raw materials.

Manufacture and design

Although several methods were used to produce the personal ornaments, the majority of the pieces were made by trepanning with grit and variously sized bamboos. Most of the disc/bangles and all the disc beads were made in this fashion. The unfinished bangles from B43 show that the artisans knew how to take shortcuts – removing the excess shell by slicing rather than grinding – which left the template with the appropriate form to make an L-shaped disc/bangle while reducing to a minimum the amount of shell to be ground. This method was probably also the simplest way of producing the disc beads made from *Tridacna* shell, but, because each bead is virtually made individually, it is a much more time-consuming way of making the thin-walled nacreous shell beads than the virtual mass-production technique used at prehistoric Ban Na Di (Higham and Kijngam, 1984:58). The latter broke the shells roughly into square tabs which were then drilled and threaded into a long string before being ground to their final circular form. The beads resulting from this technique, however, were neither as regular in shape nor as small as the Khok Phanom Di beads.

The majority of styles produced at Khok Phanom Di appear to have resulted either directly from the method of manufacture or to be a slightly modified or copied natural form. For example, the shell discs all have the same general form as the B43 discs. Even the *Conus* disc and its copy from B15 are variations on the same theme. The shape and size of the extensions and flanges are all controlled by the diameter of the central perforation, the thickness of the shell and the amount of concentric grinding away of the shell. Similar limitations appear to be applicable to the stone disc/bangles, where the artisans created the main differences in style simply by using different thicknesses of slate. There are a few fragments of stone disc/bangles that have been shaped by chipping and pecking but the use-wear on the inner surface suggests that these may have served some purpose other than as ornaments. Beads other than the disc beads are all modifications or careful copies of natural forms. In the case of the various tooth beads, the only modification required was the hole drilled through the roots. Apart from the disc beads, the shapes that were used could be cut from specific parts of shells or could be easily copied using a similar one-directional grinding technique to that used on the disc/bangles.

There is rather more freedom of design shown in the ivory disc/bangles. Although all were produced by cutting through the wide base of the tusk, the outer surface of the later ornaments was often decorated. They were either carved with sets of square concentric rings, giving the impression of several narrow bangles rather than one wide one, or had pits drilled into the surface in triangular patterns reminiscent of a pot motif. In the case of turtle-bone artefacts, the use of narrow chisels or gouges, rather than the trepans and flat grinders used on the other jewellery, allowed the artisan to produce more organic shapes. They were not constricted by the arcs or diameters of the bamboo. This resulted in the cruciform body plaques and the star-shaped disc/bangles, but, although they were more complex in outline, they were still basically two-dimensional. The outer and inner surfaces were virtually unworked and the cut edges were simply smoothed off. The form could equally well have been cut from a sheet of paper.

There is only one ornament from Khok Phanom Di that can be said to be three-dimensional in that all its surfaces have been radically modified. This is the pendant, cat. 2773 from B32 (Fig. 60). This spatula object with a fan-shaped upper portion is at first glance totally unlike anything found at the site. Yet the reconstruction of several of the body plaques including the one from B30 (cat. 991, Fig. 62) have been found to have their lateral extensions modified to produce crescent-shaped toggles which could be used to attach them to the body. Although much larger in area than the pendant, these extensions have the same general shape. Because of the curvature of the original carapace, the carved surface of the pendant would have been the original underside and its back which was ground flat would have been the original top surface. If this was a broken arm of a body plaque, the comparatively small size of the piece could be explained as the result of grinding away as much of the original material as was necessary to produce the flat spatulate area. Given the habit of grinding down shell, this piece then would not be so remarkable. What makes it unique is the careful undercutting and shaping of the fan. It is ground away over the shoulders of the spatula in one direction and then curved up into the fan in the second direction. All other undercutting or grinding down was on only one plane. It is surprising that this more sophisticated form was produced as early as MP4 and then not repeated. It would seem that its presence in a juvenile's burial marked it as a childish object of no great importance and in subsequent burials tradition prevailed.

There are still many gaps in our understanding of the Khok Phanom Di culture, but some aspects can be identified. Living, as they did, in a diverse environment, these people had time and skills to develop a number of crafts. The major craft practised must have been the pottery but they had access to various materials such as stone and shell which they modified into tools and ornaments. They had various specialised tools that they used for pottery and weaving, such as the pottery anvils and the bone bobbins, but they could use their basic tool kit for the ornaments. Apart from stone adzes this kit consisted of various shaped and graded grinders, borers or awls, bamboo trepans or trephines and chisels. In the lower layers, there is little evidence for the use of the chisel as all the ornaments were made by grinding or trepanning. The earliest of the ornaments were made from shell and stone or fish vertebrae and consisted mainly of necklaces and anklets or bracelets and bangles. From MP4, turtle bone was used for ornament or ritual and the chisel was used to create the more organic shapes.

Many of the shell ornaments were used in the embroidery of various garments. In the later burials both men and women were found to be wearing long-sleeved and belted tunics which were open down the front. The openings and edges were thickly encrusted with strings of small mother-of-pearl disc beads, while the belts consisted of strings of white disc beads. One of the women had the tunic and what may have been a long robe embroidered over the bodice with I-beads. Several of them also had head-dresses made from disc beads and larger discs. Apart from the possible length of the skirt, there seems to be little difference in dress between sexes. All types of burials had necklaces, anklets and bangles.

Few of the ornaments were gender related, but the fish-bone disc/bangles were confined to children's burials and the turtle-bone pieces were all in male or juvenile graves. The fish-bone artefacts were limited in size and their distribution may simply reflect this, but of all the other ornaments in the burials, the turtle bone stands out as a ritualistic object. Not only was it found only in male burials, but the changes through time suggest that the material became scarce while its attractiveness endured.

Two major problems remain concerning the personal ornaments. One is the source of the materials, especially the shell, and the other is the attitude of the people towards the jewellery. In other Southeast Asian sites, people were buried either with their valued goods or with representations of them (Pilditch, 1984). To some extent, this can also be said to be true of the people of Khok Phanom Di. The costume of the woman in B15 is unlikely to have been made specifically for burial, but it is certainly rich. The pieces of unworked turtle bone may represent the body plaques that had become irreplaceable. The problem is not the ornaments that are present in the burials, but rather those that are absent. Ivory bangles were recovered from the mortuary layers but not from burials. Because of their apparent scarcity, it is tempting to assume that they were imported pieces too valuable to be interred. But the patterns on the decorated bangles suggest that at least some of them were of local manufacture. Likewise, the stone bangles were found in great numbers throughout the site but were not present in any of the burials. The number of unfinished pieces attests to their local manufacture, so they were replaceable and could have found their way into burials. If these objects were of high value they would be expected to be found in the richer burials. Or if of low value why were they not recovered from the many graves with few grave goods? It cannot even be the materials themselves that were taboo, as stone tools were found in some burials.

If these two issues can be resolved, then the understanding of these peoples' social organisation and trade and exchange systems will be enhanced.

CLASSIFICATION OF SOUTHEAST ASIAN DISC/BANGLE FORMS

This classification is intended for all types and materials and may have to be added to in the future.

Style 1 discs have a ratio of internal to external diameters of 1:$\geq$1.5. The radial section consists of a wedge with a rounded or flattened narrow outer surface and a concentric flange on one edge of the wider inner surface. The result appears as an upper case L on its back. The internal diameter is > 3.5 cm.

Style 1a The basic shape is the same as above, but the internal diameter is less than 1 cm.

Style 1b The radial section of these discs is still L–shaped, but there is no internal perforation. The flange has become a solid cylinder in the centre of the disc.

Style 1c are L–shaped in radial section, but they have ratios of internal to external diameters of 1:<1.5. The L is therefore much squatter than in the previous styles and often one or more of the surfaces has been modified to produce a convex or concave curve. The internal diameter is >3.5 cm.

Style 2 have internal diameters > 3.5 cm. Their radial sections are triangular or wedge-shaped with concentric flanges on both edges of the wide inner surface. This gives the appearance of an upper case T lying on its side. The ratio of internal to external diameters is 1:1.75–2.

Style 3 are discoid ornaments with diameters > 3.5 cm and triangular sections. The longer sides are deeply concave.

Style 4 discoid items have internal diameters > 3.5 cm and wedge or triangular radial sections with no flanges. The ratio of internal to external diameters is 1:1.75–2 and the radial section is at least twice as thick as it is wide.

Style 4a have the same basic shape and dimensions as above but the wedge has been truncated forming a narrow flat outer surface.

Style 5 ornaments have internal diameters > 3.5 cm. The ratio of internal to external diameters is 1:<1.75. The outline is triangular or wedged.

Style 5a are of the same shape and dimensions as above, but are truncated at the outer edge.

Style 6 are discoid with flat ends and a single or double bevel on the outer edge. Diameter ratios are 1:$\geq$1.5 and the width/depth ratio is 1:$\geq$4.

Style 7 are discoid with flat ends and single or double bevels on the outer surface. Their internal diameter is greater than 3.5 cm and the interior to exterior diameter ratio is 1:<1.5 and the width/depth ratio is 1:<3.

Style 7a are discoid with flat ends and single or double bevels on the outer surface. Their internal diameter is greater than 3.5 cm and the interior to exterior diameter ratio is 1:<1.5 and the width/depth ratio is 1:$\geq$3.

Style 7b have a rectangular radial section. The internal diameter is > 3.5 cm and the interior to exterior diameter ratio is 1:<1.5. The width/depth ratio is 1:>1.5 and the outer surface is convex.

Style 8 are discoid with a rectangular radial section. The internal diameter is > 3.5 and the minimum dimension of the radial depth is 1.5 cm and the width/depth ratio is 1:>1.25-$\leq$2.

Style 8a have a rectangular radial section. The internal diameter is > 3.5 cm and the radial depth is $\geq$0.9 cm. The ratio of width to depth is 1:>1.25-$\leq$2.

Style 8b have a rectangular radial section. The internal diameter is > 3.5 cm and the radial depth is $\geq$0.6 cm. The ratio of width to depth is 1:>1.25-$\leq$2.

Style 8c have a rectangular radial section. The internal diameter is > 3.5 cm and the radial depth is <0.6 cm. The ratio of width to depth is 1:>1.25-≤2.

Style 9 are discoid with a rectangular radial section. The internal diameter is > 3.5 and the minimum dimension of the radial depth is 1.5 cm and the width/depth ratio is 1:>2.

Style 9a have a rectangular radial section. The internal diameter is > 3.5 cm and the radial depth is ≥0.9 cm. The ratio of width to depth is 1:>2.

Style 9b have a rectangular radial section. The internal diameter is > 3.5 cm and the radial depth is ≥0.6 cm. The ratio of width to depth is 1:>2.

Style 9c have a rectangular radial section. The internal diameter is > 3.5 cm and the radial depth is <0.6 cm. The ratio of width to depth is 1:>2.

Style 10 have radial sections that are roughly square. The internal diameters are > 3.5 cm and the radial depth is >1.5 cm. The depth/width ratio is 1:1±0.25.

Style 10a have radial sections that are roughly square. The internal diameters are > 3.5 cm and the radial depth is >0.9 cm. The depth/width ratio is 1:1±0.25.

Style 10b have radial sections that are roughly square. The internal diameters are > 3.5 cm and the radial depth is >0.6 cm. The depth/width ratio is 1:1±0.25.

Style 10c have radial sections that are roughly square. The internal diameters are > 3.5 cm and the radial depth is <0.6 cm. The depth/width ratio is 1:1±0.25.

Style 11 are discoid with a rectangular radial section. The internal diameter is > 3.5 and the minimum dimension of the radial width is 1.5 cm and the width/depth ratio is >1.25:1.

Style 11a have a rectangular radial section. The internal diameter is > 3.5 cm and the radial width is ≥0.9 cm. The ratio of width to depth is >1.25:1.

Style 11b have a rectangular radial section. The internal diameter is > 3.5 cm and the radial width is ≥0.6 cm. The ratio of width to depth is >1.25:1.

Style 11c have a rectangular radial section. The internal diameter is > 3.5 cm and the radial width is <0.6 cm. The ratio of width to depth is >1.25:1.

Style 12 have a series of concave arcs cut from the outer rim of the disc resulting in a multipointed star shape. The internal diameters are > 3.5 cm. Other features vary.

V. THE SHELL KNIVES

T. F. G. Higham

INTRODUCTION

A total of 406 prehistoric worked shell knives were identified in the laboratory, the majority being made from one valve from the freshwater mussel *Pseudodon inoscularis*, which had been ground to a concave working surface. Care was taken not to touch the worked edges of these artefacts so as not to alter any evidence of microwear. Each artefact was given a catalogue number and identified according to its context. The shells were then placed in individual plastic bags to reduce the likelihood of damage.

The examination of the wear patterns on the prehistoric shells was undertaken prior to experimentation with modern specimens and involved the observation of wear patterns on working blades using the stereoscopic microscope at x10 and x20 magnification, and S.E.M observation and photography. The aim was to isolate the characteristic wear patterns on the prehistoric tools, and then compare them for common features with any of the experimental knives.

The mechanical damage sustained by some shells hampered the identification of wear patterns, but others survived well. The removal of hard detritus and accretions adhering to some shells was attempted, but this often resulted in damage to the working edge. Complete artefacts were separated from fractured examples and examined. The lengths of each shell and its worked edge were measured. Complete shells were then cleaned in an ultrasonic cleaner. Once this was accomplished, one could observe with increased clarity the wear patterns of the shells.

All shells examined had underlying similarities; the striations that remained all ran in a perpendicular direction to the blade edge. The major difference between shells was the degree to which the striations were present, some were coarser, others smoother. During each experiment undertaken with modern shells, it was concluded that the tool would have needed resharpening after a period of work. The marked concavity on prehistoric examples was very probably the result of successive episodes of working and sharpening. This was probably undertaken with a sandstone abrader. Wear patterns are, therefore, a function of the time which elapsed following the most recent resharpening of the cutting surface. One can refer to the differences in the depth and concentration of striations between the experimental shells used for 2 and 3 hours of grass harvesting to illustrate this. The longer a tool is used, the less likely is it that sharpening striations will remain. All complete shells were worn to a greater extent in the central dorsal region (Fig. 66). The extremities of the blade were invariably less worn, and the more one moved to the left and right dorsal areas, the more one observed an increase in the coarseness and depth of the striations. The central zone was much smoother, and the remaining striations were finer and less deep. Many shell knives, depending on their condition, possessed a reflective sheen in their central dorsal regions. It was also found that the lower reaches of the blade, the zones nearest to the edge, were more likely to be smoothed and less striated than zones further up the blade. This can be seen very clearly in Figs. 67–69.

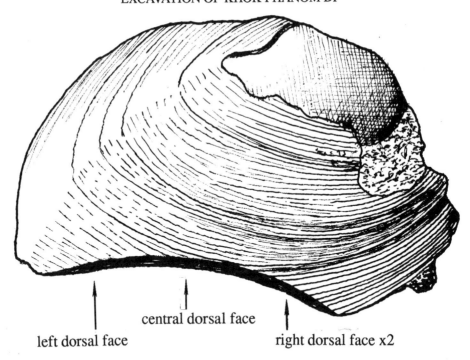

FIG. 66.   The three regions of wear on prehistoric shell knives

Fig. 70 shows a shell blade smoothed to such an extent that the striations are very difficult to see. The perpendicular lines are natural growth lines. This tool had more visible striations on its left and right dorsal regions; in the centre, where this photograph was taken, more wear had occurred and the original grinding marks were virtually obliterated.

Fig. 71 was slightly different in that fine striations covered the entire blade. It had also been fractured on its right and left dorsal sides. This may have been the result of work. It was found during the course of experiments that shells were susceptible to damage if excessive force was employed. Alternatively, this type of damage may have been sustained after abandonment.

The distribution of these artefacts within the site was interesting. All were discovered in layers 6–10, with most being found in the relatively shallow layer 9.

DESCRIPTION OF SELECTED PREHISTORIC SPECIMENS

This is not an exhaustive catalogue of each worked shell, because there are so many, and relatively few are intact. Consequently, only well-preserved knives, or those with specific and relevant characteristics will be described individually. It is axiomatic that all shells have been minutely examined, and that none departs from the general features which are set out below.

- 10:7 cat. 2959 (Fig. 92a). The striations on the cutting edge of this specimen begin from the left on the bevel as a series of vertical marks impossible to see with the naked eye, but easily

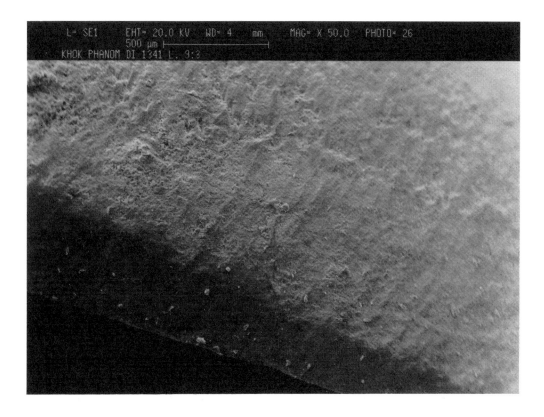

FIG. 67.   S.E.M. photograph illustrating the characteristic smoothing of the lower zone of the blade's edge

visible at x20 magnification. The upper half of the bevel may represent the original ground surface. The striations are much deeper and less worn than on the lower half. This shell may represent an example of resharpening.

- 10:4 cat. 2847. Fine striations cover the length of the cutting edge. A degree of fracturing has taken place on the right-hand side of the dorsal edge.

- 10:4 cat. 2876. The striations run parallel to the edge. Initially, it was thought that the markings were the result of use-wear, but following examination of similar patterns under the S.E.M., it was concluded that these marks are natural.

- 10:3 cat. 3166. This specimen has a very thin working edge. Striations are vertical and highly visible.

- 10:2 cat. 1653 and 10:1 cat. 1440. Striations on these two artefacts were considerably less well-defined than on most others.

- 9:6 cat. 2836, 9:3 cat. 2821 and 9:1 cat. 2851. Striations on these specimens were perpendicular to and present along the working edges.

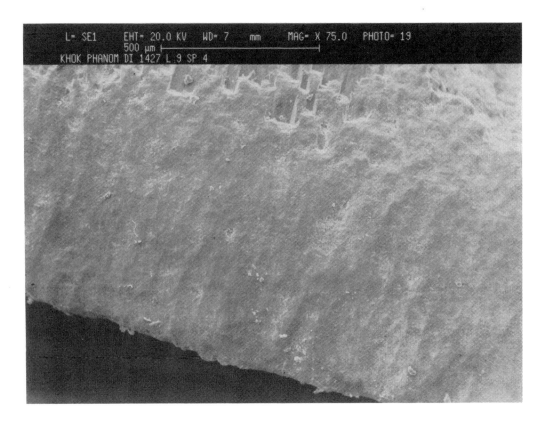

FIG. 68.   S.E.M. photograph illustrating the smoothing apparent on the lower zone of the blade's edge

- 9:6 cat. 2917 (Fig. 92c). This example possessed well-defined striations and a high bevelled edge.

- 9:3 cat. 3092 (Fig. 92f) and 9:5 cat. 3179 (Fig. 92e). These artefacts both possess a very high edge or bevel and thin, visible striations cover this area.

- 9:3 cat. 3139. Like the above example, this shell has two planes of wear, possibly indicating resharpening or the result of working the blade at a different angle to its original ground angle.

- 9:2 cat. 3052. The very wide edge, consisting of a pock-marked and poorly preserved surface, makes this shell more difficult to identify. Nevertheless the presence of striations perpendicular to the edge were noted.

- 9:1 cat. 3128. This example reveals evidence for very fine use-wear. It is likely that a greater amount of time had elapsed between sharpening and use until abandonment than on other shells.

- 8:6 cat. 2837. Despite a slightly fractured dorsal centre, this shell possessed a working bevel consisting of three distinct parts, left dorsal, right dorsal and centre dorsal. The centre

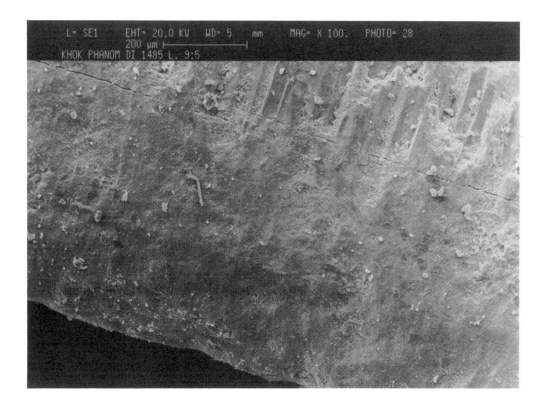

FIG. 69.   S.E.M. photograph taken at a higher magnification of the lower zone

is smoothed and somewhat reflective. This gradually merges into the outer zones where the striations are coarser and more prominent.

The prehistoric shells, almost without exception, possessed striations which ran in a perpendicular direction to the edge and exhibited a variation, both in location, depth and coarseness. The presence of striations was probably directly related to the use-time that had elapsed since sharpening. A number of shells were smoothed to such an extent that striations were not able to be identified. It therefore seems unlikely that the prehistoric tools were used on materials known to create distinctive, abrasive wear patterns, such as those formed in the processing of fish. The prehistoric wear patterning was formed not by the effects of rasping or grinding pressures, which produce widespread deformation of the edge, but by polishing. The majority of complete shells were worn to a greater extent in the central dorsal region of the blade, where a sheen or gloss was sometimes present, the result of polishing and contact with a material which smoothed and rounded pre-existing striations and formed few of its own.

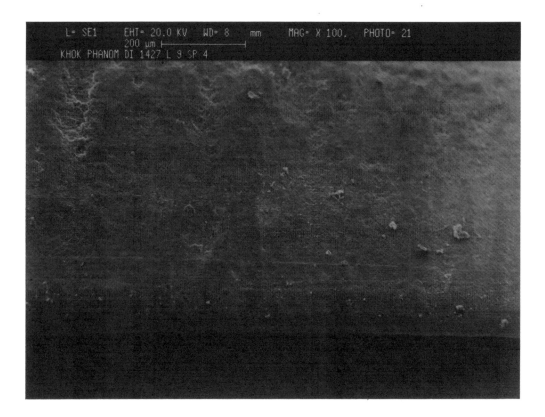

FIG. 70.   S.E.M. photograph taken of the wear patterns produced on the lower reaches of a prehistoric shell tool

METHODOLOGY

Since the appearance of Semenov's (1964) influential review of prehistoric technology, research has continued on creating a systematic approach for inferring the function of prehistoric implements. According to Keeley, the ultimate goal of any research project utilising microwear analysis is to recreate, as completely as possible, the primary economic activities of prehistoric populations. The research must attempt to obtain precise designations of functions for the tools under examination, a procedure requiring an assessment of every possibility.

Keeley and Newcomer (1977) have stressed that one must first consider what material was treated with the implements under analysis. An experimental copy can then be made, tested on the material in question, and examined for patterns of use-wear. An alternative is to find an ethnographic equivalent which had been used for a specific function for comparison with the prehistoric examples under analysis. Naturally, similar wear patterns are expected to indicate similar use.

The vast majority of microwear analyses have dealt with stone tool wear, predominantly on flint and, to a lesser extent, bone and wood (Juel-Jensen, 1988). These have only a limited value when we are dealing with shell as the raw material, although the procedural and methodological frame-

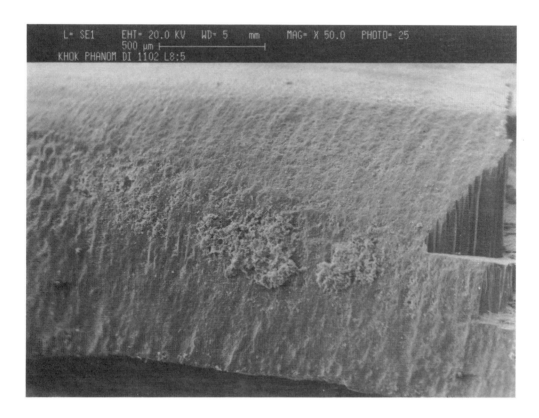

FIG. 71.   S.E.M. photograph illustrating the most common wear patterns present on the left and right dorsal areas of working blades

works employed have some relevance. Harsant (1978) worked with unmodified shell tools which possessed no wear patterns. Any microwear she discovered on her examples was thus automatically the result of contact and friction between the tool and the material in question. Despite the paucity of comparative data on shell wear patterns, she showed it is still possible through experimentation to determine function and usage from wear with some degree of success.

Wear is a physical process, which Semenov (1964) has divided into two basic types. This research is concerned with micro-deformation, which arises from friction between the tool and the object of work. Micro-deformation produces small alterations on the surface of, in this case, the ground edge of the tool.

There are three degrees of wear to be distinguished, the first of which is micro-polish. This wear pattern is produced from small specific pressures, and results in micro-plastic surface alterations generated from contact with other materials. This wear is only noticeable under high magnification. Striations are grooves and scratches probably formed from grits and abrasive materials generated in most instances from work. Edge scarring and rounding are more immediately apparent wear patterns resulting from higher specific pressures. These occur on surfaces when a larger pressure has been exerted, causing macroscopic destruction of the surface (Semenov, 1964).

It should be recognised that natural processes can act upon artefacts and alter their appearance, for example, the agents of weathering. In the post-depositional environment, soil movements can scratch and abrade the surfaces of the material. Similarly, differentiating between retouching, re-working and use-wear, is sometimes difficult (Juel-Jensen, 1988).

EXPERIMENTATION: DISCUSSION

Keeley (1980) has undertaken several analyses of micro-wear, attempting to create a framework suitable for future research ventures. His research, especially his descriptions of the different types of wear pattern formed by various materials, proved most useful to this project, as did his list of problems associated with test experiments. Odell's (1975) systematic procedure was used as a background for the experiments described below. Advice on the importance of publishing every step involved, and adequately describing changes, differences and similarities before, after and during experimentation, was followed.

There is a marked difference between the following experiments and those undertaken by Keeley and Harsant. Keeley and Newcomer (1977) used chipped tools, which lacked any form of wear pattern prior to experimentation. Harsant (1978), as described above, used unmodified shell tools. The shells discovered at Khok Phanom Di exhibited a marked concavity in the shape of their cutting edge. It was suggested that shells had been sharpened and fashioned to that shape for a specific purpose, or purposes. It was considered necessary, prior to experimentation, to fashion modern shells into a shape similar, though not as concave, as the prehistoric examples. This was accomplished using a piece of sandstone found in cultural deposits at Khok Phanom Di. Approximately 30 modern freshwater mussel shells (*Hyridella menziesii*) were ground on this block. The choice of species reflects the fact that *Hyridella menziesii* is the most similar in size and shape to *Pseudodon inoscularis*. It was found that a sharp edge could be obtained in about 20 minutes. A sawing motion was initially used, until it was discovered that the blade could be made a great deal sharper using a grinding motion (Fig. 72).

An attempt was made to replicate completely the shape of one particular prehistoric example, which was markedly concave and possessed a large cutting edge 3-4 mm in width (layer 9:6, cat. 2917 Fig. 92c). It took over two hours to create the modern equivalent, which was just as sharp as the example fashioned in 20 minutes. It was concluded that a shell implement in prehistory would probably have been resharpened a great deal, resulting in the well-worn artefacts recovered during the excavation. The modern experimental shells were ground and worked to a cutting edge. Figure 73 shows the resultant wear patterns present on a typical shell tool. Deep, coarse striations, running at right-angles to the cutting edge, cover the entire surface of the blade. Wear patterns resulting from experimental use had to be identified against this pre-worked surface. This proved understandably difficult, because one was not looking at a once-pristine surface, now covered in small striations and gouges, but a dense array of deep striations, softened, filled and smoothed by use, but often difficult to discern.

The experiments to which the modern shells were subjected were selected on the basis of the actual or likely applications during the prehistoric period at Khok Phanom Di. Every conceivable material was used in experiments in an attempt to isolate the most plausible use during prehistory.

FIG. 72.   The method used in the creation of an experimental shell knife

Tapa cloth, for example, was included, because a number of burials at the site were interred upon or wrapped in a bark covering. It is possible that the shells were used to process fish. Numerous fish bones were found, and the stomach contents of one adult interment comprised fish bone and scales. Fish bones were also found in human coprolites. Consequently, a sample of modern shells was used to head and tail, gut and scale fish. Rice chaff was found throughout the sequence. It was used as a tempering agent in clay preparation and was locally available. The faunal remains included evidence of dog, deer, macaque and pig in the early layers, with the appearance of water buffalo in the later part of the sequence. Cutting cooked and raw meat was therefore undertaken experimentally with modern shells. It was also assumed that taro or a similar tuber was present. Modern taro were therefore peeled. Since much of the prehistoric pottery bore incised designs, a modern shell knife was used to apply similar decoration to clay collected from the vicinity of Khok Phanom Di. Since bamboo is likely to have been an important source of raw material for the manufacture of traps and bows, a shell knife was used experimentally to fashion a point from a length of bamboo. Again, the preparation of hides through the removal of hair may have been undertaken at Khok Phanom Di, and the removal of hair from a modern bovid skin was attempted. Finally, it was assumed that the shells could have been used to cut hair. Doubtless there were also

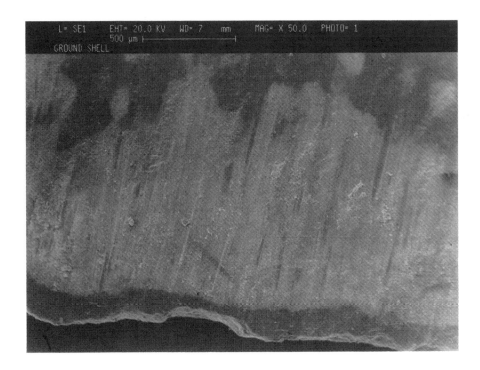

FIG. 73.   S.E.M. photograph of the blade of a modern ground shell tool

other uses to which the shell knives could have been put. The present study claims only to have isolated the most obvious in order to consider their plausibility.

Different types of physical activity were used on the experimental materials. Cutting occurred when the edge was used with bidirectional strokes, the working edge being parallel to the direction of use. One or both aspects of the edge are held at approximately a right-angle to the worked surface. Slicing is similar except that the strokes are unidirectional. Cutting and slicing methods are used on softer materials while sawing involves the application of greater pressure and is concerned with processing of harder materials. Scraping involves using the edge at a very high angle to the worked surface, and pulling it towards oneself (Keeley, 1980).

The following section includes details of observations and descriptions of wear noted at x20 and x40 magnification and also photographs and associated commentary using the Scanning Electron Microscope. A section of the cutting edge of each experimental shell and some of the prehistoric examples was taken and prepared for S.E.M. photography on a Polaron gold-coating unit (E 5000), using a vacuum of approximately 0.4 Torr. Rather than simply being a method of taking photographs, examination of the shell under very high magnification proved a most valuable diagnostic technique in its own right

THE EXPERIMENTS AND THEIR RESULTS

Experiment 1: harvesting grasses

Three freshwater mussel shells were selected for this experiment, and used for varying periods to replicate the type of use that harvesting rice probably entailed. The first was used for 2 hours, the second for 4 hours and the third for 8 hours. This plan was subject to change, depending on the efficiency of the tools, and the extent to which their effectiveness was maintained or decreased.

The harvested grasses stood *c* 50-60 cm tall, the diameter of their stems ranging from 1 to 3 mm. All were mature. Both the shell knife and the cutting technique proved most effective. The shell was placed in one of two positions, the first of which was between the index and second fingers, the ventral surface facing upwards. The thumb was used to collect a grass and hold it against the blade, whereupon the wrist would swivel, bringing the blade up into the stem, while the thumb held the plant, bending the head and forcing the cut. The second method differed in that the index finger was used to grip the rim of the shell, which was supported on its dorsal side by the second finger (Fig. 74). Both methods cut at a very fast rate – 1450 grass heads in 2 hours for the first shell – with no noticeable decrease in efficiency. An attempt to harvest grasses without using a shell knife was found to be a very difficult, painful and inefficient process. The second experimental shell was to have been used for 4 hours, but this timespan was shortened because after approximately 3 hours the tool's performance had diminished considerably and it clearly required resharpening. It had harvested 2100 grass heads in 3 hours.

The shell was observed under a stereoscopic microscope at x20 and x40 magnification. The deep, coarse manufacturing striations had been considerably modified, and the cutting surface had been smoothed and polished to such an extent that it reflected a great deal of light. The central face of the cutting edge was considerably more affected by this glossy effect than the outer ends. Here, the manufacturing striations that had previously existed across the whole blade were reduced in number, and were less visible. The wear sustained from the harvesting seemed to smooth the peaks of the striations. There was no evidence of microflaking on either the dorsal or ventral surfaces, probably due to the nature of the material, which offered limited resistance.

A number of photographs were taken to assess the type of wear present. Figure 75 was taken at x50 magnification and shows the edge of a blade used for two hours of grass harvesting. One can clearly observe the way in which the material acted on the original ground shell seen in Fig. 73. The blade edge had been considerably smoothed.

This can be seen more dramatically in figures. 76 and 77 at a greater magnification of x100. Figure 78 shows the knife used to harvest grass for 3 hours. It was very blunt at this stage and this is reflected in the photograph which shows a blade exhibiting a very smooth polished texture. The original ground striations are almost imperceptible and it is likely that this shell, were it used in prehistory, would have been resharpened some time prior to this stage being reached.

The shell knives were found to be very efficient at harvesting grasses. They severed the stalks easily and continued efficiently for up to 3 hours.

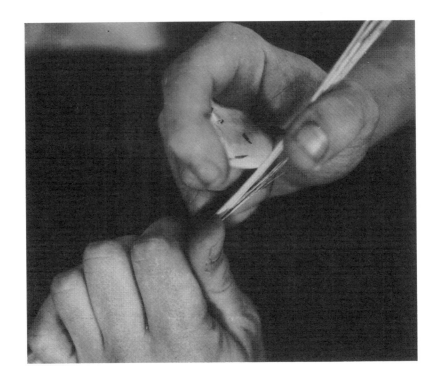

FIG. 74.   The method most commonly used in harvesting grass

Experiment 2: grass scraping

A fresh-water mussel shell was used to remove the seeds from grasses. Figure 79 illustrates how this was accomplished. The shell was used for 45 minutes, and 355 strokes were counted. The blade became blunt at this point, and finally broke due to the extra pressure that needed to be exerted. The tool was very effective, and could easily have been resharpened after blunting. An examination of the wear patterns on the blade revealed little change to the scarred remnants of the grinding stone. On the ventral surface, however, some wear had resulted, and was visible under the stereoscopic microscope. The edge here had been rounded, and a small strip, approximately 1 mm wide, ran parallel to the ventral edge. The wear pattern was smoothed and shiny, consistent with the way in which the edge was used on the material. No striations were evident (Fig. 80). The S.E.M. photograph shows the lack of wear on the blade itself, which looks similar to the original ground shell.

Experiment 3: harvesting and scraping rice

Five experimental shell tools were sent to Thailand for use in harvesting rice. Three were used to harvest the rice utilising the same method as that described above in the grass experiment, while

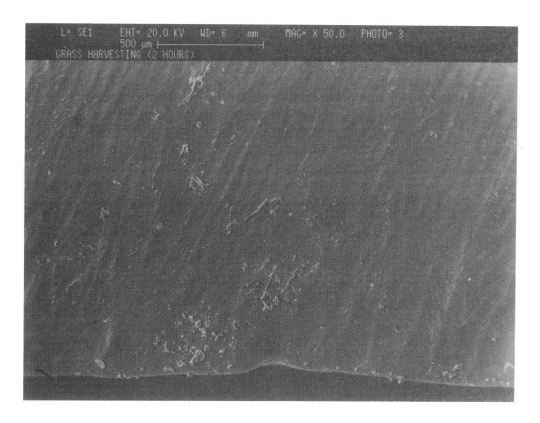

FIG. 75.   S.E.M. photograph showing the wear patterns produced after two hours grass harvesting

two were used to scrape the actual grains of rice from the stalks in an identical manner to the grass-scraping experiment. The shells were used for two, four and eight hours harvesting and for two and four hours scraping. Mr A. Grant coordinated the experiments and submitted that the tools had worked effectively until blunting. Since he was acting according to requests from New Zealand, the knives were, in effect, used beyond the point when resharpening was necessary. When the knives were returned to New Zealand, the smoothness of the blades was noted. Some wear from the grinding stone remained on the shell used for two hours harvesting (Fig. 81), while on the 4-hour shell, the blade was smoothed to such a degree that no visible striations were noted (Fig. 82). A gloss was noted on this particular example due to the extent of its smoothness. The rice-scraping wear patterns were produced on the ventral edge, while the dorsal edge remained coarsely and deeply striated, corresponding identically with the New Zealand knives used for grass scraping (Fig. 83).

Although the knives used for rice harvesting were used beyond the point when resharpening was necessary, the wear patterns produced did represent the extent to which a blade could be smoothed when used on such a substance. No noticeable wear patterns were produced by the plant material, no striations or fractures were formed. Rather, cutting the rice stalks removed and smoothed the original ground striations and replaced them with a glossy sheen.

FIG. 76.   Experimental shell knife used in grass harvesting for two hours

Experiment 4: fashioning wood

A worked shell tool, similar to the examples used in experiment 1, was fashioned on a grinding stone. It was decided to use bamboo for this exercise, as bamboo is common in Southeast Asia, and remains widely used. An attempt was made to fashion a point with the shell, which was used in a variety of angles. Each stroke measured approximately 4-5 cm.

Initially, the shell proved quite inadequate in altering the tough outer layer of bamboo. It took a great deal of pressure to remove even the smallest shavings. Once the exterior layer had been removed, slightly larger shavings were able to be removed, but again a great deal of pressure was necessary, and the shell quickly became blunt. The experiment finished after 25 minutes due to this factor. The piece of bamboo was very difficult to fashion owing to its hard exterior and soft centre. The shell knife was not sharp enough, and would have required constant resharpening, thereby diminishing its usefulness. A microscopic examination of the cutting edge revealed macro-flaking, consistent with workings on a hard surface. The bevel was smoothed, but was not glossy as were the shells used on grasses. Analysis on the S.E.M. revealed that the original rough surface was exacerbated with use on wood, the surface was not smoothed or polished, but was fractured in

FIG. 77.   Experimental shell knife used in grass harvesting for two hours

many places. The striations present from the grinding stone were difficult to discern and the edge had been flaked (Fig. 84).

Experiment 5: scraping hide

A unionid shell was ground, and sharpened as much as possible. Some off-cuts of skin from butchered cattle were obtained and pieces were selected, which included the outer hide of the animal, to be used on a later experiment, and possessed flesh and fat adhering to the inner side. The purpose of the experiment was to assess the usefulness of a shell blade in cutting and removing flesh from cowhides. The length of each stroke was kept at a constant 10-15 cm, and directed towards the operator. The angle of the working edge was alternated during the course of the experiment in order to pinpoint the best position and maximise efficiency. The hide was scraped for 30 minutes.

The duration of this experiment was abbreviated because the shell proved ineffective. The blade was not sharp enough and most of the little flesh removed was accomplished by crude tearing and pulling. The striations on this example were still deep, but were rounded in many places. There was widespread macro-flaking on the cutting edge itself. Due to the pressure required to remove flesh, the edge was very damaged, even after such a short working period. Scars and striations extended from the blade itself onto the dorsal surface. These findings indicate that the use of shell knives to

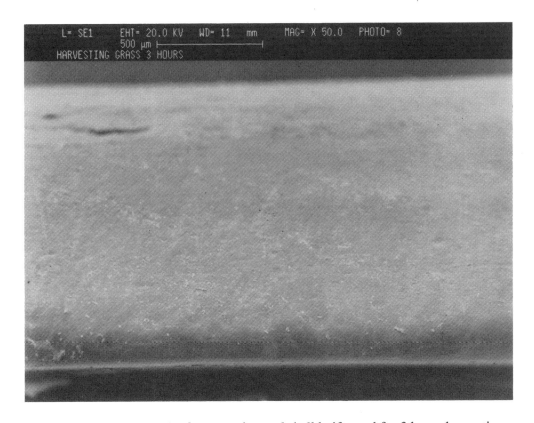

FIG. 78.   S.E.M. photograph of an experimental shell knife used for 3 hours harvesting grass

prepare hides in prehistory is implausible. The shells were neither sharp nor robust enough. The concave cutting edge of the prehistoric shells was clearly not the result of working with meat and S.E.M. analysis was deemed unnecessary.

Experiment 6: cutting bark cloth

A worked shell was sharpened and used to cut a piece of beaten bark cloth. The blade was used in a sawing motion, as it cut more effectively. The bark cloth itself was composed of strips approximately 1 m long and 50 mm wide, and the shell knife was used to cut the bark cloth width-wise. The knife was used over an initial 30-minute period, and 61 strokes were counted. A great deal of time was consumed in preparing each piece for cutting, the shell being more effective if the material was held taut. During the next 40 minutes another 175 strokes * were made, making a total of 236. After approximately 175 strokes, the blade had lost much of its keenness and needed resharpening.

' A stroke in this experiment consisted of between 6 and 10 sawing movements until the bark cloth was cut right through

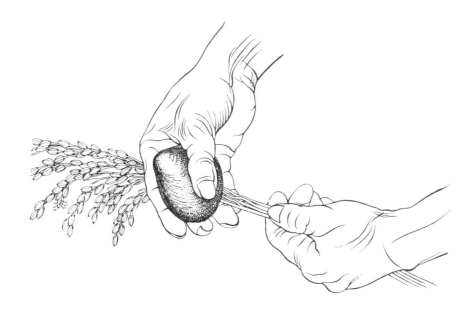

FIG. 79.   The technique used in the grass-scraping experiment

The shell knife was very effective in cutting bark cloth, although resharpening was found to be necessary. A major problem encountered was the difficulty in cutting a straight line along the tapa, and it was usual for a pattern of semi-circular lines to be formed. A microscopic examination of the knife revealed wear on the margins of the edge, but very little wear higher up the blade. Deep striations left by the grinding stone had been rounded on the edge margins, and a distinctive gloss was formed. On the ventral surface, one could clearly see this glossy finish, most noticeable towards the lower face. The major zone of wear was the ventral edge margin and the entire dorsal face (Fig. 85).

Experiment 7: processing fish

Four shell knives were used in this experiment. Seven specimens of Moki (*Latridopsis ciliaris*) were obtained for this experiment. The first shell was used to scale, gut and tail one fish, which was 28 cm long. It worked very efficiently. During the gutting and tailing operations, the shell knife was used in a sawing motion, while in scaling, the blade itself was pressed flat to the side of the fish, and moved in the direction of the operator. A great deal of striation damage was observed

FIG. 80.   S.E.M. photograph taken of the wear patterns produced in the grass-scraping experiments

on this example. Striations consisted of two types, first those moving at 45° from the edge, and secondly, those moving at 120° from the edge. These markings formed a criss-cross pattern, and ranged from very deep gouges, to smaller finer scratches. A scalar scar on the blade's edge was also observed, probably caused by the hardness of the fish bone, especially the tail bone. No polish was observed.

The second shell was used to tail, gut and scale two fish, the first of which was 25.5 cm and the second, 32 cm long. The wear patterns on this blade were very similar to those of the first, despite the fact that it was used to do twice the work. Instead of the criss-crossing series of striations along the whole edge, the second shell possessed striations which ran parallel to the edge. They were not deep but very straight and long. Two short (c 5 cm) semi-circular striations were also observed, beginning parallel to the edge and curving to a position at 90° to the blade. No polishing was observed. The edge was considerably rounded, and it was noted that, during work on the second fish, the degree of sharpness had diminished considerably. Extra pressure was applied, and this fractured the knife.

The third shell was used for scaling three fish, and it was very effective. Two different areas of wear were formed. On the right face, a criss-cross formation of striations was present, but on the rest of the face the effect of the scaling had smoothed the surface. There were no new striations

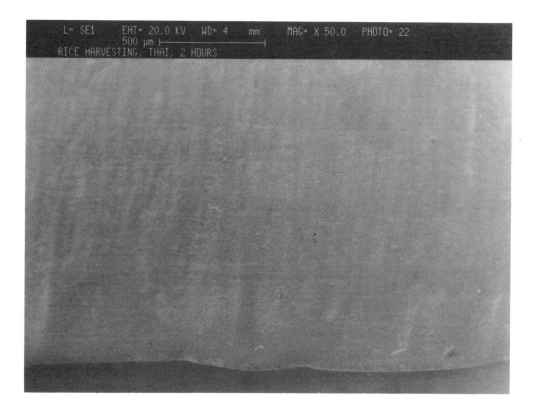

FIG. 81.   S.E.M. photograph taken of the wear patterns produced in the rice-harvesting experiments. This example was used for 2 hours

here, and the scars remaining from the effects of the grinding stone had been rounded and softened. A certain degree of polish was in evidence and would probably increase with further usage.

A fourth knife was used to gut three fish. Once again, it proved effective. Like shell number 2, striations could be seen running parallel to the edge, and close to the blade (*c* 1–2 mm), indicative of a sawing movement. The striations formed during grinding remained, though they were not as coarse. Cutting efficiency declined during the course of the experiment, and this was reflected in the edge, which was rounded and blunt. The blade was not polished in any way. The S.E.M. photographs illustrate the types of wear pattern formed. In Figs. 86 and 87 one can clearly see the characteristic parallel and criss-cross striations.

Experiment 8: cutting hair

A shell was used for cutting head hair over a 25-minute period. During the course of the experiment 565 strokes were counted. The shell was used in a sawing motion. A great deal of pressure was needed, and the hairs had to be held taut to enable the shell to cut at all. It was tedious for the operator and painful for the person whose hair was being cut. Nevertheless, the shell did cut hair, albeit slowly, and we must seriously consider depilation as a possible factor for prehistoric

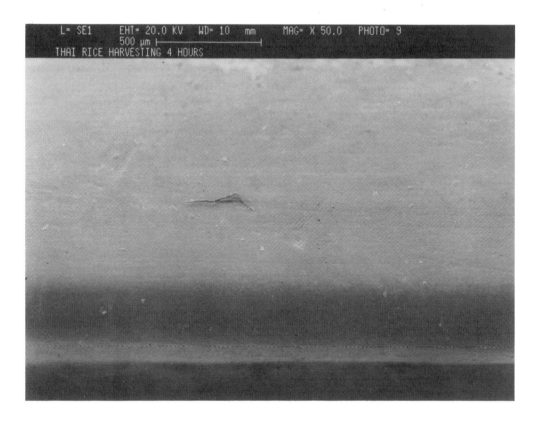

FIG. 82.   S.E.M. photograph taken of the wear patterns produced in the rice harvesting experiments, this example was used for 4 hours

usage. An examination of the wear patterns revealed very little damage. The deep, coarse striations formed from grinding still remained on most of the blade's surface. On the lower edge however, some glossy, reflective sheen was evident, some small striations running parallel to the edge were also noted, though none rivalled those on the shell used to incise lines on clay.

Experiment 9: duplicating decorations on pottery from Khok Phanom Di

It was a distinct possibility that shells may have been used to decorate and mark pots, because a number of the vessels discovered at the site were incised with straight lines. A sample of clay from Khok Phanom Di was used in this experiment. Water was added to the clay to soften the material, then it was spread out over a wooden board, and left to harden. According to Vincent (pers. comm.), the decoration of pots is undertaken when the clay is leather hard. A ground fresh water mussel was used to incise 60 lines in the clay. Each stroke was approximately 40 mm long and the method used was a sawing movement. A microscopic examination of the cutting blade revealed that the action had smoothed the area adjacent to the edge. This zone was more worn than

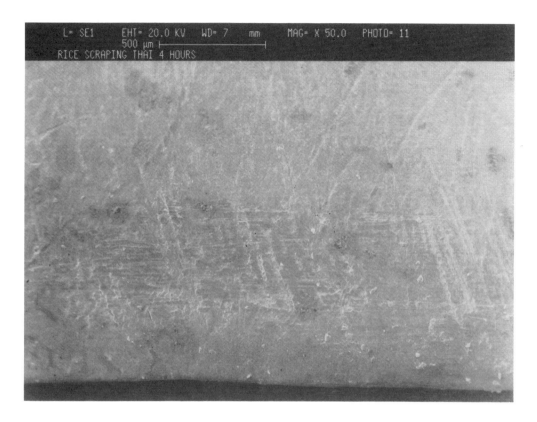

FIG. 83.   S.E.M. photograph taken of the wear patterns produced in the rice-scraping experiments. This example was used for four hours

any seen previously in these experiments. Fine, long striations, running parallel to the edge, were visible along the blade. This area was no more than 1 mm wide and was polished to a dark sheen (Fig. 90). The shell knife was effective enough and, although the clay was perhaps a little too hard, it still incised adequately.

Experiment 10: cutting cooked meat

A shell knife was used for 25 minutes on a quantity of cooked beef. (Bovid bones and the remains of water buffalo (*Bubalus bubalis*) were found at the site). The length of each stroke was approximately 6-8 cm, in a sawing motion, in the same manner as a carving knife. The shell was very effective, easily cutting the meat, and maintaining its sharpness throughout. Approximately 150 cuts were made, each consisting of between 1 and 5 strokes.

The cutting surface was smoothed and the cutting edge was greatly modified from the formerly deep, coarse ground surface which resulted from the initial grinding of the concave cutting edge. The edge was very reflective (much more so than that on the knife used to cut raw meat). There

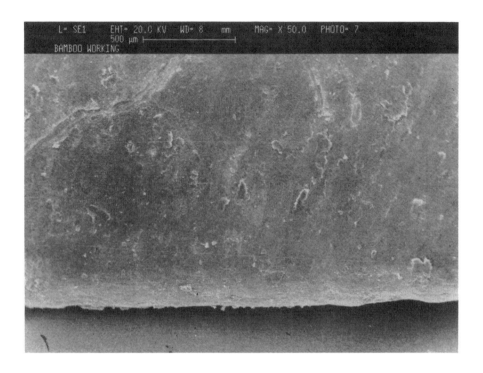

FIG. 84.   S.E.M. photograph of the blade of an experimental shell knife used to work bamboo

were a small number of parallel striations, but in general there were few marks, perhaps indicative of the soft nature of the meat. Very little edge damage was evident and the surface looked slightly worn.

Experiment 11: cutting raw meat

A sharpened shell was used in an attempt to cut raw meat. The experiment lasted 20 minutes, and 120 cuts were counted consisting of 5-6 strokes each. Like the previous experiment, the shell worked very efficiently and the same technique was used. The angle of the working edge was kept constant at the point where cutting efficiency was highest. It was found that this occurred when the angle between the meat surface and the blade was approximately 45°.

The wear patterns on the blade were observed through a microscope at x20 magnification. The striations formed as a result of grinding on the sandstone block were a great deal more rounded. On the left face of the blade there were a number of striations running parallel to the edge, i.e. directionally at right-angles to the original scars. There were also semi-lunar scars which began on the edge itself and curved backwards to a position parallel to the edge. This type of wear pattern

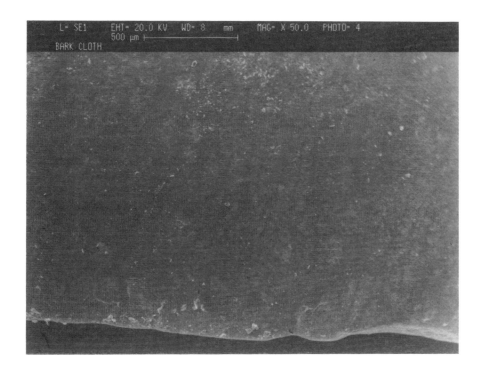

FIG. 85.   S.E.M. photograph showing the wear patterns resulting from the cutting of bark cloth

does not correlate with those found on the prehistoric shell artefacts, in which one usually finds a sheen, or glossy effect on the blade. The shell used to cut raw meat exhibited a dull finish and scars and striations that differed markedly from the Khok Phanom Di shell wear.

Experiment 12: peeling taro

It is possible that the prehistoric inhabitants of the site, having access as they did to freshwater swamps, might have consumed tubers such as taro. Three taro were peeled and scraped with a ground shell for approximately 20 minutes. The tool was most effective, cutting the soft material and showing no signs of blunting. Microscopic examination of the shell revealed that an overall smoothing of the original striations had occurred, the coarse gouges had been rounded and softened and the blade seemed shiny. The edge possessed additional striations, however, running from right to left at a 45°angle on the right edge. This may have been formed as a result of the wrist motion used to lever off pieces of taro (Fig. 91). It is possible that taro were not peeled in a hardened form such as they were in this experiment. In Polynesia, for example, the taro tubers are commonly peeled when soft and directly from the ground. They are then beaten into a pulp and stored. The

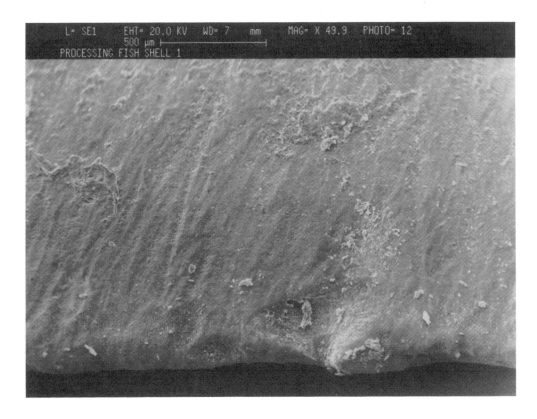

FIG. 86.   S.E.M. photograph of the wear patterns produced when scaling, gutting and tailing one Moki specimen (*Latridopsis ciliaris*)

features observed during the course of the experiments described above were collated in Table 34.

BLIND TESTS

As outlined above, the paucity of available evidence on shell microwear means that stone microwear methodology assumes great importance. A study of the relevant literature led to the choice of Hurcombe's (1988) methodology, on a slightly modified basis, for the procedure of blind tests. This procedure is the acid test for the validity of identifying the use or uses to which the shell knives may have been put. Duplicate experiments were undertaken by another party, and the author then attempted to identify tool function from the wear patterns. If successful, this experiment will show that it is possible to identify variation in patterns of wear and that, by comparing prehistoric shell tools with modern equivalents, we may be able to assess the probable uses of these tools in prehistory. The modified version of Hurcombe's (1988) methodology is listed below; it is essentially a means for defining and recording some of the surface alterations that are termed microwear traces.

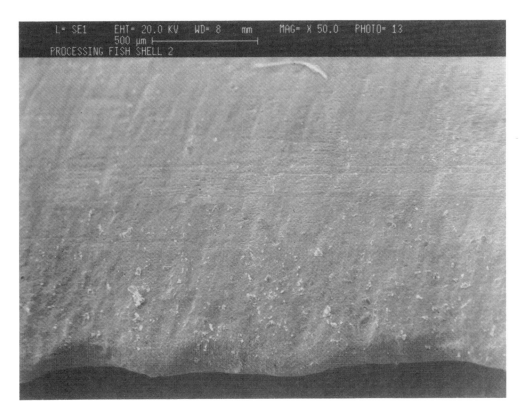

FIG. 87. S.E.M. photograph of the wear patterns produced when scaling, gutting and tailing two Moki specimens (*Latridopsis ciliaris*)

1. Polish variables

- Polish brightness (a) intense (b) bright (c) dull

- Polish texture (a) very smooth (b) smooth (c) matt

- Distinctiveness of the altered surface from the unaltered (a) very distinct (b) distinct (c) merging gradually (d) almost imperceptible gradation

- Predominant area of polishing (a) central dorsal face (b) central ventral face (c) entire dorsal face (d) entire ventral face (e) edge ridge

2. Striation variables

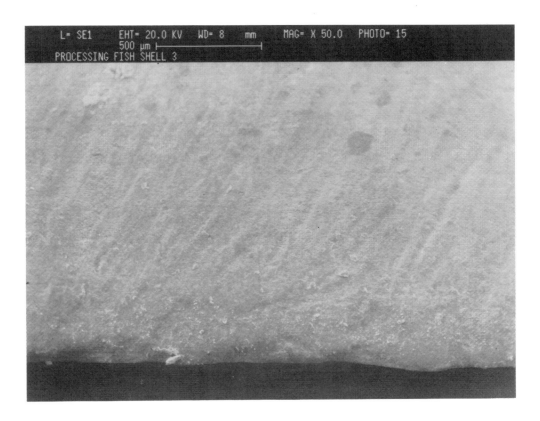

FIG. 88.   S.E.M. photograph taken of the wear patterns produced when scaling three Moki specimens (*Latridopsis ciliaris*)

- Striation depth (estimated): shallow (width greater than depth) deep (depth greater than width)

- Predominant striation orientation in relation to edge axis: parallel; perpendicular; crossed diagonals; one diagonal

- Presence of microscopic flaking or crushing: a great deal; some; none

The following experimental shells were included in the blind tests on the grounds of their effectiveness. Others, used previously for such functions as cutting hair and bark cloth were rejected for blind testing because it was deemed highly unlikely that shells had been used on these materials in prehistory.

1. Harvesting grasses.

2. Cutting cooked meat

3. Incising marks on pottery

FIG. 89.   S.E.M. photograph taken of the wear patterns produced when gutting three Moki specimens (*Latridopsis ciliaris*)

4. Processing fish

5. Grass scraping

Experimental shells and a microscope (x10 and x20 magnification) were used in the blind testing. No SEM images were used. Each shell was examined and assigned a use type. It was found that the knife used to gut, tail and scale two fish was easily recognised on the basis of the extensive flaking on the cutting edge, and the many clear striations along the worked surface. The implements used to incise clay and scrape grass were also identified with little difficulty. It was found less easy, however, to distinguish with confidence between the knives which had been used for grass harvesting and cutting cooked meat. There was a gloss present on both which made it difficult to set them apart with confidence and they were incorrectly identified. According to Keeley (pers. comm.)[†], the problem which led to this misidentification could have been avoided if all samples, both prehistoric and modern, had been cleaned uniformly prior to analysis. The micro-surfaces resulting from the two types of use were quite different, the uncertainty centred on the 'gloss' or

---

[†]The author is most grateful to Professor L.H. Keeley for his helpful comments on a draft of this chapter

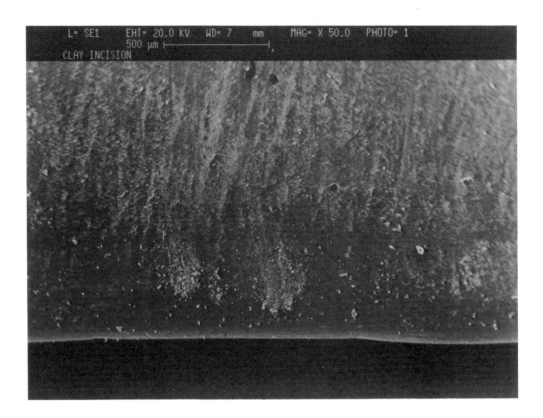

FIG. 90.   S.E.M. photograph taken of the wear patterns produced in incising clay

'sheen' dominating both blades. The sheen on the meat cutting implement is likely to have been protein residue, while the gloss found on the grass harvesting tool was probably due either to deposited plant opal silica or to fine abrasion from it (Keeley, pers. comm.). Cleaning with weak solvents or detergent water would have removed the former and made differentiation between the two simpler.

The blind testing of the knives, then, was partially successful. The shell knives used for scraping grass, incising clay and processing fish were correctly ascribed to their experimental uses. The shell knives used for cutting meat and harvesting grass were incorrectly identified, that used on meat being identified as a grass harvesting implement and vice-versa.

Despite this result, it is suggested that there is a reasonable likelihood of a correct conclusion, with two reservations. The first is that it is difficult, at least on the basis of single samples, to distinguish between cutting meat and scraping grasses. The major reason for this is inadequate cleaning procedures, since there is ample evidence to distinguish the two on the basis of microwear alone. The second is that any further pursuit of this aspect of the research will necessarily entail larger numbers of knives in the blind-testing procedure and the use also of SEM photographs, which are able to identify microwear traces more clearly.

FIG. 91.   S.E.M. photograph taken of the wear patterns produced in peeling taro

CONCLUSIONS

The modern experiments have permitted the elimination of a number of possible uses to which the prehistoric knives could be been put. Relevant information is summarised in table 34. All experimental shells which possessed striations which ran parallel to the edge, those used for scaling three fish, gutting three fish, cutting hair, incising clay, cutting cooked meat and processing one fish, were rejected. Similarly, those exhibiting deep and coarse striations, such as the shells used to scrape hides, scale, gut and tail two fish and cut raw meat were deemed to be highly unlikely alternatives. The predominant area of polishing on prehistoric shells was the central dorsal zone and the majority of experimental wear patterns differed in this respect. Most wear occurred on the entire dorsal edge, the only exceptions being the shells used for cutting hair and incising clay (edge ridge-wear predominated), the shell used for grass scraping (central ventral face-wear) and the grass harvesting and wood fashioning shells (central dorsal face). The shells possessing edge ridge-wear were dissimilar to the prehistoric examples, while dorsal edges of the grass-scraping shells were relatively pristine and wear concentrated on the ventral side.

These findings suggest that the most likely material upon which the shell tools were used in prehistory was a grass, and that they were probably used in a cutting rather than a scraping motion.

Certainly the presence of a gloss or sheen has been associated with wear attained from a grass or grass-like material. There is considerable debate concerning the mechanics of 'sickle gloss' and whether it is additive or abrasive (subtractive) in nature. Witthoft (1967) claimed that gloss formed on stone blades was the result of the spread of plant opal, from the phytoliths in the grass. He suggested the substance affects the tool by filling in striations, causing the fluid appearance on polished stone surfaces and concluded that the presence of corn gloss is a clear indicator that the tool was once used on a grass material, for example as a sickle. Implements used on wood also exhibit a certain brightness but lack the filled-in striations and range of polish (Keeley and Newcomer 1977). Others disagree, suggesting polish gloss may be related to the amount of water and fluid contained in the material upon which the tool is used (see Juel-Jensen, 1988). Keeley (pers. comm.) suggests the micro-wear polish may result from silica forming a gel in the combined presence of water and friction.

It is likely that determining the exact reasons for gloss on shell tools will be similarly problematic. Whatever the reason, the experimental and prehistoric shell knives used in the harvesting of grass and rice showed a distinctive sheen, which is probably related to the richness of the silica in the plants which they harvested or cut.

This study has addressed the possible use or uses to which a sample of knives fashioned from freshwater bivalves were put. The possible range of uses was based upon the material recovered from the site. For each possible function, a modern equivalent of the prehistoric artefact was used to judge its usefulness and examine the resulting use-wear. It was found that a series of distinctively different wear patterns resulted, each distinguishable from the other. With one exception, these patterns were able to be identified in a blind test situation. By defining the predominant wear patterns present on the prehistoric artefacts and comparing them with the shells used in experiments, it was possible to determine the most likely prehistoric usage. The material deemed most likely to have created the prehistoric wear patterns was rice. This conclusion was supported by the amount of rice found in the site, and the fact that, in a sample of many hundreds of thousands of bivalves dominated numerically by marine species, those selected for use as knives were of a freshwater mussel adapted to ponds and streams likely to be located near ricefields.

The site is located remote from good sources of stone, and therefore shell was used as a readily available and very important local resource. Within the site, it is notable that the knives are concentrated more in layers where burials are absent, suggesting that a possible domestic activity was being undertaken. On the basis of the palynological evidence presented by Maloney, it seems likely that the ricefields may have been close to the site, while McKenzie has identified some freshwater ostracodes in the site deposits which are adapted to conditions of freshwater or slightly saline ricefields. In association with these knives, we can also point to leucogranite hoes and grinding stones as being part of an assemblage of artefacts devoted to the cultivation, harvesting and processing of rice. The importance of resharpening blades was well attested in all the experiments carried out in this project.

Hodges (1964) has suggested that the working of shell, perhaps because of its normally fragile nature, is seldom of great interest to the archaeologist. Data on shell knives from other prehistoric Southeast Asian sites are so rare as to be virtually non-existent. There is, however, some evidence for harvesting using metal implements, for example, the bronze sickles from Go Mun

a. L. 10:7 cat. 2959

b. L. 9:7 cat. 2920

c. L. 9:6 cat. 2917

d. L. 9:3 cat. 3136

e. L. 9:5 cat. 3179

f. L. 9:3 cat. 3092

0   1   2   3   4   5 CM

FIG. 92.   The shell knives

(Ha Van Phung and Nguyen Duy Ty, 1982) and O Pie Can (Lévy, 1943) and the iron examples from Ban Na Di (Higham, 1988). There are also some relevant archaeological and ethnographical references that describe a variety of tools similar to the Khok Phanom Di examples. Moszkowski (1908) noted, for example, that in Sumatra, shell harvesting knives were included among objects assembled for the harvesting ceremony, adding that prior to the development of iron knives, shell was the material most commonly employed for harvesting knives. Colani (1940) recognised several types of harvesting knife in Southeast Asia, made from bamboo, iron and shell. She noted that the use of such knives was more prevalent than the use of a sickle or scythe, because the knife can be concealed in the hand and thus does not offend the rice spirit. Skeat (1900) has also referred to the ritual association between the tool and rice amongst the Batak, where the harvesters believed the rice grains were not frightened by the sight of the knife as opposed to a larger implement. It seems that the perpetuation of this belief may have contributed significantly to the long continuation in the usage of such knives in many regions. Another major advantage in using such a tool, according to Colani, is that it is ideal for harvesting crops which ripen unevenly. Bray (1984) has described how the farmer can cut individual heads with a knife (impossible with a sickle), selecting those grains that are ready to be harvested. Since the stem is cut just below the ear, the farmer does not need to stoop so low, and straw left in the field may be used for stock fodder, or burned. Finally, and most importantly, the use of the harvesting knife, while enabling the harvest of individual ears, also encourages the individual examination of each head, and thus facilitates the propagation and selection of new strains.

There is evidence for the extensive use of knives and sickles in Northern China as early as 6500-5000 B.C. at the site of Peiligang and its associated pre-Yangshao cultures. According to Chang (1986), polished and semi-polished stone sickle knives were found, shell being an important material for agricultural knives. The assemblage indicated that the inhabitants habitually harvested plants. Shell knives and sickles were also found at sites of the Longshan and Dawenkou cultures of Northern China. These cultures were, of course, primarily concerned with cultivating millet, but knives were also found in the south, where rice was the staple crop. During the Miaodigou culture phase polished semi-lunate and sickle-shaped knives were found, indicating to Chang the presence of a more advanced agricultural system. The sole date for this culture is *c* 2415-3015 B.C. (Chang, 1986). Stone and shell knives were also common in the site of Erlitou, and the Erlitou culture (*c* 1800-2100 B.C.). Chang has also described the use of 'semi-lunar and rectangular stone sickles (knives)', as being one of the ten major characteristics of the Chinese Neolithic. He assumes that these implements were used for stalked plants. In the south this was probably rice. At Qianshanyang, the remains of *Oryza indica* and *Oryza japonica* were found in association with rectangular and semi-lunar knives (with holes, probably for the attachment of strings) and sickles.

Grist has described how the knives are used in harvesting:

> Using the small knife, the harvester bends the finger around the stem of the plant, and draws the ear onto the blade, which severs it a few cm below the collar. When a few heads have been cut and retained in the cutting hand, they are transferred to the left hand, until a large enough bunch is obtained. This is then placed in a basket for removal from the field (Grist, 1975:161).

According to Grist, women perform the task of harvesting. Freeman (1955) timed Iban women harvesters in Sarawak severing 40 heads in 30 seconds. Working 10 hours each day, one woman could harvest one ha in 42 days (Grist, 1975). Bray, referring to Chinese material, has noted that the harvesting implement is:

> a small flat knife, often with a curved blade ... held in the palm of the hand, usually between the middle and ring fingers. The heads of grain are cut just below the ear by drawing the stem across the blade with the index finger (Bray, 1984:323).

She also noted that such harvesting knives are still used in many parts of Southeast Asia, in Java, (where they are called *ani-ani* by the local inhabitants), Malaya (*uai* or *ketaman*, in Kelantan), Sarawak (*ketap*), and the Philippines (*yatab*). In parts of Northern China the tool is still used (Bray, 1984). At the Tabon cave site on Palawan island in the Philippines, Fox (1970) found a number of bivalve shells which possessed a high sheen along their edge and were recognised by the Tagbanwa and Pula'wan workers as being rice scrapers.

There is little doubt, then, that the shell knife was and is an extremely useful tool, and widespread in its distribution. There is, however, no known sample as large as that described above. Indeed, apart from ceramics and shell jewellery, these reaping knives are the single most abundant type of artefact found at Khok Phanom Di. The fact that the sample has to be extracted from thousands of unmodified bivalves might help explain why it is that more have not been recognised in the past. A future understanding of rice exploitation in prehistory requires that large samples of shells be rigorously scrutinised.

TABLE 34: *The identifiable features represented on the experimental shell tools, based on the methodology presented by Hurcombe (1988)*

1: POLISH VARIABLES	1	2	3	4	5	6	7	8	9	10	11	12	13	14	15	16
Polish brightness																
• Intense	⊕	⊕				~						⊕			⊕	⊕
• Bright			⊕			~				⊕			⊕	⊕		
•Dull				⊕	⊕	~	⊕	⊕	⊕		⊕					
Polish texture																
• Very smooth		⊕														⊕
• Smooth	⊕				⊕	~		⊕		⊕		⊕		⊕	⊕	
• Matt			⊕	⊕		~	⊕	⊕			⊕		⊕			
Distinctiveness of altered from unaltered surface																
• Very distinct		⊕								⊕					⊕	⊕
• Distinct	⊕				⊕	⊕	⊕		⊕				⊕	⊕		
• Merging gradually			⊕	⊕				⊕		⊕		⊕				
• Almost imperceptible gradation																
Predominant area of polishing																
• Central dorsal face	⊕	⊕	⊕													
• Central ventral face														⊕		
• Entire dorsal face				⊕	⊕	⊕	⊕	⊕	⊕			⊕	⊕		⊕	⊕
• Entire Ventral face																
• Edge ridge										⊕	⊕					
2: STRIATION VARIABLES	1	2	3	4	5	6	7	8	9	10	11	12	13	14	15	16
Striation depth																
• Shallow	⊕	⊕	⊕		⊕			⊕				⊕		~	~	~
• Deep				⊕		⊕	⊕		⊕	⊕	⊕		⊕	~	~	~
Predominant striation orientation in relation to edge axis																
• Parallel						⊕		⊕	⊕	⊕	⊕	⊕	⊕			
• Perpendicular	⊕	⊕	⊕		⊕			⊕	⊕	⊕						
• Crossed diagonals						⊕										
• One diagonal																
• Microscopic flaking			⊕	⊕		⊕	⊕									
• A great deal																
• None														⊕	⊕	⊕

⊕: present, ~: not applicable or observable

1: Harvesting grass for 2 hours, 2: Harvesting grass for 3 hours, 3: Fashioning bamboo, 4: Scraping hide, 5: Cutting bark cloth, 6: Processing 1 fish, 7: Processing 2 fishes, 8: Scaling 3 fishes, 9: Gutting 3 fishes, 10: Cutting human hair, 11: Incising clay, 12: Cutting cooked mead, 13; Cutting raw meat, 14: Scraping rice and grass, 15: Rice harvesting for two hours, 16: Rice harvesting for 4 hours

TABLE 35: *The dimensions of shell sickles*

Context	Cat. no.	Width	Width of cutting edge	Context	Cat. no.	Width	Width of cutting edge
10:10	2879	61.1	29.5	10:7	2959	51.0	42.7
10:4	2847	52.9	35.7	10:4	2876	47.7	42.4
10:3	3166	50.0	30.3	10:3	2980	49.3	21.5
10:1	3126	51.1	35.2	10:1	3000	50.6	29.7
9:7	2983	42.0	32.8	9:7	3081	43.8	22.8
9:6	2942	45.7	31.3	9:6	2917	53.2	42.5
9:6	2836	47.3	33.6	9:6	3193	47.7	33.9
9:6	3006	44.6	27.2	9:6	3195	44.6	29.8
9:6	3192	42.4	28.2	9:6	3031	48.5	30.7
9:6	3191	45.1	30.1	9:6	2871	39.0	11.9
9:6	3007	43.4	18.7	9:5	3177	55.1	35.0
9:5	3179	58.3	46.1	9:4	3104	34.2	18.3
9:4	3070	46.8	23.9	9:4	1427	51.0	38.6
9:3	2865	35.9	20.7	9:3	3094	45.2	29.4
9:3	2821	50.0	22.7	9:3	3092	62.6	43.9
9:3	3139	52.6	29.7	9:3	3117	38.9	36.3
9:2	3156	48.0	30.1	9:2	3052	49.3	36.3
9:2	2817	48.1	19.3	9:2	3051	45.9	40.9
9:2	3152	46.6	28.7	9:2	2824	40.6	23.2
9:2	3154	48.3	42.6	9:2	2828	43.5	25.8
9:2	2986	48.4	30.5	9:1	3032	49.0	25.4
9:1	2851	48.1	35.9	9:1	3128	48.6	28.4
8:7	3084	36.2	19.9	8:7	2838	63.1	43.4
8:7	2894	52.2	28.6	8:7	3212	44.7	27.0
8:7	2992	37.2	31.3	8:7	3211	53.2	38.2
8:7	3042	47.7	31.4	8:7	3213	38.6	27.1
8:6	3036	41.6	17.0	8:6	3089	46.6	36.4
8:6	2837	50.9	40.9	8:5	3072	41.2	17.6
8:5	2867	38.2	21.5	8:5	3074	40.8	20.3
8:5	2940	43.0	24.7	8:5	2878	54.0	44.3
8:4	2985	50.3	24.5	8:4	2855	42.2	24.2
8:4	2979	44.6	40.5	8:4	2853	51.8	21.6
8:3	2841	43.5	38.4	8:3	3174	50.6	31.1
8:3	3163	43.3	21.3	8:3	3025	51.4	33.2
8:2	2896	48.9	37.5	8:1	3096	42.1	31.6
7:7	2961	55.0	30.8	7:7	3120	43.9	20.9
7:6	2862	45.2	35.4	7:5	2863	43.9	25.0
7:5	3221	41.8	11.8	7:5	3122	52.6	35.8
7:2	3180	48.6	41.6	7:2	2953	62.2	45.7
7:2	2900	53.2	31.2				

VI. MISCELLANEOUS SHELL ARTEFACTS

C. F. W. Higham

WORKED SHELL OF THE GENUS *PINCTADA*

THIS is the only example of the large *Pinctada* sp. in the site (Fig. 93). It comes from 10:3 (cat. 3336). It has been worked by grooving and splitting along one side, forming a straight, probably ground surface. An adjacent side has been worn or modified to a sharp edge. The nacreous surface of the shell, however, reveals neither grinding nor use striations.

WORKED SHELL OF THE GENUS *NAUTILUS*

There is one specimen of this genus represented in the site (burial 72, cat. 1365). Mason has identified it as *Nautilus pompilius* and it was found on the lower left arm of B72, an adult male in cluster C, mortuary phase 3 (Fig. 93). This deep-water species is not known in the Gulf of Siam, and probably arrived in the vicinity of Khok Phanom Di via tidal currents. This suggestion is supported by the presence of two polychaete worm casts on the shell's interior, and two adhering members of the gastropod family Vermetidae. These would have colonised the shell as it floated.

The shell itself has been modified by the cutting of a scalloped edge along the right lateral adapertural wall. These edges have been worn smooth. There is one complete and one broken hole along the scalloped edge, suggesting that the shell had been suspended. The larger of the two, with a diameter of 9 mm, has fractured. The smaller has a diameter of only 1.5 mm. Such suspension, presumably on the person, could also account for the wear gloss found on the vermetid gastropods, and on the surface of the shell itself. Numerous small striations also suggest that the surface had suffered abrasive contact during wear.

THE WORKED EXAMPLES OF *OLIVA* SP.

Four of the five specimens of this genus have been worked by the removal of the top of the spire apex (Fig. 93). In the case of cat. 1208 (layer 10:3), the hole is circular, with a diameter of 6 mm. The edges of the hole are worn to a smooth and glossy sheen. The hole in cat. 1168, layer 10:1, is 2.8 mm across and was neatly cut and rounded. Striations which reflect preparation of the perforation are visible in the case of cat. 732 (layer 7:1), where the hole has a diameter of 4.5 mm. No such striations are in evidence for cat. 1065, also from 7.1. Rather, the surface is polished, probably through use. The perforation in this case is 4.5 mm.

No use can be ascribed with confidence to these four specimens. The most likely interpretation is that they were threaded as beads. This would account for the polish present round the perforation.

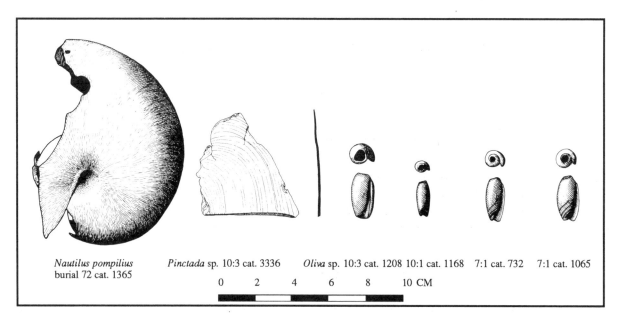

Nautilus pompilius
burial 72 cat. 1365

Pinctada sp. 10:3 cat. 3336

Oliva sp. 10:3 cat. 1208 10:1 cat. 1168   7:1 cat. 732   7:1 cat. 1065

0   2   4   6   8   10 CM

FIG. 93.   Worked shell of the genus *Pinctada*, *Oliva* and *Nautilus pompilius*

THE SHELL SPOKESHAVES

A number of robust bivalve shells revealed major modification through use. The outer surface reveals modification to level the ribs, while the ventral surface usually has a marked concavity or worn segment caused through repetitive contact with a medium being worked. The general direction of the wear marks is at right-angles to the ventral surface, suggesting that the shell implement was moved along the length of the object under modification (Fig. 94).

The individual items are as follows:

- 10:18 cat. 3298 *Polymesoda erosa* (Fig. 94l). This specimen has a concavity along the ventral margin *c* 30mm long. Use has resulted in a clear facet, the surface of which is smooth and polished, and bears striations running at 90° to the edge. A section of this worked edge fractured in antiquity, but use continued and the break has been smoothed over striae partially obliterated by use. These reach back over about 10 mm of the outer surface. The interior of the shell has a wear-gloss corresponding to the use facet on the exterior, but there are no matching striations, suggesting that the abrasive contact with the implement being modified was confined to the outside. This artefact was fashioned from an adult valve with a maximum width of 69 mm.

- 10:22 cat. 1812 *Anadara uropigimelana*. The outer surface of this bivalve bears striations over virtually the whole surface. These criss-cross each other, but trend at an angle of 90° to the edge of the shell. Vestiges of a concave, worn facet survive, but breakage in antiquity removed further information on the working surface. Certainly, part of the dorsal surface of the shell has been worn smooth, blurring some of the striations.

- 10:21 cat. 3299 *Anadara secticostata* (Fig. 94k). The entire exterior surface including the umbo has been ground to smooth and level the ribs. Grinding striations crossing each other at wide angles are visible. The exterior surface bears a concave depression, on the outer surface of which use-striae run back at right-angles over a distance of 3 mm. At least six small flakes of shell were detached from the working edge, but subsequent use partially obliterated these and covered them with striations and a wear gloss. Although the interior surface of the concave worked area has a gloss, there are no working striations corresponding to those on the exterior. The shell has a width of 58.2 mm, of which the concave working surface covers *c* 38.5 mm.

- 10:20 cat. 3300 *Meretrix lusoria*. The exterior surface is almost entirely covered by cross-hatched striations. Only within 3–4 mm of the worked surface do these follow a more consistent, parallel pattern which lies at right-angles to the outer edge of the valve. These have not formed a concavity. The parallel striations have formed a glossy, reflective surface over a width of 53 mm. The total width of the valve is 56.8 mm. No striations are visible on the interior surface, but this too has a smoothed, reflective surface along the outer rim.

- 10:20 cat. 1848 *Anadara uropigimelana*. The ribs on the dorsal surface of this specimen have been worn down both by some form of grinding, which has left surface striations, and then by smoothing or polishing after a medium was repeatedly passed over its surface. The edge of the shell has also been worn through scratching and polishing. Fracturing to most of this edge, however, makes it impossible to identify the extent to which it has been worn to the point that a facet was formed.

- 10:19 cat. 3301 *Anadara uropigimelana* (Fig.94d). This shell has a broad concavity, *c* 52 mm wide, along the surface of which are numerous areas where small chips have been removed during use. These have been smoothed over with subsequent wear. The outer surface of the shell along the working surface has numerous parallel striations lying at a 90° angle to the surface itself. The interior of the same edge is polished but has no similar striations. Apart from the working surface, the outer surface including the umbo is covered by numerous striations lying at angles to each other which probably result from the smoothing of the surface with a grinding stone. The shell has a width of 68 mm.

- 10:19 cat. 3302 *Anadara* sp. An almost straight working facet lies along part of the ventral margin of this specimen, which lacks the concavity of most of this class of artefact. This may reflect a brief period of use. Parallel striations run along the outer surface of this facet, disposed at right-angles to its long axis. Most of the shell has been corroded and the original surface is lost. Consequently, the extent to which it was shaped cannot be determined. The working facet is 34.5 mm wide, against a total shell width of 67 mm.

- 10:16 cat. 1730 *Anadara uropigimelana*. The top of this specimen bears striations and a marked gloss over the surface, the striations trending increasingly towards a parallel configuration 90° to the edge of the shell. Here, there is a marked sheen and worn, slightly concave facet. There are further striations along this working edge, but few progress onto the underside of the shell.

- 10:15 cat. 3303 *Anadara secticostata* (Fig. 94i). This artefact has faint striations over the exterior surface and a polish, associated with dense, parallel striations along a slightly concave working surface. No such striations are found along the interior surface. It is not possible to measure the length of the working surface due to breakage in antiquity. The valve itself was at least 64 mm wide.

- 10:15 cat. 3311 *Anadara* sp. (Fig. 94b). This fragment has all the hallmarks of this group, with a concavity on the outer edge bearing striations at an angle of 90° to the long axis of the shell.

- 10:12 cat. 3304 *Anadara secticostata*. Only part of this specimen survives. The concave worked surface is *c* 25 mm across, and bears a marked sheen with parallel striations along the outer surface. The surviving part of the exterior surface of the shell has cross-hatched striations.

- 10:9 cat. 3305 *Anadara secticostata* (Fig. 94g). This fragment of shell has the hallmarks of this class of artefact: cross-hatched striations on the outer surface and a glossy sheen associated with parallel striations on the surviving section of the working edge.

- 10:9 cat. 3308 *Anadara secticostata* (Fig. 94j). This is the best-preserved specimen in this class of artefact. The concave area which reveals concentrated working is 29 mm wide, and wear has formed a depression *c* 9-10 mm deep. The outer surface of this concavity is worn smooth, has a marked surface sheen and parallel striations. This smoothed surface extends 10 mm back from the working edge. No corresponding wear marks are seen on the interior. The rest of the outside surface is covered with cross-hatched striations and the shell is smooth and worn to the touch.

- 10:7 feature 29 cat. 1437 *Anadara uropigimelana*. This specimen has striations and polishing over its exterior surface, but breakage to the edge makes it impossible to determine the nature of the presumed working facet there.

- 10:5 cat. 3306 *Meretrix lusoria* (Fig. 94e). While there is a band characterised by a sheen and faint striations on the ventral margin of this shell, both sheen and parallel striations running back from the edge concentrate in a concavity formed as a result of restricting most work at this part of the artefact. This concave depression is 17 mm wide, against a total width of the valve of 60 mm. The whole exterior is covered in cross-hatched striations.

- 10:1 cat. 3307 *Anadara uropigimelana* (Fig. 94c). This valve has seen little use, sufficient only to wear a slightly concave facet 23 mm long on the edge. This area is smooth, has a slight sheen, and some superficial striations.

- 9:6 lens 9 cat. 1126 (Fig. 94h). *Anadara uropigimelana*. This is one of the best-preserved artefacts in this assemblage. The outer surface of the shell is covered in striations and parts have been worn so smooth that the ribs have all but disappeared. The central part of the shell has been worn right through. A deep concavity has also developed through wear, about 8 mm of shell having been removed. Along this, the presumed working edge, we encounter clear, deep striations on the outer, bevelled edge. The interior, however, has no such striations.

- 8:3 cat. 2010 *Anadara secticostata* (Fig. 94a). The surface of this fragment of bivalve shell has been ground and is now smooth, with striations along the edge suggesting that it belongs to the class of artefact under review.

- 8:2 cat. 1406 *Anadara secticostata* (Fig. 94f). The valve was broken in half in antiquity. It is unusual in this class of artefact because it has two worked surfaces. Apart from the striations found over the exterior, there is a concave facet on the exterior ventral margin of the shell bearing parallel striae and a sheen which parallels the artefacts described above. This has a number of flake scars which have been smoothed over with subsequent use. There is also a concave surface on the end of the shell which has a further series of faint striations partially obliterated by a smoothed, glossy surface. No corresponding striations are visible on the interior surface of the shell.

- 8:2 cat. 1071. *Anadara uropigimelana.*The working edge of this specimen has been broken, but the outer surface bears numerous criss-cross striations and signs of a wear polish.

- 6:1 cat. 3309 *Polymesoda erosa* (Fig. 94n). This specimen has not survived well, the surface being corroded. However, the ventral margin reveals a characteristic concave depression characteristic of this group of artefacts, and a few faint striations have survived.

- 5 cat. 3310 *Polymesoda erosa* (Fig. 94m). This specimen differs from the rest of this group in two respects. First, the working edge forms a straight rather than a concave surface. Secondly, this edge comprises a clear facet, with a maximum depth of *c* 1 mm. There are two sets of striations along this edge. Most are at 90° to the long axis of the edge, but a series of other striations run almost parallel with this long exis. On the umbo behind this facet, there are the characteristic striations at 90° with the long axis. There is well-polished zone of roughly triangular shape on the umbo behind the facet, formed presumably by the regular passage of the medium being treated. Behind this area, the striations are cross-hatched, and occur in swathes as if imparted with one brush of the grinding stone or other medium employed. The working facet is 40 mm wide, and the shell employed has a width of 70.5 mm.

Most of these valves were ground over the outer surface to create and smooth the surface, and then used in such a way that a concave edge was formed. The wear striations and area of polish are found only on the outer surface, suggesting that the implement was used as a spokeshave.

WORKED SHELL OF THE GENUS *ISOGNOMON*

Two species of this genus are found at Khok Phanom Di, *I. isognomum* and *I. ephippium*. *Isognomon* species are littoral bivalves, usually found in semi-sheltered inlets, byssally attached to large stones (Reid, 1985). They are opportunistic filter feeders, and are very flat. This gives them the advantage of being able to turn side on to the current in rough weather, presenting a minimal surface area to the drag, while in calmer waters they can utilise their large valve surface as a food trap (Reid, 1985). The favoured habitat of *Isognomon* species, according to Reid, is a substrate of gravelly clay, with a surface covering of silt. Siung (1980), studying *I. alatus* (which he described as very similar to *I. ephippium*), noted that it is well-adapted to mangrove swamp conditions. He also stressed that attachment by byssus rather than by cementation makes *Isognomon* easy to handle and harvest.

The shell of *Isognomon* has a smooth surface, to reduce the drag of moving water (Siung, 1980), and Reid (1985) noted that the valve margins often have a concentrically flaky appearance, which he attributed to the repeated withdrawal of the mantle edge during periods of wave action and high turbidity. The interior of *I. alatus* is described by Siung as a pearly, nacreous layer. It could have been locally available. Three out of four specimens have been worked, and the remaining shells are fragmentary and some, at least, of them could also have been modified. There is little doubt, therefore, that *Isognomon* was selected for conversion into artefacts. The following are the specimens which have been modified and bear traces of either use-wear, manufacturing striations or processing into blanks (Fig. 95).

- 10:14 cat. 3313 (Fig. 95f). This specimen has been ground in a straight line to form a bevelled edge at an angle of *c* 35°. The facet so created is 2.5 mm deep. The bevelled edge bears use striations at right-angles to the cutting surface, and similar striations are seen on the reverse side. Two flake scars are present on the edge, and these have been smoothed over with subsequent use. The cutting edge has a width of 21.2 mm.

- 10:13 cat. 3316. The surviving bevelled surface of this shell implement is only 13 mm wide. Faint grinding or use marks are visible on the bevelled facet, but not on the reverse side.

- 10:12 cat. 3317 (Fig. 95d). There is a bevelled edge on this fragment of shell 13 mm long. The majority of the striations on this bevel run parallel with the cutting edge. These occur as swathes overlapping each other, suggesting successive contact with an abrader. The horizontal bands are overlain by single striations at a right-angle to the cutting edge. The latter might be the result of use.

- 10:11 cat. 3314 (Fig. 95m). This specimen has a surviving cutting edge 14.5 mm wide. The adjacent edge comprises a nearly straight line which was probably formed through incising a line and then snapping the shell to create, in effect, a backed blade. The cutting edge is bevelled, and bears faint striations and a sheen which probably reflects use.

- 10:11 cat. 3315 (Fig. 95c). Both the sides on the long axis of this artefact comprise straight cuts or snaps of the shell. A third edge has been worked to a bevelled cutting edge with a width of 19.5 mm. It has use striations on both edges of the cutting surface. These, however, markedly concentrate on the bevelled surface, which may indicate that a grinding stone was used to create or sharpen the bevel, and that the artefact was later used to cut a soft medium which was responsible for smoothing over rather than creating the striations.

- 10:9 cat. 3322 (Fig. 95i). One side of this piece has been ground to a bevelled edge. The uppermost surface of the bevel has a few striations running back from the edge which might be the result of use. Two other edges have been fractured in straight lines, so that the resulting artefact is almost rectangular.

- 10:3 cat. 3323 (Fig. 95g). There is a fashioned bevel along one edge of this piece of shell, which has a few striations on it resulting either from fashioning the bevel or using the artefact as a knife.

- 10:3 cat. 3324 (Fig. 95o). One edge of this artefact has been snapped along a straight line, the opposite edge being bevelled along a slightly convex line, the bevel bearing a few faint striations.

- 9:6 lens 6 cat. 3325. Two edges of this piece reveal the snapped edges, while a third edge has been ground to a bevelled shape, wear or grinding sriations being visible on the edge. This bevelled edge is straight.

In addition to the specimens described above which have been clearly modified and used, there are examples of *Isognomon* shell which have straight or curved edges. These result from deliberate modification, although in the absence of any further grinding or shaping, it seems most likely that they were blanks of this nacreous shell which were not subsequently worked in any way. It seems that the most likely technique employed to effect a break along a predicted line was to incise a line and one side of the shell and snap it along the resulting weakness.

- 10:10 cat. 3318 (Fig. 95a). This specimen has been shaped on two sides to form one concave and one convex contour on opposite sides.

- 10:10 cat. 3319 (Fig. 95h). This piece has been shaped on three sides, one edge being straight and two others convex and concave.

- 10:9 cat. 3320 (Fig. 95n). This is a large section of the shell, which has been cut in a straight line directly through the hinge. There are no signs of subsequent working along the broken surface, supporting the interpretation that these represent blanks of nacreous shell for further manufacture.

- 10:9 cat. 3321 (Fig. 95b). This piece has a curved, concave form and bevelled edge to one side which was formed by grinding.

- 9:6 lens 9 cat. 3327 (Fig. 95k). This specimen was cut directly through the hinge to leave a concave edge. A second cut was made running parallel with the hinge in a straight line, and a third small round piece was removed from the hinge line itself.

Further shaped specimens come from layer 10:10, 10:9 (2), 10:6, 10:4, 10:3 (7), 10:1 (2), 9:7, 9:6 (2) 8:5, (2), 8:4, 5:2.

A very high proportion of the fragments of *Isognomon* shell were worked. Some have bevelled edges and striations suggesting that the implement was used for cutting. Others reveal clear evidence of having been grooved and then snapped so as to create straight lines. These were not subsequently worked, and may represent tabs or blanks of attractive, thin nacreous shell destined for further modification. Most of these concentrate in layer 10.

THE WORKED EXAMPLES OF *POLINICES TUMIDUS* AND *P. CUMINGIANUS*

There are nine specimens of *Polinices tumidus* from the site, and a single example of *P. cumingianus*. All except one of the former have a hole through the side of the shell. *Polinices tumidus* occupies sand bars and sandy beaches, while *P. cumingianus* prefers sandy mud under deep water. Individual specimens are as follows. All are *P. tumidus* except for cat. 3335.

- 10:15 cat. 3328 (Fig.95r). The perforation in this specimen measures 5 by 4 mm. It has jagged edges and clearly was not bored as one process. There is no polish or use-wear round the rim of the hole.

- 10:14 feature 11 cat. 3329 (Fig. 95q). The jagged perforation in this shell measures 4.5 by 4.2 mm. Unlike the previous specimen, there are signs of a sheen round the edge of the hole suggesting that the shell was suspended.

- 10:12 cat. 3330 (Fig. 95p). This specimen has a jagged perforation measuring 10 by 6.1 mm. The edges reveal faint traces of a wear-polish.

- 10:3 cat. 3331 (Fig. 95s). The perforation in this specimen measures 6.5 by 4.5 mm and there is some evidence in the contour of the edge that several holes were bored through the shell in order to create the final aperture. The surface of the shell is also covered by a number of striations, but no pattern is involved.

- 9:7 cat. 3332 (Fig. 95u). The aperture in this shell measures at least 9 mm in length, but breakage in antiquity has removed part of it. It has a width of 6 mm. The edges of the hole have been smoothed and have a gloss from wear.

- 9:6 lens 9 cat. 3333 (Fig. 95t). This specimen has a circular hole with a diameter of 3.5 mm. There are faint striations over the body of the shell, but no particular pattern of alignment.

- 8:4 burial 28 cat. 3334 (Fig. 95w). This shell has fractured across the perforation. It, too, is covered in striations.

- 10:4 cat. 3335 (Fig. 95x). This is the only specimen of *Polinices cumingianus* recovered at Khok Phanom Di.

WORKED SHELL OF THE GENUS *CYPRAEA*

Cowrie shells were almost exclusively found in burials. Six specimens of *Cypraea miliaris* were worked. Two were found with B133 (cat. 1672), and had the upper part of the shell removed. A further such modified specimen came from 7:4 cat. 3344. The other three had holes cut through the anterior and posterior ends of the dorsum. These come from 10:6 feature 21 cat. 3337, 10:3 cat. 1205 (Fig. 95cc) and 8:2 cat. 3343 (Fig. 95bb). There is a hint of smoothing along edges of the holes, and it may well be that the shell was pierced for suspension. Twelve examples of *Cypraea errones* and three of *Cypraea helvola* come from B133, all having had their upper surfaces removed. Two further examples of this species from 10:2 cat 3338 (Fig. 95aa) and 9:7 cat. 3339 have two holes cut through the upper surface, the edges of which appear to have a glossy, worn surface, perhaps as a result of suspension. The same treatment was accorded two specimens of *Cypraea helvola* (B133 cat. 3340, 9:4 lens 7 cat. 3341, Fig. 95z). The only example of *Cypraea onyx* in the site, from layer 10 lens 2 cat. 3342, (Fig. 95y) was also pierced twice on the dorsum for suspension.

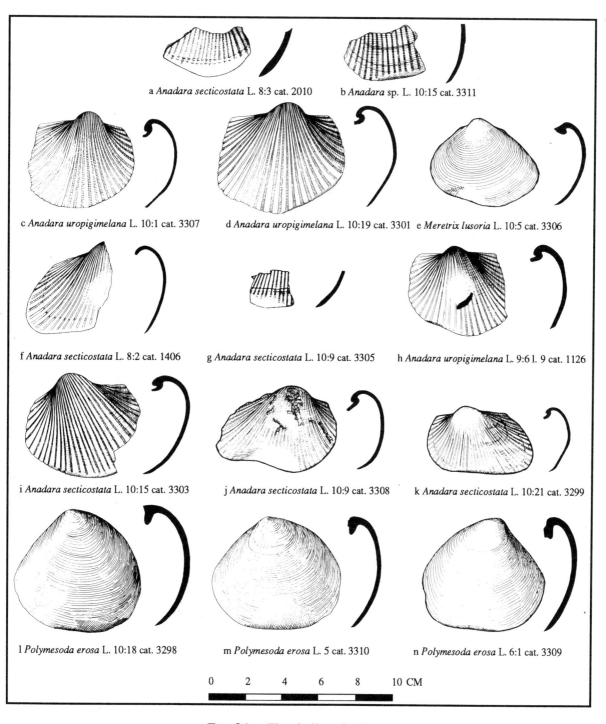

a *Anadara secticostata* L. 8:3 cat. 2010   b *Anadara* sp. L. 10:15 cat. 3311

c *Anadara uropigimelana* L. 10:1 cat. 3307   d *Anadara uropigimelana* L. 10:19 cat. 3301   e *Meretrix lusoria* L. 10:5 cat. 3306

f *Anadara secticostata* L. 8:2 cat. 1406   g *Anadara secticostata* L. 10:9 cat. 3305   h *Anadara uropigimelana* L. 9:6 l. 9 cat. 1126

i *Anadara secticostata* L. 10:15 cat. 3303   j *Anadara secticostata* L. 10:9 cat. 3308   k *Anadara secticostata* L. 10:21 cat. 3299

l *Polymesoda erosa* L. 10:18 cat. 3298   m *Polymesoda erosa* L. 5 cat. 3310   n *Polymesoda erosa* L. 6:1 cat. 3309

0   2   4   6   8   10 CM

FIG. 94.   The shell spokeshaves

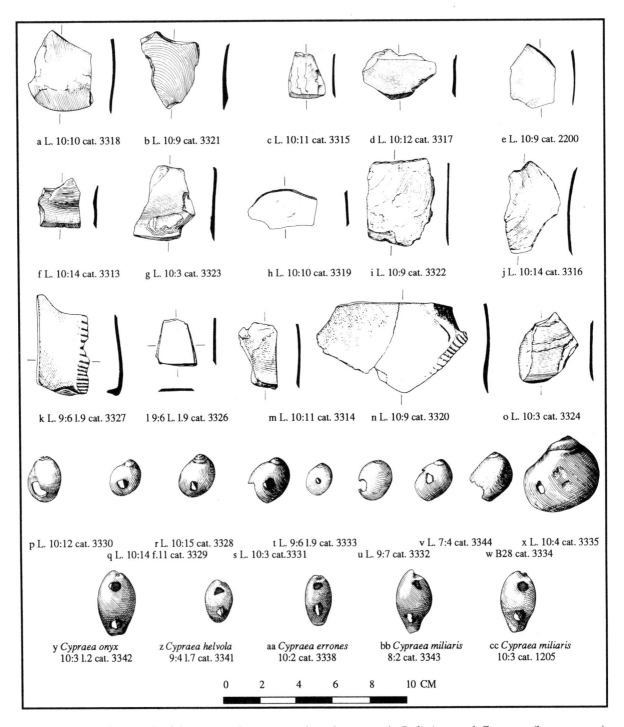

a L. 10:10 cat. 3318   b L. 10:9 cat. 3321   c L. 10:11 cat. 3315   d L. 10:12 cat. 3317   e L. 10:9 cat. 2200

f L. 10:14 cat. 3313   g L. 10:3 cat. 3323   h L. 10:10 cat. 3319   i L. 10:9 cat. 3322   j L. 10:14 cat. 3316

k L. 9:6 1.9 cat. 3327   l 9:6 L. 1.9 cat. 3326   m L. 10:11 cat. 3314   n L. 10:9 cat. 3320   o L. 10:3 cat. 3324

p L. 10:12 cat. 3330   r L. 10:15 cat. 3328   t L. 9:6 1.9 cat. 3333   v L. 7:4 cat. 3344   x L. 10:4 cat. 3335
    q L. 10:14 f.11 cat. 3329   s L. 10:3 cat.3331   u L. 9:7 cat. 3332   w B28 cat. 3334

y *Cypraea onyx*   z *Cypraea helvola*   aa *Cypraea errones*   bb *Cypraea miliaris*   cc *Cypraea miliaris*
10:3 1.2 cat. 3342   9:4 1.7 cat. 3341   10:2 cat. 3338   8:2 cat. 3343   10:3 cat. 1205

0   2   4   6   8   10 CM

FIG. 95.   Worked shell of the genera *Isognomon* (top three rows), *Polinices* and *Cypraea* (bottom row)

VII.   THE WORKED SHELL OF THE GENUS *PLACUNA*

D. M. Higham

INTRODUCTION

THE group of shells to be analysed in this section is dominated by *Placuna placenta*, with the remainder being *Placuna sella*. They take a variety of forms, the most common theme being a shape exhibiting some kind of wear on the edges, resulting either from use or shaping. These artefacts are unusual in that they have not been reported from any other sites of this period. Reports from sites such as Samrong Sen (Mansuy, 1923) and Ban Kao (Sørenson and Hatting, 1967) contain no mention of them, nor of anything like them. None of the artefacts can be ascribed to a particular function, and many, if not all, may never have been finished. The aim of this section is to identify why these shells were worked and suggest what form the finished product took. It will then be possible to provide a working hypothesis as to their use and their significance to the people of Khok Phanom Di.

There are five species in the genus *Placuna*, *P. placenta* being the most common. *P. placenta* and *P. sella* are the species represented at Khok Phanom Di. They are found from the Gulf of Aden, around India and the Malay peninsula to the south coast of China, and along the north coast of Borneo to the Philippines (Yonge, 1977). Their natural habitat is the surface of mud flats, from the mid-tide levels to depths of up to 20 m. Due to their need for a muddy surface, they are often associated with a mangrove-covered coastline, but are not known from a coralline habitat. The ideal environment for *P. placenta* is a mixture of mud and fine sand, and estuaries associated with mangroves (Magsuci *et al.* 1980). *P. placenta* is sessile, although older individuals are possibly capable of maintaining their position by expelling water 'forward' between the valves. This places them at the mercy of wave action, and so they commonly congregate in shallower waters, where they are easily harvested. Young (1980) describes his observation of adult *P. placenta* found piled up in large numbers in water 3–5 m deep following a storm.

The shell of *P. placenta* is extremely flat laterally, with the right valve being slightly concave and the left marginally more convex (Yonge, 1977). They are sub-orbicular, with a straight hinge line. They have no distinct internal layer, so the outer calcareous layer (which has a high organic content) effectively forms the entire substance of the shell (Yonge, 1977). Their final thickness is about 1 mm, and they are very delicate and easily damaged, although readily repaired. Young and medium-sized shells are transparent and usually colourless, but larger specimens become sub-opaque, white and somewhat friable.

In the Philippines, *P. placenta* is an important commercial species, known as *kapis*. It is gathered in the summer months (February–April), by divers who grope for the shellfish with their fingers and toes, then pick them up and place them in bamboo baskets. An average day's work can yield two baskets, containing about 6000 pieces of *kapis* (Magsuci *et al.*, 1980). They are then opened and the meat removed. The meat is a rich source of protein, with 23.3gm of protein in every 100gm of fresh meat, but there is very little in each shell.

223

TABLE 36:   *The distribution of* P. placenta

Layer	Group A	Group B	Group C
10	24	14	65
9	22	7	12
8	14	7	9
7	8	5	10
6	4	-	7
5	2	-	1
4	1	-	-

After the meat is removed, the shells are cleaned by soaking them in fresh water overnight. They are then scraped with a flat piece of metal, or a brush, to produce the desired lustre. The edges are smoothed by rubbing them against a rock or an earthen jar. They are then used for the manufacture of shellcraft products such as lampshades, lanterns, screens, trays, place cards and picture frames. *P. placenta* is considered to be the best of the various shells exported from the Philippines, and commands a high price. Originally, *P. placenta* was collected extensively as a substitute for glass in glazing, and Hornell (1909) has suggested that this use developed in China.

ALTERNATIVE INTERPRETATIONS

These shells may have been collected for food, for conversion into artefacts or for ornament. A combination of these possibilities may also be in question. Before reviewing these alternatives, the shells will be described. There are 216 specimens of *Placuna placenta* and 16 of *Placuna sella*. They were distributed between layers 4 and 10, and were not found in regular association with any particular feature. In no case were they found as grave goods, nor were they regularly associated with hearths, pits or middens.

The first division of the shells into groups was undertaken on a species level. As *P. placenta* was the dominant group numerically, it has provided the bulk of the data, and this will be presented first.

Description of *P. placenta* specimens

The main group comprises *Placuna placenta* shell. On examination of the whole range, a dominant form could be discerned: a shell modified to a semi-lunate shape exhibiting some kind of wear on various parts of the edges. No other recurring form could be identified. Using the degree to which each piece approximated to this form, the *P. placenta* group was further subdivided into those which were clearly of a semi-lunate shape (group A), those which were a close approximation of this (group B) and those which did not seem to exhibit this form at all (group C). Group A comprised 75 samples, group B 33, and group C 104. The distribution of the three groups within the site is set out in Table 36.

Each specimen was examined to ascertain whether it had been worked or was natural. Where necessary, the pieces were cleaned before being examined under the microscope. An ultrasonic cleaner was used, after first establishing that the process would not damage the rather brittle shell. A mixture of one teaspoon of sonate cleaning solution to every litre of warm water was used, and each piece was placed in the ultrasonic cleaner for three minutes, with a further three minutes for heavily encrusted specimens. They were then examined under x15 magnification. Care was taken to avoid excessive handling or abrasion, as they are susceptible to scratches.

The group A pieces were examined first, in an attempt to identify some kind of pattern associated with this shape in terms of size and degrees of working and wearing. First, the width and length of each piece was measured, and the results tabulated and graphed. These can be seen in Table 39 and Figure 96. Next, the edge of each individual was examined under the microscope in order to establish whether it had been cut, cut and worked to produce a smooth edge, snapped or left as natural. Each piece was placed with the shell interior facing upwards, the shorter curve was designated 'A', the longer 'B', the edge to the left 'C' and the edge to the right 'D'. The results of this are set out in Table 37.

TABLE 37:   *Worked* Placuna placenta: *the edges of the group A pieces*

L	Cat.	Side A	Side B	Side C	Side D	L	Cat.	Side A	Side B	Side C	Side D
4:5	629	C-R	C-R	S	S	9:3	1346	C-R	C-R	SC	C or S
4:5	629	C-R	C-R	S	S	8:7	3306	C-R	C-R	C	?
4:5	629	C-R	C-R	S	S	9:4	1369	C-R	C-R	S	S
5:5	2409	C-R	C-R	C	S	9:4	1895	C-R	C-R	C	S or C
5:5	889	C	C	S	S	9:4	1096	C-R	C	S	C
6:1	164	C-R	C-R	S	S	9:4	3307	C-R	C-R	C	C
6:4	1532	C-R	C-SR	S	C	9:6	1176	C-R	C-R	S	S
6:7	713	C-R	C-SR	S	S	9:6	1932	C	C	C	C
7:1	1497	C-R	C-R	S	S	9:6	1499	C-R	C-R	S	S
7:3	1048	C-R	C-SR	S	C-SR	9:6	1140	C-R	C-R	SC	S
7:3	1048	C-R	C-R	C	C-R	9:6	1107	C-R	C-R	C	C
7:3	851	C-R	C-R	S or C	S or C	9:6	1107	C-R	C-R	C	S
7:5	1193	C-R	C-R	S	S	9:7	1575	C-R	C-R	SC	SC
7:5	1193	C-R	C	C	C	9:7	1575	C-R	N	C	C or S
7:6	1007	C-R	C-R	S	C	9:7	1150	C-R	C-R	C	C

Abbreviations: L, layer; C-R, cut and rounded; C, cut; C-SR, cut, semi-rounded; N, normal; SC, scored; S, shaped

Worked Placuna placenta: *the edges of the group A pieces* (cont.)

L	Cat.	Side A	Side B	Side C	Side D	L	Cat.	Side A	Side B	Side C	Side D
7:6	848	C-R	C	C	C	10:1	1958	C-R	C	C	C
7:6	1058	C-R	C-R	?	?	10:1	1195	C-R	C-R	C-R	C
7:8	879	C-R	C-R	S	C or S	10:1	1625	C-R	C-R	C	C
8:2	1476	C-R	C-R	C	S	10:1	1197	C-R	C	C	C
8:3	963	C-R	C-R	SC	S	10:1	1194	C-R	C	C	C
8:3	1564	C-R	C	S	S	10:1	1196	C-R	C	C	C
8:3	1564	C-R	C-SR	SC	C	10:2	1327	C-R	C-R	C	SC
8:3	1083	C-SR	C-SR	SC	SC	10:2	1203	C-R	C-R	C	SC
8:4	1012	C	N	S	S	10:2	1402	C-R	C	C	S
8:4	1173	C-R	C-R	S	C or S	10:2	1402	C-R	C-R	S	S
8:4	1173	C-R	C-R	C	S	10:2	1402	C-R	C	S	S
8:4	955	C-R	C-R	C	C or S	10:3	1694	C-R	C-SR	C	C or S
8:4	993	C-R	C-SR	C or S	C	10:3	1694	C-R	C-SR	C-SR	C-SR
8:4	1080	C-R	C-R	C	S	10:3	1212	C-R	C	C	C
8:6	1226	C-R	C-R	S	S	10:3	1220	C-R	C-R	C	C
8:6	1225	C-R	C-SR	C	S	10:14	2325	C-R	C-R	C	C
8:7	3305	C-R	C-R	C	C or S	10:14	2325	C-R	C-R	C	S
8:7	1305	C-R	C	C	C or S	10:15	2386	C-R	C-R	C	C
8:7	1059	C-R	C-R	C	S	10:16	1733	C-R	C-R	C	C
8:7	1059	C-R	C-SR	C	S	10:17	1423	C-R	C-R	C	C
8:7	1059	C-R	C-R	S	C or S	10:17	1423	C-R	C-R	C	C or S
9:1	1055	C-R	C	S	S	10:18	2447	C-R	C	C	S
9:1	1361	C-R	C-R	C	S	10:18	1770	C-R	C-R	S	S
9:2	1345	C-R	C-R	S	C	10:18	1853	C-R	C-R	C	S or C
9:3	1061	C-R	C-R	C	S	10:19	1839	C-R	C-R	C	C
9:3	1052	C-R	C	S	S	10:19	1839	C-R	C-R	C	C
9:3	1052	C-R	C-R	C	S	10:19	1837	C-R	C-R	S	S
9:3	1770	C	S	S	S	10:19	1837	C-R	C-R	C	SC
9:7	1948	C-R	C	C	C	10:22	1880	C-R	C	C	C
9:7	1134	C-R	C	C	C	10:22	1878	C-R	C-R	C	C
9:7	1160	C	C	C	C	10:19	1837	C or S	C	C	S
9:7	1159	C-R	C-R	C	C	10:25	2563	C-R	C-R	C	C
9:7	1500	C	C	C	C or S	10:25	2563	C-R	C-R	C	C or S
						10:25	2563	C-R	C-R	C	C

Abbreviations: L, layer; C-R, cut and rounded; C, cut; C-SR, cut, semi-rounded; N, normal; SC, scored; S, shaped

Side 'A' seems to have been fairly constantly cut and rounded, with 90.7 per cent of the samples showing this, increasing to 92.8 per cent when those which only exhibit a certain degree of rounding are included. A similar pattern emerges for side 'B', with 85.6 per cent showing some degree of rounding after cutting. A different pattern, however, is revealed by sides 'C' and 'D'. The former was most often cut, without being rounded (56.7 per cent), although a fairly high proportion were snapped (30.9 per cent). The latter was snapped relatively often (39.2 per cent), with 31.9 per cent being cut, and 71.1 per cent being either cut or snapped (which could have been interpreted as having been scored and then snapped).

On the whole, a pattern emerges of the pieces being deliberately cut into this form, and the edges worked in some way to produce a smooth, rounded edge. It is not certain whether this is a function of the method used to cut the shell, or whether the working was completed after cutting by some technique used to produce the smooth finish. Magsuci *et al.* (1980) described a method employed in the Philippines to smooth the cut edges of these shells, involving 'grinding' the edge against a rock, or an earthen jar. During examination of the Khok Phanom Di pieces, it was noted that the edges were often tinted with a darker brown colour – possibly the residue left by this method.

During the examination of the group A pieces, it was noted that fifteen bear deliberately cut notches. These are always on side 'B', that is, the outer edge of the curve. These notches varied in size and number, but always displayed an even wear pattern over the entire notch. The notches were never shaped to a point.

The group B pieces were examined next. All showed some sign of working, with most exhibiting an approximation of the semi-lunate shape. Others were included in this group because they resemble a broken version of this shape. A brief description of each piece is given in Table 38.

These pieces confirm that they represent unfinished or broken specimens of the more complete pieces found in group A. One particularly interesting piece appears to have had a hole drilled through it. The implications of this will be discussed below.

The group C pieces, despite exhibiting no identifiably dominant form, all showed some degree of working. They often consisted of quite large pieces of shell compared to groups 'A' and 'C', and may represent an earlier stage of the manufacturing process. Two samples from this group were found to have holes drilled through them.

TABLE 38: *Worked* Placuna placenta: *the edges of the group B pieces*

Context	Cat.	No. of pieces	Description
6:7	197	1	broken end piece
7:2	1158	3	broken halves
7:2	583	1	plain
7:4	665	1	unfinished
7:5	669	3	rough
8:2	919	1	broken at ends
8:2	1081	4	3 have notches
8:4	993	1	plain
8:5	1693	1	plain
9:1	1775	1	broken
9:2	1803	1	plain
9:2	3087	2	shallow notch
9:4	1875	1	plain
9:5	1845	1	unfinished
9:6	1531	3	fragments
9:6	1174	2	plain
9:7	1565	5	2 with wavy edges
9:7	1565	1	with hole
9:7	1565	2	fragments
10:5	2080	2	rough
10:6	2098	1	large, rough
10:6	1884	1	fragment
10:9	2111	1	large, plain
10:14	2364	1	small, plain
10:15	2386	2	large, rough
10:16	2418	3	1 plain
10:16	2418	2	fragments
10:17	2441	3	1 plain
10:17	2441		2 fragments
10:17	2439	5	2 plain
10:17	2439	3	fragments
10:17	2429	5	fragments
10:18	2450	1	large
10:18	2454	6	5 plain
10:18	2454	1	large, rough
10:19	2473	1	rough
10:25	2563	2	plain

TABLE 39: *The length and width of the* Placuna placenta *group A pieces*

Context	Cat.	No.	Length	Width	Context	Cat.	No.	Length	Width
4:5	629	3	4.5	2.0	9:4	3305	1	5.8	2.2
4:5	629	-	1.7	2.0	9:4	1369	1	6.0	2.7
4:5	629	-	1.8	2.5	9:4	1895	1	8.0	2.6
5:5	2409	1	5.1	2.2	9:4	1096	2	8.5	3.2
5:5	889	1	2.7	1.9	9:4	1096	-	6.8	3.5
6:1	164	1	4.3	1.8	9:6	1176	1	7.9	2.4
6:4	1532	1	6.6	3.5	9:6	1932	1	4.9	2.5
6:7	713	1	6.0	2.3	9:6	1499	1	7.7	1.9
7:1	1497	1	6.1	2.5	9:6	1140	1	5.8	2.3
7:3	1048	2	5.2	2.3	9:6	1107	2	8.4	2.3
7:3	1048	-	3.9	2.0	9:6	1107	-	3.1	3.0
7:3	851	1	5.2	2.2	9:7	1575	2	5.9	2.1
7:5	1193	2	6.1	3.2	9:7	1575	-	4.7	2.0
7:5	1193	-	7.5	2.4	9:7	1150	1	6.7	2.1
7:6	1007	1	4.0	1.3	9:7	1948	1	7.0	2.4
7:6	848	1	7.7	2.1	9:7	1134	1	3.1	1.6
7:6	1058	2	5.3	2.6	9:7	1160	1	5.9	2.3
7:6	1058	-	6.7	1.6	9:7	1159	1	4.8	2.1
7:8	879	1	6.6	1.0	9:7	1500	1	3.8	2.3
8:2	1476	1	4.0	2.2	10:1	1958	1	6.5	3.3
8:3	963	1	4.3	2.6	10:1	1195	1	6.0	2.0
8:3	1564	2	7.0	2.7	10:1	1625	1	7.5	1.6
8:3	1564	-	5.5	3.0	10:1	1197	1	5.0	3.0
8:3	1083	1	7.1	2.7	10:1	1194	-	4.0	2.2
8:4	1012	1	6.8	3.3	10:1	1196	1	6.0	2.3
8:4	1173	2	4.5	1.7	10:2	1327	1	6.8	2.7
8:4	1173	-	2.8	1.8	10:2	1203	1	5.8	2.5
8:4	955	1	8.4	2.3	10:2	1402	3	4.6	2.8
8:4	993	1	5.0	2.5	10:2	1402	-	4.5	3.1
8:4	1080	1	6.1	3.3	10:2	1402	-	7.0	1.5
8:6	1226	1	4.0	1.7	10:3	1694	2	4.0	2.2
8:6	1225	1	5.0	1.9	10:3	1694	-	3.5	2.3

The length and width of the Placuna placenta *group A pieces* (cont.)

Context	Cat.	No.	Length	Width	Context	Cat.	No.	Length	Width
8:7	3306	1	5.4	2.5	10:16	1733	1	6.5	3.0
8:7	1305	1	5.1	2.6	10:17	1423	2	6.5	3.3
8:7	1059	3	8.6	3.0	10:17	1423	-	6.6	2.6
8:7	1059	-	4.7	2.6	10:18	2447	1	4.0	1.3
8:7	1059	-	3.0	3.2	10:18	1770	2	7.6	3.1
9:1	1055	1	5.8	3.0	10:18	1770	-	8.5	3.7
9:1	1361	1	4.0	2.4	10:19	1839	2	6.5	3.3
9:2	1345	1	6.1	2.2	10:19	1839	2	6.0	2.2
9:3	1061	1	6.5	2.6	10:19	1837	3	6.8	3.5
9:3	1052	2	5.5	2.3	10:19	1839	-	7.5	4.0
9:3	1052	-	6.0	3.1	10:19	1837	-	8.8	2.6
9:3	1346	1	6.7	2.6	10:21	1853	1	6.4	2.9
10:3	1212	1	4.9	1.9	10:22	1878	1	5.8	1.9
10:3	1220	1	5.7	2.2	10:23	1880	1	5.9	1.9
10:14	2325	2	5.2	2.0	10:25	2563	2	5.0	2.6
10:14	2325	-	3.5	1.7	10:25	2563	-	5.2	3.0
10:15	2386	1	5.5	3.5					

DESCRIPTION OF THE *PLACUNA SELLA* SPECIMENS

Only sixteen samples of *P. sella* were found. Athough they have all been worked in some way, they do not exhibit a regular shape. Some could be interpreted as approximations of the semi-lunate form seen in so many of the *P. placenta* pieces, but none shows the same degree of completion. On the whole, they appear to be irregularly shaped and roughly cut tabs. Table 40 sets out brief descriptions of these specimens.

DESCRIPTION OF THE INDIVIDUAL ARTEFACTS

As there are too many specimens to describe each individually, the following is a description of the most complete pieces, or those which exhibit characteristics of relevance to this study (Fig. 97). All are *Placuna placenta*.

- 10:23 cat. 1880. This is unique among the group A pieces in that it is the only one that has had a hole drilled through it. The outer edge is quite irregular, with a rather unusual feature being a series of small serrations on either side of one notch.

- 10:19 cat. 1839 (Fig. 97a). A large, regularly-shaped piece. Quite unusual in that it is slightly concave rather than flat, but this can be attributed to the shape of the shell used in its manufacture, and is probably not a deliberate feature.

TABLE 40:   *The provenance of worked* Placuna sella

Context	Cat.	No. of pieces	Description
7:2	1017	1	possible semi-lunate some notching
7:8	821	1	possible semi-lunate rough
8:4	1012	1	possible semi-lunate uneven shape
8:4	1037	1	standard semi-lunate
8:5	1102	2	1 rough semi-lunate 1 notched semi-lunate
8:5	1060	1	rough semi-lunate
8:6	1190	1	rough semi-lunate notched
9:6	1499	1	rough semi-lunate
10:1	1584	2	1 possible semi-lunate 1 semi-lunate fragment
10:7	2131	1	fragment
10:10	2238	1	large slab
10:10	2288	1	no identifiable shape
10:12	2240	1	small fragment
10:12	2239	1	large slab
10:13	2231	1	no identifiable shape
10:16	2418	1	fragment

- 10:18 cat. 1770 (Fig. 97b). An unusually large specimen, rather broad in relation to its length, although this could be explained by the fact that it appears to have been broken off at one end. The interior side of the shell displays a high polish.

- 10:18 cat. 2447. A small, extremely delicate piece. This was probably made from a young shell, as it is very thin, and of an almost translucent quality.

- 10:14 cat. 2325 (Fig. 97c). This sample consists of two pieces, of very similar form. They do not appear to represent two parts of one specimen, however, as one is noticeably wider than the other. Both have an extremely distinctive serration pattern on the outer edge, and their identical pearly sheen suggests that they were manufactured from the same shell.

- 10:13 cat. 1609. The fragility and brittleness of the shell used in the manufacture of this piece has prevented it from being preserved as well as some of the more robust specimens. The edges all show signs of damage, and the surface is flaky, although it is possible to distinguish the attractive, almost translucent quality it would have possessed. The most significant feature of this piece is the hole drilled through it, which is perfectly round, and positioned at the outer edge.

- 10:3 cat. 1711. This specimen involves two pieces, neither of which appears to be finished. Both are rather roughly cut, the first in what could be interpreted as the early stages of the typical semi-lunate form and the other into a 'tab'. Again, the important feature is the drilled holes which both possess. On the first piece the hole is situated at the outer edge, and is circular, while the hole on the second piece is fairly central and more oval in shape.

- 10:3 cat. 1212. This piece is of a fairly standard shape, and is a particularly attractive colour – a kind of pearly ivory. The interior is smooth and may well have been polished to give it a lustre. Faint traces of notching can be discerned on the outer edge.

- 10:2 cat. 1203. The edges of this piece have been cut and ground into a remarkably smooth curve. A series of parallel scratches running lengthwise are easily visible to the naked eye, and under a x15 magnification some additional scratches across the width can also be seen. The cause of these is not clear.

- 10:1 cat. 1958 (Fig. 97d). This piece is of an unusual form, being considerably wider at one end (3.6 cm) than the other (2.3 cm), resulting in a trumpet-like shape. The interior has a strangely ridged texture, undoubtedly a property of the shell rather than the result of deliberate working.

- 10:1 cat. 1625. The outer edge of this piece is very irregularly shaped, including two clear notches as well as some disfiguration through breakage.

- 9:7 cat. 1150 (Fig. 97e). Another classically shaped piece, and again possessing an attractive opalescent sheen. This piece is particularly notable for its remarkable symmetry, suggesting a rather sophisticated manufacturing technique.

- 9:7 cat. 1948 (Fig. 97f). A large, robust piece, cut in a classic semi-lunate form and possessing a pearly surface.

- 9:6 cat. 1176 (Fig. 97g). A large, roughly finished piece. This has been manufactured from a rather inferior shell of no particular colour, and extensively bent and warped, suggesting that *P. placenta* shell may have been scarce enough to justify using even sub-standard pieces.

- 9:6 cat. 1107 (Fig. 97h). The shape of this piece is reminiscent of cat. 1958, in that one end is wider (at 3 cm) than the other (2 cm). The outer edge is rather unusual, as it is cut into a series of about twelve small notches, as well as 'ripples' between these, giving it a serrated appearance. Another piece found in association with this one appears to be a broken fragment of a similar specimen, displaying the same serrations on the outer edge.

- 9:6 cat. 1499 (Fig. 97i). A fairly standard piece, of regular shape and size. Again, it appears to have been manufactured from a relatively inferior shell.

- 9:3 cat. 1061. This specimen is of a standard shape, and exhibits a small degree of notching on the outer edge. It is of a rather attractive pearly colour.

- 8:6 cat. 1225. A rather delicate piece. The outer edge has been cut and rounded, with a pointed notch cut into it. This artefact is interesting in relation to the suggestion elsewhere in this paper that the discoloration regularly observed on the edges is caused by grinding with a piece of pottery, or a pebble, to achieve the rounded finish. The inner and outer curves of this piece exhibit the discolouration, and have a rounded finish, while the notch is not rounded and the discolouration is not present.

- 8:3 cat. 1083 (Fig. 97k). This specimen is large and robust. It is cut into a regular, semi-lunate shape.

- 8:2 cat. 1120 (Fig. 97j). These two pieces are distinctive in that they have a series of unusually deep notches carved into the outer curve. They appear to be a variation on the serration pattern theme.

- 7:8 cat. 879 (Fig. 97l). This piece is of a very unusual shape, being particularly long and narrow. The edges are extremely well finished, and it is an attractive pearly white colour.

- 7:6 cat. 1007. A small, narrow piece, this displays a 'rippled' outer edge.

- 7:6 cat. 1058 (Fig. 97m). This piece is slightly wider at one end than the other, but is otherwise of a characteristic form. It has a series of regular serrations along its outer curve.

- 7:6 cat. 848 (Fig. 97n). This large, regularly shaped piece includes a pattern of wide, shallow serrations on its outer curve.

- 6:3 cat. 1531. This appears to be a broken part of a larger specimen. It is most distinctive in that it has two deep, evenly spaced notches on the outer edge. One is triangular and the other curved.

REVIEW AND CONCLUSIONS

Two sources of evidence argue against the suggestion that the shells were collected for food only. The meat provided by each shellfish, although high in protein, is minimal in quantity. Where this species is used today, the meat is relatively worthless, and is often given to workers as a bonus, or sold at a low price (Magsuci *et al.*, 1980). The value of these species lies in the shell. The other reason for rejecting this hypothesis is that the shells, without exception, show some degree of working. If the utilisation of the meat as a food source was the primary objective in the gathering of these shellfish, then only a proportion of the shells would be expected to have been worked, as the majority (or at least a percentage) of shells would have been discarded after removing the meat. It is possible (and even likely, given its high protein value) that the people of Khok Phanom Di did consume the meat of these shellfish, but it is not likely that this constitutes the main reason for their collection. It is argued that this hypothesis be rejected as the primary reason for the presence of this species.

The second hypothesis argues that the shell was used to make some kind of tool. The evidence does not support this hypothesis. Ethnographic studies have not yet revealed any society which uses this type of shell for this purpose, mainly because of its brittle and flaky nature. It can be made into a sharp edge, but is highly susceptible to damage, to an extent that would make it virtually worthless as a tool requiring any kind of pressure. The *Isognomon* shell seems to be slightly more robust and its use as a cutting tool cannot be rejected altogether.

Another factor which does not support this hypothesis is the wear patterns observed. None of the pieces exhibited an edge which could be interpreted as a blade. The worn edges were present on each side of the curve, which is highly impractical for an unhafted knife. In the case of the notched specimens, utilisation of these as cutting implements would result in the presence of signs of wear only on the top curve of the notch, or at least differential wear would occur on different parts of the notch. This is not the case. The edges have been uniformly smoothed and rounded. This implies that the worn down edges were produced deliberately, as a part of the manufacturing process, rather than as a result of practical use. This, in turn, suggests that this hypothesis can also be rejected as an explanation of the function of these shells.

The last possible interpretation holds that this type of shell was used for ornamentation. On examination of the pieces, this hypothesis remains plausible. No evidence was found to disprove it, and ethnographic data reveal that modern societies use it almost exclusively in a decorative role. The shell is delicate and translucent, and responds well to polishing. Again, the shape of the more intact pieces, and the fact that the Khok Phanom Di people are known to have used shell jewellery, supports this hypotheses.

However, a number of questions remain. First, what kind of ornament do these pieces represent? At first the possibility that they are the broken fragments of circular bracelets was considered, but the observation that the relevant edges were cut rather than snapped does not support this. The most likely explanation is that they were worn suspended around the neck, and this is supported by the discovery of three samples with holes drilled through them. The possibility that they were suspended by tying a thread around the middle can be discarded, as none of them exhibits the more heavily worn area that this would produce.

The next problem is that none of the group A pieces (which were the most nearly complete) had holes drilled through them. Also, no specimens were found in grave goods assemblages, which is unusual for a type of ornament. These problems cannot be resolved given the data available, but one plausible explanation can still be advanced.

The number of unfinished specimens, and the absence of any complete ones (assuming holes were necessary for suspension) at Khok Phanom Di suggests two possibilities – first that the finished pieces were exported from the site, and secondly that the nearly complete pieces represented by group A were exported and finished elsewhere. This, combined with the absence of this type of artefact in any other site thus far excavated in Southeast Asia, has interesting implications. It may be that these shells represent a unique trade item, manufactured only at Khok Phanom Di and exported either as a finished product or a partially completed 'blank' to other sites. This suggestion does have its faults, the most basic of which is that none of these pieces has been found as part of any grave assemblages, which is extremely unusual for what appears to be a type of prestige jewellery. However, this could be explained in part by the ready availability (and thus decreased value) of this type of shell to the Khok Phanom Di inhabitants. Another problem is the absence of these pieces in other sites, but excavations in the area inland of Khok Phanom Di have not been sufficient to rule this out as a future possibility.

Another possible use for these pieces is as ornamentation for clothing, which could explain the extreme scarcity of drilled holes in the pieces. A needle has been found at Khok Phanom Di, and the presence of some kind of thread is indicated by the 'strings' of beads found with some of the burials. Again, a comparative study using modern examples would be useful, to establish whether the prehistoric specimens exhibit any kind of polish, due to being worn against the skin or cloth.

There is a further plausible hypothesis, which draws upon modern ethnographic observations in Northeast Thailand. Shaped specimens of *Placuna* have been seen there attached to the eaves of houses, and placed there as wind chimes (Mason, pers. comm.). If, indeed these artefacts were used in this manner, then it is likely that they were to be found on mortuary structures.

To answer these questions satisfactorily, two areas of evidence need to be explored more fully. Comparative work on modern examples would help to establish how the pieces were manufactured, and whether the techniques employed were those already known to have been used by the Khok Phanom Di inhabitants. More extensive excavations at both Khok Phanom Di and throughout the surrounding area may provide some clues as to the distribution and form of the finished pieces.

Although it has not been possible to identify the precise nature of these pieces, it has been fairly certainly established that they represent some kind of ornament. Three possibilities have been advanced, that they were worn in the form of a pendant, that they were used for decoration on items of clothing, or that they were used as wind chimes. The scarcity of group A pieces (the most complete forms) in comparison to the relative abundance of unfinished pieces suggests that the final product was exported from the site. This is supported by the ready availability of this type of shell to the Khok Phanom Di inhabitants, compared to its rarity and therefore likely increased value to people inhabiting sites further inland. More data are needed concerning the presence or absence of these pieces at inland sites of the area, and comparative studies on modern examples would be helpful in contributing to an understanding of the working processes involved.

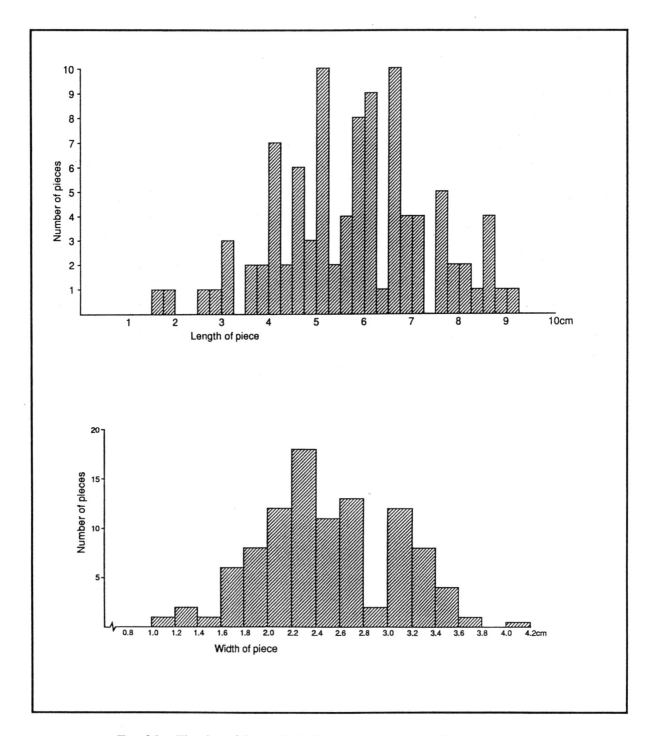

FIG. 96.　The size of the worked *Placuna placenta* from Khok Phanom Di

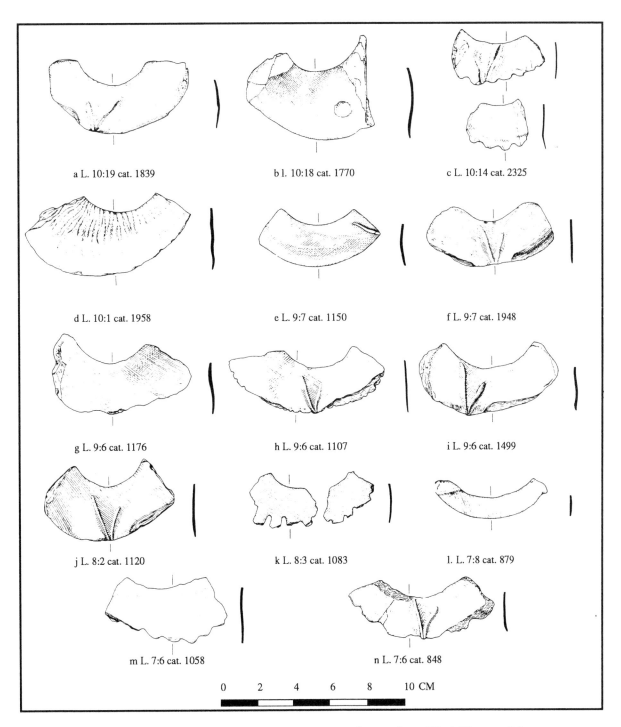

a L. 10:19 cat. 1839

b l. 10:18 cat. 1770

c L. 10:14 cat. 2325

d L. 10:1 cat. 1958

e L. 9:7 cat. 1150

f L. 9:7 cat. 1948

g L. 9:6 cat. 1176

h L. 9:6 cat. 1107

i L. 9:6 cat. 1499

j L. 8:2 cat. 1120

k L. 8:3 cat. 1083

l. L. 7:8 cat. 879

m L. 7:6 cat. 1058

n L. 7:6 cat. 848

0 2 4 6 8 10 CM

FIG. 97. The worked *Placuna placenta* specimens from Khok Phanom Di

VIII. ASPECTS OF THE POTTERY DECORATION

M. D. Hall

INTRODUCTION

THE excavation of Khok Phanom Di yielded a large sample of pottery derived from burials, associated ritual activity and domestic and manufacturing contexts. A proportion was decorated, many techniques and motifs being encountered. This section will first describe this decorated pottery, and then consider its social implications. In doing so, the sample is divided into two major contexts: the complete or reconstructed pots from burials, and the non-mortuary material.

Quantifying motif categories and chronological change in the non-mortuary context was an area of some complexity, as was measuring large quantities of sherds. There is no received technique for the latter and two methods are often employed: counting and weighing. Orton (1980) favours the latter, as raw numbers are greatly influenced by sherd size.

There has been considerable debate on motif category analysis. Plog (1980) has argued that there has been much subjectivity in this area. Good classification is apparent if, when the work is repeated, the results are the same. Rice (1987) has noted the critiques that have challenged the validity of the procedures used in stylistic studies. One area of focus has been the difficulty of distinguishing elements from motifs. Because of the diversity of opinion on the method for this analysis, the Khok Phanom Di decoration was studied under one category, the motif. Motif groups were allocated on the basis of mode of application: incised, impressed, incised and impressed combination, cord-marked incised and smoothed, paddle-impressed, ridged and appliqué. Motifs that were burnished were noted as evidence of added energy expenditure. When the zone was identifiable, it was recorded.

The variables employed are as follows:

Incising. The execution, in a freehand manner, of this decoration is usually produced by a narrow-ended tool that is applied to the surface of the clay with sufficient pressure to cut it. Rye (1981) states that a wide range of aesthetic effects can be achieved by the skill of the potter. Variations in the size and shape of the tip, the amount of pressure and the dryness of the clay can all contribute to the result. Any manner of tool may be used, such as sticks of varying widths and points, bones, shells and combs. Combing is a special form of incising in which a multiple-pronged tool is used. Single incised lines are used to demarcate design fields and motif boundaries. Striations, present on some incised lines, suggest that plant material was utilised for decorating tools. The majority of the incised lines on the mortuary pots are extremely uniform. It is possible that a pot was placed on two stones to allow the rotation movement similar to the wheel. This would account for neatness of line and design elements that are demonstrated on these pots. Curvilinear incised lines are not common and are predominantly found on cord-marked sherds or pots. Gouge incising is very rare, but three examples were found in the non-mortuary context.

Impressing.   This is formed by the pressing of a textured surface or tool into the clay. The negative impression leaves a surface of various patterns depending on the instrument used. A large variety of tools can be used. At Khok Phanom Di, natural objects such as shells are common while stems or hollow canes produce effects described as punctation. Carved and cord-wrapped paddles can be specially made for impressing. Designs carved into paddles or other suitable tools will create a raised decoration while the opposite effect is achieved with a relief pattern.

Combination incised and impressed.   The use of both techniques has provided the basis for the highest number of individual and most innovative of the motifs at Khok Phanom Di.

Cord-marked and incised.   The smoothed-line decoration is only to be found on the cord-marked ware and is uneven in both application and design. The technique appears to have been a finger or stick dragged across the surface to apply these markings. The other decorative technique to be found on the cord-marked ware is incising.

Paddle-impressed.   This is a sub-branch of impressing but the motifs have been classified separately.

Ridged and notched.   Ridged decoration is the technique of removing clay by scraping and creating a raised thin band. Notching is an addition to the ridging process with slashes being applied, often diagonally, to the relief edge.

Appliqué.   Pieces of clay are applied to the surface of the vessel by pressure, sometimes into a pattern.

Painting.   A few sherds were painted.

The motifs which have been identified and numbered are as follows:

1. Incised

1:1   Single or multiple incised lines. They vary in thickness and some are uneven in execution (Fig. 98a-c).

1:2   Incised horizontal lines form bands which are filled with small dashes. There is considerable variation between the width of the filled bands and the dashes are, in the main, randomly placed. In layer 8, one sherd had incised vertical lines, 1 cm in length, evenly spaced between the horizontal lines. On some sherds there was clear evidence that the horizontal line had been added after the dashes (Fig. 98d-f).

1:3   Diagonal incised lines bounded by single or double horizontal lines. The space between the diagonal lines varies in width between 1 and 4.5 mm. The diagonal line is present in both directions (Fig. 98g-i).

1:4   Wavy and zigzag line. This motif is utilised on a variety of surface patterning: cord-marked, paddle-impressed, and stamped-impressed. It is rare to find it on a plain surface. On one sherd, a wavy line is utilised to bound stamped impressions and in layer 10 there is one example of a continuous pattern of horizontal wavy lines (Fig. 98j-k).

1:5   This motif is exclusive to the burial context and is present on two pots. The image is not identical on each pot but the variations are minor so the same classification has been allocated for these similar motifs (Fig. 98l-n).

1:6   Hatching bounded by incised lines (Fig. 98o).

1:7   Hatching bounded by curvilinear incised lines (Fig. 98p).

1:8   Pattern of rhythmic vertical incising (Fig. 98q).

1:9   Vertical zigzag with incised infill (Fig. 98r).

1:10   Two-directional comb incising (Fig. 99a).

2. Impressed

2:1   Stamped impressions. A variety of tools used creating small needle-like indentations to larger impressions. This method creates an interesting texture to the surface (Fig. 99b-c).

2:2   Horizontal lines of small impressions. Very rare (Fig. 99d-e).

2:3   Horizontal line of shell-edge impressions either single or multiple. Shell-edge impressions also used as a mode for decorating the internal space of motifs (Fig. 99f).

2:4   Impressions of small shells. It is possible that some of these impressions are not part of the decorative scheme but were acquired unintentionally while the clay was plastic. Shell images are also found on the internal surface of some sherds (Fig. 99g-h).

2:5   Square impressions possibly achieved by a blunt bone or wood instrument. (Fig. 99i).

2:6   Small relief chequer-board pattern of impressions (Fig. 99j).

2:7   Pattern of fine stamped impressions (Fig. 99k).

3. Incised and impressed

3:1   Bands of stamped impressions bounded by incised lines (Fig. 99l-n).

3:2   Bands of random punctation between incised lines (Fig. 99o).

3:3   Diagonal impressions between incised lines. Shell-edge impressions and cord-marked impressions commonly used for infill, though a variety of tools appear to have been used giving considerable variation in terms of visual effect (Figs. 99p-100b).

3:4   Small ridges every 2 mm bounded by incised lines. Difficult to ascertain method of execution. Possibly a small stick impressed on clay though the effect is textured with fine striations present between the thin ridges (Fig. 100c).

3:5   Multiple, oblong impressions dissected by incised lines (Fig. 100d).

3:6   Punctate impressions, either in rows or individually. A variety of tools has been used with a corresponding diversity of shapes. Some punctation achieved with a hollow tool as only outer ring impressed while others are complete indentations. Elliptical shapes are also present. Effective use of this technique is seen in curvilinear and diagonal bands (Fig. 100e-g).

3:7   Double rows of very fine indentations between incised lines (Fig. 100h-i).

3:8   A black, burnished lenticular motif surrounded by stamped impressions (Fig. 100j).

3:9   Small, comet-like impressions between incised lines (Fig. 100k).

3:10   A double triangle filled with shell-edge impressions (Fig. 100l).

3:11   A band of repeating, shell-impressed triangles (Fig. 101a).

3:12   A bi-convex lens is bisected by an oblong/oblate figure filled with small impressions. This motif is contained in a band of stamped impressions (Fig. 101b).

3:13   Geometric motif surrounded by a band of stamped impressions (Fig. 101c).

3:14   Two opposing geometric forms are surrounded by stamped impressions (Fig. 101d).

3:15   An undulating band with oval shapes positioned on the downward trajectory of the band (Fig. 101e).

3:16   A panel of contrasting shapes containing comet-like dashes bounded by double incised lines (Fig. 101f).

3:17   A row of semicircles filled with shell-edge impressions (Fig. 101g).

3:18   A row of opposing and alternating semi-circles with shell-edge impressions (Fig. 101h).

3:19   A combination of shell-edge impressed triangles, base uppermost, with alternating narrow zigzag of plain burnishing and shell impressions (Fig. 101i).

3:20   This incised, curvilinear motif, possibly symbolic, is surrounded by areas of shell-edge impressions. The only example of this motif in the non-mortuary context had gouge-incising for the motif outline. A variation is present on one non-mortuary sherd. The curvilinear motif is filled with shell impressions with the surrounding space plain (Fig. 102a-b).

3:21   A combination of diagonal and vertical cord-marked impressions (Fig. 102c).

3:22   Multiple, fine lines of impressions bounded by incised lines (Fig. 102d).

3:23   A band of intersecting stamped impressions (Fig. 102e).

3:24   A band of zigzag stamped impressions bounded by incised lines (Fig. 102f).

3:25   Deep, thick pointed impressions bounded by gouge-incised lines (Fig. 102g).

3:26   A row of deep, alternate impressions bounded by incised lines (Fig. 102h).

3:27   A pattern of angular stamping bounded by incised lines (Fig. 102i).

3:28   A cord-impressed doublet motif surrounded by both plain and stamped areas (Fig. 102j).

3:29   Paw-print motif. A rosette of three impressions probably applied individually to create the band. The impressions are deeper on the left of each design imprint (Fig. 102k).

3:30   A plain, burnished zigzag band enclosed in a panel of stamped impressions (Fig. 102l).

3:31   A line of lenticular shapes filled with stamped impressions contained in a plain panel (Fig. 102m

3:32   Small punctation pattern bounded by a straight and wavy incised line (Fig. 103a).

3:33   A curvilinear motif of burnished bands and plano-convex lens (Fig. 103b).

3:34   A stepped, black-burnished band surrounding a band of impressions (Fig. 103c).

4. Cord-marked with smooth bands and incised

4:1   Cord-marked ware with a smooth line or band usually irregular and uneven in execution. Effect possibly created by dragging a finger or stick along plastic clay (Fig. 103d).

4:2   Cord-marked ware with incising. Curvilinear incising is present on this ware but often sherds are too small to illustrate the complete motif (Fig. 103f).

4:3   A band of cord-marking with incised zigzagging (Fig. 103g).

5. Paddle-impressed

5:1   Multiple-directional paddle-impressing (Fig. 103h-j).

5:2   Two directional paddle-impressing. Possible diamond pattern but sherds too fragmentary for complete pattern (Fig. 103k-l).

6. Ridged and notched

6:1   A raised thin band resulting from the removal of clay from both sides by scraping (Fig. 104a).

6:2   A raised band with slashes, usually diagonal (Fig. 104b).

7. Appliqué

7:1   Added pieces of clay, some smooth and round while other examples are more angular. Impressing on the top of some strips (Fig. 104c-f).

8. Burnished bands

8:1   A variety of widths are present.

FIG. 98.　　Incised motifs 1:1–1:9 on pottery

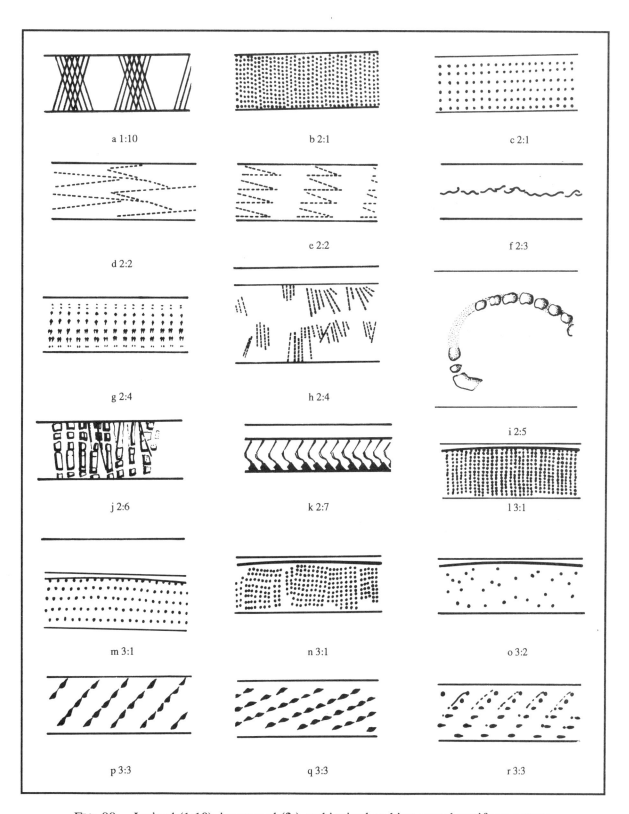

FIG. 99.   Incised (1:10), impressed (2:) and incised and impressed motifs on pottery

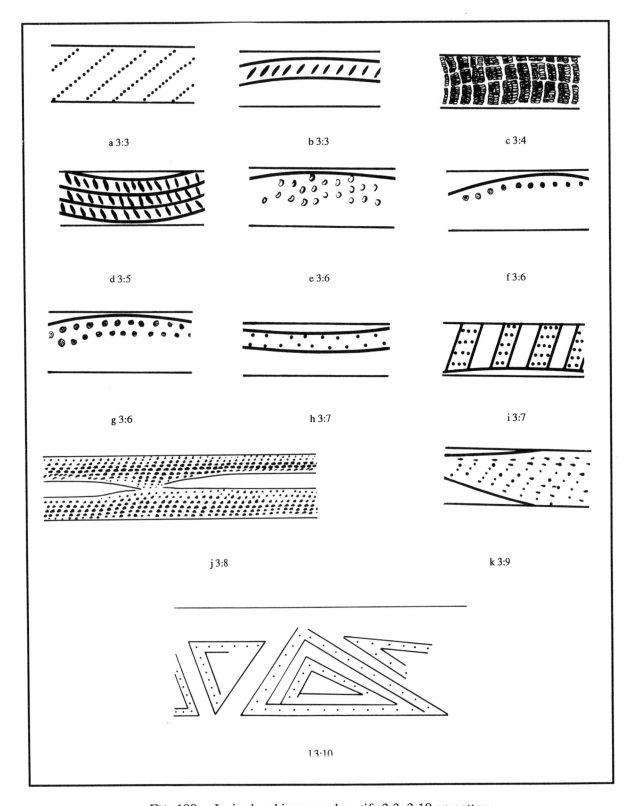

a 3:3 b 3:3 c 3:4

d 3:5 e 3:6 f 3:6

g 3:6 h 3:7 i 3:7

j 3:8 k 3:9

l 3:10

FIG. 100.   Incised and impressed motifs 3:3–3:10 on pottery

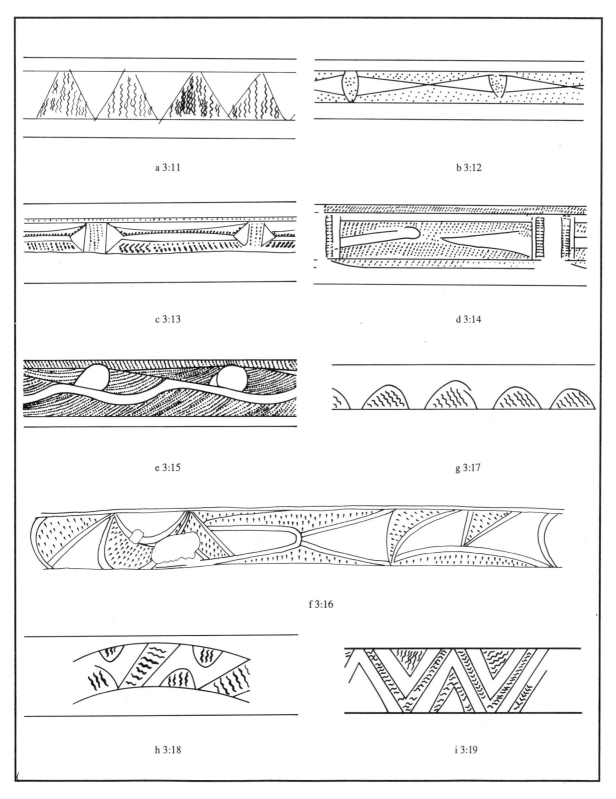

a 3:11

b 3:12

c 3:13

d 3:14

e 3:15

g 3:17

f 3:16

h 3:18

i 3:19

FIG. 101. Incised and impressed motifs 3:11–3:19 on pottery

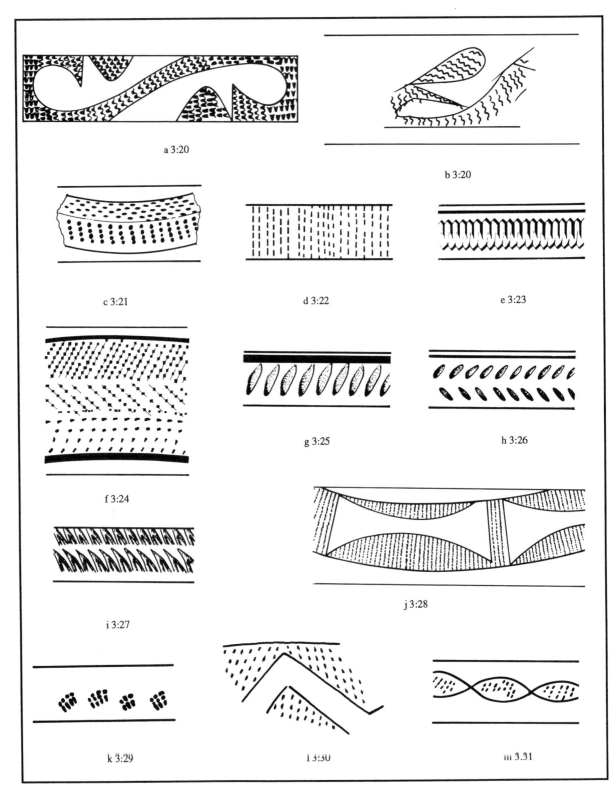

a 3:20

b 3:20

c 3:21

d 3:22

e 3:23

f 3:24

g 3:25

h 3:26

i 3:27

j 3:28

k 3:29

l 3:30

m 3:31

FIG. 102. Incised and impressed motifs 3:20–3:31 on pottery

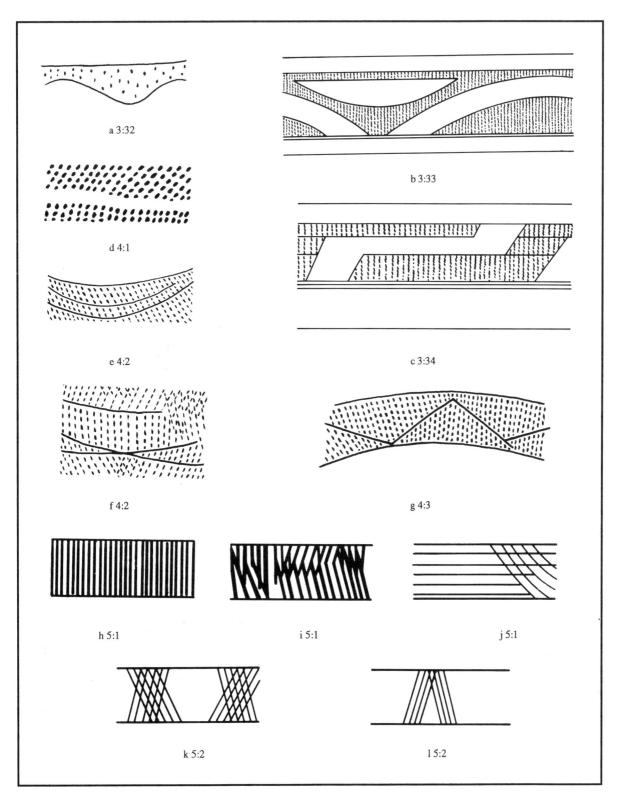

FIG. 103.   Incised and impressed (3:), cord-marked with smooth bands with incised lines (4:) and paddle-impressed motifs (5:) on pottery

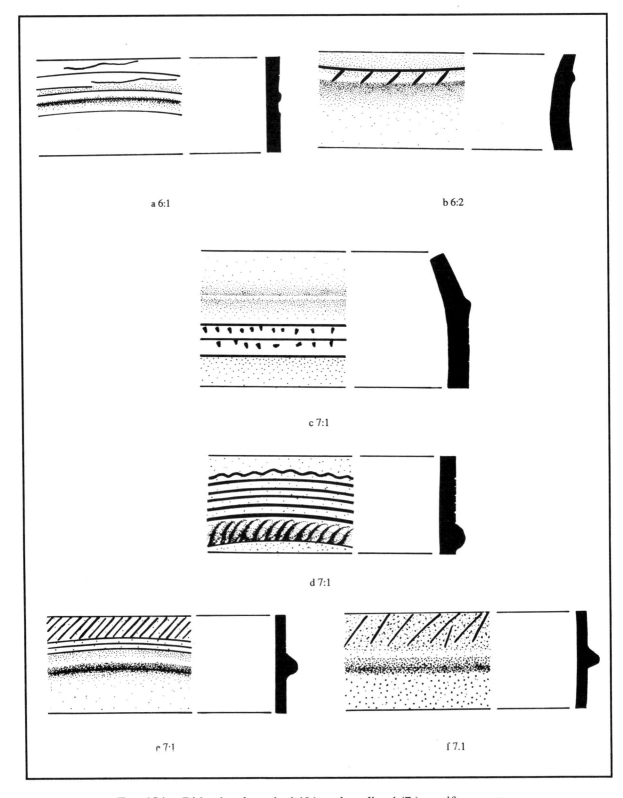

FIG. 104.   Ridged and notched (6:) and appliqué (7:) motifs on pottery

FIG. 105.   The distribution of motifs by layer

TABLE 41: *The weight of sherds with specific motifs from non-mortuary contexts*

Motif	Layer Burn.	Layer N/Burn.	Feature Burn.	Feature N/Burn.	Lens Burn.	Lens N/Burn.	Raised structure Burn.	Raised structure N/Burn.	Weight (gm)
Layer 11									
1:1	167	304	-	111	-	-	-	-	582
1:2	49	211	-	90	-	-	-	-	350
1:3	-	61	-	-	-	-	-	-	61
1:4	60	42	-	111	-	-	-	-	213
2:1	179	227	-	-	-	-	-	-	406
2:3	78	18	-	-	-	-	-	-	96
2:5	7	-	-	-	-	-	-	-	7
3:1	260	68	-	-	-	-	-	-	328
3:2	24	-	-	-	-	-	-	-	24
3:3	107	123	-	-	-	-	-	-	230
3:4	8	-	-	-	-	-	-	-	8
3:5	-	9	-	-	-	-	-	-	9
3:6	24	-	-	-	-	-	-	-	24
3:7	-	16	-	-	-	-	-	-	16
3:9	5	-	-	-	-	-	-	-	5
5:1	14	10	-	-	-	-	-	-	24
5:2	53	24	-	-	-	-	-	-	77
6:1	-	18	-	-	-	-	-	-	18
6:2	-	35	-	-	-	-	-	-	35
7:1	6	22	-	-	-	-	-	-	28
Total	1041	1188	-	312	-	-	-	-	2541
Layer 10									
1:1	2078	1292	18	-	850	536	-	-	4774
1:2	105	112	3	-	44	181	-	-	445
1:4	179	290	-	-	116	54	-	-	639
1:6	5	46	-	-	8	-	-	-	59
1:8	-	4	-	-	-	-	-	-	4
2:1	504	640	-	-	161	439	-	-	1744
2:2	65	91	-	-	-	-	-	-	156
2:3	65	66	3	-	46	-	-	-	180
2:4	-	-	-	-	4	275	-	-	279
2:5	-	30	-	-	3	159	-	-	192
2:6	-	21	-	-	-	-	-	-	21
2:7	14	-	-	-	-	-	-	-	14
3:1	2282	955	2	-	1184	317	-	-	4740
3:2	86	4	-	-	60	36	-	-	186
3:3	1118	135	5	-	451	67	-	-	1776
3:5	8	16	-	-	-	4	-	-	28

Table 41 (cont.) The weight of sherds with specific motifs from non-mortuary contexts

Motif	Layer Burn.	Layer N/Burn.	Feature Burn.	Feature N/Burn.	Lens Burn.	Lens N/Burn.	Raised structure Burn.	Raised structure N/Burn.	Weight (gm)
Layer 10 (cont.)									
3:6	20	257	-	-	75	82	-	-	434
3:7	256	42	-	-	26	-	-	-	324
3:9	-	6	-	-	-	-	-	-	6
3:10	-	-	-	-	10	-	-	-	10
3:21	-	-	-	-	-	10	-	-	10
3:22	16	-	-	-	37	-	-	-	53
3:23	12	7	-	-	-	-	-	-	19
3:24	11	15	-	-	-	-	-	-	26
3:25	-	5	-	-	-	12	-	-	17
3:26	19	26	-	-	-	-	-	-	45
4:1	-	1713	-	-	-	617	-	-	2330
4:2	-	4785	-	-	-	439	-	-	5224
5:1	83	527	-	-	37	176	-	-	823
6:1	58	8	-	-	-	47	-	-	113
7:1	-	17	-	-	-	-	-	-	17
8:1	349	-	5	-	89	-	-	-	443
Total	7333	11110	36	-	3201	3451	-	-	25131
Layer 9									
1:1	602	218	-	-	184	33	-	-	1037
1:6	-	7	-	-	-	-	-	-	7
1:7	7	-	-	-	-	-	-	-	7
1:8	7	-	-	-	-	-	-	-	7
2:1	129	87	-	-	27	53	-	-	296
3:1	1011	328	-	-	200	75	-	-	1614
3:2	4	-	-	-	-	5	-	-	9
3:3	222	18	-	-	59	-	-	-	299
3:6	-	12	-	-	-	-	-	-	12
3:7	38	12	-	-	-	-	-	-	50
3:11	-	8	-	-	-	-	-	-	8
3:20	30	-	-	-	-	-	-	-	30
3:22	11	-	-	-	-	-	-	-	11
4:1	-	714	-	-	-	11	-	-	725
4:2	-	643	-	-	-	103	-	-	746
7:1	-	109	-	-	-	-	-	-	109
8:1	60	-	-	-	-	-	-	-	60
Total	2121	2156	-	-	470	280	-	-	5027

Table 41 (cont.) The weight of sherds with specific motifs from non-mortuary contexts

Motif	Layer Burn.	Layer N/Burn.	Feature Burn.	Feature N/Burn.	Lens Burn.	Lens N/Burn.	Raised structure Burn.	Raised structure N/Burn.	Weight (gm)
Layer 8									
1:1	307	294	4	-	49	66	-	-	720
1:4	-	29	-	-	-	-	-	-	29
1:8	7	-	-	-	-	-	-	-	7
2:1	212	85	-	-	-	18	-	-	315
2:3	20	-	-	-	-	-	-	-	20
2:4	-	-	-	-	-	10	-	-	10
2:5	-	18	-	-	-	38	-	-	56
3:1	715	339	13	-	72	14	-	-	1153
3:2	5	-	-	-	-	-	-	-	5
3:3	162	25	4	-	16	7	-	-	214
3:7	6	-	-	-	-	-	-	-	6
3:11	11	-	-	-	-	-	-	-	11
3:27	11	-	-	-	-	-	-	-	11
3:28	62	-	-	-	-	-	-	-	62
4:1	-	1595	-	43	-	122	-	-	1760
4:2	-	967	-	-	-	68	-	-	1035
5:1	3	16	-	-	-	-	-	-	19
7:1	-	77	-	-	-	-	-	-	77
8:1	134	-	6	-	40	-	-	-	180
Total	1655	3445	27	43	177	343	-	-	5690
Layer 7									
1:1	550	250	25	7	14	20	-	-	866
1:2	9	24	-	-	-	-	-	-	33
1:4	13	-	-	-	-	-	-	-	13
1:6	-	39	-	-	-	-	-	-	39
2:1	125	19	-	-	-	-	-	-	144
2:3	39	-	-	-	-	-	-	-	39
3:1	1160	189	39	15	53	-	-	-	1456
3:2	37	-	-	-	-	-	-	-	37
3:3	113	10	16	-	15	-	-	-	154
3:7	12	-	5	-	-	-	-	-	17
3:11	-	18	-	-	-	-	-	-	18
3:22	48	7	-	-	-	-	-	-	55
3:29	9	-	-	-	-	-	-	-	9
4:1	-	676	-	59	-	-	-	-	735
4:2	-	2163	-	20	-	168	-	-	2351
5:1	5	14	-	5	-	-	-	-	24
7:1	-	97	-	-	-	-	-	-	97
8:1	237	-	-	-	-	-	-	-	237
Total	2357	3506	85	106	82	188	-	-	6324

Table 41 (cont.) The weight of sherds with specific motifs from non-mortuary contexts

Motif	Layer Burn.	N/Burn.	Feature Burn.	N/Burn.	Lens Burn.	N/Burn.	Raised structure Burn.	N/Burn.	Weight (gm)
Layer 6									
1:1	395	347	169	178	7	92	-	-	1188
1:2	58	-	7	26	-	-	-	-	91
1:6	-	-	-	-	-	81	-	-	81
2:1	24	77	21	52	-	161	-	-	335
2:3	-	-	-	11	-	-	-	-	11
3:1	609	357	277	134	49	70	-	-	1496
3:3	26	-	25	8	-	-	-	-	59
3:7	-	-	4	-	-	-	-	-	4
3:11	-	30	-	24	-	-	-	-	54
3:17	27	-	-	-	126	-	-	-	153
3:22	59	14	-	-	-	19	-	-	92
3:23	18	-	-	-	-	-	-	-	18
4:1	-	544	-	-	-	121	-	-	665
4:2	-	4428	-	1294	-	852	-	-	6574
5:1	34	126	-	6	4	46	-	-	216
7:1	-	166	-	43	-	-	-	-	209
8:1	103	-	61	-	45	-	-	-	209
Total	1353	6089	564	1776	231	1442	-	-	11455
Layer 5									
1:1	175	765	81	234	-	-	59	15	1329
1:6	-	46	-	-	-	-	-	-	46
2:1	68	31	-	4	-	-	11	57	171
2:3	-	65	53	27	-	-	-	21	166
3:1	327	162	24	14	-	-	132	-	659
3:2	-	-	-	-	-	-	-	18	18
3:3	130	18	-	4	-	-	-	-	152
3:4	-	11	-	-	-	-	-	-	11
3:11	71	-	-	-	-	-	-	-	71
3:17	32	44	53	-	-	-	-	-	129
3:22	5	-	-	-	-	-	-	-	5
4:1	-	75	-	10	-	-	-	62	147
4:2	-	2473	-	1325	-	-	-	193	3991
5:1	11	469	-	293	-	-	-	52	825
7:1	-	215	-	8	-	-	-	29	252
8:1	221	-	44	-	-	-	53	-	318
Total	1040	4374	255	1919	-	-	255	447	8290

Table 41 (cont.) The weight of sherds with specific motifs from non-mortuary contexts

Motif	Layer Burn.	Layer N/Burn.	Feature Burn.	Feature N/Burn.	Lens Burn.	Lens N/Burn.	Raised structure Burn.	Raised structure N/Burn.	Weight (gm)
Layer 4									
1:1	49	1393	37	317	-	-	-	-	1796
1:2	-	15	-	-	-	-	-	-	15
1:6	-	29	-	-	-	-	-	-	29
1:9	-	-	-	25	-	-	-	-	25
2:3	36	322	24	65	-	-	-	-	447
3:1	75	242	-	16	-	-	-	-	333
3:2	-	24	-	-	-	-	-	-	24
3:3	-	40	-	-	-	-	-	-	40
3:6	-	10	-	5	-	-	-	-	15
3:11	-	38	-	-	-	-	-	-	38
3:20	-	-	-	50	-	-	-	-	50
3:21	-	24	-	-	-	-	-	-	24
3:27	-	-	-	11	-	-	-	-	11
3:30	25	-	5	-	-	-	-	-	30
4:1	-	29	-	-	-	-	-	-	29
4:2	-	13894	-	3896	-	-	-	-	17790
4:3	-	304	44	229	-	-	-	-	577
5:1	19	2299	-	815	-	-	-	-	3133
7:1	238	127	-	40	-	-	-	-	405
8:1	54	-	6	-	-	-	-	-	60
Total	496	18790	116	5469	-	-	-	-	24871
Layer 3									
1:1	26	3732	-	-	-	-	-	-	3758
1:6	-	438	-	-	-	-	-	-	438
2:1	-	32	-	-	-	-	-	-	32
2:3	-	1099	-	-	-	-	-	-	1099
3:1	-	791	-	-	-	-	-	-	791
3:2	-	115	-	-	-	-	-	-	115
3:3	-	88	-	-	-	-	-	-	88
3:5	-	44	-	-	-	-	-	-	44
3:6	-	21	-	-	-	-	-	-	21
3:11	-	150	-	-	-	-	-	-	150
3:23	-	46	-	-	-	-	-	-	46
3:30	10	39	-	-	-	-	-	-	49
3:31	-	80	-	-	-	-	-	-	80
4:2	-	15008	-	-	-	-	-	-	15008
4:3	-	1520	-	-	-	-	-	-	1520
5:1	-	7671	-	-	-	-	-	-	7671
7:1	-	231	-	-	-	-	-	-	231
Total	36	31105	-	-	-	-	-	-	31141

Table 41 (cont.) The weight of sherds with specific motifs from non-mortuary contexts

Motif	Layer Burn.	N/Burn.	Feature Burn.	N/Burn.	Lens Burn.	N/Burn.	Raised structure Burn.	N/Burn.	Weight (gm)
Layer 2									
1:1	-	1742	-	-	-	-	-	-	1742
1:6	-	72	-	-	-	-	-	-	72
2:1	-	121	-	-	-	-	-	-	121
2:2	-	18	-	-	-	-	-	-	18
2:3	-	467	-	-	-	-	-	-	467
2:4	-	22	-	-	-	-	-	-	22
3:1	-	393	-	-	-	-	-	-	393
3:11	-	602	-	-	-	-	-	-	602
3:17	-	32	-	-	-	-	-	-	32
3:32	-	90	-	-	-	-	-	-	90
4:2	-	14298	-	-	-	-	-	-	14298
4:3	-	82	-	-	-	-	-	-	82
5:1	-	4245	-	-	-	-	-	-	4245
6:1	-	103	-	-	-	-	-	-	103
7:1	-	356	-	-	-	-	-	-	356
Total	-	22643	-	-	-	-	-	-	22643

TABLE 42: *The distribution of motifs on non-mortuary pottery by layer and context*

Motif	Layer	Within layer Burn.	N/Burn.	Feature Burn.	N/Burn.	Lens Burn.	N/Burn.	Raised structure Burn.	N/Burn.	Weight (gm)
1:1	2	-	1742	-	-	-	-	-	-	1742
1:1	3	26	3732	-	-	-	-	-	-	3758
1:1	4	49	1393	37	317	-	-	-	-	1796
1:1	5	175	765	81	234	-	-	59	15	1329
1:1	6	395	347	169	178	7	92	-	-	1188
1:1	7	550	250	25	7	14	20	-	-	866
1:1	8	307	294	4	-	49	66	-	-	720
1:1	9	602	218	-	-	184	33	-	-	1037
1:1	10	2078	1292	18	-	850	536	-	-	4774.
1:1	11	167	304	-	111	-	-	-	-	582
1:2	4	-	15	-	-	-	-	-	-	15
1:2	6	58	-	7	26	-	-	-	-	91
1:2	7	9	24	-	-	-	-	-	-	33
1:2	10	105	112	3	-	44	181	-	-	445

Table 42 (cont.) The distribution of motifs on non-mortuary pottery by layer and context

Motif	Layer	Within layer Burn.	N/Burn.	Feature Burn.	N/Burn.	Lens Burn.	N/Burn.	Raised structure Burn.	N/Burn.	Weight (gm)
1:2	11	49	211	-	90	-	-	-	-	350
1:3	11	-	61	-	-	-	-	-	-	61
1:4	7	13	-	-	-	-	-	-	-	13
1:4	8	-	29	-	-	-	-	-	-	29
1:4	10	179	290	-	-	116	54	-	-	639
1:4	11	60	42	-	111	-	-	-	-	213
1:6	2	-	72	-	-	-	-	-	-	72
1:6	3	-	438	-	-	-	-	-	-	438
1:6	4	-	29	-	-	-	-	-	-	29
1:6	5	-	46	-	-	-	-	-	-	46
1:6	6	-	-	-	-	-	81	-	-	81
1:6	7	-	39	-	-	-	-	-	-	39
1:6	9	-	7	-	-	-	-	-	-	7
1:6	10	5	46	-	-	8	-	-	-	59
1:7	9	7	-	-	-	-	-	-	-	7
1:8	8	7	-	-	-	-	-	-	-	7
1:8	9	7	-	-	-	-	-	-	-	7
1:8	10	-	4	-	-	-	-	-	-	4
1:9	4	-	-	-	25	-	-	-	-	25
2:1	2	-	121	-	-	-	-	-	-	121
2:1	3	-	32	-	-	-	-	-	-	32
2:1	5	68	31	-	4	-	-	11	57	171
2:1	6	24	77	21	52	-	161	-	-	335
2:1	7	125	19	-	-	-	-	-	-	144
2:1	8	212	85	-	-	-	18	-	-	315
2:1	9	129	87	-	-	27	53	-	-	296
2:1	10	504	640	-	-	161	439	-	-	1744
2:1	11	179	227	-	-	-	-	-	-	406
2:2	2	-	18	-	-	-	-	-	-	18
2:2	10	65	91	-	-	-	-	-	-	156
2:2	11	65	109	-	-	-	-	-	-	174
2:3	2	-	467	-	-	-	-	-	-	467
2:3	3	-	1099	-	-	-	-	-	-	1099
2:3	4	36	322	24	65	-	-	-	-	447
2:3	5	-	65	53	27	-	-	-	21	166
2:3	6	-	-	-	11	-	-	-	-	11
2:3	7	39	-	-	-	-	-	-	-	39
2:3	8	20	-	-	-	-	-	-	-	20
2:3	10	65	66	3	-	46	-	-	-	180
2:3	11	78	18	-	-	-	-	-	-	96

Table 42 (cont.) The distribution of motifs on non-mortuary pottery by layer and context

Motif	Layer	Within layer		Feature		Lens		Raised structure		Weight (gm)
		Burn.	N/Burn.	Burn.	N/Burn.	Burn.	N/Burn.	Burn.	N/Burn.	
2:4	2	-	22	-	-	-	-	-	-	22
2:4	8	-	-	-	-	-	10	-	-	10
2:4	10	-	-	-	-	4	275	-	-	279
2:5	8	-	18	-	-	-	38	-	-	56
2:5	10	-	30	-	-	3	159	-	-	192
2:5	11	7	-	-	-	-	-	-	-	7
2:6	10	-	21	-	-	-	-	-	-	21
2:7	10	14	-	-	-	-	-	-	-	14
3:1	2	-	393	-	-	-	-	-	-	393
3:1	3	-	791	-	-	-	-	-	-	791
3:1	4	75	242	-	16	-	-	-	-	333
3:1	5	327	162	24	14	-	-	132	-	659
3:1	6	609	357	277	134	49	70	-	-	1496
3:1	7	1160	189	39	15	53	-	-	-	1456
3:1	8	715	339	13	-	72	14	-	-	1153
3:1	9	1011	328	-	-	200	75	-	-	1614
3:1	10	2282	955	2	-	1184	317	-	-	4740
3:1	11	260	68	-	-	-	-	-	-	328
3:2	3	-	115	-	-	-	-	-	-	115
3:2	4	-	24	-	-	-	-	-	-	24
3:2	5	-	-	-	-	-	-	-	18	18
3:2	7	37	-	-	-	-	-	-	-	37
3:2	8	5	-	-	-	-	-	-	-	5
3:2	9	4	-	-	-	-	5	-	-	9
3:2	10	86	4	-	-	60	36	-	-	186
3:2	11	24	-	-	-	-	-	-	-	24
3:3	3	-	88	-	-	-	-	-	-	88
3:3	4	-	40	-	-	-	-	-	-	40
3:3	5	130	18	-	4	-	-	-	-	152
3:3	6	26	-	25	8	-	-	-	-	59
3:3	7	113	10	16	-	15	-	-	-	154
3:3	8	162	25	4	-	16	7	-	-	214
3:3	9	222	18	-	-	59	-	-	-	299
3:3	10	1118	135	5	-	451	67	-	-	1776
3:3	11	107	123	-	-	-	-	-	-	230
3:4	5	-	11	-	-	-	-	-	-	11
3:4	11	8	-	-	-	-	-	-	-	8
3:5	3	-	44	-	-	-	-	-	-	44
3:5	10	8	16	-	-	-	4	-	-	28

Table 42 (cont.) The distribution of motifs on non-mortuary pottery by layer and context

Motif	Layer	Within layer		Feature		Lens		Raised structure		Weight (gm)
		Burn.	N/Burn.	Burn.	N/Burn.	Burn.	N/Burn.	Burn.	N/Burn.	
3:5	11	-	9	-	-	-	-	-	-	9
3:6	3	-	21	-	-	-	-	-	-	21
3:6	4	-	10	-	5	-	-	-	-	15
3:6	9	-	12	-	-	-	-	-	-	12
3:6	10	20	257	-	-	75	82	-	-	434
3:6	11	24	-	-	-	-	-	-	-	24
3:7	6	-	-	4	-	-	-	-	-	4
3:7	7	12	-	5	-	-	-	-	-	17
3:7	8	6	-	-	-	-	-	-	-	6
3:7	9	38	12	-	-	-	-	-	-	50
3:7	10	256	42	-	-	26	-	-	-	324
3:7	11	-	16	-	-	-	-	-	-	16
3:9	10	-	6	-	-	-	-	-	-	6
3:9	11	5	-	-	-	-	-	-	-	5
3:10	10	-	-	-	-	10	-	-	-	10
3:11	2	-	602	-	-	-	-	-	-	602
3:11	3	-	150	-	-	-	-	-	-	150
3:11	4	-	38	-	-	-	-	-	-	38
3:11	5	71	-	-	-	-	-	-	-	71
3:2	4	-	24	-	-	-	-	-	-	24
3:2	5	-	-	-	-	-	-	-	18	18
3:2	7	37	-	-	-	-	-	-	-	37
3:2	8	5	-	-	-	-	-	-	-	5
3:2	9	4	-	-	-	-	5	-	-	9
3:2	10	86	4	-	-	60	36	-	-	186
3:2	11	24	-	-	-	-	-	-	-	24
3:3	3	-	88	-	-	-	-	-	-	88
3:3	4	-	40	-	-	-	-	-	-	40
3:3	5	130	18	-	4	-	-	-	-	152
3:3	6	26	-	25	8	-	-	-	-	59
3:3	7	113	10	16	-	15	-	-	-	154
3:3	8	162	25	4	-	16	7	-	-	214
3:3	9	222	18	-	-	59	-	-	-	299
3:3	10	1118	135	5	-	451	67	-	-	1776
3:3	11	107	123	-	-	-	-	-	-	230
3:4	5	-	11	-	-	-	-	-	-	11
3:4	11	8	-	-	-	-	-	-	-	8
3:5	3	-	44	-	-	-	-	-	-	44
3:5	10	8	16	-	-	-	1	-	-	20

Table 42 (cont.) The distribution of motifs on non-mortuary pottery by layer and context

Motif	Layer	Within layer		Feature		Lens		Raised structure		Weight (gm)
		Burn.	N/Burn.	Burn.	N/Burn.	Burn.	N/Burn.	Burn.	N/Burn.	
3:5	11	-	9	-	-	-	-	-	-	9
3:6	3	-	21	-	-	-	-	-	-	21
3:6	4	-	10	-	5	-	-	-	-	15
3:6	9	-	12	-	-	-	-	-	-	12
3:6	10	20	257	-	-	75	82	-	-	434
3:6	11	24	-	-	-	-	-	-	-	24
3:7	6	-	-	4	-	-	-	-	-	4
3:7	7	12	-	5	-	-	-	-	-	17
3:7	8	6	-	-	-	-	-	-	-	6
3:7	9	38	12	-	-	-	-	-	-	50
3:7	10	256	42	-	-	26	-	-	-	324
3:7	11	-	16	-	-	-	-	-	-	16
3:9	10	-	6	-	-	-	-	-	-	6
3:9	11	5	-	-	-	-	-	-	-	5
3:10	10	-	-	-	-	10	-	-	-	10
3:11	2	-	602	-	-	-	-	-	-	602
3:11	3	-	150	-	-	-	-	-	-	150
3:11	4	-	38	-	-	-	-	-	-	38
3:11	5	71	-	-	-	-	-	-	-	71
3:11	6	-	30	-	24	-	-	-	-	54
3:11	7	-	18	-	-	-	-	-	-	18
3:11	8	11	-	-	-	-	-	-	-	11
3:11	9	-	8	-	-	-	-	-	-	8
3:17	2	-	32	-	-	-	-	-	-	32
3:17	5	32	44	53	-	-	-	-	-	129
3:17	6	-	-	-	-	126	-	-	-	132
3:20	4	-	-	-	50	-	-	-	-	50
3:20	9	30	-	-	-	-	-	-	-	30
3:21	4	-	24	-	-	-	-	-	-	24
3:21	10	-	-	-	-	-	10	-	-	10
3:22	5	5	-	-	-	-	-	-	-	5
3:22	6	59	14	-	-	-	19	-	-	92
3:22	7	48	7	-	-	-	-	-	-	55
3:22	9	11	-	-	-	-	-	-	-	11
3:22	10	16	-	-	-	37	-	-	-	53
3:23	3	-	46	-	-	-	-	-	-	46
3:23	6	18	-	-	-	-	-	-	-	18
3:23	10	12	7	-	-	-	-	-	-	19
3:24	10	11	15	-	-	-	-	-	-	26

Table 42 (cont.) The distribution of motifs on non-mortuary pottery by layer and context

Motif	Layer	Within layer Burn.	Within layer N/Burn.	Feature Burn.	Feature N/Burn.	Lens Burn.	Lens N/Burn.	Raised structure Burn.	Raised structure N/Burn.	Weight (gm)
3:25	10	-	5	-	-	-	12	-	-	17
3:26	10	19	26	-	-	-	-	-	-	45
3:27	4	-	-	-	11	-	-	-	-	11
3:27	8	11	-	-	-	-	-	-	-	11
3:28	8	62	-	-	-	-	-	-	-	62
3:29	7	9	-	-	-	-	-	-	-	9
3:30	3	10	39	-	-	-	-	-	-	49
3:30	4	25	-	5	-	-	-	-	-	30
3:31	3	-	80	-	-	-	-	-	-	80
3:32	2	-	90	-	-	-	-	-	-	90
4:1	4	-	29	-	-	-	-	-	-	29
4:1	5	-	75	-	10	-	-	-	62	147
4:1	6	-	544	-	-	-	121	-	-	665
4:1	7	-	676	-	59	-	-	-	-	735
4:1	8	-	1595	-	43	-	122	-	-	1760
4:1	9	-	714	-	-	-	11	-	-	725
4:1	10	-	1713	-	-	-	617	-	-	2330
4:2	2	-	14298	-	-	-	-	-	-	14298
4:2	3	-	15008	-	-	-	-	-	-	15008
4:2	5	-	2473	-	1325	-	-	-	193	3991
4:2	6	-	4428	-	1294	-	852	-	-	6574
4:2	7	-	2163	-	20	-	168	-	-	2351
4:2	8	-	967	-	-	-	68	-	-	1035
4:2	9	-	643	-	-	-	103	-	-	746
4:2	10	-	4785	-	-	-	2439	-	-	7224
4:3	2	-	82	-	-	-	-	-	-	82
4:3	3	-	1520	-	-	-	-	-	-	1520
4:3	4	-	304	44	229	-	-	-	-	577
5:1	2	-	4245	-	-	-	-	-	-	4245
5:1	3	-	7671	-	-	-	-	-	-	7671
5:1	4	19	2299	-	815	-	-	-	-	3133
5:1	5	11	469	-	293	-	-	-	52	825
5:1	6	34	126	-	6	4	46	-	-	216
5:1	7	5	14	-	5	-	-	-	-	24
5:1	8	3	16	-	-	-	-	-	-	19
5:1	10	83	527	-	-	37	176	-	-	823
5:1	11	14	10	-	-	-	-	-	-	24
6:1	2	-	103	-	-	-	-	-	-	103
6:1	10	58	8	-	-	-	47	-	-	113
6:1	11	-	18	-	-	-	-	-	-	18

Table 42 (cont.) The distribution of motifs on non-mortuary pottery by layer and context

Motif	Layer	Within layer		Feature		Lens		Raised structure		Weight (gm)
		Burn.	N/Burn.	Burn.	N/Burn.	Burn.	N/Burn.	Burn.	N/Burn.	
6:2	11	-	35	-	-	-	-	-	-	35
7:1	2	-	356	-	-	-	-	-	-	356
7:1	3	-	231	-	-	-	-	-	-	231
7:1	4	238	127	-	40	-	-	-	-	405
7:1	5	-	215	-	8	-	-	-	29	252
7:1	6	-	166	-	43	-	-	-	-	209
7:1	7	-	97	-	-	-	-	-	-	97
7:1	8	-	77	-	-	-	-	-	-	77
7:1	9	-	109	-	-	-	-	-	-	109
7:1	10	-	17	-	-	-	-	-	-	17
7:1	11	6	22	-	-	-	-	-	-	28
8:1	4	54	-	6	-	-	-	-	-	60
8:1	5	221	-	44	-	-	-	53	-	318
8:1	6	103	-	61	-	45	-	-	-	209
8:1	7	237	-	-	-	-	-	-	-	237
8:1	8	134	-	6	-	40	-	-	-	180
8:1	9	60	-	-	-	-	-	-	-	60
8:1	10	349	-	5	-	89	-	-	-	443

THE DECORATED NON-MORTUARY CERAMICS

Certain motifs were restricted to part of the sequence. Two of the most common are biased in terms of weight analysis. Thus, motif 1:1 exhibits one or several incised lines. On a small sherd, the incised line was clearly identifiable, but if a more complex motif was only partially complete on a sherd, it was discarded due to the uncertainty of the diagnosis. Motifs 4:1–2 are decorated cord-marked, and they are consistently thicker and therefore heavier than non cord-marked motifs. However, the wide margin between the weights indicates that they are still more frequent.

The number of motifs for each layer, apart from layer 10, was relatively uniform. Some were very rare, with only one or two sherds being identified in one layer throughout the sequence. In layer 5, paddle-impressed decoration increased and remained frequent in the upper layers. Throughout zone C, the less labour-intensive motifs were dominant. Layer 10 contained the highest number of the more complex and time-consuming motifs. The number of burnished motifs dropped significantly in layer 4. It is present on only two motifs in layer 3 and ceased by layer 2.

Sherds painted with a red pigment are only found in non-mortuary contexts. They are very rare, and the use of colouring appears to be an ornamental adjunct rather than a dominant decorative device. It was applied over incised and impressed designs, or is present in spaces between motifs. It is non-figurative. Frequencies of painted sherds in gm were as follows: layer 10, 33; L. 9, 14;

L. 8, 73; L. 7, 59; L. 6, 53; L. 5, 33 and L. 4, 69 gm. The use of powdered ochre to emphasise the decorative motif was present on a small number of sherds throughout the layers. Occasionally, these were decorated on both exterior and interior surfaces. If more than one motif was represented, it was incorporated in each category.

Burnishing has been categorised as a decorative technique due to the added energy expenditure involved. However, where burnishing was found only on the interior, it is possible that it was functional rather than decorative, due to compression of the surface. This resulted in a harder texture which was more impervious to water. A few highly burnished sherds are present in the non-mortuary context: 30 gm in layer 9, 50 gm in layer 4. The sherds in layer 9 are heavily encrusted in the interior with red pigment. This suggests that some burial motifs, such as 3.20, even though they are present in the non-mortuary context, are associated with ritual-orientated ceramics.

THE DECORATED MORTUARY CERAMICS

When reviewing the vessels from burials, several issues will be considered, their implications being deferred until later in this report. These issues include the degree to which decoration, and particular styles of decoration, were restricted to mortuary contexts. It is then possible to enquire whether certain motifs were gender, age or cluster specific. The 122 vessels available for analysis comprised 83 decorated with motifs, 12 plain burnished, 13 plain, 2 cord-marked with burnishing and 12 cord-marked. Several of the damaged pots exhibited evidence that the initial construction of the vessel had been undertaken with a cord-marked paddle. The secondary process was smoothing followed by the decorative treatment, such as burnishing. Clearly, making burial ceramics involved a high labour input. During MPs 2–4, more infants and children were buried than were adults. It is noted that 69 per cent of the decorated pots are located in MPs 2–4. Only decorated pots were found in MP6 burials.

TABLE 43:   *A comparison of decorated (D) to plain (P) pots by gender and mortuary phase*

MP	Male		Female		Child		Infant		No.	No.	Ratio	%	%
	D	P	D	P	D	P	D	P	D	P	D/P	D	P
2	6	-	3	1	-	-	12	1	21	2	10.5:1	22	8
3	16	3	6	4	-	-	1	-	23	7	3:1	24	28
4	8	5	7	2	3	1	4	-	22	8	3:1	23	32
5	1	-	5	3	-	-	7	1	13	4	3:1	13	16
6	2	-	7	-	5	-	2	-	16	-	16:0	16	0
7	-	-	-	-	2	4	-	-	2	4	1:2	2	16

Mortuary motifs

Only 24 motifs out of a repertoire of 60 were found on the burial pots, 13 of which are gender related. Eight of the 10 motifs exclusive to the mortuary context were also related to gender.

The five gender-related motifs found in the non-mortuary context are 1:7, 3:10, 3:3, 4:2 and 3:20. Three of these are very rare: 1:7, 7 gm; 3:10, 10 gm; and 3:20, 80 gm. Both 4:2 and 3:3 are common in the non-mortuary material. Motif 4:2 is present in B15 on a cord-marked domestic ware vessel. This rich female burial contained eight vessels. The two motifs exclusive to females are found on pots from B15.

The pots associated with infants exhibit more individual motifs than are found with males and females, but it would be more constructive to look at the distribution in relation to burials with pots per mortuary phase, as out of the 61 individuals that were interred without grave goods, there were 48 infants, 4 children, 3 males and 6 females. The decoration on the infants' pots was innovative and individual throughout the mortuary phases with high-energy expenditure and artistic skill expended on the grave goods of some of the young.

TABLE 44:   *The distribution of gender-related motifs*

Motif	MP	M	F	C	I	Motif	MP	M	F	C	I
1:7	2	-	-	-	1	3:10	-	-	1	-	-
3:12	-	-	-	-	2	3:13	-	-	-	-	1
3:14	3	1	-	-	-	3:15	-	1	-	-	-
3:16	-	-	-	-	1	3:3	4	-	-	-	2
3:19	-	-	-	1	-	3:33	5	-	-	-	1
3:34	-	-	1	-	-	4:2	-	-	1	-	-
3:20	6	-	-	1	-						

The distribution of motifs by zone

This analysis is to ascertain if the Khok Phanom Di potters made a deliberate choice to decorate certain zones with particular motifs. The following figure illustrates the position of zones on form. Out of the 24 motifs present in the mortuary context, nine motifs are restricted to one zone, five motifs are present on two zones, three motifs are present on three zones, and the remaining seven are common throughout the majority of zones.

The association between individuals interred close to each other in space and time and the motifs found on their mortuary vessels provides an avenue for appreciating the possible significance of the ceramics and their decoration. Thus, the highest number of exclusive motifs is associated with cluster F (Table 48). It is found that motif 3:12 links Bs 99 and 101, two infants interred alongside each other during stage 1, MP2. Again, motif 4:2 links Bs 15 and 13. In the analysis of the burials from this site, presented below, it will be found that these two burials are linked genealogically with cluster F. The connection between these two women is given support by the

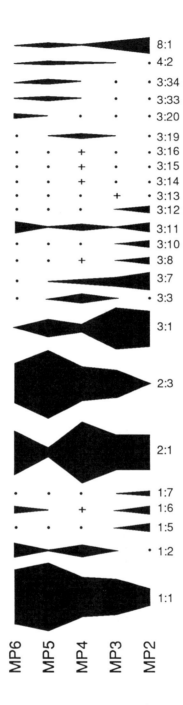

FIG. 106.   Distribution and frequency of motif by mortuary phase

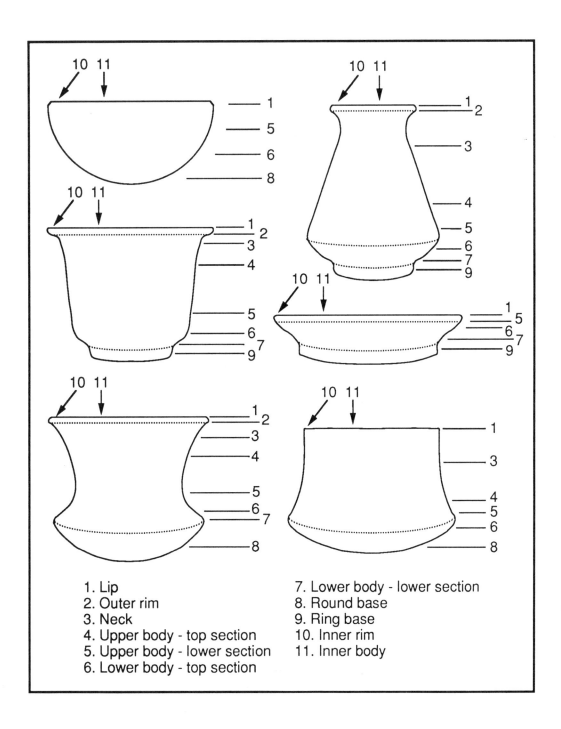

1. Lip
2. Outer rim
3. Neck
4. Upper body - top section
5. Upper body - lower section
6. Lower body - top section
7. Lower body - lower section
8. Round base
9. Ring base
10. Inner rim
11. Inner body

FIG. 107.   Zone positions for motif placement

TABLE 45:   *Frequency of gender-related motifs to burials with pots*

MP		Male	Female	Child	Infant
2	No. burials	8	11	3	34
	No. burials with pots	2	4	-	8
	GR motifs	1	-	-	4
3	No. burials	10	9	-	23
	No. burials with pots	10	7	-	3
	GR motifs	2	-	-	1
4	No. burials	9	10	5	5
	No. burials with pots	6	7	3	2
	GR motifs	-	-	1	2
5	No. burials	1	1	-	2
	No. burials with pots	1	1	-	2
	GR motifs	-	2	-	1
6	No. burials	1	4	3	4
	No. burials with pots	1	2	2	2
	GR motifs	-	1	1	-
7	No. burials	-	-	2	2
	No. burials with pots	-	-	1	1
	GR motifs	-	-	-	-

GR mot./p.bur.: the percentage of burials containing pottery vessels
which incorporate gender motifs

link provided by this enquiry. Table 49 also shows that there are chains of similar motifs running through the female line, including infants and children. Thus, motifs 2:1-3 are present on the pots of burials found in MPs 2–6 inclusive for the combined clusters F, MP5 and H.

CONCLUSIONS

The analysis of the non-mortuary decorative motifs suggests a number of interesting trends. There is continuity over time for the popular but low energy expenditure motifs such as the incised lines and the cord-marked incised ware. Many of the more complex motifs are confined to the burial sequences so are not present in the non-mortuary material.

Out of the 50 motifs present in the non-mortuary context, 44 per cent show continuity over time, albeit intermittently for some; 48 per cent of these terminate at the end of layer 5 and 8 per cent are new motifs for zone C. This zone saw a change in site use, the area excavated being a pottery workshop. It may well be that domestic wares were produced there, for there is no evidence for the production of the burnished and decorated mortuary vessels. The presence of this workshop could explain the 44 per cent continuity of the non-mortuary motifs aligned with a 48 per cent

TABLE 46: *The distribution of motifs by zone on the pottery vessel*

Motif	Zone 1	2	3	4	5	6	7	8	9	10	
1:1	-	28	14	8	2	3	-	-	3	-	58
1:2	1	1	2	-	1	-	-	-	-	-	5
1:5	-	-	2	2	-	-	-	-	-	-	4
1:6	-	1	-	1	-	-	3	-	-	-	5
1:7	-	-	1	-	-	-	-	-	-	-	1
2:1	24	1	-	-	21	1	-	-	-	4	51
2:3	19	1	10	1	18	-	-	-	-	-	49
3:1	-	4	6	3	14	5	7	1	2	-	42
3:3	-	-	-	-	2	-	-	-	-	-	2
3:7	1	1	2	-	-	2	-	-	3	-	9
3:8	-	-	-	2	-	-	-	-	-	-	2
3:10	-	-	1	-	-	-	-	-	-	-	1
3:11	-	-	-	-	2	4	-	-	-	2	8
3:12	-	-	-	1	2	1	-	-	-	-	4
3:13	-	-	1	-	1	-	-	-	-	-	2
3:14	-	-	1	-	-	-	-	-	-	-	1
3:15	-	-	-	1	1	-	-	-	-	-	2
3:16	-	-	-	-	-	1	-	-	-	-	1
3:19	-	-	1	-	-	-	-	-	-	-	1
3:20	-	-	-	-	-	-	-	-	-	2	2
3:33	-	-	1	1	1	-	-	-	-	-	3
3:34	-	-	1	-	1	-	-	-	-	-	2
4:2	-	-	-	-	-	-	-	-	-	2	2
8:1	-	4	4	2	5	3	3	-	2	-	23
Total	45	41	47	22	71	20	13	1	10	10	280

Zone codes: 1, lip; 2, outer rim; 3, neck; 4, upper body - upper section;
5, upper body - lower section; 6, lower body - upper section; 7, lower
body - lower section; 8, round base; 9, ring base; 10, inner rim

motif termination. A potter or workshop group would be unlikely to utilise the total design range but specialise within a smaller category of decorative schemes.

Of the 24 motifs utilised on the mortuary pots, 42 per cent were exclusive to the burial contexts. Seven of the ten exclusive motifs are present in MPs 2–3, suggesting that individuality was more important in the earlier rather than later mortuary phases. Of the ten mortuary-exclusive motifs, eight are gender-related, with infant burials having 50 per cent of the gender-related exclusive motifs. There is, however, a predominance of infant burials at Khok Phanom Di. They comprise 48 per cent of the total burials.

	Cluster A	B	C	D	E	F	G	I
M.P. 2 M.		120				91		
F.	110				102	113		
C.								
I.		130	125	123		88,89,99,101,105		
3 M.	57		67,72,90,93 64,73,77,79	92,103		74	86	
F.						56,58,60		
C.								
I.	75							
4 M.	28,30			44		24		
F.	31		35,36,45,47			27,38,39		
C.			37			20		
I.						41		
5 M.						15		
F.								
C.								
I.						14,16		
6 M.						9		
F.			19			13		
C.						8		
I.						72		
7 M.								
F.								
C.								1
I.								

FIG. 108.   Distribution of burials with pottery vessels within cluster

The undecorated sherds have a very high concentration in comparison to the decorated ware, which comprises 2.3 per cent of the total sherd density in the non-mortuary context. This trend is reversed in the mortuary sequence, where the decorated pots comprise 80 per cent of the burial vessels. These figures illustrate very clearly that the decorated pots were an important element in the Khok Phanom Di mortuary ritual.

An important objective in the mortuary ceramics analysis was to examine the decoration in order to elicit social information. The skeletal material provided an opportunity to pursue the wider dimensions of the decorative interpretation in order to explore the possibilities of gender-related and cluster-affiliated designs. No definite conclusions were reached, though it is clear that the infant burials of Khok Phanom Di contained pots that were decorated in an innovative and labour-intensive manner throughout the mortuary phases. The pots associated with infants exhibited more individual motifs than those found with adult males and females. If the potters were predominantly female, as is suggested by the pottery accoutrements in the grave goods, it is probable that energy

TABLE 47: *The distribution of burials with decorated pots by cluster and sex*

Cluster	Sex	No. burials	%	Burials dec. pots	%
A	Male	4	17.0	1	25.0
	Female	3	13.0	2	67.0
	Child	2	9.0	–	–
	Infant	14	61.0	1	7.0
B	Male	2	25.0	1	50.0
	Female	1	12.5	–	–
	Infant	5	62.5	1	50.0
C	Male	7	17.5	4	57.0
	Female	15	37.5	2	29.0
	Child	2	5.0	1	14.0
	Infant	16	40.0	–	–
D	Male	4	40.0	3	75.0
	Female	2	20.0	–	–
	Infant	4	40.0	1	25.0
E	Male	2	25.0	–	–
	Female	2	25.0	1	100.0
	Child	1	12.5	–	–
	Infant	3	37.5	–	–
F	Male	8	18.0	7	32.0
	Female	13	30.0	4	18.0
	Child	1	2.0	2	9.0
	Infant	22	50.0	9	41.0
G	Male	2	100.0	1	100.0
I	Child	1	33.0	–	–
	Infant	2	67.0	–	–

and artistic skill would be expended on the grave goods of infants, stressing the role of the young in supplying the next generation of potters.

Out of the 155 burials excavated at Khok Phanom Di, 15 are not associated with clusters. Due to the edge effect, only clusters A, C and F will be considered. The percentages of burials with decorated pots in the clusters are, A: 17 per cent, C: 17.5 per cent and F: 50 per cent. It is clear that in cluster F burials, the decorated pot is an important grave good. One interpretation of this analysis is that the master potter in B15 was allied to this cluster. The importance of the female in B15, is attested by the size of her grave and the wealth of her offerings. The presence of an anvil and burnishing stones in such a rich burial indicate the high status a female potter could aspire to.

TABLE 48: *The frequency of exclusive motifs per cluster*

MP	A	B	C	D	E	F	G
2	-	-	-	3:13	-	1:7	-
	-	-	-	-	-	3:8	-
	-	-	-	-	-	3:12	-
	-	-	-	-	-	3:12	-
3	3:16	-	-	3:14	-	-	3:15
4	-	-	3:19	-	-	-	-
5	-	-	-	-	-	3:33	-
	-	-	-	-	-	3:34	-
	-	-	-	-	-	4:2	-
6	-	-	1:2	-	-	4:2	-
	1	-	2	2	-	8	1

No. of burials with decorated pottery vessels

	4	2	7	4	1	22	1

TABLE 49: *Motifs associated with cluster F, MP5 and cluster H burials through the female line*

B.No.	Sex															Motif No.
113	F	1:1	-	1:6	-	-	-	-	3:7	3:11	-	-	-	-	8:1
99	I		1:5	1:6	-	2:1	-	3:1	-	-	3:12	-	-	-	8:1
101	I		-	-	1:7	-	-	-	-	-	3:12	-	-	-	8:1
60	F	1:1	-	-	-	-	2:3	3:1	-	-	-	-	-	-	-
58	F	1:1	-	-	-	2:1	2:3	3:1	-	-	-	-	-	-	-
58	1F	1:1	-	-	-	2:1	2:3	3:1	-	-	-	-	-	-	-
39	F		-	-	-	2:1	-	-	-	-	-	-	-	-	-
41	I		-	-	-	2:1	-	-	-	-	-	-	-	-	-
39	F		-	-	-	2:1	-	-	-	-	-	-	-	-	-
27	F		-	-	-	2:1	2:3	-	-	-	-	-	-	-	-
27	F		-	-	-	2:1	2:3	-	-	-	-	-	-	-	-
20	C	1:1	-	-	-	2:1	2:3	-	-	-	-	-	-	-	-
15	F	1:1	-	-	-	-	2:3	3:1	-	-	-	-	3:34	4:2	8:1
14	I	1:1	-	-	-	-	2:3	3:1	-	-	-	3:33	-	-	-
16	I	1:1	-	-	-	-	2:3	-	-	-	-	-	-	-	-
13	F		-	-	-	2:1	-	-	-	-	-	-	-	4:2	-
7	I	1:1	-	1:6	-	-	-	-	-	3:11	-	-	-	-	-
2	I	1:1	-	-	-	-	2:3	-	-	3:11	-	-	-	-	-

Both clusters A and F contain decorated pots in MP2, but it is not until MP3 that decorated ware is present in cluster C burials. Cluster F has a short hiatus during MPs 3 and 4 when 10 out of 12 burials are without decorated pots. Cluster F, the most enduring of the clusters, had the highest number of exclusive motifs, 8.

Each cluster produced a different result in terms of the predominant sex with decorated pots in burials. In cluster A, females comprised 13 per cent of the burials which contained 67 per cent of the decorated pots. In cluster C, males comprised 17.5 per cent of the burials which contained 57 per cent of the decorated pots. In cluster F, infants comprised 50 per cent of the burials which contained 41 per cent of the decorated pots.

The analysis of the distribution of the motifs suggested that some recurred through successive stages of a given cluster, though the majority of these motifs were also present in other clusters. Cluster F has one example of an exclusive motif retained in the same stage, motif 3:12 being present in both Bs 99 and 101 (Fig. 109). There also appears to be a correlation of vessel shape with motif. The carinated pots show a consistent combination of motifs. The four plates also demonstrate a common selection of motifs. That Khok Phanom Di potters seem to have made a deliberate choice to decorate certain zones with particular motifs suggests that this practice was quite widespread; the highest number of motifs, 37.5 per cent, is restricted to one zone. The most popular zones utilised were the upper body, lower section; the neck and lip; and the upper body, upper section. The majority of the pots had round bases, but where ring bases were utilised, the base was frequently decorated.

The non-mortuary ceramics contain examples of three-dimensional decoration in the form of appliqué and ridging; these are present at the earliest level indicating a high degree of expertise from the founding potters. Three-dimensional decoration is absent from the burial ceramics, as is the painted ware which is present, albeit rarely, from L. 10 to L. 4 inclusive.

The pottery vessel was the commonest grave good to be excavated at Khok Phanom Di. It is evident that high energy expenditure and artistic skill featured on the majority of the burial pots. There is no clear division between sacred and profane motifs, but 42 per cent of the mortuary motifs were exclusive and could, therefore, be assigned to a sacred category. There is, however, compelling evidence that pottery decoration was a ritual preference in the mortuary practices of Khok Phanom Di and the decorated burial ceramics played a significant role in the ritual of death.

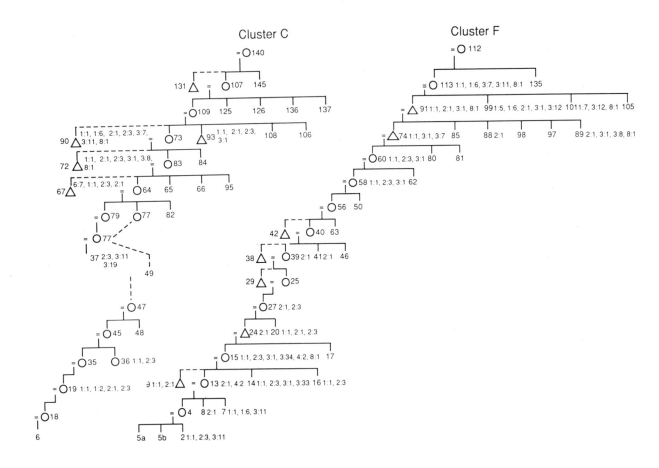

FIG. 109.   Motifs associated with clusters C and F. The burials are set out as putative genealogies, an issue which will be discussed fully in the final volume of the report on Khok Phanom Di. Triangles: male, circles: female

BIBLIOGRAPHY

Birks, L., 1972. Artefacts from Tonga and Fiji. *Asian Perspectives*, 15:93–6.

Blackwood, B., 1950. The technology of modern stone age people in New Guinea. In Penniman, P. K. and Blackwood, B. M., editors, *Occasional Papers on Technology*, 3, pages 1–57. Oxford University Press, Oxford

Bray, F., 1984. *Science and Civilisation in China. Vol. 6, Biology and Biological Technology. Part II: Agriculture.* Cambridge University Press, Cambridge

Bulmer, S., 1977. Waisted blades and axes. In Wright, R. V. S., editor, *Stone Tools as Cultural Markers: Changes, Evolution and Complexity*, pages 40–59. Australian Institute of Aboriginal Studies, Canberra.

Chang, K. C., 1986. *The Archaeology of Ancient China.* Yale University Press, New Haven

Colani, M., 1940. Origine et évolution du couteau de moissoneur. In Chasen, F. N. and Tweedie, M. W. F., editors, *Proceedings of the Third Congress of Prehistorians of the Far East*, pages 194–9. Government Printing Office, Singapore

Dalton, G., 1977. Aboriginal economics in stateless societies. In Earle, T. K. and Ericson, J. E., editors, *Exchange Systems in Prehistory*, pages 191–212. Academic Press, London

Duff, R., 1970. *Stone Adzes of Southeast Asia.* Canterbury Museum, Christchurch

Earle, T. K., 1982. Prehistoric economy and the prehistory of exchange. In Ericson, J. E. and Earle, T. K., editors, *Context for Prehistoric Exchange*, pages 1–11. Academic Press, New York

Ericson, J. E., 1981. *Exchange and Production Systems in Californian Prehistory.* British Archaeological Reports (International Series) 110, Oxford

Ericson, J. E., 1984. Towards the analysis of lithic production systems. In Ericson, J. E. and Purdy, B. A., editors, *Prehistoric Quarries and Lithic Production*, pages 1–10. Cambridge University Press, Cambridge

Flannery, K. V., 1976. Contextual analysis of ritual paraphernalia from formative Oaxaca. In Flannery, K. V., editor, *The Early Mesoamerican Village*, pages 333–44. Academic Press, New York

Fox, R. B., 1970. *The Tabon Caves: Archaeological Explorations and Excavations on Palawan Island, Philippines.* National Museum of Manila, Monograph no. 1, Manila

Freeman, J. D., 1955. *Iban Agriculture. A Report on the Shifting Cultivation of Hill Rice by the Iban of Sarawak.* H.M.S.O., London

Grist, D. H., 1975. *Rice.* Longmans, London

Ha Van Phung and Nguyen Duy Ty, 1982. *Di Chi Khao Co Hoc Go Mun.* Nha Xuat Ban Khoa Hoc Xa Hoi, Ha Noi

Harsant, W., 1978. Unmodified shell tools: their use in prehistoric New Zealand. Master's thesis, University of Auckland

Higham, C. F. W., 1983. The Ban Chiang culture in wider perspective. *Proc. Brit. Acad.,* LXIX:229–61

Higham, C. F. W., 1988. Prehistoric metallurgy in Southeast Asia: some new information from the excavation of Ban Na Di. In Maddin, R., editor, *The Beginning of the Use of Metals and Alloys,* pages 130–55. Massachusetts Institute of Technology Press, Cambridge, Mass.

Higham, C. F. W., Bannanurag, R., Maloney, B. K., and Vincent, B. A., 1987. Khok Phanom Di: the results of the 1984-5 excavation. *Bulletin of the Indo-Pacific Prehistory Association,* 7:148–78.

Higham, C. F. W. and Kijngam, A., 1984. *Prehistoric Investigations in Northeast Thailand.* British Archaeological Reports (International Series) 231(1-3), Oxford

Hodges, H., 64. *Artefacts: an Introduction to early Metals and Technology.* John Baker, London

Hornell, J., 1909. Report upon the anatomy of *Placuna placenta,* with notes upon its distribution and economic uses. *Report to the Government of Baroda on Marine Zoology,* 1:43–97

Hurcombe, L., 1988. Some criticisms and suggestions in response to Newcomer *et al. Journal of Archaeological Science,* 15:1–10

Juel-Jensen, H., 1988. Functional analysis of prehistoric flint tools by high power microscope: a review of West European research. *Journal of World Prehistory* 2:53-88

Keeley, L. H., 1980. *Experimental Determination of Stone Tool Uses.* University of Chicago Press

Keeley, L. H. and Newcomer, M. H., 1977. Microwear analysis of experimental flint tools: a test case. *Journal of Archaeological Science,* 4:29–62

Lévy, P., 1943. *Recherches préhistoriques dans la region de Mlu Prei.* Publications de l'École Française d'Extrême Orient: 30, Paris

Magsuci, H., Conlu, A., and Moyano-Aypa, S., 1980. The window-pane oyster (*kapis*) fishery of western Visayas. *Fisheries Research Journal of the Philippines,* 5(2):74–80

Mansuy, H., 1902. *Stations préhistoriques de Samrong-Seng et de Longprao (Cambodge).* F.H. Schneider, Hanoi

Mansuy, H., 1923. Contribution a l'étude de la préhistoire de l'Indochine. Résultats de nouvelles recherches effectuées dans le gisement préhistorique de Samrong Sen (Cambodge). *Mémoires du Service Géologique de Indochine,* 10:1

Maranet, S. and Boonsue, S., 1984. *Petrological Identification of Khok Phanom Di Stone Artefacts*. Department of Mineral Resources, Bangkok

Moszkowski, M., 1908. Enstehungsgeschichte des Malayischen reismessers. *Zeitschrift f. Ethnologie*, XL:961–3

Nakinbodee, W. S., Maranet, S., and Chaturonkawanich, S., 1976. *Report on the Bangkok and Rayong Geological Surveys*. Department of Mineral Resources, Bangkok

Odell, G. H., 1975. Microwear in perspective: a sympathetic response to Lawrence H. Keeley. *World Archaeology*, 7(2):226–40

Orton, C., 1980. *Mathematics in Archaeology*. Collins, London

Pilditch, J. S., 1984. The jewellery from Ban Na Di. In Higham, C. F. W. and Kijngam, A., editors, *Prehistoric Investigations in Northeast Thailand*, pages 57–222. British Archaeological Reports (International Series) 231, Oxford.

Plog, S., 1980. *Stylistic Variation in Prehistoric Ceramics: Design Analysis in the American Southwest*. Cambridge University Press, Cambridge.

Rajpitak, W. and Seeley, J., 1984. The bronze metallurgy. In Higham, C. F. W. and Kijngam, A., editors, *Prehistoric Investigations in Northeast Thailand*, pages 102–12. British Archaeological Reports (International Series) 231, Oxford.

Reid, R., 1985. *Isognomon*: life in two dimensions. In Morton, J. and Dudgeon, D., editors, *Proceedings of the Second International Workshop of the Malacofauna of Hong Kong and Southern China*, pages 311–19. Hong Kong University Press, Hong Kong

Renfrew, A. C., 1969. Trade and culture process in European prehistory. *Current Anthropology*, 10:151–69

Renfrew, A. C., 1975. Trade as action at a distance: questions of integration and communication. In Sabloff, J. A. and Lamberg-Karlovsky, C. C., editors, *Ancient Civilisation and Trade*, pages 3–60. University of New Mexico Press, Albuquerque

Rice, P. M., 1987. *Pottery Analysis: a Sourcebook*. University of Chicago Press, Chicago

Rye, O. S., 1981. *Pottery Technology, Principles and Reconstruction*. Taraxacum Inc, Washington D. C.

Semenov, S. A., 1964. *Prehistoric Technology*. Cory, Adams and MacKay, London

Siung, A. M., 1980. Studies on the biology of *Isognomon alatus* (Bivalvia: Isognomonidae) with notes on its potential as a commercial species. *Bulletin of Marine Science*, 30(1):90–101

Skeat, W. W., 1900. *Malay Magic*. London

Sørensen, P. and Hatting, T., 1967. *Archaeological Investigations in Thailand. Vol.II, Ban Kao, Part 1: The Archaeological Materials from the Burials*. Munksgard, Copenhagen

Thompson, G. B., 1992. *Archaeobotanical Investigations at Khok Phanom Di, Central Thailand.* PhD thesis, Australian National University

Torrence, R., 1986. *Production and Exchange of Stone Tools.* Cambridge University Press, Cambridge

Tugby, D. J. and Tugby, E., 1964. A stone artefact from Lower Mandailing Sumatra. *Asian Perspective*, 8:166–70

Turner, F. J. and Verhoogen, J., 1960. *Igneous and Metamorphic Petrology.* McGraw-Hill, New York

Vincent, B. A., 1987. The ceramics, in Higham, C. F. W. Maloney, B. Bannanurag R. and Vincent B. A. Khok Phanom Di: the results of the 1984–5 excavation. *Bulletin of the Indo-Pacific Prehistory Association*, 7:148–78

Webb, M., 1974. Exchange networks: prehistory. *Annual Review in Anthropology*, 3:357–383

White, J. C., 1982. *Ban Chiang. The Discovery of a Lost Bronze Age.* University of Pennsylvania Press, Philadelphia

Williams, H., Turner, F. J., and Gilbert, C. M., 1958. *Petrography: an Introduction to the Study of Rocks in Thin Section.* W. H. Freeman and Co, San Francisco

Witthoft, J., 1967. Glazed polish on flint tools. *American Antiquity*, 32:383–8

Yonge, C. M., 1977. Form and evolution in the Anomiacea (Mollusca: Bivalvia) *Pododesmus, Anomia, Patro, Enigmonia* (Anomiidae); *Placunanomia, Placuna* (Placunidae *Fam. Nov.*). *Philosophical Transactions of the Royal Society of London*, B, 276 (950):453–527

Young, A. L., 1980. Larval and post-larval development of the window-pane shell, *Placuna placenta* Linnaeus, with a discussion on its natural settlement. *Veliger*, 23(2):141–8

INDEX